MONASTIC WISDOM SERIES: NUMBER FORTY-ONE

Thomas Merton

Charter, Customs, and Constitutions of the Cistercians
Initiation into the Monastic Tradition 7

MONASTIC WISDOM SERIES

Simeon Leiva, ocso, General Editor

Advisory Board

Michael Casey, ocso
Lawrence S. Cunningham
Patrick Hart, ocso
Robert Heller

Terrence Kardong, osb
Kathleen Norris
Miriam Pollard, ocso
Bonnie Thurston

INITIATION INTO THE MONASTIC TRADITION SERIES
BY
THOMAS MERTON

Cassian and the Fathers:
Initiation into the Monastic Tradition (MW 1)

Pre-Benedictine Monasticism:
Initiation into the Monastic Tradition 2 (MW 9)

An Introduction to Christian Mysticism:
Initiation into the Monastic Tradition 3 (MW 13)

The Rule of St. Benedict:
Initiation into the Monastic Tradition 4 (MW 19)

Monastic Observances:
Initiation into the Monastic Tradition 5 (MW 25)

The Life of the Vows:
Initiation into the Monastic Tradition 6 (MW 30)

MONASTIC WISDOM SERIES: NUMBER FORTY-ONE

Charter, Customs, and Constitutions of the Cistercians
Initiation into the Monastic Tradition 7

by
Thomas Merton

Edited with an Introduction by
Patrick F. O'Connell

Preface by
John Eudes Bamberger, ocso

Cistercian Publications
www.cistercianpublications.org

LITURGICAL PRESS
Collegeville, Minnesota
www.litpress.org

A Cistercian Publications title published by Liturgical Press

Cistercian Publications
Editorial Offices
161 Grosvenor Street
Athens, Ohio 54701
www.cistercianpublications.org

Cover design by Ann Blattner. Drawing by Thomas Merton. Copyright of the Merton Legacy Trust and the Thomas Merton Center at Bellarmine University. Used with permission.

© 2015 by Merton Legacy Trust. All rights reserved. No part of this book may be reproduced in any form, by print, microfilm, microfiche, mechanical recording, photocopying, translation, or by any other means, known or yet unknown, for any purpose except brief quotations in reviews, without the previous written permission of Liturgical Press, Saint John's Abbey, PO Box 7500, Collegeville, Minnesota 56321-7500. Printed in the United States of America.

Library of Congress Cataloging-in-Publication Data

Merton, Thomas, 1915–1968.
 Charter, customs, and constitutions of the Cistercians : initiation into the monastic tradition 7 / by Thomas Merton ; edited with an introduction by Patrick F. O'Connell ; preface by John Eudes Bamberger, OCSO.
  pages   cm. — (Monastic wisdom series ; 41)
 Includes index.
 ISBN 978-0-87907-041-0 (paperback) — ISBN 978-0-87907-480-7 (ebook)
 1. Cistercians—Rules. 2. Trappists—Rules. I. O'Connell, Patrick F. II. Title.

BX3404.Z5M46   2015
271'.12—dc23   2014043311

TABLE OF CONTENTS

Preface   vii

Introduction   xiii

CARTA CARITATIS   1

THE CONSUETUDINES   15

CONSTITUTIONS OF THE ORDER OF CISTERCIANS OF THE STRICT OBSERVANCE   57

Appendix A: Textual Notes   205

Appendix B: For Further Reading   229

Index   231

PREFACE

When Thomas Merton, whom we knew as Fr. Louis in those early days, was serving as master of novices at the Abbey of Gethsemani, he expended immense energy in research of the monastic sources of the current norms, practices, and spirituality of the Cistercian life. He undertook this exacting labor by way of preparing the conferences he gave to novices as part of their training and introduction to our community's way of life. The result of this exploration of the sources that originated from earliest times (the text of the *Charter*) to the twentieth century (the *Constitutions*) is evidenced by the texts published in this volume. He was at pains to "return to the sources" in order to maintain continuity with traditional monastic values while adapting them to the men and conditions of the mid-twentieth century. He had already entered on such a program of thorough research some years before his appointment as novice master in his talks to the young monks in simple vows. For four years (1951–1955) he had functioned as master of juniors. I can still recall how he would rapidly glance at his extensive notes and, skipping over some paragraphs, spontaneously comment at length on selected passages. Regularly he had prepared more material than he could cover in the allotted time. I was impressed with the extensive and conscientious preparation he obviously brought to bear on each of his conferences which he presented in an alert and attractive manner. Such serious and friendly dedication translated into a respectful concern to provide us with an authentic exposure to the values of our life as Cistercian monks. We eagerly attended his talks that he was able to make interesting as well as informative.

Although buttressed by the authority of considerable learning, Fr. Louis managed to avoid a sense of heaviness by his style of presentation. For Merton invariably brought an enthusiasm to the sessions, imparting a liveliness of spirit that added markedly to the interest we felt even in regard to legislative materials. This light touch did much to render more palatable what on paper might seem to anyone reading the printed text rather heavy and even dull in some particulars. Merton, invariably lively and given to spontaneous comments, possessed a sense of humor that provided welcome relief even when treating of disciplinary and legal matters. He had a way of conveying teachings rooted in the past so as to render them suited to our current times. A few years after Fr. Louis wrote and taught these documents, Pope John XXIII was to refer to the same approach he recommended to Vatican Council II as "aggiornamento."

The commentaries on the *Charter*, the *Customs*, and the *Constitutions* published in this volume were composed at the end of a long period of development. The *Charter* text that Merton commented on is a writing of the early twelfth century that applied the earlier *Rule* of Saint Benedict to the new requirements of religious communities of the Middle Ages and that continues in large part to be suited to modern times. The *Customary* and *Constitutions* reflect an evolution that took place over the intervening centuries. The form these texts had assumed at the period when Merton commented on them reflects the circumstances of monastic life and its practices at the very end of a long period following the Council of Trent. By his dynamic and personal contributions to monastic spirituality and observance in his teaching and various writings, Merton contributed appreciably to the climate that prepared for the Second Vatican Council. Shortly after these conferences were written and presented, the event of Vatican II marked the beginning of a new phase in monastic life as well as in the Church as a whole. That Merton contributed to the thought and spirit of the Council, and had some measure of influence on Pope John himself, is evident by the symbolic gift of his own stole the pope sent to him at Gethsemani[1] as well as from the fact he was invited to contribute to a text on monastic spirituality for the postconciliar synod of October 1967.[2]

Although less obvious in these commentaries on legislative documents than in more personal writings such as his autobiography and his diaries, there are at places even in these texts glimpses of a more profound spiritual insight than appears on the surface. In reading these commentaries we do well to recall that Merton was a poet and a master of words. Pope Benedict XVI has cogently observed: "Every great human utterance reaches beyond what was consciously said into greater, more profound depths; there is always, hidden in what is said, a surplus of what is not said, which lets the words grow with the passing of time."[3] Fr. Louis wrote, and more freely spoke, in such

---

1. See Merton's April 13, 1960, journal entry (Thomas Merton, *A Search for Solitude: Pursuing the Monk's True Life. Journals, vol. 3: 1952–1960*, ed. Lawrence S. Cunningham [San Francisco: HarperCollins, 1996], 383).

2. See "Contemplatives and the Crisis of Faith," written jointly by Carthusian Procurator General J.-B. Porion, Cistercian Abbot André Louf, and Merton for the synod (Thomas Merton, *The Monastic Journey*, ed. Brother Patrick Hart [Kansas City: Sheed, Andrews & McMeel, 1977], 174–78); see also the related "A Letter on the Contemplative Life," written slightly earlier at the request of Pope Paul VI (*Monastic Journey*, 169–73). On the latter text, and an unpublished intermediate version, see the journal entries for August 21 and 28, 1967 (Thomas Merton, *Learning to Love: Exploring Solitude and Freedom. Journals, vol. 6: 1966–1967*, ed. Christine M. Bochen [San Francisco: HarperCollins, 1997], 280–81, 282–83); the August 21 and 22, 1967, letters to Abbot Francis Decroix, ocso (Thomas Merton, *The Hidden Ground of Love: Letters on Religious Experience and Social Concerns*, ed. William H. Shannon [New York: Farrar, Straus, Giroux, 1985], 154–59); and the August 29, September 6, and October 13, 1967, and March 30, 1968, letters to Filiberto Guala, ocso (Thomas Merton, *The School of Charity: Letters on Religious Renewal and Spiritual Direction*, ed. Patrick Hart [New York: Farrar, Straus, Giroux, 1990], 344–45, 346, 349–50, 371–73).

3. Joseph Cardinal Ratzinger, *Truth and Tolerance: Christian Belief and World Religions*, trans. Henry Taylor (San Francisco: Ignatius Press, 2004), 254–55.

a manner as to cause even his words to young beginners in the art of monastic living to suggest much more than they explicitly state, if the reader knows how to listen. He himself was alive to this hidden dimension of his style of writing as is evidenced by the concluding words of his preface to the Japanese translation of *The Seven Storey Mountain:*

> Therefore, most honorable reader, it is not as an author that I would speak to you, not as a story-teller, not as a philosopher, not as a friend only: I seek to speak to you, in some way, as your own self. Who can tell what this may mean? I myself do not know. But if you listen, things will be said that are perhaps not written in this book. And this will be due not to me, but to One who lives and speaks in both![4]

Not only in this account of his life that has spoken to the hearts of readers in many different countries and cultures but also in other works does the tone, and the unstated but ever-present background, resonate in Merton's words. In another context, he refers to the same phenomenon in a more poetic strain in his preface to the Japanese translation of *Thoughts in Solitude*:

> No writing on the solitary, meditative dimensions of life can say anything that has not already been said better by the wind in the pine trees. These pages seek nothing more than to echo the silence and peace that is "heard" when the rain wanders freely among the hills and forests. But what can the wind say where there is no hearer? There is then a deeper silence: the silence in which the Hearer is No-Hearer. That deeper silence must be heard before one can speak truly of solitude.[5]

This contemplative dimension, in a less obvious manner, is a feature even of these commentaries composed and delivered for

---

4. Thomas Merton, *"Honorable Reader": Reflections on My Work*, ed. Robert E. Daggy (New York: Crossroad, 1989), 67.

5. Merton, *"Honorable Reader,"* 111.

young beginners in the spiritual life. The words of these writings point to more than they explicitly state. Arising from such a background as Merton's broad and sophisticated culture and his extensive studies of the traditions, by their roots in personal experience these commentaries rendered more accessible to novices of that period these documents that can seem rather formal and exterior.

The rapidity of changes in the period since these commentaries were produced has meant that they were composed in a cultural period strongly marked by very different values than our present times. We can observe the striking change of style and tone in comparing these documents with the version of customs and constitutions elaborated by the Order in the General Chapters beginning some ten years after Merton's commentaries were first produced. For it was in the General Chapter of 1969 that a major adaptation of the Order's uniform legislation was to effect a new approach to maintaining the unity of life of the monasteries while avoiding strict uniformity. The chief instrument of this fresh approach to Cistercian practice is the Statute on Unity and Pluralism. The increased presence of monasteries in countries outside Europe that live in social, geographic, and economic circumstances at considerable variance from those prevailing in a European environment had revealed the need for special exceptions to practices suited to quite different requirements. This statute was accepted by the 1969 Chapter and has provided the flexibility within acceptable limits that responded to these different practices and needs. Daily life in cultures as different as the Congo and northern Canada presented monks with conditions affecting lifestyle and physical requirements in divergent ways. The concept of a statute that allowed for greater flexibility while preserving sufficient limits as would assure an effective unity of practice and support the same spirituality originated at Gethsemani and was presented to the Order by its abbot, Flavian Burns, who was formed to our life by Merton's teaching and example. The texts included in this present book eventually gave rise to the Cistercian way of spiritual living that continues to contribute to the Church's witness in this new millennium. This publication is a witness to the process of transformation that assures the continuity of the Catholic monastic tradition, which witnesses to the God who, as Saint Augustine observed, is "ever old and ever new."

Abbot John Eudes Bamberger, ocso
Abbey of the Genesee, Piffard, NY

INTRODUCTION

In specifying the duties of the Cistercian master of novices, the official *Usages* of the Order that had been approved by the General Chapter of 1926 indicate the topics to be discussed during "repetitions," as the regular conferences for the aspiring monks were called: "At Repetition, he explains the Holy Rule, the Constitutions, the Regulations, the Ceremonies, the signs, and everything relating to monastic education; he also teaches the history of our Order."[1] The three interrelated sets of conferences included in the present volume are evidence of the seriousness with which Thomas Merton took these directives as he began his decade-long tenure as novice master at the Abbey of Gethsemani in October 1955. The brief set of conferences on the *Carta Caritatis*, or *Charter of Charity*, the foundational document of the Order of Cîteaux, must have been presented soon after Merton assumed the position and would have been followed immediately by the somewhat longer series of conferences on the *Consuetudines*, the twelfth-century collection of customs and regulations of the Order. That in turn was followed in 1956 by the more extended presentation of the twentieth-century *Constitutions* of the Order, approved in 1924, the basic rules by which Merton and his students actually lived at the time. The conferences on the *Consuetudines* and the *Constitutions* (but probably not on the *Carta Caritatis*) were given a second time in 1960–1961, begun shortly after Merton had stopped giving the somewhat

---

1. *Regulations of the Order of Cistercians of the Strict Observance Published by the General Chapter of 1926* (Dublin: M. H. Gill & Sons, 1927), 257–58 (#545).

similar series of conferences on the Cistercian observances in February 1960,[2] but were not repeated again in the remaining years before Merton resigned as novice master to take up full-time residence in his hermitage on August 20, 1965. Taken together, these conferences on the *Charter, Customs,* and *Constitutions* of the Cistercians give evidence of Merton's own deep familiarity with both the traditional and the current regulations governing monastic life and his recognition of his responsibility to make clear to those preparing to become vowed members of the Order what such a commitment involved in terms of the actual prescriptions and demands of day-to-day life in the monastery.[3] While even at the outset of his mastership, and increasingly as he moved into the period of his "turning toward the world" in the last decade of his life, Merton consistently emphasized the priority of the spiritual over the institutional dimension of the monastic vocation, he recognized, and wanted the novices to recognize, that Trappist life in the mid-twentieth century was a highly regulated, tightly organized way of living, in which ideally the myriad rules provided a framework for nurturing a rich

---

2. See Thomas Merton, *Monastic Observances: Initiation into the Monastic Tradition* 5, ed. Patrick F. O'Connell, Monastic Wisdom [MW], vol. 25 (Collegeville, MN: Cistercian Publications, 2010), xvi; these conferences began during late February or early March 1957 (xiii–xiv), so probably occupied most if not all of the period between the first and second presentations of the *Consuetudines / Constitutions* conferences.

3. See Merton's October 18, 1955, letter to Cistercian Abbot General Dom Gabriel Sortais concerning his recent appointment as novice master by Gethsemani Abbot James Fox: "Perhaps you will say that Dom James is quite imprudent to make this choice. To protect him, and to protect the house and the novices, I have made a vow (it is only the third private vow I have made!) not to say anything to the novices that would diminish their respect for the Cistercian cenobitic life and orientate them towards something else. If I happen to violate this promise, I will have to notify the Father Abbot. I will try to do all that is possible to give them a truly Cistercian life, cenobitical and liturgical" (Thomas Merton, *The School of Charity: Letters on Religious Renewal and Spiritual Direction*, ed. Patrick Hart [New York: Farrar, Straus, Giroux, 1990], 93).

personal and communal relationship with God. Whatever his own problems with the sometimes far from ideal ways in which authority was exercised in the Order as well as in the wider Church, he certainly knew that the young monks in training would be able to make a mature decision about their future only if they had clear and detailed information not just on such topics as the spiritual teachings of the desert fathers,[4] or the Christian mystical tradition,[5] or the rich texts and rituals of the liturgical cycle,[6] or the lives and writings of the great contemplative Cistercians of the first generation,[7] but on the much more mundane details of schedules and governance, of meals and dormitory arrangements, of monastic jobs and monastic sanctions, of the influence of canon law and of General Chapter decisions and of annual visitations on the life of the cloister. Thus these sets of conferences, along with those on monastic observances, on the vows,[8] as well as much of the material on the Benedictine *Rule*,[9]

---

4. See Thomas Merton, *Cassian and the Fathers: Initiation into the Monastic Tradition*, ed. Patrick F. O'Connell, MW 1 (Kalamazoo, MI: Cistercian Publications, 2005); and Thomas Merton, *Pre-Benedictine Monasticism: Initiation into the Monastic Tradition 2*, ed. Patrick F. O'Connell, MW 9 (Kalamazoo, MI: Cistercian Publications, 2006).

5. See Thomas Merton, *An Introduction to Christian Mysticism: Initiation into the Monastic Tradition 3*, ed. Patrick F. O'Connell, MW 13 (Kalamazoo, MI: Cistercian Publications, 2008).

6. See Thomas Merton, "Liturgical Feasts and Seasons," included in volume 24 of Merton's "Collected Essays," the twenty-four-volume bound set of published and unpublished materials assembled at the Abbey of Gethsemani and available both there and at the Thomas Merton Center, Bellarmine University, Louisville, KY.

7. See Thomas Merton, "The Cistercian Fathers and Their Monastic Theology" ("Collected Essays," vol. 20).

8. See Thomas Merton, *The Life of the Vows: Initiation into the Monastic Tradition 6*, ed. Patrick F. O'Connell, MW 30 (Collegeville, MN: Cistercian Publications, 2012).

9. See Thomas Merton, *The Rule of Saint Benedict: Initiation into the Monastic Tradition 4*, ed. Patrick F. O'Connell, MW 19 (Collegeville, MN: Cistercian Publications, 2009).

form an essential if subordinate part of the overall picture of Cistercian monastic life that Merton provided as part of his project of "initiation into the monastic tradition" that is evident in the broad variety of courses that he put together and taught over the period of his mastership, so broad that no single group of novices actually heard more than a relatively small proportion of the material during the two years of their own novitiate.

****

Merton's material on the *Carta Caritatis* survives only as an eight-page typescript with his own handwritten additions and alterations. It was apparently never retyped and reproduced in multigraphed form for the novices, as was his usual practice, and as was done for the two other sets of conferences in this volume. The only clear evidence that it was in fact presented in conferences is a line typed at the top of the first page of the typescript of a subsequent series of conferences on "THE LIFE, WORKS AND DOCTRINE OF ST. BERNARD."[10] Merton had written: "HISTORY OF THE ORDER—(to follow Carta Caritatis and Consuetudines)"—a clear indication that these two topics were closely linked to one another and were conceived by Merton as part of a succession of presentations on early Cistercianism.

Though consisting of only eight pages, the material actually has three distinct sections. A single introductory page[11] focusing on "recent studies" (1)—actually a single recent study, the 1954 article of J. -A. Lefèvre, "La Véritable Carta Caritatis Primitive et

---

10. The typescript of this set of conferences, an earlier version of "The Cistercian Fathers and Their Monastic Theology," is found in the archives of the Thomas Merton Center.

11. This somewhat technical and arcane discussion might initially seem to have been an afterthought subsequently prefixed to the rest of the material, but the fact that it is headed: "jhs / Carta Caritatis–" in two centered lines suggests that it was indeed intended by Merton from the start to begin his consideration of the *Carta*.

Son Évolution"[12]—is followed by two pages initially headed "Original Text of the Carta Caritatis," changed by hand to "*An Early Summary of the Carta Caritatis.*" These two sections report on the preliminary stages of what would become an extremely contentious scholarly controversy about the development of the document, in which Lefèvre theorized that the form of the *Carta* presented to Pope Callistus II for approval in 1119 was the so-called *Summa Cartae Caritatis*, joined with the brief historical prelude on Cistercian origins given the name *Exordium Cistercii*, and followed by a set of *Capitula* or early General Chapter decrees, and that an early version of the *Carta* published by Msgr. Josip Turk in 1945 (now generally known as the *Carta Caritatis Prior*) was that approved by the Cistercian Pope Eugene III in 1152. This proposal was soon challenged and has subsequently been rejected by a consensus of scholars—most recently and most thoroughly by Fr. Chrysogonus Waddell of Gethsemani (who had been one of Merton's students during his 1951–1955 tenure as master of scholastics, immediately before becoming novice master) in his 1999 edition of these and related early Cistercian texts.[13]

At the time Merton was writing the controversy still lay largely in the future and he simply summarizes (not completely accurately[14]) the current state of the question without challenging Lefèvre's proposals. He was mainly interested in alerting his students to the existence of newly discovered texts of this seminal

---

12. J.-A. Lefèvre, "La Véritable Carta Caritatis Primitive et Son Évolution," *Collectanea Ordinis Cisterciensium Reformatorum* 16 (1954): 5–29.

13. *Narrative and Legislative Texts from Early Cîteaux*, ed. and trans. Chrysogonus Waddell, ocso, Studia et Documenta, vol. 9 (Cîteaux: Commentarii Cistercienses, 1999), 162–66, 261–82, 371–88, 441–50, 498–505.

14. His statement (3–4) that the text of the *Exordium Cistercii*, the *Summa Cartae Caritatis*, and the *Capitula* transcribed and published in *Collectanea Ordinis Cisterciensium Reformatorum* 16, no. 2 (1954): 97–104 is that of the Trent ms., discovered and first described by Jean Leclercq, osb, is not accurate; it is actually that transcribed by Lefèvre from ms. 1207 of Ste. Geneviève, Paris, supplemented by the Trent ms.

document in Cistercian development and to some of the implications of their discovery in coming to a clearer understanding of the early history of the Order. The discussion of the "early summary" also provides an opportunity for a brief overview of the founding of Cîteaux as found in the *Exordium Cistercii*, emphasizing the founders' motive for leaving the Abbey of Molesme as the "desire to live their vows more fully" (5), particularly with respect to poverty and simplicity of life; the precarious existence of the "new monastery" (as it was called) until the arrival of Bernard and his companions; and then the composition by Abbot Stephen of a *"wise document, to prevent divisions and to preserve mutual peace"* (5), the *Carta Caritatis* itself, the provisions of which this document provides in summary form, followed by key regulations from the *Institutes*, including dedication of all the Order's abbeys to the Blessed Virgin, their location in isolated settings, the importance of the monks' manual labor in providing for their own sustenance, and the innovative institution of the laybrotherhood as an integral part of the monastic community. As Merton sums up this early but recently recovered epitome of the Cistercian way of life: "Together with the principles of observance in the *Exordium Parvum*, these give us the essential outline of our Fathers' idea of what the Cistercian Order was supposed to be" (7).

Following his brief forays into current scholarly research on these earlier texts, Merton turns to a summary explication of the five sections of the traditional version of the *Carta* (now called the *Carta Caritatis Posterior* to distinguish it from the other two versions of the text). The most important, in Merton's view, is the first, in which uniformity of observance in all the monasteries founded from Cîteaux is seen as a fundamental means of preserving and fostering a sense of community throughout the Order, a reaction to the interminable disagreements over observance among Benedictine houses of the period. Merton notes:

> The Fathers of Cîteaux were writing perfectly in the spirit of St. Benedict. They did not assume that they were wiser or more perfect than anyone else, that they alone had the right interpretation of the *Rule*. But they insisted that they

should define precisely what was *their* interpretation of the *Rule*, and that they should impose on the Order the obligation of following their interpretation, in order to keep peace and avoid controversies. This part of the *Carta* clarifies a basic principle—that unity and charity come first. (9–10)

He also remarks rather wryly, "If we {do not} forget that the purpose of the *Carta Caritatis* was to produce peace and eliminate pretexts for argument, we will not be inclined to make the *Carta* itself a starting point of new controversies" (9), an indication that he is evidently aware that heated disagreements about the document's textual development have already started to emerge.

Discussing the second section, on visitations, Merton points out the *Carta*'s careful balance between the authority of the Abbot of Cîteaux and of the father immediate of any particular monastery (the abbot of the monastery from which a daughter house was founded) and the autonomy of each individual abbey: "The Abbot of Cîteaux must be careful not to make *any decision* about the affairs of the house he visits against the will of the local abbot or the brethren. But if the *Rule* is not being kept, he will 'strive to correct the brethren with the advice of the local abbot and with charity'" (10–11). He notes as well the provision that Cîteaux itself, though the original house of the Order, is not thereby immune from all oversight, being visited annually by the "four First Fathers" (11), abbots of the earliest daughter houses.

The third section focuses on the annual General Chapter of all Cistercian abbots as the legislative and disciplinary body for the entire Order, whose function is described in the *Carta* in such precise terms that Merton quotes it in the original Latin (typed in upper case to emphasize further its importance): "*DE SALUTE ANIMARUM SUARUM TRACTENT: IN OBSERVATIONE SANCTAE REGULAE VEL ORDINIS SI QUID EST EMENDANDUM VEL AUGENDUM ORDINENT, BONUM PACIS ET CARITATIS INTER SE REFORMENT*" ("Let them consider about the salvation of their souls; if anything should be amended or added with regard to the observance of the holy *Rule* or of the Order, let them make the decision, and renew among themselves the good of peace and charity") (12). Here legislative responsibility is directly linked with the underlying purpose of any alteration in observance—the renewal of peace and charity in the Order. The discussion of this section also finds Merton drawing for the first time on particular decisions of later General Chapters as applications of various regulations (here the requirement that abbots attend the annual meetings)—a procedure he will follow extensively in both the *Consuetudines* and the *Constitutions* conferences.

The two final sections both focus on how abbots are replaced—a brief consideration in part 4 of the role of the father immediate in the election process of the abbot of a daughter house (and of the "First Fathers" in the election of a new abbot of Cîteaux) and a somewhat lengthier consideration in the final section of the circumstances of an abbot's voluntary resignation (strongly discouraged in most instances) or forced deposition—after no less than four warnings from the father immediate (or in the case of Cîteaux itself from the First Fathers) for personal violations of the *Rule* or culpably lax leadership. As a final historical note Merton points out that the role of the First Fathers in the affairs of Cîteaux would lead in the following century to a power struggle between Cîteaux and its most influential daughter house, the Abbey of Clairvaux, that would be a central contributory factor in the Order's subsequent decline.

The *Carta Caritatis* is primarily practical rather than inspirational in tone and content, and Merton's largely matter-of-fact summary and commentary does not try to turn it into something other than what it is, the key document in creating a unified and a smoothly functioning religious order, the first of its kind, primarily through the organizational genius of Cîteaux's third abbot, St. Stephen Harding. At the same time, it is not simply a charter, but a "Charter of Charity," and when the opportunity presents itself Merton does point out the underlying commitment to love of the brethren as the strongest bond that holds together the community of communities that makes up the Order, rooted of course in the desire to fulfill as perfectly as possible the spirit and letter of the Benedictine *Rule* that led to the foundation of Cîteaux in the first place. This was certainly the central motivation that prompted

Merton to deepen his novices' familiarity with this foundational document at the very beginning of his time as their master.

Considering the brevity of the typescript (and of the document itself), it is doubtful whether Merton spent more than two or three classes on the *Carta*, though given his penchant for creative (usually pertinent) digression it is impossible to know for certain in the absence of recordings of these conferences.[15] It seems unlikely that the *Carta* material was reused when Merton repeated the *Consuetudines* and *Constitutions* material in 1960–1961—the information on earlier versions, in particular, would have become outdated in the light of continued research and publication in the intervening years, and the fact that Merton's own text had not been reproduced for distribution as had the two related series of conferences means that it would not have been available to this second group of novices and therefore is set apart from the other material, making it more convenient for Merton to omit than to include it. In the absence of documentation, however, this conclusion remains speculative.

* * * * * * *

In a February 11, 1956, letter to his friend and former Columbia professor Mark Van Doren, Merton writes of his first months as master of novices at Gethsemani: "For the rest I lecture the novices on Cassian and on the customs of twelfth century monks and on the behavior of twentieth century novices and secretly I pry into the psychoanalysts. These are the occupations which God has given to Masters of Novices in Cistercian monasteries. I have no other, except the felling of trees, and the praying of prayers."[16] Some months later he writes in an undated letter to Dom Jean Leclercq, OSB: "I have spent the year teaching

---

15. Merton's novitiate conferences began to be recorded in late April 1962; for details see *Cassian and the Fathers*, xlvii.
16. Thomas Merton, *The Road to Joy: Letters to New and Old Friends*, ed. Robert E. Daggy (New York: Farrar, Straus, Giroux, 1989), 28.

a course on Cassian, on the Cistercian *Consuetudines,* and now on St. Bernard—I am just beginning."[17] Both letters refer to the second set of conferences included in this volume, on the Cistercian *Consuetudines,* which presumably followed immediately those on the *Carta Caritatis* and evidently continued through much of the summer of 1956, even though Merton's typescript consists of only twenty-two pages of text.[18] As Merton points out in introducing this material (15), the document consists of three sections, the *"Ecclesiastica Officia"* or "Religious Duties"; the *"Instituta Capituli Generalis,"* early regulations of the General Chapter; and the *"Usus Conversorum,"* the rules governing the laybrothers. Merton's conferences will focus only on the first of these three sections,[19] the customs of the Order in its earliest days,

---

17. Thomas Merton and Jean Leclercq, *Survival or Prophecy? The Letters of Thomas Merton and Jean Leclercq,* ed. Brother Patrick Hart (New York: Farrar, Straus and Giroux, 2002), 75–76; the letter is assigned by the editor to "Fall 1956"—presumably on the basis of Merton's reference to "the year" of his novitiate teaching, which would be completed in October 1956; but according to a handwritten calendar for conferences to be given between Friday August 31 and Friday September 14, 1956, inserted into the typescript for his "The Life, Works and Doctrine of Saint Bernard" conferences, by the end of August Merton was already well into his discussion of Bernard's *De Diligendo Deo,* which had been preceded by a biographical overview of Bernard's life, so if he was in fact "just beginning" this set of conferences at the time of the letter it would have been written in mid- or late summer. At least one or the other reference must be approximate at best.

18. After an unnumbered introductory page, the next page of the typescript is numbered "1" by hand and is followed by pages with the running head "consuetudines" 2–9, followed by "consuetudines" 10 and 11 (misnumbered 9 and 10 and corrected by hand), and "consuetudines" (sometimes "Consuetudines") 12–21.

19. In his conference calendar for August 31–September 14 Merton writes next to "Mon. Sept 3"—"Finish Institutes." So he may have devoted a few conferences to an overview of the *"Instituta"* section of the *Consuetudines,* but if so they would have overlapped the early section of the St. Bernard conferences, which were to follow those on the *Consuetudines* according to Merton's note on the opening page of his St. Bernard typescript. These

"the ancient usages of St. Stephen Harding and our first Fathers" (15), and in fact omits any discussion of the first 69 of the 121 chapters of the *"Ecclesiastica Officia,"* the first two *"Distinctiones"* on the celebration of Mass and of the divine office with their "details of rubrics and ritual" (16), to focus on the three subsequent *"Distinctiones"* that make up the rest of the text. The aim, he writes, is to get to know "the way in which our Cistercian Fathers carried out the monastic observances, so as to gain something of their spirit and their outlook" (15–16). It may seem strange that he omits the liturgical material here, but it is likely that he is already planning to put together sets of conferences on the monastic *horarium*[20] and on the Church year and its important feasts,[21] so he does not need to discuss similar material in this context.

The third Distinction begins with four chapters (70–73) on general matters including the daily chapter, the periods for reading, the "regular places" or principal areas of the monastery, and the light meal known as mixt. These are followed by nine chapters (74–82) on the daily schedule in winter and six (83–88) on the schedule in summer. As written, the material on the chapter and the *"tempus lectionis"* are straightforward summaries of the regulations in the *Consuetudines*. In the former most attention is given to the proclamation of faults—not necessarily because it is most important, but because it is the most complicated in detail. The chapter on reading concerns itself not with what is read by the monks but with regulations as to proper deportment while engaged in reading, including instructions on how to handle situations in which more than one monk is interested in using

---

may have been a rather informal "postscript," as apparently no text of this material is extant.

20. I.e., *Monastic Observances*, which includes material on the Night Office or Vigils (38–75), Lauds (92–103), the Mass (104–20), and Prime (189–205) and was originally intended to discuss subsequent sections of the liturgy of the hours as well.

21. I.e., "Liturgical Feasts and Seasons," which includes material dating from as early as Advent 1955.

the same book—one who wants to look at a book in another's possession should have something to exchange in return, but "if he does not want to oblige his brother in this manner, let him who asks bear it in peace, until such time as he may proclaim him for it in chapter" (19). (It is unfortunate that Merton's conferences were not yet being recorded at this time, as one can easily imagine the mordant "riff" that he would have provided on such statements as this, particularly the juxtaposition of "bear it in peace" with the final "until such time . . ." clause!)

With the discussion of the various "regular places"—i.e., places provided for in a rule—Merton begins to supplement the *Consuetudines* materials in various ways. In discussing the kitchen, he brings in the later chapter (108) on the weekly cooks. The brief description of the refectory begins by noting that no one is allowed there outside of mealtimes, then lists the exceptions (including "anyone who wants a drink"!) and concludes, "In other words, quite a few people could enter the refectory!" (21)—again, a likely opportunity for Merton to leaven what could be a rather dry discussion with a touch of humor. The section on the warming room, or calefactory, includes the instruction not to let bare feet be seen if another monk is present (!), refers to a story about the early Cistercian Amadeus of Bonnevaux (not spelled out in the text but surely elaborated in some detail in the oral presentation), contrasts the original twelfth-century customs to those at seventeenth-century La Trappe (don't sit down; keep your shoes on), cites the contemporary Cistercian *Usages* for modern regulations (don't take off your socks and make sure not to set your clothes on fire!), and provides the first of many references in these conferences to a later General Chapter ruling. Merton begins the next section by calling attention to the fact that what were currently designated as "parlors" (places for speaking—from the French "parler") were called "*auditoria*" (places for listening) by the early Cistercians. After running through the regulations Merton goes on to cite no less than fourteen General Chapter statutes on speaking and silence dating from 1152 through 1245, commenting on the early regulations that it is "interesting to note the tone and the style of these statutes—laconic, clear, strict" (23), and then including one with a somewhat different "tone and style" from 1217, about the Abbot of Tintern (the monastery best known today from its appearance in the title of Wordsworth's famous poem[22]) who "is in trouble for talking to the bishop after compline and having a party with the bishop together with some monks after compline" ("*solemniter biberit*," the Chapter comments—"he was doing some serious drinking") and who also "has women working at the granges" (24). Finally the section on the dormitory, after providing details on using the "*domus necessaria*," where even the face should be concealed in one's hood, supplements the information from the *Consuetudines* (for example, don't shake out your clothes or beat the dust out of them in the dormitory) with that available in Marcel Aubert's two-volume work on Cistercian architecture ("not always to be trusted," Merton notes [25]), and charts the gradual loosening and retightening of regulations in later centuries, including the statute of the Abbey of La Val Sainte (Trappists in Swiss exile during the aftermath of the French Revolution) which justifies the common dormitory by declaring that it is "a consolation for religious who really love one another to sleep together in {the} same room like children around their parents" (27) and which "recommended blankets . . . made of moss" (27)—another rather piquant detail Merton no doubt highlighted in his presentation.

The final introductory chapter, on the taking of mixt, the optional breaking of the fast in the morning, simply summarizes the twelfth-century regulations, followed by those from La Trappe, then by reference to current practice. This chapter is oddly placed, apparently inserted here in the *Consuetudines* rather than in the midst of the following discussion of the daily schedule to indicate that it was not originally regarded as part

---

22. William Wordsworth, "Lines Composed a Few Miles above Tintern Abbey," *William Wordsworth*, Oxford English Authors, ed. Stephen Gill (New York: Oxford University Press, 1984), 131–35.

of the "normal" monastic routine—though Merton himself takes no note of its rather anomalous position.

Merton summarizes the chapters on the winter schedule rather succinctly, proceeding through the various activities of the day, with the regulations for work and for proper conduct in the refectory getting most attention, and then looks even more quickly at the somewhat different *horarium* for the summer season until he reaches chapter 84 on the special regulations for harvest time, in which the entire community regularly participated, including the reader, who "went along, took his mixt under a tree with the cook after tierce {and} read to the community during {a} picnic dinner" (34). Since the crops were often grown at the abbey's granges, generally in the charge of the brothers, this was the one occasion when the other monks were present at these outlying properties, and their mention at this point in the *Consuetudines* prompts Merton to refer to numerous General Chapter statutes on granges, including the vexed question of whether wine and beer could be drunk there, clandestine meat-eating at granges, and the matter of hospitality—or lack of it—at granges, including thirteenth-century instances of one grange refusing to provide abbots on their way to a General Chapter with any provisions other than hay and straw, and another grange which "armed the hired help to drive away some abbots who wanted to stop off on {the} way to {the} General Chapter" (37)—another occasion for commentary that Merton and his listeners must have enjoyed.

There follows a detailed recounting of Cistercian practices concerning shaving and tonsuring in chapter 85 of the *Consuetudines* and subsequently—increased from six to nine by the close of the twelfth century, to twelve by the middle of the following century, to every two weeks in 1293, to a monthly shave and tonsure in the nineteenth-century Trappist *Usages*, to the current custom of shaving at least once a week and a monthly renewal of the "crown" of tonsure, still associated with specified feasts as had been the case from the earliest days. The whole sequence appears as an exemplification of the degree of continuity and change over the course of Cistercian history.

The final chapter of this third division provides detailed instructions for journeys outside the monastery, beginning with the basic principle that the monk "does not go out for any purpose except for the common good—one's own good must be also common good before one can go out" (39). The survey of General Chapter statutes that follows, more than twenty in all, makes clear that this ideal was not always observed in practice, that "there was such a thing as journeying out of mere restlessness" (41), as well as for penance, and in the later decadent period, for virtually no reason at all, or to "go to *festa locorum* (festivals of towns and villages) or weddings or shows or taverns" (44). While Merton notes that enclosure is strictly enforced in Cistercian monasteries at the present time, the spirit underlying the rules still needs to be cultivated:

> Abuses in this regard are a sure sign of decadence. We must be warned by the history of the Order and guard against this danger. For ourselves, it is most important to cultivate the spirit of enclosure and stability and not deceive ourselves by indulging in vain desires for which there is an apparent "reason." Above all, avoid pretexts for travelling later on, when in office. For a true monk, travelling is a nuisance and a burden, a meritorious penance when imposed by the will of God. (41)

He concludes his discussion of travel with a couple of vivid incidents described in the statutes. The first is the early thirteenth-century laybrothers' rebellion at the Welsh abbey of Margam, in which they "rose up in rebellion against the abbot, threw the cellarer off his horse, chased the abbot fifteen miles with weapons, barricaded themselves in the dormitory and refused to allow the monks to get at the food supplies" (45), and consequently had to journey on foot to Clairvaux before being dispersed to houses throughout the Order. The other is the altercation some years later between two travelling Portuguese abbots and the guestmaster at Marmoutier who "gives them some evil-smelling kind of smoked fish," which they gripe about; they then buy their own fish in town the next day, which the guestmaster refuses to cook unless he is paid to do so; instead he provides bread and wine, but only if they leave the monastery, which they do—as far as the area immediately outside the front gate where they "park" themselves conspicuously for their scanty meal; in consequence "the abbots were forbidden fish for a year" (45) (the inhospitable guestmaster, being a Benedictine rather than a Cistercian, apparently goes unadmonished). Once again Merton brings a section of his presentation to a conclusion that must have amused and delighted his audience.

Moving on to the fourth "*Distinctio*," Merton jumps ahead to the chapter (102) on the novitiate, which he combines with the chapter on the novice master (113) from the final section. These regulations, and the subsequent General Chapter statutes that Merton summarizes, of course invite comparison with the situation in which the current Gethsemani novices find themselves and so have an intrinsic interest. For example, novices were originally clothed with the habit at the time of profession rather than at the end of postulancy (initially only a three-day period) so that elements of the current clothing ceremony had been shifted from the time of first entrance into the community. A good deal of attention was given to the minimum age of the novice (fifteen, raised to eighteen by 1175), as well as to his degree of physical and psychological maturity—his ability for instance to get along without three meals a day. Merton mentions one early thirteenth-century abbot who "has a novice who eats three times a day" and—he notes with an eye for the gratuitous but droll detail—has "peacocks in the cloister" (48). The duties of the novice master are outlined in the later chapter (including "*in ecclesia excitare*—wake them in church" [50]), with a particular emphasis in the *Consuetudines* not only on his training the novices in monastic discipline but on his role in smoothing the transition from the novitiate to the professed community after first vows (the novitiate lasting only a single year rather than the two-year period currently required).

Having jumped ahead to the fifth "*Distinctio*," on monastic officials, Merton goes on to describe the duties of the cantor and subcantor (c. 115), the cellarer (c. 117), the sacristan and his assistant (c. 114) and finally the weekly reader (c. 106). All of this is fairly straightforward, with no additional details drawn from other sources, and with no discussion of the chapters on other offices. One gets the impression that at this point Merton is ready to be finished with this set of conferences and is willing to omit material to get to the end quickly, though he does turn back to the fourth Distinction to consider the four chapters on the sick, in part, perhaps, to be able to include details on what to do if a priest saying Mass gets a nosebleed, or when someone leaves choir—or the refectory—to vomit, as well as the quaint customs associated with regular bleeding (three or four days of rest, better food, and exemption from the night office), though the actual conclusion is rather more staid with its instructions for the sick whether outside the infirmary or in it. By intention or not, Merton's final sentence, referring to the latter group—"They work if work is assigned to them" (56)—suggests that being bled is a surer guarantee for a bit of rest than being sick.

Inserted in Merton's typescript immediately before the page that begins to discuss the winter monastic schedule[23] is a small note page of jottings in Merton's hand referring to announcements to be made to the novices—customarily written on the verso sides of his typescript pages rather than on a separate sheet, as here. The topics are various, including an upcoming retreat, procedures for a novitiate chapter of faults, and a reminder not to slam screen doors. Among these notes are three that provide important clues about a second cycle of presentations of these conferences on the *Consuetudines*. On one side of the sheet, immediately below mention of cold-weather clothes, is the note: "Bellarmine retreat"; on the other, following the screen door instructions, are found the notes: "Heschel book" and "St Malachy." In Merton's journal entry for October 24, 1960, he refers to presentations he made to a faculty

---

23. A bracketed note in the top left hand corner of the paper, apparently not made by Merton, reads: "attached to p. 8" (the following page), and the outline of a paper clip is visible on one side of the sheet.

group from Bellarmine College in Louisville and to "Msgr. Horrigan," the college president, "who brought the Bellarmine group here"; he writes, "The Bellarmine conferences last week. These busy but rewarding days, talking on wisdom, talking boldly, offending pious ears (that wanted to be offended) urging a broadening of horizons in every direction. . . . Impression that it was a warm and responsive group."[24] Five days later, on October 29, he mentions in the journal that "Abraham Heschel wrote an amiable and humble letter and sent three books. I am happy and consoled. He is the most significant spiritual writer in this country at the moment. I like his depth and his realism."[25] Four days later, on November 2, the abbey celebrated the feast of Saint Malachy, the Irish archbishop and friend of Saint Bernard who died at Clairvaux and was buried there. It is therefore evident that these notes must date from the end of October 1960, and the clear inference is that Merton must have begun presenting these conferences for a second time shortly before the notes were written.

One additional piece of evidence lends further support to this supposition. Unlike the *Carta Caritatis* notes, those on the *Consuetudines* were retyped on stencils (also consisting of an introductory page and twenty-one numbered pages) and reproduced to be distributed to the novices as well as sent to formation directors in other houses of the Order. One copy of this version of the text, bound with a similar reproduction of the *Constitutions* conferences to be discussed below, is clearly Merton's personal copy since it contains an initial page in his own hand consisting in a small cross and three brief lines: "1. Consuetudines / 2.

---

24. Thomas Merton, *Turning Toward the World: The Pivotal Years. Journals, vol. 4: 1960–1963*, ed. Victor A. Kramer (San Francisco: HarperCollins, 1996), 59.

25. *Turning Toward the World*, 61–62; see also Merton's December 17, 1960, letter thanking Rabbi Heschel for the books and inviting him to visit the monastery—which Heschel finally did in July 1964 (Thomas Merton, *The Hidden Ground of Love: Letters on Religious Experience and Social Concerns*, ed. William H. Shannon [New York: Farrar, Straus, Giroux, 1985], 430–31).

Constitutions of O.C.S.O. / Novitiate 1955-56," along with a few handwritten corrections to the *Constitutions* text. On the cover of this copy is a label reading: "NOTES ON THE CONSTITUTIONS / of the O.C.S.O. / and on the Consuetudines of St / Stephen." Over the lower part of the label (the two lines on the *Consuetudines*) is an ink-stamped identification "FR LOUIS" made by a very young postulant, Nelson Richardson, just before he left the monastery in early August 1960.[26] Thus it can be concluded with confidence that Merton once again presented these conferences in the autumn of 1960. It can likewise be assumed that this was the last time he gave them; it is certain that he did not do so once his novitiate classes began to be taped in late April 1962.

* * * * * * *

The final set of conferences in this volume is more than twice as long as the two preceding ones combined, running seventy-seven pages in Merton's own typescript (of which the first twenty-three are missing) and eighty-five in the multigraphed reproduction.[27] While from a historical perspective the conferences on Saint Bernard functioned as a continuation of the early Cistercian focus of the *Carta* and *Consuetudines* material, as Merton himself indicated in the introductory note on his Saint Bernard typescript, the content of the *Constitutions* makes this document a very close twentieth-century equivalent to the *Consuetudines*.[28] The note in Merton's bound copy of the multigraphed versions

---

26. In his August 5, 1960, journal entry Merton writes, "So now he is gone and has left no memorial other than a spot of wine on the altar cloth—and the little India rubber eraser on which he carved my name so that with our ink pad I can stamp it on books, etc. I like the way it is done, rough and crude and simple" (*Turning Toward the World*, 25).

27. Included in volume 15 of the "Collected Essays."

28. Merton's handwritten calendar of conferences between August 31 and September 14, 1956, shows that the *Constitutions* conferences and the St. Bernard conferences were being given simultaneously, those on the *Constitutions* on Wednesdays and those on Bernard on Fridays.

of the two latter texts linking them together as presented in 1955–1956 suggests that, at least in retrospect, he considered the *Constitutions* conferences also to be in their own way a kind of sequel to the *Consuetudines*.

Merton mentions in the text itself (99) that he is giving the conferences some time in 1956. Various notes for announcements in the *Constitutions* typescript provide somewhat more precise information about the chronology of the course. On page 31v [29] he mentions the feast of the Solemnity of Saint Benedict, celebrated on July 11, as well as that of Saint John Gualbert, celebrated the following day. On page 32v [30] a note reads: "Novices—Collegeville—classes," a reference to Merton's trip to Saint John's Abbey in Minnesota between July 22 and August 4, 1956, [31] and evidently to whatever arrangements were being made concerning novitiate conferences during his absence. On page 40v [32] are found brief notes on Saint Thérèse and Saint Francis, presumably from October when their feasts were celebrated on successive days (October 3 and 4). A note on page 63v [33] mentions Christmas, another on 66v [34] mentions "New Year" and one on 68v [35] refers to an exam scheduled for Monday, January 14. Two final notes refer to the annual retreat: on 74v [36] Merton mentions that there will be no novice conference on the upcoming Friday due to the retreat, and on 76v, [37] directly opposite the very end of the final page of the typescript, is a series of five brief jottings on retreat

29. Page 119 of this edition.
30. Page 120 of this edition.
31. See Thomas Merton, *A Search for Solitude: Pursuing the Monk's True Life. Journals, vol. 3: 1952–1960*, ed. Lawrence S. Cunningham (San Francisco: HarperCollins, 1996), 49–63 [journal entries from July 22 through August 4, 1956].
32. Page 138 of this edition.
33. Page 176 of this edition.
34. Page 182 of this edition.
35. Page 186 of this edition.
36. Page 198 of this edition.
37. Page 202 of this edition.

Introduction xxxiii

material. As the retreat concluded on January 25,[38] the conferences must have been completed by the end of January 1957. It is impossible to know for certain when they began, but as it took almost seven months to present the material from the last forty-five pages of his typescript, if Merton proceeded at the same rate from the outset, the conferences in their entirety would have run just about a year, so they probably began sometime in January or early February of 1956. While it is impossible to prove definitively that they too were given a second time along with the *Consuetudines* conferences, the fact that Merton's copies of the two sets are bound together and that eight of the pages of the *Constitutions* notes have markings in Merton's hand of one sort or another, some of them brief but substantive additions, lends strong support to the hypothesis that he repeated this series of conferences immediately after completing those on the *Consuetudines*, probably beginning sometime in early 1961 and definitely completed before the recording of conferences began in April 1962.

The Cistercian *Constitutions* in force at the time of Merton's lectures date from 1924; they were a revision of the *Constitutions* written in the aftermath of the unification of the three Trappist congregations to form the Order of Cistercians of the Strict Observance in 1892, modified to take into account the provisions of the Code of Canon Law promulgated in 1917. As Merton notes, the *Constitutions* consist of three parts, the first concerned with the governing structure of the Order, which "includes not only {the} General Chapter, {the} Abbot General, {the} abbots and their election and deposition, but also rules for visitations and for the foundations of new monasteries"; the second focuses on the observances that make up the Cistercian way of life, "{the} office, mental prayer, reading, silence, work, studies, fasting, sleep, habit, enclosure and the care of the sick"; while the final section "governs above all the admission of postulants, the novitiate, simple and solemn profession, change of stability and the reception of

---

38. See Merton's January 25 and January 26, 1957, letters to Dom James Fox (*School of Charity*, 98–99).

fugitives and apostates" (58). Merton comments (at times very briefly, particularly in the early sections) on virtually every one of the 192 individual provisions of the *Constitutions*, supplemented frequently with references to relevant modern General Chapter decrees—a procedure similar to, if probably less entertaining than, that used in the *Consuetudines* notes—as well as with extensive citations from the Code of Canon Law in certain sections. The overall impression made by the text of this material is that it is a good deal more sober, less sprightly, than its predecessor, as might be expected of regulations governing current Cistercian structures and practices. While Merton no doubt strove to make the material as accessible and as engaging as possible for his audience, evidence of such efforts is less recoverable from the written text. Before turning to the text proper of the *Constitutions*, Merton first distinguishes this document and its level of authority from the Benedictine *Rule* itself and from the Cistercian usages—each the topic of its own novitiate course. Whereas the *Rule* is "a *permanent* norm" (57) applicable to all Benedictine religious of whatever order, the *Constitutions* are unique to the reformed Cistercians, formulated by its General Chapter and approved by the Holy See, which "*define* how we are to understand the *Rule* of St. Benedict, and in what particular ways we are to carry out the prescriptions of the *Rule*," and which can be altered, subject to pontifical approval, to adapt to changing circumstances. The usages, in turn, are a "mode of observance" that apply *Rule* and *Constitutions* to the specifics of monastic life and can be changed by the General Chapter or even modified by local superiors if conditions warrant (58).

Merton then looks at *Monachorum Vita*, the 1924 Apostolic Letter of Pope Pius XI approving the revised *Constitutions*, which is included as a preface to the English translation of the document. The letter provides a capsule history of monastic life, and particularly of monastic reform movements, leading up to the foundation of the Abbey of Cîteaux in 1098, through the seventeenth-century Trappist reform, to the 1892 Strict Observance reunion, then goes on to highlight the Cistercian regimen of silence, labor and prayer, especially the regular performance of the divine office, as means of perfection of the individual religious through participation in the prayer and work of Christ and as a uniquely fruitful way of giving glory to God. Elements of "enclosure, stability, retirement and solitude" (63) are mentioned, as well as reparation for the world's rejection of God (a very "Trappist" perspective). Remarks on Eucharistic devotion and the "characteristic Cistercian observance" (63) of the little office of the Blessed Virgin (actually about to disappear from the Trappist *horarium* at the very time these conferences were being composed [39]) round out the letter's appreciative depiction of the life which the *Constitutions* are designed to foster.

Merton's discussion of the first part of the *Constitutions*, on the governance structure of the Order, is by far the briefest. The nine chapters successively treat the roles of the General Chapter, the abbot general, the definitors, the procurator general, the fathers immediate, and the abbot, followed by chapters on visitations, abbatial elections and new foundations. For the first six chapters on the various officers Merton provides a succinct description followed by usually brief descriptive summaries of the individual numbered paragraphs—sometimes only one or two words—which of course could be expanded on in the oral presentation. The last of these, on the abbot, is more extensive, going beyond the text of the *Constitutions* themselves to distinguish the

---

39. The General Chapter of 1955 authorized a new daily schedule in which recitation of the little office was discontinued (see Michael Casey, ocso, "Evolution of Cistercian Spirituality," in Augusta Tescari, ocso, Marie Gérard Dubois, ocso, and Maria Paola Santachiara, ocso, eds., *The Cistercian Order of the Strict Observance in the Twentieth Century*, 2 vols. [Rome: Cistercian Order of the Strict Observance, 2008], 2:230). The new schedule went into effect at Gethsemani on August 13, 1956 (see Merton's comments in the journal entry for the following day [*Search for Solitude*, 64]). In discussing the monastic day in *The Silent Life* (New York: Farrar, Straus & Cudahy, 1957), Merton writes: "The Little Office of the Blessed Virgin, which used to be chanted in choir every day along with the Canonical office, has been commuted to an antiphon and collect sung before each canonical hour" (120).

two types of abbot (*nullius* and *de regimine*), to elaborate on the *Constitutions'* specification of the abbot's double responsibility of spiritual jurisdiction and temporal administration, and then to note in considerable detail the abbot's obligation to consult the community in financial matters, as spelled out in the longest single numbered section (n. 46) in the *Constitutions* themselves. The sections on visitations and new foundations are dealt with rather quickly, while that on the election of abbots, particularly the regulations on who is permitted to vote, is given greater attention. Despite the general brevity, Merton already begins in this section to make reference to the Code of Canon Law as it pertains to particular aspects of these regulations, for example the authority of a general superior of a religious order (67), the legality of contracts (for which the *Constitutions* themselves cite the relevant canons) (73) and various provisions for electing a superior (76–77). He also draws on various General Chapter statutes, some of which are actually earlier than the 1924 *Constitutions*, that provide more specific direction for meeting the requirements set forth there—for example, how often abbots of non-European monasteries are expected to attend the General Chapter (66), similar timetables for visitation of distant houses (75), the extent of the authority of the father immediate in dealing with the papers of a deceased abbot (76). There are even occasional references to the *Carta Caritatis* (67, 75), the *Exordium Parvum* (77), and the twelfth-century *Instituta* (75) as providing background for modern procedures and structures. But the overall impression is given that Merton wishes to proceed through this material as expeditiously as possible.

Part II, on monastic observances, is actually significantly shorter in the text of the *Constitutions* themselves than Part I—eleven pages in the English translation as compared to fifteen for the first part[40]—but Merton's own discussion of this material is

---

40. *Constitutions of the Order of Cistercians of the Strict Observance* (Dublin: M. H. Gill & Sons, [1925]), 7–21, 22–32.

roughly five times as lengthy.[41] The reason is evident when the topics of the seventeen chapters of this part are considered: after an initial chapter on uniformity of observance throughout the Order, subsequent topics are all ones of practical significance for daily living of Cistercian monastic life: the office and mental prayer, confession and communion, reading, silence, work and studies, fasting and meals, regulations for sleeping, the habit, provisions for sickness, rules for enclosure and for journeys outside the monastery. All this obviously would have a much more immediate effect on the lives of monks and even of novices than how the General Chapter is organized or what the procurator general does or even who is eligible to vote for a new abbot on the relatively infrequent occasions when such an election is held; consequently Merton provides a much more detailed treatment of each of these chapters, with a considerably expanded use of supplementary materials. His general methodology soon becomes evident: he weaves together various elements in differing proportions, depending on the topic of a particular chapter; to a basic synopsis of the *Constitutions* text he adds relevant materials from early Cistercian sources, as well as from the Benedictine *Rule*; references to pertinent canons from the 1917 Code, along with occasional clarifications by commentators; extensive citations from General Chapter statutes since the Trappist reunion of 1892; and when appropriate his own brief reflections on the practical and spiritual implications of particular regulations, which often may well have been more developed in the conference presentation itself than in the written text.

The emphasis on uniformity is traced back to the very origins of the Order (citing the *Carta Caritatis*), but Merton also notes the legitimate development of specific customs characteristic of each particular house that give it "its own physiognomy" (78).

---

41. Thirty-six pages in the multigraph version of the text, as compared to seven for Part I. The comparison is somewhat inexact because much of the second part is reproduced in pica rather than elite type, but the disparity is still quite evident.

His focus is on the need for common sense, for discretion on the part of superiors, as the multiplication of various "extra" devotional practices at various monasteries (including Gethsemani during his early years there) could be *"harmful to regularity"* (79) by upsetting the necessary balance of a well-integrated life composed of public prayer, private reading and meditation, and manual labor. He also notes that certain adjustments can be made by the General Chapter due to the poverty of individual houses, and that even the regulations of the *Constitutions* concerning work, fasting, vigils, and the like can be modified by local superiors in individual cases when there is evident need.

The placement of the chapter on the office as the first of those on particular monastic practices is an obvious indication of its importance for the Cistercian life. The provisions, summarized by Merton, include the obligation of each monastery to the daily recitation of the office; the regulations concerning the (soon to be discontinued) little office of the Blessed Virgin; the rule that the office, except for the night office and lauds, is to be sung, as is the conventual Mass; circumstances, particularly the size of the community, which may reduce the amount of the office required to be sung; and monks' individual obligation to attend choir. Amid this material, Merton intersperses the first of his numerous references to the canonist Timothy Schaefer's commentary on the Code as it applies to religious (noting that the obligation to attend choir becomes a matter of sin if it is imposed by a superior); points from twelfth-century statutes on the background of the little office, along with a recent (1953) ruling dispensing from its recitation on days of Marian feasts (to be replaced two years later by its complete disappearance); strictures against affected singing of chant dating from the earliest legislation of the Order, against polyphonic chant from the early thirteenth century, and against unauthorized alterations in the service books and in the chant itself from various twentieth-century General Chapters. Only in commenting on the final paragraph of the chapter, on absence from the office, does Merton provide any personal instruction to his charges: "{The} principle {is} 'to let nothing be preferred to the Work of God.' When God's will manifestly calls us to something else temporarily, then we are not preferring that to the office. Regard the office as a privilege—as a burden, no" (84).

Chapter 3, on mental prayer, includes not only the direction for twice daily periods of personal prayer but the similar requirement for examination of conscience twice a day and the provisions for a yearly retreat. Here also Merton supplements the material by noting the 1920 General Chapter recommendation for a monthly retreat, the *Usages'* requirement for such retreats for those holding office, and the Gethsemani custom of a monthly day of recollection for all and weekly retreat days for certain officers. Once again he also provides his own brief interpretation—"We need to get back to the attitude which regards the time of *lectio divina* as also {a} time of mental prayer" (84)—supported by references to the *Rule*, to the *Consuetudines* and to the twelfth-century English abbot Gilbert of Hoyland.

The material on confession in chapter 4, three paragraphs taking up less than a page in the English translation of the *Constitutions*, occupies more than five in the multigraphed version of Merton's text, mainly concerned with a clear delineation of the respective roles of confessors and of superiors in regulating the monks' interior and exterior lives. Drawing extensively on canon law as well as on General Chapter decrees, Merton points out that superiors rather than confessors have the authority to require or dispense from regular observances, considers at great length the extent of a confessor's power to absolve a penitent from censures and reserved sins, and the rights of superiors to release community members from excommunications. Special attention is given to the appointment of confessors for novices, noting that confession to the novice master is and should be relatively rare, as the role of discerning a novice's vocation and that of absolving sins are distinct and may be in tension, though "the father master should know everything in the internal forum which will help him to make a correct judgement regarding the fitness of the novice for the life, his spirit, and the manner in which he fulfills the obligations of the Order" (92). Conversely, the confessor has no role in the monastic formation of a novice or in the conduct of the novitiate. The same basic principle applies to subject and superior generally: while the faculties of a confessor to absolve sins derive from the authority of the abbot, a superior hears a subject's confession only exceptionally, for a serious reason, and has no authority to require a monk to manifest his conscience, that is, to reveal the state of his soul in a nonsacramental forum. Having explained in great detail these juridical regulations, formulated to safeguard against abuse of authority on the part of superiors, Merton then concludes his discussion by looking at the other side of the matter, the spiritual rather than just the narrowly legal aspects of such relationships:

> {Note} *the advantage of openness* with superiors. The superior still has a special grace of state, especially in Benedictine life. We cannot say it is obligatory to manifest one's conscience to Reverend Father but it is certainly worthwhile. The abbot has graces of state to judge his subjects. He should be regarded as Christ in the monastery. However, it is not true to assert that the superior alone, for example, is the sole judge whether or not one has a vocation, etc., etc. (95)

Regardless of his own complicated relationship with his abbot, Merton takes care that the novices do not misinterpret the canonical and constitutional norms as in any way intended to lessen or distort the respect, confidence and affection that a monk should have toward his abbot and the other officers of the monastery.

The chapter on holy communion that follows is considerably less involved than that on confession, focused mainly on the days that all members of the community are expected to receive communion, on the practice of daily communion, and on the circumstances in which a superior can prohibit a monk from receiving communion. Once again Merton develops the spiritual implications of a typically laconic statement in the text: where the *Constitutions* mandate that "Superiors shall promote frequent and even daily communion" (96), Merton comments:

Introduction   xli

{The} obligation of {the} superior {is} not merely to urge a great number of communions but *to foster a eucharistic life* in the community, because this is the safeguard of the community itself; in a sense this obligation is more important than any other, because if the monks lead a true eucharistic life they will live united in fervor of charity and will spontaneously keep all the rules. They will aid one another to rise to high perfection. (96–97)

In discussing the following chapter, on spiritual reading, Merton emphasizes the integration of reading, meditation, and prayer, notes the *Constitutions'* strictures "against the introduction of secular curiosities or other things that do not pertain to the contemplative life" (98), cites the General Chapter's recommendation of the *Rule* and the Trappist *Spiritual Directory* as suitable reading matter, along with Scripture and the Fathers (especially Saint Bernard and other early Cistercians), and points out the prohibition of newspapers and severe restriction of even religious periodicals in Trappist monasteries. He appends a summary of Dom Gabriel Sortais' 1952 letter on *lectio divina*, in which the abbot general stresses that both the matter and the intention of monks' reading should be "divine," and that such contact with the riches of the Christian tradition is essential to spiritual progress: "IS IT NOT BECAUSE SO MANY OF THE MONKS AND NUNS OF OUR ORDER DRAW FROM THEIR READING SO LITTLE TO GAZE UPON AND CONTEMPLATE AND LOVE, THAT THERE ARE SO FEW REAL CONTEMPLATIVES EVEN IN AN ORDER LIKE OUR OWN WHERE EVERYTHING IS ORGANIZED TO LEAD SOULS TO CONTEMPLATION?" (100). Merton would certainly agree with this assessment, if not with some of the ways Dom Gabriel and the Order in general would continue to maintain a narrowly restrictive view of what constituted appropriate reading material for a Trappist. One might wonder to what extent Merton presented this material differently if it was discussed in a second round of conferences in 1961 from the way it may have been considered in 1956.

Merton calls attention to the unusual character of the opening sentence of the following chapter—"There is nothing which conduces more to the practice of regular discipline than the religious practice of silence" (101)—noting that whereas the *Constitutions* generally provide "no ascetic explanations or statements of spiritual policy" but simply "statements of fact—we do this; we don't do that" (101), silence is so essential to the Cistercian way of life that the text moves beyond its customary apodictic tone. This prompts Merton himself to quote a range of authorities from the wider Church on religious silence, from John Cassian and John Climacus to the Cluniac abbot Peter the Venerable to a preliminary draft of a schema from the First Vatican Council and a decree of an eighteenth-century pope (101–102)—an equally unusual extension of citations in these conferences beyond the more juridical sources. This context provides the rationale for the strictness of Trappist silence as decreed in the *Constitutions*, which make no provision for periods of recreation when conversation is permitted. At the same time, he notes, superiors may allow for speech in appropriate circumstances, and he warns against a kind of rigid adherence to silence as an end in itself. "Cultivate silence, but not mutism. Practice silence in a spirit of discipline, but be able to speak when you have to" (103). Also considered in this chapter, as a kind of extension of the principle of no conversation with seculars, is the necessity to submit all letters to the superior, with the exception of those sent to higher religious authorities. This particular requirement, Merton notes, "seems to have received the most elaboration from the General Chapters in recent years" (104), leading Merton to summarize almost a dozen of these statutes, such as that extending the meaning of "letters" to include other forms of communication like telegrams and phone calls, the reminder that this regulation is still in force even when a monk is physically outside the monastery, and the admonition about what properly characterizes the exempt correspondence with higher superiors.

    The centrality of manual labor to Cistercian life, as outlined in chapter 8 of this second part of the *Constitutions*, is traced by Merton back to the very foundations of the Order: "One of the main reasons for manual labor is to make us independent of powerful benefactors and thus free to live a purely monastic life. This was one of the reasons for the break from Molesme to Cîteaux" (108). Begging, including solicitation by mail, is regarded as inconsistent with this spirit, as even more fundamentally is parochial work—though Merton notes that in Europe during World War I some Trappists by necessity had to staff parishes, a situation that postwar General Chapters addressed vigorously. The somewhat related issue of retreats for laypeople at Cistercian monasteries is not considered in the *Constitutions*, Merton points out, but "closed retreats have been specifically praised and encouraged, in our monastery, by the Holy Father" (111). Still, he cautions, "The retreat 'movement' should not become too much of a 'movement' with publicity and ballyhoo surrounding it" (111) to the point that the retreat masters become overworked and lose the time for cultivating their own interior life.

Given his audience, it is not surprising that Merton's commentary on the chapter concerning studies is among the most detailed. The prescriptions for the course of studies leading to ordination as mandated by the 1917 Code of Canon Law are recognized as modifying earlier regulations formulated by General Chapters, and the canonical requirement to appoint a master of scholastics is seen as binding on Cistercians (at least in larger houses) despite there being no mention of the position in the *Constitutions*. The Cistercian house of studies in Rome receives extended attention, as does the importance of continuing studies by priests after ordination. The final provision of this chapter, for monthly theological, liturgical, and scriptural conferences, prompts Merton to cite both General Chapter statutes and Gethsemani practices aimed at insuring that the conference "does not degenerate into a dispute." He notes rather mordantly: "Due to our silence, when we talk on subjects which seem for some reason to arouse emotion, the discussion easily degenerates into a free-for-all, at least in some communities" (121). One strategy at Gethsemani for reducing the likelihood of direct arguments is to have the speaker leave the podium before any comments from the floor, which should "attempt to throw light on the matter discussed rather than to discredit the one who spoke" (121), are entertained. (One gets the impression that these provisions are the fruit of hard-earned experience.)

The next three chapters all concern food. Merton amplifies from other sources the rather meager regulations on abstinence (c. 10) and fasting (c. 11) in the *Constitutions*, then proceeds even more briskly through the following chapter on the quantity of food. The abbot's authority to dispense sick and weak monks from the requirement to abstain from meat is traced back to Saint Benedict, the rule for the ordinary exclusion of fish is cited from General Chapter statutes dating from the very beginning of the Trappist reunion, the *Usages* are quoted repeatedly as providing instruction as to what can and cannot be eaten on various kinds of journeys; *Constitutions*, *Usages*, General Chapter rulings, and even the abbot general's direction to serve coffee on a particularly cold Good Friday during a 1947 visitation are all brought to bear on the matter of proper Lenten abstinence. With regard to fasting, the *Constitutions* note that the expectations of Saint Benedict's time, even for nonmonastics, can no longer be considered normative. The principle is rather "that it is sufficient to fast *proportionately* to the rest of the Church. Our fast remains stricter, but is proportionately diminished" (125). While the regulations in the *Constitutions* concerning the amount of food are fairly straightforward, Merton uses the chapter's initial mention of meals taken at the common table to insert a short reflection on the spiritual meaning of monastic table fellowship:

> {Note the} importance of eating in common at the same time. {It is} an expression of common life—sharing the fruits of our labor together—{an} expression of unity and peace in the community. This makes eating together a supernatural act, blessed by special prayers and graces. Christ is in the midst of us in the refectory, as everywhere else. {There} should be an atmosphere of peace, recollection, decency, modesty, joy, {a} family spirit. The refectory should not become merely a place of clatter and tension in which the assembled victims develop ulcers. (126–27)

Moving from the refectory to the dormitory, the following chapter prescribes the arrangements for sleeping in partitioned cells, separate accommodations for those with particular jobs, the custom of sleeping in the habit (modified—even down to the socks—only with permission) and the appointed hours for sleeping (just changed by the 1955 General Chapter). Merton notes the difference between adaptation, which preserves the principle in the *Rule* while altering some details, and mitigation, which relaxes what the *Rule* prescribes, and notes that dispensing from some articles of clothing in warm weather is an instance of the former rather than the latter since its purpose is simply to allow the monk to get the proper amount of sleep allowed for by Saint Benedict. This consideration of nighttime attire leads into the brief chapter (14) that follows on the habit itself, which also includes mention of shoes, to be those typically worn in the country in which a monastery is located, and of the monthly renewal of the monastic crown. Merton notes in passing the difference of the Strict Observance cowl from that of the Common Observance, and the attachment to the Cistercian scapular of the indulgences associated with various nonmonastic scapulars.

The chapter on the sick covers the infirmary, its chapel, the requirement to provide for the "needs and comfort" (132) of the ill, allowance for meat and for a softer bed, the need for a God-fearing, experienced, and prudent infirmarian, and the special duty of the abbot to take responsibility for both the physical and spiritual needs of the sick. Merton uses this opportunity to instruct the novices on the way in which the treatment of those who are ill reveals the spiritual state of the community as a whole:

> the attitude taken toward the sick, the care given to them and the charity shown to them are of the greatest importance in the monastic life. If a community takes a harsh and indifferent attitude towards its suffering members, it is a sign of a bad spirit. . . . Remember—the sick are very often those who have reached the end of their course. They are completing their gift of themselves to God, and are at a crucial point in their lives: (a) help them by charity not to

lose their morale; (b) support them—give *aid* for their spiritual life; their sickness is their sacrifice—our penances will make up for what they cannot do; (c) {do} not forget and reject them! (131)

The penultimate chapter of this second part, on monastic enclosure, is, Merton points out, "one of the most essential, for we are a contemplative and monastic order, and for us separation from the world is even more strict and more vital than it is in other religious orders" (133) and consequently receives a detailed exposition of both active enclosure—the obligation of the religious not to leave the monastery and its immediate surroundings without permission—and passive enclosure—the prohibition of unauthorized outsiders, women in particular, from entering cloistered space. Regulations about automobiles (luxury models are forbidden), publicity (no recognizable photographs of monks to be published), radio and television broadcasts (neither to be produced nor watched in monasteries), and making and listening to phonograph records (allowed by exception with a due application of prudence) are discussed as extensions of the rule of enclosure. The exact circumstances of excommunications imposed for violation of the papal enclosure of monasteries by women as spelled out in canon law are examined, as are the exceptions for wives of heads of state (extended in the past to the first lady of Kentucky by Gethsemani abbots) and for a nine-day period following the dedication of a church, a rite that directly concerns the entire Mystical Body of Christ. Merton concludes that the purpose of enclosure is "to protect the monks against undue disturbance and distraction from outsiders, to allow them to live their life of prayer and solitude which are with us serious obligations," so that the spirit of the regulation can be violated even by "frequent visits in the parlor etc.," or by a monk's efforts "to procure for himself a job in which he will have contact with visitors or other seculars" (140). The point, Merton tells the novices, is not simply to observe the letter of the law but to recognize and respond positively to its underlying purpose.

Introduction

xlvii

The final chapter of this second part logically follows that on enclosure by considering legitimate reasons for and proper deportment during journeys outside the monastery, another topic that has elicited numerous specifications and clarifications from the General Chapter, emphasizing that only *"necessary business of the house"* (140) or "most grave reasons" (141) (normally excluding even sickness or death of relatives) justify such trips. A few cultural differences between European and American houses of the Order come into play here, including the exceptional but possible permission to "take a cure" (141) at a French or Swiss health spa, and the difference in travel apparel (clerics rather than the habit being customary in America). Thus the discussion of Part II concludes, quite by chance, with some indication that uniformity is not quite so absolute as one might presume from its opening chapter.

The third and final part of the *Constitutions* is headed "On Entrance into the Order," broadly understood as including not just the circumstances of admission but the period of the novitiate, both simple and solemn profession, transfers from and to other religious orders, and even change of stability from one Cistercian house to another and circumstances of expulsion and/or readmission. As one would expect from the relevance of the subject matter to Merton's immediate audience, his discussion of this part of the document is quite detailed. The proportion of text to commentary matches almost exactly that for Part II: once again the text in the English translation is eleven pages (though divided into eight chapters rather than seventeen),[42] and the multigraph reproduction of Merton's commentary takes up thirty-nine pages, three more than in the previous part.

The first chapter of Part III, on the admission of postulants, runs more than three pages in the translation, the second longest (after that on the abbot) of any chapter in the text, and the twelve-plus pages of the commentary, almost one-third of the material on this part, is the most extensive of that on any single chapter of

---

42. *Constitutions*, 33–43.

the *Constitutions*. The importance of testing prospective vocations and of thorough formation of those admitted has been emphasized by the Church since the time of the Council of Trent and is of vital concern to the Cistercian Order in particular. Merton immediately points out, commenting on the opening clause of the chapter, "The greatest care shall be taken in the admission of novices," that the approach taken by the *Constitutions* and thus by his own commentary as well focuses primarily on "the mystery of our vocation from a canonical point of view, rather than from the viewpoint of spirituality." He acknowledges that such a perspective "may seem cold and heartless" but maintains that "this aspect of the question is vitally important. Vocation is an expression of the inner life of the Church, and consequently it belongs to the Church herself to say whether or not an individual belongs in this or that state of life. Unless we allow ourselves to be guided by her, the Order cannot remain for long in a healthy state" (142). Yet while carefully describing the exterior signs of a religious vocation, explaining the various impediments that invalidate a novitiate and distinguishing them from those that make a novitiate illicit (and therefore in need of dispensation), but not invalid, and discussing the official documentation needed from ecclesial authorities attesting to a candidate's good standing, Merton repeatedly reminds his audience that conforming to the juridical norms outlined in the *Constitutions* and detailed in canon law is a necessary prerequisite but not the most important factor in discerning a genuine vocation. Aptitude for the life, he emphasizes, involves not only basic physical, psychological, and intellectual capacities but a holistic commitment that sounds more like the greatest commandment than the dry provisions of the *Constitutions* and the Code: "we have to be able to serve God in our chosen vocation *with everything we have*—with body, heart, mind, will and our whole being. If we are so constituted that one or other of these *cannot* be used, we generally lack aptitude for a given vocation" (144). He picks up on the phrase *"divine vocation,"* used in a 1931 curial decree (143), to emphasize that the point of all the canonical criteria is ultimately "to discover whether the person is *called by*

God" (146). While not considered explicitly in the *Constitutions*, which simply speak of "a true desire of a higher and more perfect life, and of being able to serve God with greater freedom" (159), the signs of a contemplative and specifically of a Cistercian Benedictine vocation are clearly in Merton's mind at the center of any process of vocational discernment. Is there a "desire to seek God above all else"? Is there a *"love of prayer*, especially of the divine office, . . . love of {the} common life, with emphasis on simplicity and strictness and greater solitude . . . love for our special poverty, silence, manual labor, etc."? Are Saint Benedict's own criteria as found in the *Rule* present in the candidate: "zeal for {the} *office*, {for} *obedience*, {for} *humiliations*"? According to Merton, "If we take people who lack these qualities, we will ruin the Order" (145). Thus while providing an exhaustive investigation of the specifics of the requirements for valid admission to religious life in general and to Cistercian life in particular, Merton finds it impossible to limit himself to the parameters found in the legal documents under discussion.

The treatment of the novitiate itself in the following chapter of the *Constitutions* is rather straightforward, covering the reception of the habit; food (though not fasting), and a *horarium* identical to what applies to the professed; identical application of the principle of rank based on time of entrance; prohibition of offices and studies to the novices; and separation of the novitiate from the professed side of the house with provision for minimal contact between novices and professed monks. The qualifications of the novice master, both formal (age, length of profession, ordination) and spiritual (devoted to prayer and mortification, marked by prudence and charity) receive the most detailed attention. Merton expands somewhat on some of this material but not all of it—simply mentioning "The habit of the novices" (162) as the focus of n. 152 without bothering even to repeat the text's list of its component parts, which of course his listeners had no need to be told. He does mention such additional details as the necessity for approval by the abbot's private council in order to be admitted to the novitiate; the need for "a spirit of docility and abandonment" (163) in accepting mitigations decided upon by superiors; various provisions of the *Usages* relating to the determination of rank; an explanation of the apparent duplication of the regulations on separation of the novitiate from the professed side (nn. 155 and 158) as due to the second iteration apparently being based on the ancient legislation of the Order and the first on modern canon law, which, as he goes on to consider at some length, focuses more on keeping novices apart from the professed—protecting against premature exposure to the inevitable imperfections of community life and preserving the consistency of a monastic formation provided by a single master. Not surprisingly, the role of the novice master receives the most detailed attention, drawing on canon law, Cistercian *Usages*, and the General Chapter to delineate the juridical responsibilities of the office, but placing particular emphasis on the expectation that "the novice master must be deeply imbued in the spirit of the Order and must be able to impart that spirit to others, not only by words but above all by example," which he calls "a terrible responsibility" (167). Formation of novices involves the threefold activity of "*instruction*—imparting doctrine about the *Rule*, monastic life, {the} virtues, etc.; *training*—giving them things to do, showing them how to do them well; *probation*—testing their virtue and their spirit" (168). All this involves a complementary dedication on the part of the master and the novice to both the letter and the spirit of the *Rule* and the observances. "The training of the novice in the monastic way of life is a *disciplina* which is learned more by doing what is right than by merely hearing it told to him. Hence the father master is bound most seriously to see that the novice cultivates the fundamental monastic virtues and outlook" (170). The novice in turn must "take regularity very seriously; although perfection does not consist merely in the exterior observance of the rules and usages, nevertheless the fundamental duty of the monk is to obey his rule and *use it as a means to perfection*. This is impossible if he neglects it in order to prefer his own will and his own fancies" (171). A sense of balance, Merton maintains, is the essential quality for being an effective guide in formation—"not being either excessively severe or rigorous or too gentle and complacent towards fallen nature" (170).

The third chapter, on temporary profession, "is naturally one which is most important for novices studying the laws of the Order, since temporary profession is the immediate term of the novitiate training" (171). Thus Merton's discussion here consists largely of factual information. He provides a succinct definition of profession itself, "a public taking of vows of religion in an institute approved by the Church, a *juridical act* by which the professed *assumes the religious state* and becomes a religious in the strict sense of the word" (171). A mutual obligation is established in which the religious commits himself to follow the rule of the institute and the orders of superiors, and the order commits itself to care for the physical and above all the spiritual well-being of its members. Merton makes sure his charges are aware of the precise conditions for a valid profession, particularly what does and does not constitute an uninterrupted novitiate (spelled out in great detail). He lists no less than twelve effects of simple profession, involving both the privileges and the duties of incorporation into a religious community, rooted in the vows. He discusses valid reasons for extending the period of simple profession and for the dismissal of a simple professed, and closely follows the explanation in the *Constitutions* about the retention of ownership—but not use—of property during the period of simple vows. Merton's concluding comment that "In effect, the time of simple profession is really a prolongation of the novitiate" may seem somewhat oversimplified, given that the simple professed is now a vowed religious, but it emphasizes that the profession is to be recognized as temporary and can be brought to an end (at the proper time and in the proper circumstances) by either party. "It extends the time of formation and probation of the young monk," he points out. "In this period he must continue to show zeal and regular spirit—if he loses them it is certainly a reason for barring him from solemn profession" (180).

The remaining chapters, of less immediate relevance to the novices, are considered in more summary fashion. Both in the text of the *Constitutions* and in Merton's commentary, the material on solemn profession in chapter 4 receives less detailed attention than that on temporary profession, despite its definitive character of permanent commitment to religious life, with its implication of "a complete and irrevocable giving of oneself" (181) that involves the total renunciation of property and the promise of perpetual obedience, in a public rite of notable solemnity described in the Cistercian *Ritual* and further specified in various General Chapter statutes.

The discussion of the brief chapter five, on change of stability, is expanded somewhat by considering just what the *Constitutions'* provision of "grave necessity" (185) might or might not entail (questions of physical health, and in exceptional circumstances spiritual well-being, but not simply failure to "fit in" to one's present community), as well as questions about which community may have rights to the monk's former property (according to the General Chapter, it is the original house, but justice may require sharing or transfer of resources if the monk in question is likely to be a financial burden to his new community). He also notes that "change of stability is very likely to imply a dishonor" since it suggests a failure to live up to the "vow to live and die" (186) in a particular monastery, though it must be remembered that there may be legitimate reasons for a change in stability—such considerations would determine what rank the transferred monk takes in his new community: according to a General Chapter statute referred to but not quoted in the *Constitutions*, that of proper seniority if "the change is honorable and publicly known as such," but the lowest place if "the reason is notoriously unfavorable" (186).

The following chapter, on admission of religious from other orders, is brief, as is Merton's discussion. He spells out the provisions of the relevant canon (n. 633) mentioned but not quoted in the *Constitutions*: the requirement to make a full novitiate while vows made in the former order are suspended, and the obligation to return to the original institute should the candidate not make profession in the new one. He identifies the canon that follows

(n. 634) as the source for the *Constitutions'* subsequent specifications that the period of probation may be extended for an additional year, appending an additional note, not based on the *Constitutions*, from the next canon (n. 635) to the effect that, as with change of stability, the former house of the *"transiens"* legally retains possession of whatever goods had come to it under the vow of poverty, though he also points out that any of these goods that had accrued during the period of his new novitiate might by right belong to the house the religious is entering.

Merton begins his consideration of the penultimate chapter, on the laybrothers, by pointing out that the rather disconcerting, seemingly patronizing references to the brothers being "under our care" and to be "treat[ed] . . . like ourselves" (188) are a reflection of the situation in the earliest days of the Order when the brothers were almost always illiterate and thus in need of guidance and tutelage. He comments that in the present not only is there more equality between brothers and choir monks in the Cistercians than in many other orders, but from one perspective the "somewhat 'simpler' choir religious" (188) are actually being taken care of by the brothers, who generally possess considerably greater technical competence and run the material affairs of the monastery. He goes on to point out that recent General Chapters have been moving in the direction of greater parity between the two classes, including professed brothers in the visitation process, providing for solemn profession of brothers, and authorizing alterations in the daily schedule allowing the brothers more time for reading and an opportunity to participate in the choir at certain times. (This process of greater integration would continue with the combining of the choir and brothers novitiates in 1963 and eventually the full participation of the brothers, now having equal status as monks, in the office and in the conventual chapter. [43]) Merton stresses the importance of treating the brothers "in

---

43. See Merton's June 13, 1966, letter to Dom Inácio Accioly, osb: "The two novitiates, brothers and choir, were united into one. Both classes of novices received exactly the same formation. Since then the two classes,

every way like the choir religious" (189) with regard to respect and affection, and on the brothers' part the importance of cultivating practices of "prayer and *lectio divina*" and developing a "spirit of silence, recollection and obedience" (192) that is all the more crucial given their somewhat more autonomous patterns of work, "since the brothers too are obliged to lead a monastic and contemplative life" (192).

Finally the *Constitutions* consider the situation of those who have left the Order—fugitives and apostates—and the conditions under which they may or may not be readmitted. Merton's extensive discussion of this eighth and final chapter begins with the warning that "Even good and fervent religious can sometimes lose their zeal and fervor and end up in a betrayal of their vocation," that "it can happen to anyone," particularly if "fidelity [is] based on fear" or if "exterior regularity" is a substitute for rather than an expression of "a genuine and humble love of our vocation" (192). He explains the distinction (taken for granted in the *Constitutions*) between flight (illegitimate absence from a religious house with an intention to return) and apostasy (desertion of religious life with no intention to return by one under perpetual vows); describes the various applicable penances, including excommunication, both for fugitives and for apostates who return; outlines the procedures for dismissal from the Order of "notoriously incorrigible" (197) monks or brothers (including apostates); and considers the various processes for readmission—more and more stringent as the degree of separation increases—of those

---

brothers and choir, have been officially merged into one class of 'monks' in the whole community. There are however two offices, one in English and one in Latin, and those who participate in the English office also usually have longer hours of work; that is to say they prolong the kind of life that was led by the brothers and which they sought when they entered the monastery, but there is no difference of habit, of status, or anything else" (*School of Charity*, 305). The separate Latin and English offices were of course ended when the liturgy of the hours began to be celebrated completely in the vernacular.

who had received permission for temporary exclaustration; those who had been granted a leave of absence; those who had left at the time of expiration of temporary vows; those who had obtained an indult of secularization.

At this point Merton's *Constitutions* conference notes proper come to a rather abrupt end (somewhat surprisingly omitting any mention of the actual final stipulation of the *Constitutions* themselves that they be publicly read annually on appointed days), but they are followed in the typescript (though not in the multigraphed reproduction) by a page and a half of instruction on the chapter of faults,[44] described as "a very important observance" (202) but one that can easily be ineffective or harmful if conducted in the wrong spirit. Consequently Merton outlines practical norms for making proclamations of the faults of one's fellow monks: they must be simple and objective (based on the *Rule*, the usages or the known will of the superior); charitable (both in intention and in tone); and selfless (not motivated by self-righteousness or irritation, and never including faults committed against oneself). Merton's final comments relate specifically to the novitiate chapter of faults, to be understood as a "training ground" where "proclamations may be taken apart and analyzed and criticized" in order to learn the proper procedures, and where customs specific to the novitiate may be included, but not in such a way as to develop "a seed-ground for innumerable new 'rules'" (204). With that bit of salutary advice, the text of this set of conferences reaches its final conclusion.

Of course in many ways the *Constitutions* conferences are the most dated of the three included in the present volume. Those on the foundational documents retain their historical interest, while these, along with the 1917 Code of Canon Law to which they conform, were about to be rendered obsolete in the wake of the

---

44. Merton provides a much more extensive discussion of the chapter of faults in *Monastic Observances*, 215–39; for Merton's later thoughts on the chapter of faults in the context of monastic renewal, see his April 7, 1964, letter to Guerric Couilleau, ocso (*School of Charity*, 212).

Second Vatican Council. But looked at from another angle they become historical in their own right, reflecting the end of an era reaching back beyond the 1892 reunion to the seventeenth-century reform of La Trappe itself, and are also indicative of Merton's own understanding of his formative role as novice master in the initial phase of his decade-long tenure in that position. Not content simply to quote and paraphrase the text of the document itself, Merton has thoroughly researched relevant sections of canon law and more than a half-century of Cistercian General Chapter decrees to flesh out the rather compressed and laconic provisions of the *Constitutions* themselves with all the relevant information he could assemble, in order to make clear to the novices what obligations this fundamental legislative document of the Order would require of them. If the impression is given that this exhaustive investigation was more dutiful than enthusiastic on Merton's part, it nevertheless serves as evidence of the seriousness of his sense of responsibility as novice master both to the Order and to his charges.

Still, it is unlikely that he relinquished this particular task with much regret. In the wake of the Second Vatican Council, Merton wrote from his hermitage on November 25, 1966, to his friend Fr. Charles Dumont, editor of the Order's journal *Collectanea Cisterciensia*, who had evidently mentioned plans to bring the *Constitutions* up to date:

> I am glad to hear about the commission for the revisions of the Constitutions. If I get any ideas I will let you know. As a matter of fact, living in the woods, I find I have a quite different perspective and probably if I had any ideas at all on this subject they would be useless. But if something does occur to me I will suggest it. My present thought is: if the Constitutions could be kept down to two pages it would be fine.[45]

In point of fact, the new Cistercian *Constitutions*, which had to wait for the revised Code of Canon Law to be promulgated in

---

45. *School of Charity*, 323.

1983, were not finally approved and published until 1990 (though already in 1969, the year after Merton's death, the Cistercian General Chapter passed the Statute on Unity and Pluralism, which approved "the principle of diverse usages, within specified limits"[46] and so fundamentally altered the requirement laid down in the very first sentence of Part II of the 1924 *Constitutions*: "A uniform observance of the Rules shall be maintained, this being required by the very nature of our Order"[47]). While the 1990 *Constitutions* were rather longer than two pages, the text embodies a more flexible, more contemporary vision of the spirit and the practice of the Order than its predecessor, a vision that Merton would no doubt have found to be more in harmony with his own evolving sense of the meaning and purpose of Cistercian monastic and contemplative life.[48]

* * * * * * *

The copy texts for the first two sets of conferences in this volume are the respective typescripts with their handwritten additions and alterations that Merton himself typed and would have had in front of him as he presented the material to the novices. The *Carta Caritatis* material is extant only in this version, and while the *Consuetudines* notes are also reproduced in a multigraphed (spirit master) text that was typed by one (or more) of the novices and made available to the novices, it is clear that this

---

46. John Eudes Bamberger, ocso, "The Office of Secretary General," in *Cistercian Order in the Twentieth Century*, 2:79.

47. *Constitutions*, 22.

48. *Constitutions and Statutes of the Monks and Nuns of the Cistercian Order of the Strict Observance and Other Legislative Documents* (Rome: Cistercian Order of the Strict Observance, 1990); the text of the current *Constitutions*, as modified by the 2005 General Chapter, is available (along with the Statute on Unity and Pluralism and other relevant texts) on the official OCSO web site: http://www.ocso.org.

second version is dependent on the original typescript and therefore has no independent textual authority.[49]

The situation with the *Constitutions* text is somewhat more complicated. The first twenty-three pages of Merton's own typescript for this material, from the beginning up to the end of the commentary on section 95 of the *Constitutions*,[50] are lost. Therefore the copy text for this segment of the notes is the only available witness, the first twenty-four pages of the eighty-five-page multigraph (spirit master) version.[51] It is therefore impossible to be sure that the extant text for this material is exactly as Merton intended it, particularly in any handwritten additions or alterations, as the typist was not always accurate in deciphering Merton's difficult handwriting.[52] But it can be assumed that any divergences

---

49. Unlike most of the other multigraphed texts of Merton's novitiate conferences, the *Consuetudines* material is not found in the twenty-four-volume "Collected Essays."

50. Pages 57–103 of this edition.

51. It is evident from the multigraph that there was some confusion on the part of the typist at precisely this point in the typing of the stencils. Interpolated in the multigraph immediately before the commentary on section 96 is a full page plus eight lines headed "THE NOVITIATE" that is in fact a transcription of page 16 of Merton's *Consuetudines* typescript (pages 46–48 of this edition), which must somehow have been misplaced and interleaved into the *Constitutions* typescript at this point. The page is crossed out with a large X and the eight lines on the following page are likewise cancelled with an undulating mark. The misplaced page has been returned to its proper place in the *Consuetudines* text, but it seems likely that in the confusion at this point the earlier pages of the *Constitutions* text—everything preceding this erroneous interpolation—must have been mislaid and have subsequently not been recovered and reunited with the rest of the text.

52. For example, on pages 133–34 of the present edition, a handwritten addition written on the verso of the previous page and marked for insertion in the typescript reads: "What is the enclosure? *Materially*, it is that space immediately surrounding and including a religious house and which is clearly designated as set aside for the exclusive use of the religious. *Formally*, it is the law which obliges the religious not to leave these premises without permission. *Active* {enclosure is} where the religious can go without special

would be relatively minor and not seriously affect Merton's main points. For the rest of the text, as well as for the brief appendix on the chapter of faults, Merton's own typescript serves as the copy text, but with certain modifications. In Merton's personal copy of the *Constitutions* multigraph (bound together with his copy of the *Consuetudines* multigraph as mentioned earlier), there are almost two dozen alterations[53]—about half of these are simply underlinings (rendered as italic in this edition), but the rest are brief substantive additions in Merton's own hand, presumably made at the time of the second presentation of this set of conferences, but in any case to be accepted as part of the final version of the text. Therefore the copy text for the material found on pages 103–204 of this edition is Merton's typescript as supplemented by the further alterations found in his copy of the multigraph. There are also two anomalous passages, nine lines on pages 150–51 of the present text ("*Note on* . . . without vows"), and three words on page 156 ("by civil law") that are found in the multigraph text itself but not in the typescript. Presumably they were given to the typist by Merton either on a separate slip of paper or perhaps orally.

The textual notes as presented in Appendix A thus consist of two lists of additions and alterations. The first records all changes found in Merton's typescripts of the three sets of conferences included in this volume, including those made in the process of typing as well as those that are handwritten. The second, much briefer list records the changes Merton made on his copy of the *Constitutions* multigraph along with the two unique multigraph readings. Appendix B includes suggestions for further reading, consisting first of other sources in Merton's published works

---

permission (v.g., St. Ann's). *Passive* {enclosure is} strictly protected by law and {the} penalty of excommunication." The typist omitted "*Materially*" (which had been interlined in the original); read "enclosing" for "including"; omitted "as set aside"; read "enclosure" for "exclusive"; read "denies" for "obliges"; and omitted "(v.g., St. Ann's)."

53. There are also various check marks and vertical lines in the margin that do not affect the substance of the text.

dealing with the life, organization, and history of the Cistercian Order, and also of recent volumes on the Order's early and contemporary legislation.

All substantive additions made to the text, in order to turn elliptical or fragmentary statements into complete sentences, are included in braces, as are the few emendations incorporated directly into the text, so that the reader can always determine exactly what Merton himself wrote. No effort is made to reproduce Merton's rather inconsistent punctuation, paragraphing, abbreviations, and typographical features; a standardized format for these features is established that in the judgment of the editor best represents a synthesis of Merton's own practice and contemporary usage: e.g., all Latin passages are italicized unless specific parts of a longer passage are underlined by Merton, in which case the underlined section of the passage is in roman type; all other passages underlined by Merton are italicized; words in upper case in the text are printed in small caps; periods and commas are uniformly included within quotation marks; patterns of abbreviation and capitalization, very inconsistent in the copy text, are regularized. All references to primary and secondary sources are cited in the notes. Untranslated Latin passages in the original text are left in Latin but translated by the editor in the notes. Scriptural citations are taken from the Douay-Rheims translation, as was Merton's usual practice in his conferences.

****

In conclusion I would like to express my gratitude to all those who have made this volume possible:

- to the Trustees of the Merton Legacy Trust, Peggy Fox, Anne McCormick, and Mary Somerville, for permission to publish the *Charter, Customs, and Constitutions of the Cistercians* conferences;
- to the late Robert E. Daggy, former director of the Thomas Merton Center, Bellarmine College (now University), Louisville, Kentucky, for first alerting me to the project of editing

Merton's monastic conferences, and for his encouragement in this and other efforts in Merton studies;

- to Brother Patrick Hart, ocso, the founding editor of the Monastic Wisdom Series, for his friendship and guidance in the publication of this series of volumes of Thomas Merton's monastic conferences;

- to Father Simeon Leiva, ocso, the present editor of the Monastic Wisdom Series, for his careful editorial guidance and continued encouragement in publishing these conference volumes;

- to Abbot John Eudes Bamberger, ocso, student of Thomas Merton and a major figure in the postconciliar renewal of the Cistercian Order, for his insightful Preface to this volume that situates Merton's work in his own time and in the present;

- to Paul M. Pearson, director and archivist of the Merton Center, and Mark C. Meade, assistant archivist, for their gracious hospitality and valued assistance during my research visits to the Center;

- to Colleen Stiller, production manager at Liturgical Press, for guiding this and previous volumes of Merton's conferences through the publication process with grace and efficiency;

- to the Gannon University Research Committee, which provided a grant that allowed me to pursue research on this project at the Merton Center and at various libraries;

- to Mary Beth Earll of the interlibrary loan department of the Nash Library, Gannon University, for once again providing invaluable assistance by locating and procuring various obscure volumes;

- to library staff of the Hesburgh Library of the University of Notre Dame, the Latimer Family Library of St. Vincent College, and the Institute of Cistercian Studies Collection at the Waldo Library of Western Michigan University, especially

Neil Chase, for assistance in locating important materials in their collections;
- again and always to my wife Suzanne and our children for their continual love, support, and encouragement in this and other projects.

CARTA CARITATIS

{For} recent studies, {see} *Collectanea*, 1954: J.-A. Lefèvre: "La Véritable Carta {Caritatis} Primitive et Son Evolution."[1] The original text of {the} *Carta Caritatis* had been a problem all along. {In} 1945, Msgr. Turk publishes a text[2] from {the} University of Laibach, which was older than those in Guignard,[3] {the} *Nomasticon*[4] {and} Canivez.[5] He believed that this was the actual text of St. Stephen. He also thought this was the text approved by Callistus II in 1119, and he thought it had been written in 1119. {However,} evidence of interpolations in the text of Turk shows that it cannot be the original. The Turk text was obviously revised by the General Chapter after difficulties had arisen. Lefèvre believes[6] there were four main revisions: (a) before 1118; (b) 1118–1119; (c) before 1119; (d) after 1119. He believes that the original was written by St. Stephen in 1113–1114. {The} steps of development {were as follows}:

1. J.-A. Lefèvre, "La Véritable Carta Caritatis Primitive et Son Évolution," *Collectanea Ordinis Cisterciensium Reformatorum* 16 (1954): 5–29.

2. Josip Turk, "Charta Caritatis Prior," *Analecta Sacri Ordinis Cisterciensis* 1 (1945): 11–61.

3. Philippe Guignard, ed., *Les Monuments Primitifs de la Règle Cistercienne* (Dijon: Imprimerie Darantière, 1878), 79–84.

4. *Nomasticon Cisterciense, seu Antiquiores Ordinis Cisterciensis Constitutiones A.R.P.D. Juliano Paris . . . Editio Nova*, ed. Hugo Séjalon (Solesmes: E Typographeo Sancti Petri, 1892), 68–81.

5. J.-M. Canivez, ed., *Statuta Capitulorum Generalium Ordinis Cisterciensis ab Anno 1116 ad Annum 1786*, 8 vols. (Louvain: Bureaux de la Revue d'Histoire Ecclésiastique, 1933–1941), 1.xxvi–xxxi.

6. See Lefèvre, "Véritable," 10.

1. There was a General Chapter, deliberating and legislating at Cîteaux in 1116, because William of C. received permission to look after St. Bernard's health.[7]

2. Certain statutes presuppose that there are not yet any second generation houses, and that the Abbot of Cîteaux is the Father Immediate of all (*matrem suam* novum videlicet monasterium[8]).

3. Other statutes, dating from 1118 or 1119 at least, reflect the presence of a second generation (Trois-Fontaines, 1118: *Cum vero aliqua ecclesia adeo creverit* . . . etc.[9]).

4. Other statutes are clearly before 1119, since they appear in the *Summa Cartae Caritatis* which is proved to be of 1119.[10]

---

7. I.e., William of Champeaux, the Bishop of Châlons-sur-Marne (William of Saint-Thierry, *Sancti Bernardi Vita Prima*, 1.7.32 [J.-P. Migne, ed., *Patrologiae Cursus Completus, Series Latina* [*PL*], 221 vols. (Paris: Garnier, 1844–1865), vol. 185, col. 246AB], cited in Lefèvre, "Véritable," 11).

8. "their mother, that is, the New Monastery" (*Carta Caritatis*, c. 9, as transcribed in Josip Turk, "Cistercii Statuta Antiquissima," *Analecta Sacri Ordinis Cisterciensis* 4 [1948], 111, quoted in Lefèvre, "Véritable," 12).

9. "When any church [i.e., abbey] has already grown to such an extent [as to be able to found another monastery] . . ." (*Carta Caritatis*, c. 8 [Turk, "Statuta," 110, quoted in Lefèvre, "Véritable," 11, n. 12]).

10. Lefèvre, "Véritable," 12. Lefèvre considered the brief *Summa Cartae Caritatis* to be the text presented to Pope Callistus II for approval in 1119 and the *Carta Caritatis Prior* that presented to Pope Eugene III in 1152, with the *Carta Caritatis Posterior* (the standard text) a later revision from c. 1190. This theory has been generally rejected by more recent scholars, who date the *Carta Caritatis Prior* to 1119 and the *Carta Caritatis Posterior* to 1152, with the *Summa Cartae Caritatis* being an abridgment of the *Carta Caritatis Prior*, dating from early in the abbacy of Raymond de Bar of Cîteaux (1133/34–1150). For a thorough discussion of the evidence and new editions of the relevant texts, with translations, see *Narrative and Legislative Texts from Early Cîteaux*, ed. and trans. Chrysogonus Waddell, ocso, Studia et Documenta, vol. 9 (Cîteaux: Commentarii Cistercienses, 1999), 162–66, 261–82, 371–88, 441–50, 498–505.

5. One other is clearly after 1119 (because not in the *Summa*) {which} forbids a particular "chapter" of a certain line of filiations, besides the General Chapter.[11]

Turk includes this last,[12] and is therefore hybrid, and not the actual text approved by Callistus II in 1119.

The Preface (which is in Guignard,[13] Turk[14] etc., and therefore later) begins by saying that *before* the abbeys began to "flourish"[15] (i.e., to make foundations), Stephen etc., drew up the *Carta*. Lefèvre argues this means there was an original version before 1119, to which the preface was later added.

Division: in the *Carta* as we have it ({in the} *Nomasticon*[16]) there is a separation (by style, etc.) between two "blocks": {in} chapters 1–3, obviously by St. Stephen, {the} tone is one of paternal authority of a Father calling together his sons to deliberate on their common spiritual interests; chapters 4–7 {are} less personal—more the tone of a contract. Here instead of the "we" of St. Stephen, we have {the} third person—*abbas novi monasterii*;[17] {there is} much glossing in this section, while there is none in the first, {as well as a} progressive restriction of the authority of Cîteaux. Chapters 8–13 {form} a second contractual block.

An Early Summary of the Carta Caritatis: Dom Leclercq discovered a manuscript containing a résumé of the *Exordium*

---

11. Lefèvre, "Véritable," 14.
12. *Carta Caritatis*, c. 8 (Turk, "Statuta," 111).
13. Guignard, 79.
14. Turk, "Statuta," 109.
15. "*Antequam abbacie cistercienses florere inciperent* . . ." ("Before the Cistercian abbeys began to flourish . . .") (*Nomasticon*, 68).
16. Actually the *Nomasticon* text is arranged into the five main sections to be discussed below, rather than into the thirty chapters found in Canivez and elsewhere.
17. "the abbot of the New Monastery" (c. 6 [Canivez, 1.xxvii]; the numeration is that found in Canivez and elsewhere, but not in the *Nomasticon*, which has only the five major divisions of the *Carta*).

Parvum,[18] the basic elements of the *Carta Caritatis*, and some statutes of the General Chapter;[19] and this composite was the dossier presented by the Cistercians to Callistus II in 1119.[20] It is printed in *Collectanea*, 1954, p. 97ff.[21] Let us resume its contents:

1. {It} describes the departure from Molesme and the reasons for it: (a) Molesme is described as *fama celeberrimum, religione conspicuum . . . nec minus amplum possessionibus quam clarum virtutibus*;[22] (b) but *possessionibus virtutibusque diuturna non solet esse societas*;[23] (c) the founders of Cîteaux ELEGERUNT POTIUS STUDIIS CELESTIBUS OCCUPARI QUAM TERRENIS IMPLICARI NEGOTIIS;[24] (d) their first step was to "think about poverty" (*de paupertate fecunda virorum*[25]); (e) they note that the life at Molesme is regular ("*sancte honesteque viveretur*"[26]), yet it is not what they were seeking

---

18. In fact the "*Exordium Cistercii*" found in this document is an independent composition not textually related to the better known *Exordium Parvum*; see Waddell, *Narrative and Legislative Texts*, 139–61.

19. Jean Leclercq, OSB, "Une Ancienne Rédaction des Coutumes Cisterciennes," *Revue d'Histoire Ecclésiastique* 47 (1952): 172–76.

20. For the more recent theory dating the *Carta Caritatis Prior* to 1119 and its abridgment, the *Summa Cartae Caritatis*, to a later date, see n. 10 above.

21. Actually this transcription of the *Exordium Cistercii*, the *Summa Cartae Caritatis*, and the *Capitula* is not directly from the Trent ms. discovered and described by Dom Leclercq, but is that of Lefèvre, from ms. 1207 of Ste. Geneviève, Paris, supplemented by the Trent ms., published as an appendix (97–104) to his article "La Véritable Constitution Cistercienne de 1119," *Collectanea Ordinis Cisterciensium Reformatorum* 16. 2 (1954): 77–104.

22. "most highly regarded in reputation, outstanding in religious observance . . . no less extensive in possessions than illustrious in virtues" (n. 1) (Lefèvre, "Véritable," 97).

23. "a connection of possessions and virtues is not accustomed to be ongoing" (n. 1) (Lefèvre, "Véritable," 97).

24. "chose to be occupied with heavenly pursuits rather than to be wrapped up in worldly business" (Lefèvre, "Véritable," 97).

25. "about poverty, fruitful source of men" (n. 1) (Lefèvre, "Véritable," 97).

26. "it might be lived out in a holy and honest way" (n. 1) (Lefèvre, "Véritable," 97).

("*minus tamen pro suo desiderio et proposito*"[27]); they desire to live their vows more fully; (f) under the leadership of Robert "of blessed memory,"[28] they plan to go *communi consilio, communi perficere nituntur assensu quod uno spiritu conceperunt;*[29] (g) IGITUR, *post multos labores ac nimias difficultates quas omnes in Christo pie vivere volentes pati necesse est, tandem desiderio potiti cistercium devenerunt locum tunc scilicet horroris et vastae solitudinis;*[30] and they thought it very appropriate for their purpose, receiving it as prepared for them by God.

2. The beginning of the monastery of Cîteaux: with the support of authorities, *inventam heremum in abbatiam construere coeperunt.*[31] Robert returns to Molesme; under Alberic the community prospers. He is succeeded by Stephen, *religionis paupertatis disciplinaeque regularis ardentissimus amator, fidelissimus emulator.*[32] But they are poor and without vocation until the providential arrival of thirty novices. There are twelve foundations. *Then St. Stephen wrote a wise document, to prevent divisions and to preserve mutual peace.* UNDE SCRIPTUM ILLUD CARTAM CARITATIS COMPETENTER VOLUIT NOMINARI QUOD EA TANTUM QUAE CARITATIS SUNT TOTA EJUS SERIES REDOLEAT, ITA UT PENE NIL ALIUD UBIQUE SUI PROSEQUI VIDEATUR QUAM NEMINI

---

27. "still, it was less in accord with their own desire and purpose" (n. 1) (Lefèvre, "Véritable," 97, which reads: ". . . *pro sui desiderio atque proposito*").

28. "*beate videlicet memorie*" (n. 1) (Lefèvre, "Véritable," 97).

29. "they strive by common counsel and common assent to bring about what they have conceived in one spirit" (n. 1) (Lefèvre, "Véritable," 97).

30. "Therefore, after many labors and very great difficulties, which it is necessary for all wanting to live piously in Christ to endure, at last, fulfilling their desire, they reached Cîteaux, then a place of horror and of vast solitude" (n. 1) (Lefèvre, "Véritable," 97, which reads: ". . . *vaste* . . .").

31. "They began to build the desert place they had found into an abbey" (Lefèvre, "Véritable," 97, which reads: ". . . *in abbatia construe ceperunt*").

32. "a most ardent lover and most faithful promoter of religious life, of poverty and of discipline according to the *Rule*" (n. 2) (Lefèvre, "Véritable," 98, which reads: ". . . *disciplineque* . . .").

CUIQUAM DEBEATIS NISI UT INVICEM DILIGATIS.[33] *Then follows a summary of the Carta.*

3. The provisions of the *Carta* are outlined:

    a) Fathers Immediate cannot impose exactions on filiations.

    b) {They} cannot receive novices of filiations to profession, or to change of stability, without {the} consent of {the} abbot of {the} filiation.

    c) {They} can do nothing against the will of {the} abbot of {the} filiation except what is for the good of souls, {such as} correct irregularities.

    d) {The Father Immediate} takes precedence over {the} abbot of {the} filiation in the daughter house.

    e) {He} must visit filiations once a year, and eat in {the} refectory, not in {the} guest house (to show {that} he is {the} father of {a} family, not a mere visitor);

    f) The General Chapter {meets} each year at Cîteaux for the purpose of visiting one another, repairing {the} *ordo* {and} confirming peace and charity. Under {the} presidency of {the} Abbot of Cîteaux, they correct errors, proclaim for faults {and} help one another materially if need be. {Abbots are} only allowed to stay away from {the} General Chapter for two reasons: sickness and solemn profession (!); then {they} send {the} prior as {their} vicar.

    g) *De culpis abbatum*:[34] {with regard to the question of} what to do with an irregular abbot, the four First Fathers[35] will advise and correct Cîteaux. La Ferté takes care of Cîteaux if the

---

33. "Thus he wished that document to be appropriately named the Charter of Charity, because the entire series of its provisions focuses just on what pertains to charity, so that almost nothing else seems to be sought everywhere other than to 'owe no one anything except to love one another'" (n. 2) (Lefèvre, "Véritable," 98, which reads: "*Unde et scriptum . . . que sunt caritatis tota . . . nemini quicquam . . .*"; the closing quotation is from Rom. 13:8).

34. "Concerning the Faults of Abbots" (n. 5) (Lefèvre, "Véritable," 100).

35. I.e., the abbots of the first four daughter houses of Cîteaux: La Ferté (1113), Pontigny (1114), Clairvaux (1115), Morimond (1115).

abbotship is vacant. {They} cannot elect an abbot from outside the Order. {An abbot must} yield place to {a} visiting abbot (*honore invicem prevenientes* [36]).

h) Other problems: {one must} not attract to one's own abbey a vocation headed for another. If a fugitive comes, {one should} try to persuade him to return to his monastery; if he will not, {he} cannot stay over one night.[37]

i) *Instituta*:[38] foundations {are} all to be in honor of Our Lady. {They are} not to be founded in cities, towns or villages. Foundations must be made with twelve men, a superior and books (listed), and the following places constructed: oratory, refectory, dormitory, guest house, gate house; {there must be} no dwelling places outside the enclosure—only barns, etc. {All houses should have the} same interpretation of the *Rule*, {the} same books, {the} same customs. {With regard to} food and clothing, {there are} some special prescriptions, {and} special fast days. Monks must get {their} living from manual labor—farming and stock-raising. {They} can own woods, fields, vineyards (away from {the} haunts of men) and animals ("except those which excite curiosity"[39]); {they} can have granges, manned by brothers—monks should not live in granges. Laybrothers {are} received as coadjutors, under our care, {as} brothers and sharers in spiritual and temporal goods.

Here we have the basic early legislation of the Order as such. Together with the principles of observance in the *Exordium Parvum*, these give us the essential outline of our Fathers' idea of what the Cistercian Order was supposed to be.

---

36. "outdoing one another in showing honor" (n. 5) (Rom. 12:10, quoted in the Benedictine *Rule*, cc. 63, 72 [*The Rule of St. Benedict in Latin and English*, ed. and trans. Justin McCann, osb (London: Burns, Oates, 1952), 144,160]) (Lefèvre, "Véritable," 101).

37. Nn. 7–8 (Lefèvre, "Véritable," 101).

38. Nn. 7–26 (Lefèvre, "Véritable," 101–104).

39. "*preter illa que magis solent provocare curiositatem*" (n. 15) (Lefèvre, "Véritable," 103).

The Carta Caritatis—{the} Prologue ({written} later?): (a) {emphasizes} avoiding conflicts with bishops about foundations—{one is} not to move without previous agreement; (b) "mutuae pacis *futurum praecaventes naufragium*":[40] they decreed qua caritate *monachi* {. . .} corporibus divisi animis indissolubiliter conglutinarentur.[41]

Outline of the *Carta Caritatis* (after {the} Prologue): {there are} five parts: (1) uniformity of observance and charity (without material exactions) for the good of souls—{the} "common salvation" of the members of the Order; (2) visitations; (3) the General Chapter; (4) elections of abbots; (5) resignation and deposition of abbots.

Part I: *Uniformity of Observance and Unity in Charity (De singulari consensione*[42]): we are all servants of one King and Lord. He has in His love dispersed the members of the Order in many different places, there to live under one *Rule*. Because of this equality under God, no one house (Cîteaux) shall impose material exactions on the others. Cîteaux imposes no burden on the other houses of the Order, in order to avoid avarice, which is the "service of idols."[43] However, Cîteaux will retain the care for the souls of all in the Order, out of charity—meaning {that} the Abbot of Cîteaux and abbots of the General Chapter will strive to prevent any house from wavering in its purpose and deviating from the *Rule*: *ut si quando a sancto proposito et observantia sanctae Regulae declinare (quod absit) tentaverint, per nostram sollicitudinem ad rectitudinem vitae redire possint.*[44] Hence {the} most important pre-

---

40. "taking precautions as to a future shipwreck of mutual peace" (*Nomasticon*, 68).

41. "by what charity the monks, . . . separated in body, might be held together indissolubly in mind" (*Nomasticon*, 68).

42. "On the unique consensus" (*Nomasticon*, 68–69).

43. "*idolorum servitus*" (*Nomasticon*, 69).

44. "so that, if they ever were tempted (may it not happen) to turn away from their holy purpose and from observance of the holy *Rule*, they could return through our solicitous care to the right way of life" (*Nomasticon*, 69).

scription {is} UT REGULAM BEATI BENEDICTI PER OMNIA OBSERVENT SICUTI IN NOVO MONASTERIO OBSERVATUR.[45] This means:

a) The *Rule* is not to be *interpreted* differently: *Non alium inducant sensum . . . sed sicut antecessores nostri sancti patres, monachi scilicet novi Monasterii, intellexerunt et tenuerunt, et nos hodie intelligimus et tenemus, ita et isti intelligant et teneant.*[46]

b) All books and observances should conform to those accepted at Cîteaux.

c) QUATENUS IN ACTIBUS NOSTRIS NULLA SIT DISCORDIA, SED UNA CARITATE, UNA REGULA, SIMILIBUS VIVAMUS MORIBUS.[47] And no member of the Order can secure a *privilege* from the Holy See contrary to these accepted norms, thus going over {the} heads of {the} General Chapter to introduce something new. (This {is} a later addition.)

{d})[48] {This} must be seen distinctly in the light of the historical context {of} Molesme, Cluny, and the *interminable struggles between different monasteries* about points of observance, usages, chant, alleged "superiority" of one over another, etc., etc. If we {do not} forget that the purpose of the *Carta Caritatis* was to produce peace and eliminate pretexts for argument, we will not be inclined to make the *Carta* itself a starting point of new controversies. See all this in terms of flesh and spirit (cf. 1 Corinthians,[49] James[50] etc.). The Fathers of Cîteaux were writing perfectly in the spirit of St. Benedict. They did not assume that

---

45. "so that they may observe the *Rule* of blessed Benedict in all things as it is observed at the New Monastery" (*Nomasticon*, 69).

46. "Let them not bring in another meaning . . . but as our predecessors the holy fathers, that is, the monks of the New Monastery, understood and held fast, as we ourselves today understand and hold fast, so may they also understand and hold fast" (*Nomasticon*, 69).

47. "May there be no discord in our acts, but may we live with a single charity, under a single *Rule*, with common customs" (*Nomasticon*, 69).

48. "a" in text.

49. See 1 Cor. 2:14–3:4.

50. See Jas. 3:13-18.

they were wiser or more perfect than anyone else, that they alone had the right interpretation of the *Rule*. But they insisted that they should define precisely what was *their* interpretation of the *Rule*, and that they should impose on the Order the obligation of following their interpretation, in order to keep peace and avoid controversies. This part of the *Carta* clarifies a basic principle—that unity and charity come first.

II. Visitations and Precedence:[51]

1. The Abbot of Cîteaux has the right to visit all the monasteries of the Order. When he comes, the local abbot must yield place to him in order to show that Cîteaux is the Mother of all the houses of the Order.

2. When the Abbot of Cîteaux makes a visitation, he replaces the local abbot in everything, except that he does not eat in the guest house with visitors (as the local abbot was obliged to do: cf. *Consuetudines*, 110[52]) but in the refectory with the brethren—*propter disciplinam*.[53] But if the local abbot is absent, then the abbot visitor must take on the obligation of entertaining the guests. This applies to all abbots (whether on an official visitation or not). If several abbots are staying in a monastery and the local abbot is absent, then the senior of the visiting abbots must eat with the guests.

3. One big exception {is that} the local abbot, even in {the} presence of the Abbot of Cîteaux, receives the profession of his own subjects.

4. The Abbot of Cîteaux must be careful not to make *any* decision about the affairs of the house he visits against the will of the local abbot or the brethren. But if the *Rule* is not being kept, he will "strive to correct the brethren with the advice of the local

---

51. *Nomasticon*, 69–70.
52. "*in hospitio comedere*" (*Nomasticon*, 198).
53. "for the sake of discipline" (*Nomasticon*, 69).

abbot and with charity."[54] If the local abbot is absent, then the visitor shall correct the abuse.

5. {Concerning} Fathers Immediate (*abbas majoris ecclesiae*[55]), {each} must visit his filiations once a year; {he} *may* visit them more often. *Si fratres amplius visitaverit, inde magis gaudeant.*[56] The four First Fathers visit Cîteaux annually.

6. When another abbot comes to Cîteaux, he occupies {the} abbot's stall etc., if {the} Abbot of Cîteaux is absent, {but} not otherwise.

7. When one abbot visits another, the other yields him his place, *honore invicem praevenientes.*[57]

8. When a mother house has a number of filiations, they must not hold their own annual "general chapter."[58]

III. The General Chapter:[59]

1. All the abbots must meet at Cîteaux each year, except those who are ill, who must send an explanation of their absence, and those far distant, whose time of attending the General Chapter will be determined by the General Chapter. All others who miss the General Chapter shall be penanced in the following year (or in the same year: cf. 1190, n. 42:[60] the Abbots of Quarr, Stonely and Ford, who did not come to the General Chapter, shall spend six days *"in levi culpa,"*[61] one of them on bread and water—for

---

54. *"cum consilio praesentis Abbatis caritative studeat fratres corrigere"* (*Nomasticon*, 70).

55. "the abbot of the senior church" (*Nomasticon*, 70).

56. "If he should visit the brothers more frequently, let them rejoice the more because of it" (*Nomasticon*, 70).

57. "outdoing one another in showing honor" (Rom. 12:10, quoted in *Rule*, cc. 63, 72 [McCann, 144, 160]) (*Nomasticon*, 70).

58. *"annuum inter se capitulum"* (*Nomasticon*, 70).

59. *Nomasticon*, 70–71.

60. Canivez, 1.126–27.

61. "for a minor fault".

levis culpa, see {the} *Rule*, {c.} 24:[62] eat late and do not intone antiphons in choir [cf. *Usages*, 352[63]]; the Abbot of L'Aumône was told to make this known to them; {the} same penance {was} imposed, at the same time, on the Abbots of Jouy and Bonnefont for not visiting {their} filiations, {and the} same penance, for forty days, to {the} Abbot of Berdoues, who did not come to {the} General Chapter—the extra days because he gave a frivolous excuse—and he must pay {the} money he owes to {the} Abbot of Toronet before Christmas; in 1192 [n. 46],[64] the Abbot of Bonaval, in Spain, who did not come to the General Chapter and sent no letter, gets three days *in levi culpa*, one of which on bread and water—three or six days *in levi culpa* seem to be the ordinary penance for this fault).

2. The function of the General Chapter: DE SALUTE ANIMARUM SUARUM TRACTENT: IN OBSERVATIONE SANCTAE REGULAE VEL ORDINIS SI QUID EST EMENDANDUM VEL AUGENDUM ORDINENT, BONUM PACIS ET CARITATIS INTER SE REFORMENT.[65]

3. Irregular abbots shall be charitably proclaimed—by abbots only—and are obliged to do the penance imposed.

4. The Chapter has the definitive right to decide all cases and judge and punish all faults (of a regular nature) brought to its attention. When a case is being judged, the interested party must be absent. If there is a serious division, the decision shall rest with the Abbot of Cîteaux and the abbots *"sanioris consilii."*[66]

5. If a house is in bad shape materially, the abbot shall make known his plight and the others in their charity will make

---

62. McCann, 72.

63. *Regulations of the Order of Cistercians of the Strict Observance Published by the General Chapter of 1926* (Dublin: M. H. Gill & Sons, 1927), 169.

64. Canivez, 1.155.

65. "Let them consider about the salvation of their souls; if anything should be amended or added with regard to the observance of the holy *Rule* or of the Order, let them make the decision, and renew among themselves the good of peace and charity" (*Nomasticon*, 71).

66. "of more mature counsel" (*Nomasticon*, 71).

haste to help him ({the} same wording {is} preserved in our *Constitutions*⁶⁷).

IV. The Election of Abbots:⁶⁸

1. The Father Immediate takes full charge of the election of a new abbot when one is to be elected. He calls the abbots of the filiations, and under the presidency of the Father Immediate (*consilio et voluntate patris abbatis*⁶⁹) the monks and abbots present elect a successor.

2. When the Abbot of Cîteaux is to be replaced, {the} four First Fathers take care of the election. They summon all the abbots of the filiations of Cîteaux, and *others whom these abbots and the brethren of Cîteaux think fit* (*ex aliis quos praedicti Abbates et {fratres} Cistercienses idoneos noverint*⁷⁰), then hold the election.

3. Any monastery can elect {an} abbot from among the monks and even abbots of the filiations, but not from another order; nor can Cistercians become abbots of houses outside the Order.

V. The Resignation and Deposition of Abbots:⁷¹

1. Resignation is frowned upon: *Si quis abbas pro inutilitate seu pusillanimitate sua . . . postulaverit ut ab onere abbatiae suae relaxetur,*⁷² the Father Abbot shall consider the case. He shall not accept the plea unless there is a very serious cause. But if such a

---

67. *Constitutiones Ordinis Cisterciensium Strictioris Observantiae a Sancta Sede Approbatae et Confirmatae* (Westmalle, Belgium: Ex Typographia Ordinis, 1925), 5 (n. 14); *Constitutions of the Order of Cistercians of the Strict Observance* (Dublin: M. H. Gill & Sons, [1925]), 9.

68. *Nomasticon*, 71–72.

69. "by the counsel and will of the father abbot" (*Nomasticon*, 71).

70. *Nomasticon*, 71 (text reads: ". . . *monachi* . . ." though the preceding translation reads: ". . . *brethren* . . .").

71. *Nomasticon*, 72–73.

72. "If any abbot on account of his own uselessness or pusillanimity . . . demands to be relieved of the burden of his abbacy . . ." (*Nomasticon*, 72).

cause exists, he will then call together some other abbots of the Order and will decide the case on their advice.

2. {In the case of} deposition, for what {cause is it imposed}? *Si quis abbas . . . innotuerit* (a) *contemptor sanctae Regulae*; (b) *Ordinis praevaricator*; (c) *commissorum sibi fratrum vitiis consentiens*.[73] How {is it effected}? The Father Immediate issues four warnings. If these are ignored, he convokes several other abbots and they depose the offender. (Today, only {the} General Chapter deposes abbots: {see} *Constitutions*, #10.[74]) Then a new election is held under the presidency of the Father Immediate.

3. If the sentence is resisted, by the abbot or {by} the monks, (a) the Father Immediate and his counselors (other abbots) impose a sentence of excommunication on them; (b) and they use other coercive measures, as they see fit; (c) if any one of the rebels repents, he shall be received back with mercy. Here is added the command that no abbot shall receive a fugitive against the will of his own superiors, indicating that the case of rebels is particularly kept in mind. {This is} to prevent a split in the Order, {with} rebels of one house received in another, forming a faction, etc., etc.

4. If the Abbot of Cîteaux is off the beam (*ab observatione Regulae . . . exorbitare*[75]), the four First Fathers shall warn him in the name of the others. They take all the measures taken against other recalcitrant abbots, except they cannot depose or excommunicate him. The General Chapter—and outside {the} time of {the} General Chapter the abbots of the filiations of Cîteaux—can however depose and excommunicate him. (Note: in {the} history of {the} Order in {the} thirteenth century, the decline really began with {a} big struggle between Clairvaux and Cîteaux on this kind of thing.) When the Abbot of Cîteaux is deposed, the General Chapter must be held at one of the other four first houses.

---

73. "If any abbot should become known as one who scorns the holy *Rule*, or deviates from the Order, or consents to the vices of the brothers committed to his care" (*Nomasticon*, 72).

74. *Constitutiones*, 4; *Constitutions*, 9.

75. "straying from the observance of the *Rule*" (*Nomasticon*, 73).

THE *CONSUETUDINES*

As given in the *Nomasticon*,[1] the text of the *Consuetudines* is divided into three parts: (i) *Ecclesiastica Officia*;[2] (ii) *Instituta Capituli Generalis*;[3] (iii) *Usus Conversorum*.[4] We are concerned only with the first part, the ancient usages of St. Stephen Harding and our first Fathers. It is divided as follows: *Distinctiones* 1 and 2: the Mass and office (nn. 1–69); *Distinctio* 3: the regular observances: (a) in general (nn. 70–73); (b) in winter (74–82); (c) in summer (83–88); *Distinctio* 4: the sick and the dead and novices: (a) {the} sick (89–92); (b) the dying (93); (c) the dead—burial (94–98); (d) prayers for the dead—different categories (99); (e) sick guests (100); (f) death of a guest (101); (g) reception and training of novices (102); *Distinctio* 5: weekly officers, officers of the monastery and various functions: (a) weekly officers (nn. 103–109); (b) permanent officers (110–120); (c) prayers at meals (121). We will consider what is most useful for us in the *monastic observances*, especially *Distinctio* 3, but also in other places.

THE MONASTIC DAY according to the *Consuetudines*, with remarks from the Cistercian Fathers (before this, *the monastery*—{its} plan, etc.): the purpose of this series is to go through the *Consuetudines* briefly, remarking on the way in which our Cistercian

---

1. *Nomasticon Cisterciense, seu Antiquiores Ordinis Cisterciensis Constitutiones A.R.P.D. Juliano Paris . . . Editio Nova*, ed. Hugo Séjalon (Solesmes: E Typographeo Sancti Petri, 1892), 84–241.
2. *Nomasticon*, 84–211.
3. *Nomasticon*, 212–33.
4. *Nomasticon*, 234–41.

Fathers carried out the monastic observances, so as to gain something of their spirit and their outlook. We will not go too much into details of rubrics and ritual, but concentrate on the monastic observances. We begin with the *morning chapter* (*Cons.* 70[5]).

CHAPTER:

1. The sacristan rings for the chapter and goes on ringing until the blessing is given. Hence the bell was probably above the chapter room and rung by a rope in the chapter. The way this article is written gives the impression that monks and {the} superior come from all directions to the chapter.

2. Rules for saluting {were} much the same as today. Note—the chapter faces *east*.

3. When all are assembled, the chapter begins with the invitator opening the book and asking a blessing before the martyrology.

4. Prayers {were} much the same ceremonies as today.

5. Reading the *tabula* (of appointments): if anyone finds that he cannot fulfill the duty appointed for the following week, he must make it known right there in chapter—or, in exceptional cases (*pro gravi necessitate*[6]) in the following chapter—but not outside of chapter.

6. The abbot receives the *Rule* book and either explains the *Rule* himself or hands it to another to explain. Presumably the *Rule* read that day is usually the passage explained. "*Cui lector ostendat sententiam quam exponere debet.*"[7]

7. The exposition of the *Rule* begins with *benedicite*[8] of the one presiding. If anyone arrives after this, he says sotto voce at his place "*benedicite*" and his neighbor says *dominus*.[9]

---

5. *Nomasticon*, 146–50.
6. "because of grave necessity" (*Nomasticon*, 147).
7. "Let the reader point out to him the passage which he is to explain" (*Nomasticon*, 147).
8. "Bless [the Lord]".
9. "Lord".

8. *Loquamur de ordine nostro*[10]—first comes absolution of the dead, if any. {The} abbot then appoints what prayers are to be said for that soul.

9. After that, anyone with a fault prostrates and presumably accuses himself.

10. Proclamations: (a) the one proclaiming apparently announces the name and the fault at the same time; the one proclaimed prostrates; (b) then the abbot says to him, *quid dicis?* {and} he replies *mea culpa*[11]—then rising, either humbly confesses his fault, if he is guilty, or if he is not guilty, he says he did not do it; the one who made the proclamation is not to repeat it and insist, unless asked, but a third party who knows can intervene and say: "He did it!"; (c) the one proclaimed cannot proclaim the proclaimer back the same day; (d) when several are proclaimed together for a common fault, the senior stands in the middle and does the talking for the group; (e) only three proclamations {are} allowed (plus {the} fault in chapter); (f) no proclamations {are permitted} on pure suspicion; (g) as punishment, the one proclaimed may be flogged—but never by the one who proclaimed him; (h) the one flogged takes off {his} cowl and puts it on his knees; he strips to the waist and bows, saying nothing except *mea culpa, ego me emendabo*;[12] afterwards {he} goes to his place when told {to do so} by the abbot.

11. After chapter, all leave, except those who wish to go to confession (presumably to the abbot, or to some other confessor).

---

10. "Let us speak of our order" (*Nomasticon*, 148); see the discussion of this phrase in Thomas Merton, *Monastic Observances: Initiation into the Monastic Tradition* 5, ed. Patrick F. O'Connell, Monastic Wisdom [MW], vol. 25 (Collegeville, MN: Cistercian Publications, 2010), 213–15, where Merton notes that its "more modern meaning . . . is taken to include news of deaths from other houses. But the original and proper meaning of this phrase is 'Let us speak of our observance . . . let us speak of the way we are keeping our rule'" (215).

11. "What do you say?" "through my fault" (*Nomasticon*, 148).

12. "through my fault; I shall reform" (*Nomasticon*, 148).

The chapter room was the ordinary place for confessions, during the *tempus lectionis*.

{Chapter} 71—D*e* T*empore* L*ectionis* [13] (the term interval is used later, quasi-distinct from "*tempus lectionis*"):

1. *Fratres egressi de capitulo sedeant ad lectionem.* [14] This is not a counsel or a permission but a command—only those are excepted who have some duty to perform or some work (*officium*) that makes it impossible then—but as soon as they are free they must apply themselves to their reading.

2. During the time of reading and all the intervals they can go to pray in church (cf. *today*), but they *may not* sit down, may not *cover*, may not use a book "except for those who do not know the psalter by heart or who have to prepare for the next office." [15]

3. "Those sitting in the cloister shall conduct themselves as befits religious, sitting by themselves and reading each in his own book, except for those who [practice] with an antiphoner, gradual or hymnal. . . . These are to be listened to by the cantor or some competent brother appointed by him." [16]

4. Let them not bother each other with questions, except concerning the accents and pronunciations which they do not know, and the way to begin the reading at table or before compline. These questions must be very brief.

5. If one is covered when reading, his hood must be so disposed that one can see if he is sleeping.

6. If one has to go somewhere, he places his book in the *armarium*, or leaves it at his place, having made a sign to his neigh-

---

13. "Concerning the Time for Reading" (*Nomasticon*, 150–52).

14. "Having come out of the chapter room, let the brothers sit for reading" (*Nomasticon*, 150, which reads: "*Fratres igitur egressi . . .*").

15. "*praeter illos qui psalterium nesciunt, & qui ad praesens opus providere, legere aut cantare aliquid necesse habuerint*" (*Nomasticon*, 151).

16. "*Qui vero in claustro sederint, religiose se habeant singuli in singulis libris legentes, exceptis illis qui in antiphonariis, hymnariis, gradualibus cantaverint, . . . quos auscultet cantor vel quilibet frater ad hoc idoneus ab ipso praemonitus*" (*Nomasticon*, 151).

bor to look after it. This sign can be made in the great silence (*post vesperas*[17]).

7. "If anyone wants to get the book which someone else is reading or singing from, it being necessary for him to find something in it, he must give him another book in exchange, and he who receives this other book should let the first one go in peace. But if he does not want to oblige his brother in this manner, let him who asks bear it in peace, until such time as he may proclaim him for it in chapter."[18]

8. {When} walking in the cloister, "*humiliter incedant*"[19] (along {the} wall??) "*discooperto capite* supplicantes *invicem obviando.*"[20] The term for "salute" (to wish health to) is rendered by *supplicantes*—"begging a blessing from." Note the implications. It seems they said "*benedicite*" when saluting. But they are not to salute or say *benedicite* at work (presumably {an} exception {is} made for when they have to speak).

9. {They are} not to make signs *per caputium*[21] (meaning what???); not to attract attention from {a} distance by voice or sound. They can wear their night cowls also during {the} time of reading (presumably to keep warm).

10. In case one has scandalized a brother (i.e., annoyed him) one makes it known to the prior; then the prior, if he sees fit, calls him, and the offender prostrates before the one offended until he is placated (note {the} application of {the} Rule in a definite sense—not just at random—read {the} Rule[22]).

---

17. "after vespers" (*Nomasticon*, 151).

18. "*Porro si quis ab aliquo librum in quo legit vel cantat accipere voluerit, necesse habens in eo videre: tradat ei alium, & ille cui tradiderit in pace ei dimittat. Quem si ei accommodare noluerit, ille qui petit in pace ferat, donec super eo in capitulo inde proclamationem faciat*" (*Nomasticon*, 151).

19. "Let them walk humbly" (*Nomasticon*, 151).

20. "with head uncovered, begging a blessing from one another when passing" (*Nomasticon*, 151).

21. "through the cowl" (*Nomasticon*, 151).

22. "*Si quis autem frater pro quavis minima causa, ab abbate vel a quocumque priore suo corripitur quolibet modo, vel si leviter senserit animos prioris cujuscumque*

Various Regular Places—which may or may not be entered at various times (72[23]):

1. *The Kitchen* (c. 72): no one but the cantors and copyists can enter {the} kitchen (except of course cooks, etc.)—to smooth out parchment and to melt ink; also {the} sacristan and thurifer, to get light etc., for {the} church, or salt to be blessed—but not if there is a fire in the calefactory. The abbot's cooks can enter, also the infirmarian, and anyone the cook calls in to help him put a pot on the fire; also the *circators*.[24] Two types of kitchens existed— those with {an} open fireplace against one wall, and those with {an} open fire in the middle of the room. {The} *abbot's kitchen* {was} separate from the rest; {he} ate with guests. If there were no guests, the abbot's cook called the two monks invited to eat with {the} abbot. {Each} brought his things from {the} common refectory. They eat in silence and after grace bow and retire. The servant brings their things back to {the} common refectory. The *weekly cooks* (108[25]) get {a} blessing and enter immediately upon their charge after {the} night office, and begin to draw water, etc., and work in {the} kitchen. If it is a feast of two Masses, one hears one Mass and other the other, and {they} receive communion if they wish; if one has to sing {the} gospel or epistle, he goes to the Mass for which this is appointed. On big feasts, both hear the conventual Mass (in Lent {they} don't go to {the} kitchen before

---

contra se iratos vel commotos quamvis modice, mox sine mora tamdiu prostratus in terra ante pedes ejus jaceat satisfaciens, usque dum benedictione sanetur illa commotio" ("If any brother, for however trifling a reason, be corrected in any way by the abbot, or any of his seniors, or if he perceive that any senior, in however small a degree, is displeased or angry with him, let him at once without delay cast himself on the ground at his feet, and lie there making reparation, until that displeasure is appeased and he bless him") (*The Rule of St. Benedict in Latin and English*, ed. and trans. Justin McCann, OSB [London: Burns, Oates, 1952], 158, 159 [c. 71]).

23. *Nomasticon*, 152–53.

24. "certain special ones charged with watch over regularity" (*Monastic Observances*, 216).

25. *Nomasticon*, 195–97.

tierce, except {on} Sundays). They serve one another the mixt. They work during the *tempus lectionis*, unless the first cook dismisses the other with a sign. They are charged with providing hot water for shaving, and when the *lavabo* freezes, they put warm water in the cloister. They have to cut wood for {the} kitchen fire. {As for} serving in {the} refectory, one rings for the novices and serves them first, then the others, preparing also necessaries for those who eat late {while} doing penance.

2. *The Refectory*: outside {the} time of meals no one could enter the refectory except the infirmarian, the cooks, the refectorian, the sacristan (to get salt), those called in to help by {the} refectorian, and anyone who wants a drink. In other words, quite a few people could enter the refectory!

3. *The Calefactory*: sacristans, thurifers, etc., can enter to get fire. The monks go there to oil their shoes (*ad subtalares ungendos*[26]) ({cf. the} story of Bl. Amadeus of Bonnevaux[27]). They can enter to warm themselves: "*Quod honeste et non nudis pedibus praesente aliquo faciendum est.*"[28] Contrast La Trappe: {according to the} *Usages* of La Trappe (1837):[29] (1) one ordinarily does not stay more than a quarter hour; (2) salute {one's} neighbors on entering and leaving; (3) don't sit down; (4) don't turn {one's} back to {the} fire; (5) don't take *shoes* off ({this was} later

---

26. *Nomasticon*, 152.

27. See *Vita Amedaei Altae Ripae*, c. 7, in which the nobly born Amadeus is found by his uncle greasing the boots of the monks of the Abbey of Bonnevaux (*Vita Venerabilis Amedaei Altae Ripae*, ed. Anselme Dimier, *Studia Monastica* 5 [1963], 293–94); Merton recounts the story in his biographical sketch of Amadeus in Thomas Merton, *In the Valley of Wormwood: Cistercian Blessed and Saints of the Golden Age*, ed. Patrick Hart, ocso, Cistercian Studies Series [CS], vol. 233 (Collegeville, MN: Cistercian Publications, 2013), 17–18.

28. "When another is present this should be done decently and not in bare feet" (*Nomasticon*, 152).

29. *Règlemens des Religieux de Choeur de la Congrégation Cistercienne de N. D. de La Trappe en France* (Paris: Imprimerie de Béthune et Plon, 1837), 178 (nn. 819, 820).

suppressed). (Read *Usages* #305[30] for modern legislation regarding {the} calefactory.) In 1497 the General Chapter[31] allowed a calefactory in the monastery of Balerne to be used as {an} infirmary refectory, although it was not in but under the infirmary, and opened out into the cloister.

4. The *Parlors* (*auditoria*): note that where we say parlors (places for talking), our Fathers said *auditoria* (places for listening). The main auditorium ("grand parlor") was next to the chapter room. {The} *Consuetudines* state that no one enters the auditorium unless in order to speak with a superior. "If anyone has need to enter, he should make a sign or some sound at the door and wait for permission to enter"[32]—ergo the prior or abbot is inside. The auditorium was probably like our prior's room. In the time of reading only two could speak with the prior at the same time "unless by chance the prior sees fit to call together more than two for some necessity."[33] They leave as soon as they have finished their business. {The} General Chapter of 1152 has legislation about visiting abbots (not {the} father immediate) speaking to monks ({1152}, n. 4[34]): (1) visiting abbots cannot keep a monk back from work in order to talk to him; (2) {a} guest abbot

---

30. "There is in each monastery a common calefactory for the religious. It should be sufficiently lighted. Silence is always kept there, and each one conducts himself in a becoming manner. We may take off our shoes to warm ourselves, but not our socks; we take care not to burn our garments. We should avoid going too often to the calefactory, or remaining there longer than necessity requires" (*Regulations of the Order of Cistercians of the Strict Observance Published by the General Chapter of 1926* [Dublin: M. H. Gill & Sons, 1927], 150 [c. 7, n. 8]).

31. J.-M. Canivez, ed., *Statuta Capitulorum Generalium Ordinis Cisterciensis ab Anno 1116 ad Annum 1786*, 8 vols. (Louvain: Bureaux de la Revue d'Histoire Ecclésiastique, 1933–1941), 6.180 (n. 36).

32. "*si aliquo opus habuerint, quaerant signo vel sonitu ad ostium, & tunc si concessum fuerit ingreditur*" (*Nomasticon*, 152).

33. "*nisi forte prior pro aliqua necessitate plures sibi convocandos judicaverit*" (*Nomasticon*, 152).

34. Canivez, 1.46 (text reads: "1154").

cannot talk to more than two monks at a time; (3) he is permitted to call them to speak *"in auditoria, vel in locum proximum auditorio"* [35] (for this he needs no permission of {the} local superior); (4) he cannot take them outside the enclosure or talk to them in the infirmary or among the farm buildings without permission of {the} local superior (n.b. this means he cannot call a healthy monk to talk in {the} infirmary, but he can talk to one or two of the sick there—but not to the servants); 1154, n. 28 says tersely: *Prohibeantur multiloquia monachorum in adventu abbatum.*[36]

Some other legislation on silence:
1157, n. 52:[37] if a monk or laybrother has to speak in church, he asks permission of the bishop, if he is there, or of the abbot or prior (1175[38] tightens {this} up: only speak to {a} bishop or king in church).

1159, n. 6: *Magister cementariorum, sutorum, vel ejusmodi artificum loquuntur diebus quibus non laborant cum subditis suis, et vespertinis horis quibus se disjunxerint ab operibus suis: Exordinatio est, ultra non fiat.*[39]

{It is} interesting to note the tone and the style of these statutes—laconic, clear, strict.

1186, n. 15:[40] there is to be no speaking in the monastery while the office is going on.

---

35. "in the parlors, or in a place next to the parlor" (*Nomasticon*, 152).
36. "Much conversing of monks at the arrival of abbots is to be forbidden" (Canivez, 1.58).
37. Canivez, 1.66.
38. Canivez, 1.83 (#14).
39. "The master of masons, shoemakers, or other such crafts speaks with his subordinates on days on which they do not work and during evening hours in which they have separated themselves from their work: this is a violation of order—let it no longer be done" (Canivez, 1.70, which reads: ". . . *horis vespertinis* . . .").
40. Canivez, 1.105.

1200:[41] for laybrothers in granges—if they break silence, they are to be on bread and water the next day, and stay away from communion until they have accused themselves in chapter (probably in the monastery).

1209, {n.} 25:[42] Abbots of Rozières and Balerne get one day on bread and water for talking to monks and brothers after compline (although it is in the *Rule*[43]).

1217, n. 30:[44] {the} abbot of Tintern is in trouble for talking to the bishop after compline and having a party with the bishop together with some monks after compline (*solemniter biberit*[45]); also he has women working at the granges (the following statute to this is the one about polyphonic chant at Tintern[46]).

1258, n. 17:[47] when monks are eating outside {the} monastery, they are only allowed to ask for bread, salt, water and *ejusmodi necessaria*,[48] when signs are not understood.

{1195}, n. 100: *Nulli detur generalis licentia loquendi*.[49]

41. Canivez, 1.251 (#13).
42. Canivez, 1.362.
43. C. 42: "*Ut post Completorium Nemo Loquatur*" ("That after Compline No One May Speak") (McCann, 101).
44. Canivez, 1.472.
45. "He was doing some serious drinking."
46. "*De abbatibus de Dora et Tinterna in quorum abbatiis, ut dicitur, triparti vel quadriparti voce, more saecularium canitur, committitur abbatibus de Neth et de Flesleya, qui ad praedicta loca personaliter accedentes, rei veritate diligenter exquisita, quae viderint emendanda diligenter corrigant et quid inde fecerint, in sequenti Capitulo denuntient*" ("Concerning the Abbots of Dore and Tintern, in whose abbeys, it is said, there is singing in three and four parts in the manner of seculars, it is entrusted to the Abbots of Neath and Flaxley to go personally to the aforesaid places, and after carefully investigating the truth of the matter, let them correct what they have seen to be in need of reform, and let them report what they have done about it at the next General Chapter") (Canivez, 1.472).
47. Canivez, 2.441, which reads: ". . . *huiusmodi necessaria* . . ."
48. "such necessities".
49. "General permission to speak is to be given to no one" (Canivez, 1.197) (text reads: "1190").

1176:[50] no laybrother shall have power to give other laybrothers permission to speak.

1185, n. 14:[51] when two monks speak in {the} presence of {the} prior or abbot, they are *only allowed to speak to one another through {a} third person*. When speaking with another, they have no permission to speak to each other through {a} third person.

1245:[52] Pontaut ({its} chapter room {is} in {the} Cloisters {in} New York) {was} signalized as having lost all discipline in {the} matter of silence.

5. *The Dormitorium*: the *domus necessaria*[53] was in the dormitory—at the end, over a stream. Hence one had to be covered there, {and} covered everywhere in {the} dormitory, for modesty's sake. "Entering the *domus necessaria* they must cover as far as possible their faces in their hoods."[54] It seems that the *domus necessaria* did not have doors or anything like that. {Thus there were} regulations for keeping covered in front. In the dormitory there were no cells, just beds, and stools by the beds. They have to know how to change their clothes without showing their nakedness. (Aubert[55] however asserts there was a low partition between beds—he is not always to be trusted.) {The monks were} not allowed to shake out their clothes or beat the dust out of them in the dormitory or to make signs there, except to superiors.

1192, n. 23:[56] {the} Abbot of Longpont, who built a dormitory not according to the rules, gets forty days outside his stall, six days *in levi culpa*,[57] of which one {was} on bread and water; he is

---

50. Canivez, 1.84 (#35).
51. Canivez, 1.99–100.
52. Canivez, 2.296 (#35).
53. I.e., the bathroom (*Nomasticon*, 152).
54. "*Intrantes autem domum necessariam quantum possunt caputia in capitibus suis*" (*Nomasticon*, 152).
55. "sa couchette isolée de la voisine par une cloison basse" (Marcel Aubert, *L'Architecture Cistercienne en France*, 2 vols. [Paris: Vanoest, 1947], 2.85).
56. Canivez, 1.150.
57. "for a minor fault".

given three years in which to alter the dormitory according to {the} rule—after that, if it is not changed, nobody can sleep in it.

What were the ordinary dispositions of the dormitory (Aubert, 2.85ff.)? {It} was always on the upper floor of the east wing. The far end was reserved for novices—sometimes an L for them. General chapters in {the} fifteenth century[58] legislate against partitions. (Benedict XII forbade private cells.[59]) But partitions were finally permitted in 1666 (says Aubert[60]—but {they were} allowed before—see *Statutes*[61]). In {the} fifteenth century fireplaces were introduced, but suppressed in 1482.[62] There were usually two stairways; one led directly to choir. At the top of the stairs leading to choir was a private cell for the abbot. {His} window looked out over the cloister and he could see everything that went on. Another room at this end of {the} dormitory was a strong room for valuables, archives, etc. The sacristan's bed and bell rope were under the belfry, against the wall of the transept. He had to ring the bell (which he could do lying in bed), then get up and light {the} lamps in the church.

(N.B. {the} dormitory mentioned in {the} statute of 1252, n. 5,[63] in which it is said the brethren enter {the} dormitory after the *Salve*;[64] the *Salve*, with versicle and oration as we now have it, was then ordained to be sung nightly by the General Chapter for the intentions of King St. Louis and his family.)

Legislation in late General Chapters on {the} dormitory:

1565, {n.} 41:[65] cubicles {were} permitted in {the} dormitory of Poblet.

---

58. See Aubert, 2.85, n. 6.
59. Benedict XII, *Fulgens sicut Stella*, c. 24 (*Nomasticon*, 426).
60. Aubert, 2.86; see Canivez, 7:430: "*Constitutio Alexandri Papae VII pro Generali Ordinis Cisterciensis Reformatione*," 5.19.
61. See 1565, n. 41 (Canivez, 7.97).
62. Canivez, 5.447; Aubert, 2.86.
63. Canivez, 2.376–77.
64. I.e., the "*Salve, Regina*," sung at compline.
65. Canivez, 7.97.

1573, {n.} 10:[66] all religious must sleep in {the} common dormitory and not have private rooms in which they could hold parties!

1601, {n.} 15[67] resumes observance at the time: they entered their dormitory cells after compline, spent some time in meditation and reading, {with} closed doors; cells {were} to be visited once a month by {the} superior, who has a common key (hence they could lock their cells). The windows of the cells were barred. It seems each cell was a real little room.

Usages of La Val Sainte:[68] after prefacing with {the} idea that it is a consolation for religious who really love one another to sleep together in {the} same room like children around their parents, {the usages} add {the} following: (a) {there are} never any private cells, even enclosed with curtains; (b) but {there is} a curtain to hide behind when changing; (c) the sacristan and infirmarian slept outside {the} common dormitory; (d) {the} dormitory {was} locked during the day; (e) the beds were simple planks without mattresses; (f) {the} recommended blankets {were} made of moss.

Chapter 73: *De Mixto*:[69] {this is} not a formal meal; {it is} taken at various times by various people: (a) on the *dies prandii*,[70] the bell for mixt is rung—three tolls before sext; (b) on fast days it is rung, three strokes after sext; (c) at the signal for mixt, the weekly reader and the cooks go to the refectory; the junior says "*Benedicite*," the senior says *Largitor*[71] and blesses the bread;

66. Canivez, 7.128–29.
67. Canivez, 7.217.
68. *Règlemens de la Maison-Dieu de Notre-Dame de la Trappe . . . Mis en Nouvel Ordre et Augmentés des Usages Particuliers de la Maison-Dieu de Val Sainte* (Fribourg: Béat-Louis Piller, 1794), 439–47 (Bk. 2, c. 5).
69. *Nomasticon*, 153.
70. "the day for dining".
71. "*Largitor omnium bonorum, benedicat cibum et potum servorum suorum*" ("May the Giver of all good things bless the food and drink of His servants") (see *Monastic Observances*, 185).

afterwards they say the *Retribuere*[72] in silence; (d) others who take mixt are the *adolescentes*,[73] who have mixt before tierce; (e) the measure of the food and drink is to be one quarter pound of bread and a third of a hemine of wine; if they did not take it all, what remained should be put back into the breadbox and poured back into the jug; (f) {there was} no mixt (for {the} reader, etc.) on fast days in Lent, rogation days, ember days, vigils of feasts of Our Lord and of the saints; (g) however, the *adolescentiores did* take mixt on fast days before tierce (General Chapter, 1134, {n.} 50[74]); (h) the *minuti* (those who had been bled) had mixt after tierce with a *pitantia*[75] and a pound of white bread, together with common bread; (i) the laybrothers, at the discretion of the abbot, took mixt (in their own refectory) consisting of a half-pound of "their bread," or a greater quantity of poorer bread, and water; they all took mixt in the granges.

In the *Usages* of the Trappists (1837): (a) mixt consists of four ounces of bread for the reader ({the} words "and for the servant of refectory" are crossed out); (b) the laybrothers all took mixt and all got six ounces of bread, or soup; (c) this was also served to "all those who come in the morning to the refectory," indicating that the mixt was optional for all;[76] (d) mixt consisted of either bread and drink or bread and soup (??); (e) the oblates get the same mixt as the infirm; (f) the infirm (les infirmes de la commu-

---

72. "*Retribuere dignare Domine omnibus nobis bona facientibus propter nomen Tuum, vitam aeternam*" ("O Lord, deign to reward with eternal life all those doing good to us on account of Your name") (see *Monastic Observances*, 186).

73. "youths".

74. Canivez, 1.24.

75. "All monasteries in fact have benefactors, and in the ancient monasteries sometimes benefactors left sums of money to be used for 'pittances' ('relief') to be served in the refectory on certain days, and the monks prayed for them in a special way in consequence. Pittances could be specified by the benefactor—that the monks should have a dish of eggs, or even of fish, or some wine of good quality, etc." (*Monastic Observances*, 186).

76. "On donne pour le mixte quatre onces de pain au lecteur et au serviteur de table, et six onces aux convers et à tous les autres qui viennent le matin au réfectoire" (*Règlemens des Religieux*, 161 [n. 739]).

nauté—e.g., those on relief) got for mixt not only good bread but also fruit, butter or cheese, or "soupe d'infirme."[77]

Present *Usages* and *Constitutions* {are as follows}: *Constitutions* 116 {specifies that} on all days when there is no fasting, "the monks shall take the mixt in the morning."[78] {According to} *Usages* 379,[79] the mixt consists of six ounces of bread with the ordinary drink or soup. *Usages* 369[80] {says that} during extraordinary work the mixt is granted to the community. Dessert may be added and the quantity of bread and drink may be increased.

Chapter 74 to 83: THE DAILY HORARIUM:[81]

1. *Winter Season* (74[82]):

1) about 3:30: after vigils {came the} interval: the servant of the church provides light before the *armarium* and in the chapter room, and the brethren read, "*nec sedeant in angulis nisi legentes*"[83] (note: it was in this interval that matins and lauds of {the} Blessed Virgin came to be said).

2) about 4:45 or 5(?): lauds.

3) {there is} another interval after lauds (light can again be furnished for reading in this interval).

4) 5:30 or 6:00: dawn—but as soon as it is dawn, prime begins: *apparente die pulsetur signum;*[84] prime is followed by High Mass and tierce.

---

77. "Le matin on leur donne des fruits ou du beurre, ou du fromage, ou bien une soupe d'infirme" (*Règlemens des Religieux*, 161 [n. 740]).

78. *Constitutions of the Order of Cistercians of the Strict Observance* (Dublin: M. H. Gill & Sons, [1925]), 29; "*Monachi mane accipiant mixtum*" (*Constitutiones Ordinis Cisterciensium Strictioris Observantiae a Sancta Sede Approbatae et Confirmatae* [Westmalle, Belgium: Ex Typographia Ordinis, 1925], 23).

79. *Regulations*, 179.

80. *Regulations*, 177.

81. *Nomasticon*, 153–66.

82. *Nomasticon*, 153–55.

83. "Let them not sit in nooks unless they are reading" (*Nomasticon*, 154).

84 "once day appears, let the signal be struck" (*Nomasticon*, 154, which reads: ". . . *apparante autem die* . . .").

5) 6 or 7:30: after tierce, chapter (it is here that the parenthesis is added: *Monacho in hieme tribus tunicis induto liceat scapulare superinduere, non tamen sine duabus cucullis*[85]).

6) 6:30 or 8: after chapter, *work* (about five hours): (a) {the} tablet {is} struck by {the} prior or subprior or anyone deputed by {the} prior; (b) at the sound of the tablet all gather except those deputed to various offices, and the sick; (c) the abbot may already in chapter have told some of the officers to do a special work and excused them from distribution of work; (d) the prior gives out work in the auditorium; (e) if the subprior gives out the work, he should do so by signs as far as possible, with only the minimum of talking; (f) silence {is} to be observed as far as possible at work; (g) it is however allowed for monks to accuse themselves (go to confession is the term used) to the superiors during {the} time of work; (h) the cooks and readers make {a} sign to leave in time for their mixt and ask what they should do after mixt; (i) rest is given and they sit in a group, without making signs; (j) reading is prohibited at work and one may not take a book to work.

7) 11 or 11:30: sext {is} usually said in the fields if they were not very close to the house; those within the enclosure left the work momentarily to say the office in church, then returned to work. After work (12:30 or 1), they put their tools in the tool room, except if it is {the} time of sheep-shearing, or pruning, or harvest, in which case they keep their tools handy by their couch in the dormitory.

{8}) 1:30: none—it seems to be foreseen that many may arrive late from work and enter choir late for none.

2:00: DINNER (c. 76: *De Refectione*[86]): (a) after none, the prior rings the bell for dinner; if it is not ready, the brethren read until the proper time; (b) the bell for dinner being rung, they enter the refectory in community, having washed their hands at the *lavabo*;

---

85. "During the winter let the monk be allowed to wear three tunics after putting on the scapular, not without two cowls as well" (*Nomasticon*, 155).

86. *Nomasticon*, 157–60.

(c) arriving at their places, they "bow towards the head table";[87] they stand waiting for the prior—if he is late (which God forbid) anyone who wishes may sit down and wait; (d) {the} prior arrives and rings {the} bell for the space of a *Miserere*[88] before grace; (e) the portions may be put out before {the} bell rings, but when the bell starts to ring they stop serving; when the reader begins, they can start serving again; (f) "The common food having been given out, if the cellarer wishes to give more to those designated to him by the abbot, he serves the pittances to them himself and gives them out as he sees fit";[89] he also provides the relief for those who have been bled; (g) rules for conduct in the refectory: they uncover the bread when the reading begins; from that moment, no one gets up and goes out; no one walks around eating; do not wipe {one's} hands or knife on the napkin without first wiping them with bread (which presumably is eaten); take salt with the knife; hold {the} cup with two hands; if one sees his neighbor lacks anything, get it from the cook or the cellarer; if the prior sends a monk anything special, that one first bows to the one who serves him, then stands up and bows to the prior; no one shares with anyone his portion of common food, but those who have pittances may share them with their immediate neighbors; they cover their bread with the napkin after the *Deo gratias* of the *Tu autem*;[90] {they} go to grace as today.

2:15: then {there is} *lectio divina*[91] {for} about {an} hour and a half, {and} the second table: while the brethren read, the reader and servants take their dinner. They say grace in common {and the} reader recites a short lesson: *"Deus caritas est et qui manet in caritate*

---

87. *"inclinent se versus principalem mensam"* (*Nomasticon*, 158).

88. Ps. 50[51]: "Have mercy [on me, O God] . . ."

89. *"Apposito itaque communi cibo, si cellararius voluerit superaddere pro misericordia illis de quibus indictum est ei ab Abbate ipsemet deferat eis, & sicut voluerit distribuat"* (*Nomasticon*, 158).

90. The prior says *"Tu autem"* when he wishes the reader to stop; the reader replies, *"Deo Gratias"* (*Nomasticon*, 159).

91. "spiritual reading" (*Nomasticon*, 159).

in Deo manet et Deus in eo."[92] If one has {a} pittance he can share it with another even on {the} other side of {the} refectory. After dinner they say the whole grace, in {the} refectory—*Miserere* etc.

3:45 or 4: vespers.[93]

4:30: *lectio divina*.[94]

5:15: *biberes*[95]—they go to {the} refectory, all say *Benedicite*, {the} prior blesses the drink. They take a drink of water, wine or beer; all must be present.

5:30: COLLATIO and compline[96]—all must be present at the blessing of the reader except {the} prior, grange master, guest master, refectorian and his helpers, master of novices and cellarer, who may be absent. But all should be present at the *Tu autem*, {or} otherwise make satisfaction (n.b. the *Salve* {was} sung at night only after 1252 [cf. Statutes of {the} General Chapter[97]] for {the} intention of St. Louis and his family).

6:30 or 7: after compline, they are blessed by {the} abbot at {the} foot of {the} dormitory stairs and go to {the} dormitory, where they sleep in cowl, robe and stockings.[98]

---

92. "God is charity: and he that abideth in charity, abideth in God, and God in him" (1 Jn. 4:16) (*Nomasticon*, 160 [c. 77]).

93. *Nomasticon*, 160–61 (c. 78).

94. *Nomasticon*, 161 (c. 79).

95. Lit. "you might drink" (*Nomasticon*, 161–62 [c. 80]); see *The Spirit of Simplicity Characteristic of the Cistercian Order: An Official Report, Demanded and Approved by the General Chapter. Together with Texts from St. Bernard of Clairvaux on Interior Simplicity. Translation and Commentary by A Cistercian Monk of Our Lady of Gethsemani* [Thomas Merton] (Trappist, KY: Abbey of Our Lady of Gethsemani, 1948), 34, n. 29: "In the golden age of the Order there was no collation, but *biberes*, that is, the monks repaired to the refectory and were served a drink to sustain them until the following afternoon, but nothing to eat."

96. *Nomasticon*, 162–63 (c. 81).

97. Canivez, 2.376–77 (n. 5) (see page 26 above).

98. *Nomasticon*, 163 (c. 82).

2. *Summer Season*:[99]

about 3:00: after vigils, interval.

about 3:45: lauds, plus lauds of {the} dead; then, "*calcient se diurnalibus et sumant cultellos.*"[100]

4:15: interval.

4:45 or 5:00: prime—"*Aspersi aqua et facta oratione secundum tempus, dicant Primam*"[101] (note {the} Cluniac practice—aspersion before office—implies also a *statio* [??][102]); *oratio*—mental or vocal?

5:30: chapter; work; work until {the} first bell for tierce.

about 9: first bell for tierce; interval.

about 9:30: tierce, high Mass.

10:30: interval.

11:30: sext; if not {a} fast day, dinner, {followed by} meridian; if a fast day, meridian after sext: "*pausent in lectis suis usque ad horam octavam*"[103] (i.e., from 12 to about 2).

From 2 to 3: work.

3: none; dinner; interval; vespers, etc., as in winter; after meridian, *coci festinent parare aquam in lavatorio ad lavandum et in refectorio ad potandum*;[104] {there was a} short interval before none.

---

99. *Nomasticon*, 163–66 (c. 83).

100. "Let them put on their shoes for daily wear and strap on their knives" (*Nomasticon*, 163).

101. "Having been sprinkled with water and having said the prayer proper to the time, let them say prime" (*Nomasticon*, 164).

102. *Statio* refers to a procession with fixed stopping places (cf. stations of the cross); in his biographical sketch of St. Alberic, Merton describes the Cluniac practice: "Instead of beginning the day with the *Deus in Adjutorium* of canonical Matins, around one in the morning, the monks started out with a procession in which all were aspersed with holy water; then they proceeded in procession to the altars of various saints, after which they went to choir for what was called the *trina oratio* consisting of groups of psalms interlaced with prayers. . . . On rising, and returning to choir for Prime, the same routine of processions, holy water and *trina oratio* began all over again" (*Valley of Wormwood*, 39–40).

103. "Let them rest on their beds until the eighth hour" (*Nomasticon*, 164).

104. "Let the cooks hasten to prepare water for washing in the lavatory and for drinking in the refectory" (*Nomasticon*, 165).

3 or 3:30: none, followed by *biberes*—all go to {the} refectory, stand at their places, and with various ceremonies, take a drink of water, then go to {the} dormitory to get ready for work; {it was} prescribed that they must not go to the cabinets without cowls on; {they} take off {the} cowls, put on scapulars, and then go to work.

3:30 to 5:30: work.

6: vespers, supper, etc., {then} to bed about 8 or 8:30.

Harvest time (84 [105]):

5:00 (or earlier): prime, high Mass (private Masses {were} permitted during {the} time of conventual Mass), or, if necessary, the community is not present even at high Mass, which is served and attended in that case by the infirm and the "*minuti.*" {The} prior, meanwhile, leaves notice for the ministers where the work is and how to get there, and they follow after Mass. "*His temporibus solet conventus usque ad Sextam laborare et ante Primam si opus fuerit exire, et extra monasterium prandere et dormire si necesse fuerit*" [106]—the reader went along, took his mixt under a tree with the cook after tierce {and} read to the community during {a} picnic dinner. They can stay in the fields right up to vespers and say vespers there, but {the} community returns after vespers. Some may stay behind, but {they} must be back for {the} second table supper (about 7:30).

Work at the granges: in harvest time the monks might go for several days to the granges. Special precautions {were in effect} to preserve regularity: (1) there must be places where they may eat and sleep in common, and where they sleep, each must be able to have his own bed; (2) they must attend especially to silence, both going there and while at {the} grange; (3) they must not make signs with the laybrothers and familiars, and must

---

105. *Nomasticon*, 166–67.

106. "During these times the community is accustomed to work right up until sext, and to go out before prime if there is need, and to eat and sleep outside the monastery if it is necessary" (*Nomasticon*, 166).

guard against sign-making among themselves (except when necessary); (4) no one may go beyond the boundaries of the grange, and they must not wander around in the fields or woods; (5) there must be reading at meals; (6) on Sundays and feasts they take the day off and read; (7) they are not to be sent to the granges except to harvest crops (not for vintage or sheep-shearing) (General Chapter, 1160, n. 3 [107]).

Further notes on granges and manual labor: (1) possession of granges, to be operated by brothers, {was} permitted by {the} first statutes (cf. 1134, {n.} 5 [108]); (2) the obligation to read and keep holy day at granges on Sundays and feasts was strict; work at such times was allowed only to bring food to {the} grange; superiors allowing their monks to work there on those days were to fast one day on bread and water for each workday so permitted; (3) statutes of {the} General Chapter bear witness to frequent disputes about a grange of Schoenthal Abbey (Wurtemburg) (cf. 1203, n. 44 [109]): {the} General Chapter of 1199 [110] legislates that the grange must not be destroyed (in settlement of {a} dispute with another abbey) because the existence of Schoenthal depends on it; 1203 says: "Of the 500 sheep and lambs [at this grange], they can stay until the feast of St. Andrew, and after that the lambs must go to other pastures, but the 500 sheep may remain" [111] ({the} sheep were evidently overflowing into lands of another abbey grange); (4) it was prescribed that when the community was at the granges, those who remained in the abbey had to keep the regular observances in everything; (5) it was strictly forbidden to say or sing Mass at the granges; altars that had been erected and blessed were taken away, and all the vessels etc., for Mass were

---

107. Canivez, 1.71.
108. Canivez, 1.14.
109. Canivez, 1.293.
110. Canivez, 1.245 (n. 62).
111. "*quingentas oves cum agnis usque ad festum sancti Andreae habeat et ex tunc, agni ad pasturas alias emittantur, quingentis ovibus in loco remanentibus usquequaque*" (Canivez, 1.293–94 [n. 44]).

to be kept out of the granges (General Chapter, 1204, n. 11 [112]); (6) if a monk was out of his monastery, he did not need special permission to eat dinner at a grange of his own monastery (1157, n. 24 [113]); (7) the brothers were not allowed to drink wine or beer at the granges, and when the monks went there they could not have it either (1180, n. 10 [114]); in some territories a concession had been granted for this, however, and {the} General Chapter of 1184 [115] sustained the concession, while at the same time forbidding granges in other territories to introduce the practice—{it was} forbidden explicitly in England, Normandy, Flanders, France, Brittany (??) (France here means not Aquitaine but Champagne) (1185, n. 9 [116]); 1186, n. 10 [117] returns to {the} same topic and declares that those who still resist this statute are considered to be conspirators, and excommunicated; 1195, n. 18 [118] {determined that} in granges where wine is permitted, there is only one portion at the dinner (and another at supper) (repeated: 1196, n. 51 [119]); 1194, n. 38 [120] {decreed that the} Abbot of Bourras (in non-wine territory), {who} allowed a monk to eat meat at a grange, {was to fast} six days *levi culpa*, of which one {was on} bread and water; 1199, n. 40 [121] {concerned} a grange at which brothers apparently ate meat—it is forbidden; 1205, n. 17 [122] {ruled that} meat-eating at granges {was} prohibited even for hired secular help and visitors; 1200, n. 64 [123] {concerned} the grange master and guest master of a grange of Obazine {who} refused to give abbots going to {the}

---

112. Canivez, 1.297–98.
113. Canivez, 1.62.
114. Canivez, 1.87.
115. Canivez, 1.97 (n. 15).
116. Canivez, 1.99.
117. Canivez, 1.104.
118. Canivez, 1.185.
119. Canivez, 1.207.
120. Canivez, 1.176–77.
121. Canivez, 1.240.
122. Canivez, 1.310–11.
123. Canivez, 1.261.

General Chapter anything but hay and straw: they must come on foot to Cîteaux to do penance; {in} 1233, n. 67,[124] it appears that {the} guest master and a brother of the grange Fons Siccus, belonging to Fontenay, armed the hired help to drive away some abbots who wanted to stop off on {the} way to {the} General Chapter; {for} penance, {they were} excommunicated {and} sent to distant houses (the two instigators) {and} the other brothers present {were to} fast on bread and water until Easter, and the hired help to be fired and not received in any other house of {the} Order; {in} 1259, n. 3,[125] {an} abbot {was} penanced for putting a secular in charge of {a} grange to avoid having to give hospitality to travelers of {the} Order (cf. 1261, n. 10[126]).

Chapter 85: *De Rasuris*:[127] originally the brethren were shaved and tonsured only at the following times: (1) during the week preceding the following: Christmas; Quinquagesima (about two months); Easter (two months); Pentecost (six weeks); St. Mary Magdalen (from four to eight weeks); Nativity of Our Lady (six weeks); All Saints (six weeks). In other words, {they were} only shaved and tonsured every six or eight weeks. What happened on the shaving days? "The cooks heat and bring water to the cloister. Combs, shears, razors and sharpeners are brought, sharpened and prepared by the one in charge of them. The abbot appoints who shall cut the hair. Those who have had their hair cut shave one another in the cloister, except for the infirm who do this in the infirmary. The crown should not be shaved too thin, and the tonsure must be above the ears. No one is to presume to shave another unless invited to do so. No one who is invited must dare to refuse. No one makes anyone a sign to shave except

---

124. Canivez, 2.125.
125. Canivez, 2.449.
126. This statute specifies that while there may be legitimate reasons to entrust the management of granges to laymen, hospitality must be given at granges to travelling members of the Order regardless of who is in charge (Canivez, 2.477).
127. *Nomasticon*, 167–68.

after the signal for work has been given."[128] Different time schedules {arise}. {The} General Chapter {of} 1191[129] increases the number of shavings to nine: Christmas, Purification, *"Oculi"* Sunday,[130] Easter, Ascension, St. John {the} Baptist, St. Peter in Chains, Nativity {of the} Blessed Virgin Mary, All Saints (roughly every five weeks). 1211, n. 20[131] punishes abbots who allowed shaving before the dedication of the church: six days *levi culpa*, two on bread and water; {for the} community, one day {on} bread and water. {According to} 1257, n. 4,[132] Cardinal John of Toledo, a Cistercian, petitioned the General Chapter on behalf of the pope that out of reverence for {the} Blessed Sacrament there should be *twelve shavings a year*—one more was added in 1258.[133] {According to} 1287, n. 14,[134] again at the petition of a cardinal and papal legate, shaving is to take place *for all members of the Order* (maybe only {the} heads of brothers) *every third Friday or Saturday* (repeated {in} 1288, n. 7[135]); 1293, n. 24[136] {decreed} *every two weeks*, on Friday

---

128. *"Coci calefaciant & deferant aquam in claustrum. Pectines, forpices, rasoria & effilatorias, custos eorum acuat & praeparet. Fratres tondeant quibus jusserit Abbas. Tonsi alterutrum radant, & in claustro; praeter infirmos qui in infirmatorio sunt. Rasura corona fiat non exigua, tonsura per desuper aures. Nullus nisi invitatus audeat refutare. Signum autem radendi alter alteri non faciat, nisi post tabulam pulsatam."*

129. Canivez, 1.136 (n. 12).

130. *"Oculi"* Sunday is *"dominicam qua canitur Oculi mei"* ("the Sunday on which '*Oculi mei*' is sung") – i.e., the Third Sunday in Lent, which begins with an introit from Ps. 24[25]:15-16: *"Oculi mei semper ad Dominum quia ipse educet de rete pedes meos. Respice in me et miserere mei quoniam solus et pauper sum ego"* ("My eyes are ever towards the Lord: for he shall pluck my feet out of the snare. Look thou upon me, and have mercy on me; for I am alone and poor").

131. Canivez, 1.382.

132. Canivez, 2.426.

133. Canivez, 2.440 (n. 12).

134. Canivez, 3.239–40.

135. Canivez, 3.241.

136. Canivez, 3.265.

or Saturday. {According to} 1303, n. 5,[137] the brothers are going too far: they are shaving their upper lip and a strip along the lower lip; if they do this in {the} future, they must have their beards cut off altogether as punishment. 1623, n. 38[138] prescribes that the shaving must be "uniform" in the whole Order. Trappist Usages[139] {decree that} crowns {are to be} renewed about once a month—about as today—done in {the} calefactory, *with public reading*. Shaving {was} permitted only at the same time, except for cellarers, guest masters and those having special permission. (Read *Usages*, 400[140]—n.b. a place and time of silence.[141])

Chapter 88: *Those Going on a Journey*:[142]

1) {The} basic principle {is}: *Nullus in via dirigatur nisi utilitate monasterii*.[143] One does not go out for any purpose except for the common good—one's own good must be also common good before one can go out; they ordinarily did not go out to hospitals—the sick were cared for in the monastery.

2) The prayers: the blessing can be received after any of the canonical hours, even after the nocturns (but it is specified that

---

137. Canivez, 3.310.
138. Canivez, 7.352.
139. *Règlemens des Religieux*, 167–68 (n. 767).
140. "The beard is shaved every week. The Superior may, however, in certain cases permit the religious to shave more often. The crowns are renewed once a month, as nearly as possible at the following times: (1) First Sunday of Advent; (2) Christmas; (3) the Conversion of St. Paul; (4) St. Matthias; (5) once before Easter, unless that feast falls in the month of March or at the beginning of April; (6) Maundy Thursday; (7) the Fourth Sunday after Easter; (8) Pentecost; (9) once or twice between Pentecost and the Assumption; (10) the Assumption; (11) the Nativity of the Blessed Virgin; (12) the Guardian Angels; (13) All Saints" (*Regulations*, 188).
141. "402. The place of shaving is a place of silence; if anyone is obliged to speak to the Superior there, he does so in a low voice and in few words" (*Regulations*, 188).
142. *Nomasticon*, 169–72.
143. "Let no one be assigned to a journey except for the advantage of the monastery" (*Nomasticon*, 169).

one gets {the} blessing after the nocturns only on ferial days). The one about to go out bows to the two choirs at the step and then bows or prostrates, depending on whether it is a ferial day or a feast. The one returning from {a} journey never bows to the two choirs and always prostrates. One can receive communion at the matutinal Mass if one is to leave before high Mass. Blessing is not received if one is only going to a grange or a dependency of the monastery for the day.

3) Leaving: if one is about to leave the monastery and the first bell rings for chapter, or an office, or for reading before compline, one returns and assists at this exercise, whatever it may be. {This} shows with what reverence our Fathers fulfilled St. Benedict's injunction to put nothing before the work of God.[144] The traveler is not allowed to eat within a half-league of the monastery. A transient monk who is not entering the monastery that day can eat just outside the monastery. {A} transient priest can say Mass after he has received {the} blessing to leave—others, no. Those going on a journey or coming from one are not allowed to speak to their companions or anyone else inside the monastery without special permission; presumably they spoke outside, except at meals.

4) Rules when on a journey: saying the office. If it is a ferial day, they kneel while saying the office, from the *Gloria Patri* at the beginning. Otherwise they may say the office while riding on horseback; if not on horseback they should stand, unless it is seriously inconvenient (*si non multum gravatur*[145]). Those going to a grange or to the *cellarium* ({the} agency of the monastery in town) do not get the blessing unless they are to stay outside overnight. Those who have eaten in town get the blessing on their return, even if they have not been out overnight (i.e., if they have eaten with seculars). {With regard to} fasting, they are obliged to keep the usual fasts even outside the monastery, unless

---

144. "*Ergo nihil operi Dei praeponatur*" ("Let nothing, therefore, be put before the Work of God") (c. 43 [McCann, 102, 103]).

145. "if one is not too greatly burdened" (*Nomasticon*, 170).

invited to eat at the abbot's table in a house of the Order, or invited to dinner by a bishop or archbishop or papal legate. In such case they do not have to keep the fasts of the Order, but are still bound to those of the Church. When out of the monastery, they do not speak at meals, they do not eat meat, they do not sleep in feather beds unless there is absolutely nothing else suitable to be had. Abbots and monks can carry a small pallet or something to lie on along with them if they like, {and} also a pillow—but not fancy bedding.

5) {Upon} returning from {a} journey, they go immediately to church. If the community is in choir saying the office, they join immediately in choir. If they are not at *canonical* office, the traveler remains praying *extra chorum*.[146] If when he arrives the church is locked, he prays outside the door. Visiting monks do not give out anything in choir.

Those on {a} journey {are considered in the} Statutes of {the} General Chapter (see index: "*Directi in Via*"[147]). Two interesting statutes in 1192 show that there was such a thing as journeying out of mere restlessness. (Stability and enclosure are so essential to our Order that the contemplative life for us depends on their strict observance. Abuses in this regard are a sure sign of decadence. We must be warned by the history of the Order and guard against this danger. For ourselves, it is most important to cultivate the spirit of enclosure and stability and not deceive ourselves by indulging in vain desires for which there is an apparent "reason." Above all, avoid pretexts for travelling later on, when in office. For a true monk, travelling is a nuisance and a burden, a meritorious penance when imposed by the will of God.) {See} 1192, {n.} 59: "A monk or laybrother who through restlessness has extorted a permission to go on a journey without any necessity for the monastery (which is forbidden) . . . must not have anything to drink except water until he returns to his own

---

146. "outside the choir" (*Nomasticon*, 171).
147. Canivez, 8.165.

house."[148] {N.} 60 {adds}: "*Non bibant nisi aquam qui de inquietudine sua equitant ad parentes*"[149]—hence they even extorted permissions to go home. (1193, n. 10[150] repeats verbatim 1192, n. 59.) Since these statutes were evidently made to *prevent such journeys*, by putting pressure on the monk himself, and since they evidently did not succeed, pressure was then put on the abbots: 1195, n. 16[151] {declares}: "Let no one receive permission to go on a journey except for the evident and certain needs of the monastery. The abbot who shall have given such a permission shall accuse himself at the General Chapter, and the prior or any other who shall have done so, shall fast three days on bread and water." However, the abuse was not altogether stamped out, {for} 1209, n. 5[152] added to the other penalties of those who go to see their parents {that} they must also travel on foot. Hence, it is first of all formally prohibited to go to see family (i.e., to travel just for that purpose); if a monk extorts that permission, then he cannot have wine on the journey and he must travel on foot; if the abbot gives that permission, he must give an account of it to the General Chapter (note {the} connection of instability and disobedience).

Other Journeys: some monks could be sent on a journey to another monastery as a penance. {See} 1209, n. 4:[153] the monk or brother who is sent to another monastery on account of a fault, or because he is restless, must go and return on foot. Those who

---

148. "*Monachus vel conversus qui per inquietationem suam licentiam extorserit quocumque ire sine utilitate domus, quod fieri non licet, . . . non bibat nisi aquam donec ad propria revertatur*" (Canivez, 1.157).

149. "Those who out of restlessness journey to their parents may not drink anything but water" (Canivez, 1.157).

150. Actually this statute (Canivez, 1.159) reads: ". . . *a Capitulo generali, ille talis non bibat . . .*" for ". . . *in Capitulo generali, non bibat . . .*"

151. "*Nulli detur licentia equitandi nisi pro certa et evidenti necessitate domus. Abbas qui huiusmodi licentiam dederit, veniam petat in capitulo generali; prior vel quilibet alius qui huiusmodi licentiam dederit, tribus diebus sit in pane et aqua*" (Canivez, 1.184).

152. Canivez, 1.358.

153. Canivez, 1.357–58.

go out on legitimate business can travel on horseback. {1219,} n. 2 repeats the sentence that monks etc., travelling *pro culpa sua* must go on foot, and adds that this fact must be stated in their "travelling letters."[154] This reminds us of the fact that a monk could not travel without letters from his abbot telling where he was to go, and how and why. Without such letters he could be considered a fugitive or apostate. {In} 1261, n. 6[155] {the} General Chapter again takes note of the fact that some monks are always pestering their abbots for permission to travel. If such permissions are extorted, the monks in question must make the fact known at the next visitation and be punished by the visitors. Here another step is taken to curb the abuse. But the measures were still not completely effective for a long time, as in 1275 it is clear the abuse has grown worse: {in} 1275, n. 8[156] the General Chapter frankly states that because of the useless travelling of many monks, numerous evils have befallen the houses of our Order. {It} renews {the} prohibition, and adds that all who extort permissions or grant such extorted permissions must be three days *in levi culpa*.

IN THE PERIOD OF DECADENCE, 1460, n. 34[157] speaks of the uninhibited wanderings of those who, pretending to transfer to another monastery, go around through towns and villages doing their own will, living in danger of damnation. They must be stabilized in regular monasteries (cf. those wandering around in Paris, in trouble with the officers of {the} College of St. Bernard [1478, n. 35[158]]). Note the *seriousness* of this state of affairs, and remember the effects of monastic decadence: the "Reformation" and schism. 1494, n. 52[159] (a sad thing to read) {specifies that} monks must not be allowed to go out to celebrate Mass in neighboring churches unless in the chapels of noblemen, who cannot

---

154. "*litteris suis viaticis*" (Canivez, 1.503) (text reads: "1218").
155. Canivez, 2.476.
156. Canivez, 3.140–41.
157. Canivez, 5.55.
158. Canivez, 5.376.
159. Canivez, 6.95.

be denied. Those who leave the monastery for this or any other cause must have permission. They cannot go without real necessity for the monastery. They must go dressed in the regular habit, with a mantle. Above all, in towns and villages they must be dressed in their habit, with mantle, under pain of imprisonment. They must no longer go to *festa locorum* (festivals of towns and villages) or weddings or shows or taverns. Still less should they sleep in taverns. They must not carry swords or lethal weapons, but if they need something to ward off the dogs, it should savor of religious gravity. They should not act as godfathers at baptisms, or take any oaths, and they must be careful not to curse or use foul language.

Further rules for travelling:

1) {The} earliest legislation (closely connected with {the} spirit of {the} *Carta Caritatis*—on relations between monasteries of the Order) {includes} 1134, {n.} 39:[160] when monks are on a journey, they shall not impose on other abbeys of the Order by demands for anything except food, shoe-repairs, horse-shoeing; only in the event of accident shall they seek anything else. {According to n.} 57,[161] abbots on a journey could of course ask for the wherewithal to say Mass, as they could not take with them chalices or vestments unless they had special permission of the General Chapter.

2) Other rules {include} 1191, n. 91:[162] monks and abbots could not join company with abbesses and nuns of the Order on a journey. They could go with them at most one day's journey. {According to} 1192, n. 6,[163] abbots in Spain who had disobeyed this and travelled more than one day with abbesses and nuns were penanced—three days *levi culpa*, one on bread and water; brothers involved got three days bread and water. {There was a}

---

160. Canivez, 1.22.
161. Canivez, 1.26.
162. Canivez, 1.146.
163. Canivez, 1.147.

further strict prohibition of joining company with women of the Order on journeys. (Note: this is the same year when legislation against monks travelling out of restlessness begins to be necessary.[164]) After 1200, {there are} references to members of the Order having to come to Clairvaux or Cîteaux or Pontigny on foot as penance. One of the most scandalous incidents is in 1206, n. 23:[165] the rebellion of the laybrothers of Margam (Wales). They rose up in rebellion against the abbot, threw the cellarer off his horse, chased the abbot fifteen miles with weapons, barricaded themselves in the dormitory and refused to allow the monks to get at the food supplies. The guilty were to come to Clairvaux on foot, thence to be scattered throughout various houses of the Order, and Margam was no longer to receive any brother novices without special permission of the General Chapter. 1208, n. 3[166] {ruled that} monks {were} not allowed to carry bottles of wine with them on journeys; 1233, n. 4[167] {specified} poverty in equipage of horses, etc.; 1217, n. 44[168] {records} another incident, regarding hospitality: two abbots from Portugal stop at the Benedictine monastery of Marmoutier (France). The guest master gives them some evil-smelling kind of smoked fish, some eggs and vegetables. They complain loudly of the fish {and} ask for water to wash the smell off their hands. The next day they send to town and get some good fresh fish and ask the guest master to prepare it for them. He refuses, unless paid. He gives them bread and wine on condition that they go and eat elsewhere. They park outside the front gate and eat there. In addition to *levi culpa* the abbots were forbidden fish for a year. ({A} pittance of fish customarily {was allowed} on journeys: {see} 1224, n. 23.[169])

164. 1192, n. 59 (see pages 41–42 above).
165. Canivez, 1.324.
166. Canivez, 1.346.
167. Canivez, 2.111–12.
168. Canivez, 1.475–76.
169. Canivez, 2.34.

THE NOVITIATE (*Consuetudines*, 102,[170] 113[171]): the postulant comes to the guest house. After at least four days in the guest house, he is brought to the chapter room {and} prostrates before the *analogium* (bookstand). {The} abbot asks: *Quid petis?* He replies: *misericordiam Dei et vestram*.[172] {The} abbot tells him to get up and exhorts him before the whole community, telling him the difficulties of the life, etc. (Note how this makes more sense out of our rite for giving the habit. The things we do at the giving of the habit—apart from giving the habit itself, which was only done at profession in the old days—are appropriate for someone *just entering*, the secular who is "*sub auditorio*,"[173] who knows nothing whatever of the life, who is officially meeting the community and presenting himself before it for the first time, etc.) After telling what the life is, the abbot asks if he is willing to embrace it. The postulant then says yes, if he means to, and returns to the guest house for three days. On the third day he is led to the *cella novitiorum*[174] ({a} special room, at the end of the north wing). There he begins his *year* of probation.

What were the conditions for admission to the novitiate? He had to be fifteen years old (1134, n. 78[175]). If he was a novice or a monk he could make his studies in the monastery, but no secular youth could make studies in one of our monasteries as a postulant (*idem*). 1154, n.16[176] states that a boy of fifteen or over could be sent away by the abbot if his growth, face and so forth made him *look* younger. {This was} a sensible measure—not merely the number of years, but childishness and lack of development were

---

170. "*De Novitiis*" (*Nomasticon*, 190–92).
171. "*De Magistro Novitiorum*" (*Nomasticon*, 201).
172. "What do you seek?"; "the mercy of God, and your own" (*Nomasticon*, 190).
173. "in the discernment process".
174. "the novices' quarters" (*Nomasticon*, 190).
175. Canivez, 1.31.
176. Canivez, 1.57.

in view. {In} 1175, n. 26,[177] the age limit is raised to eighteen ({see} 1157, n. 28[178]), and anyone who receives a postulant under eighteen will do three days *levi culpa*, one on bread and water, but those under eighteen already received before this statute may remain. {According to} 1191, n. 30,[179] {when the} Abbot of Sobrado, in Galicia, receives a boy of twelve, {he} gets six days *levi culpa* and must fast on bread and water every Friday until he puts up a screen between the brothers and the choir. {In} 1195, n. 55,[180] {the} Abbot of La Ferté had received several boys under fifteen; punishment {was} extended to priors and cellarers who had counseled him to do so. 1196, n. 65[181] {decreed that} any abbot who receives a novice under eighteen must fast on bread and water every Friday as long as the boy is in the novitiate—so too the cellarer, prior or anyone by whose advice he was received (reiterated {by} 1197, n. 10[182]). 1201, n. 4[183] {is} a long and severe statute, declaring that many abbots are introducing confusion and contemning regularity by receiving boys under eighteen against the desires of the General Chapter. The following steps were taken because of "grave scandals"[184] that had arisen: (a) former penances {were} reiterated and abbots told they are bound in conscience to perform them; (b) anyone in the monastery, having an office, who has encouraged or effected the reception of novices under age, shall be deposed; (c) {the} same penance {is imposed} for anyone who has introduced young boys into monasteries or granges to study (which is only to be permitted for very special reasons by indult of the General Chapter). The

---

177. Canivez, 1.84.
178. This statute also specifies that a novice should not be received if under eighteen years of age (Canivez, 1.62).
179. Canivez, 1.139.
180. Canivez, 1.190.
181. Canivez, 1.209.
182. Canivez, 1.212.
183. Canivez, 1.264.
184. *"gravissima scandala"*.

statute was enforced: see later decisions, for instance {the} case of a novice of Fontaine Blanche, who "seemed to be" under age (1211, n. 35 [185]). The main reason for all this seems to be that they wanted the novices to be strong, and able to take, from the start, all the austerities of the life (*maioris staturae et virioris aetatis* [186]). Specifically the novices had to be such as could get along without eating three times a day (1184, n. 2 [187]). 1190, n. 47 [188] {decreed that the} Abbot of Tennenbach, who received a novice under age, must fast on bread and water every Friday until the novice is professed. Note the General Chapter does not say that the novice, once received, must automatically be sent away. He is received now, and has a right to stay, although he should not have been received, and the abbot has to do penance for having received him. (However, in the *Libellus Antiquarum Definitionum* [189] [Dist. 11, n. 1], those under eighteen are to be sent away by the visitor.) 1194, n. 6 [190] {decrees that} a novice who contracts leprosy should be sent away, but the monastery out of charity can put him up as a secular and care for him for the rest of his life. {According to} 1206, n. {72}, [191] {the} Abbot of Pairis has a novice who eats three times a day, and {there are} peacocks in the cloister. In {the} *Libellus Antiquarum Definitionum*, [192] abbots in distant regions (Hungary, Poland, Bohemia, Livonia) could receive novices fifteen years old, because of {the} dearth of adult vocations.

Other qualities demanded in a novice: {the} *Consuetudines* [193] {require that} he had to be unmarried, unless {the} bishop gave

---

185. "*videtur esse citra annos*" (Canivez, 1.386).
186. "of taller height and more mature age".
187. Canivez, 1.95; this provision is also found in 1157, n. 28 (Canivez, 1.62).
188. Canivez, 1.127–28.
189. *Nomasticon*, 447.
190. Canivez, 1.172.
191. Canivez, 1.333 (text reads: "76").
192. *Instituta Capituli Generalis Cisterciensium*, 10.1 (*Nomasticon*, 338).
193. *Ecclesiastica Officia*, n. 102 (*Nomasticon*, 190).

{a} document saying {his} wife vowed chastity. {According to} 1234, n. 7,[194] he must not be convicted or suspect of heresy; if such a one has been received he must be sent away immediately, or locked up. Legitimate birth is not demanded until 1308, n. 1.[195] There was a special agreement between the Cistercians and Carthusians that neither order would receive a postulant from the other without the knowledge and permission of the other order (1210, n. 1[196]). In 1212, n. 10,[197] the Order promised the Canons of St. Victor in Paris that they would not try to get members of their order to join us, or allow friends of our Order to do this. ({In the} *Libellus Antiquarum Definitionum*,[198] anyone who left our Order to join another was regarded as a fugitive.) {In} 1274, n. 3,[199] it was agreed that we would not again receive any Carmelite into our Order (note {the} crisis in {the} history of the Carmelites, at the time when they were abandoning the purely contemplative life and turning to the apostolic life). N.B. novices could not be received in houses where there had been a conspiracy, until reception was permitted again by {the} General Chapter.

Life in the Novitiate: (a) the novice in community—novices take their proper rank in church, going to work, at reading before compline in the cloister, {but they} do NOT go to daily chapter; (b) at the end of the hours, they leave before the monks; (c) after compline they make a mental prayer (*oratio*) out of choir (?? what is this?); (d) they work, rest, read and sleep {at the} same times as {the} monks; (e) they eat the same food as the monks (but in the novitiate, not in {the} refectory); (f) {as for} clothing, {there is} not a special monastic novice habit: they have a cape, mantle and fur coat (*pelles*); (g) {they are} not allowed to make signs to the professed {and are} not allowed to receive tonsure or minor or-

---

194. Canivez, 2.127.
195. Canivez, 3.318.
196. Canivez, 1.368–69.
197. Canivez, 1.391.
198. *Distinctio* X, c. 3 (*Nomasticon*, 339).
199. Canivez, 3.127.

ders; (h) if he had classes, they were during the *tempus lectionis;* (i) if he dies, he receives the same privileges as a monk.

The Master of Novices (c. 113): *Magister novitiorum debet novitios ordinem suum docere*[200]—to teach the ways of {the} monastic life and observance of the *Rule; in ecclesia excitare*—wake them in church; "wherever they are negligent, to correct them by word or by sign as well as he can."[201] He does not speak to them at work, nor does he speak to them outside the novitiate, without special permission. He does not read or practice signing in the novitiate. He procures for them everything they need. He brings them to chapter on feasts of sermons, to hear the sermon. (They did not come to chapter on other days except to make their petitions.) He gives penances for public faults. He makes a record of their entry, and when they are to make their petitions. He makes this known to the abbot. He sees that they read the *Rule* each time before their petition—it could be read during {the} *tempus lectionis,* or even during time of work, and the one who did it was apart from the others. In other words, the time of reading over the *Rule* was a time of retreat. (It would be a good idea to make a short retreat—{a} day of recollection—before each one of our petitions.) He prepares them for profession one year after their entrance. He assists them in the profession ceremony, especially in putting on the habit, and after their profession he brings their things into the common refectory (previously they ate in the novitiate). He also gives him a bed in the professed dormitory, or rather shows him the one assigned to him by the prior. On the day of profession he can make signs to him about necessary things, and he retains permission to speak in the auditorium with him for two months after his profession.

---

200. "The master of novices should teach the novices his own observance" (*Nomasticon,* 201).

201. "*ubicumque se negligenter habuerint verbo vel signo quantum potuerit emendare*" (*Nomasticon,* 201).

The Cantor and his helper (115: *De cantore et solatio ejus*[202]): the job of the cantor and subcantor is first of all to see that everybody sings: "Each in his own choir must stir up the brethren to keep awake and sing."[203] Then they correct mistakes—each again in his own choir. One does not correct {a} mistake in the other choir unless the one in charge has failed to do so. The cantor can always cross over to the other side to make corrections; the subcantor can cross over to the cantor's side for an "intolerable"[204] state of affairs only. Ordinarily the subcantor does not interfere with the cantor. The cantor is in charge of the choir books and of the copying of manuscripts. He has to regulate the office. The sacristan (in charge of {the} time piece) lets him know when to go faster, or when to cut short some of the lessons or responsories. He obeys the signs of the sacristan in this regard. He intones antiphons etc., and prepares the books for those who have to sing something special. For instance, on feasts of twelve lessons, he prepares a twelfth lesson appropriate to the day (lessons were not as rigidly fixed as they are today). He makes appointments for singing, etc. (Note: on the weekly tablet—read on *Sundays*—there was also one for the *mandatum hospitum*.[205]) He makes intonations (alone) at Mass. He does not conduct a formal chant class, but he individually helps those who practice their lessons, etc. He is also {an} archivist, at least to the extent that he is in charge of all the schedules of profession. He is in charge of the *armarium*, or common box. He provides books for reading in {the} refectory and cloister. He can go to the door of the novitiate to demand the return of common-box books. He locks up the *armarium* after compline, during work time and {at} mealtimes. He distributes the Lenten books in chapter {on the} First Sunday of

---

202. *Nomasticon*, 203–5.

203. "*unusquisque in choro suo fratres ad vigilandum & cantandum excitare*" (*Nomasticon*, 203).

204. "*pro intolerabili*" (*Nomasticon*, 203).

205. "the washing of guests' feet".

Lent (hence the cantor does so in our usages,[206] though there is no longer any real reason for him to do so). In the absence of the abbot, it was the cantor's place to anoint the dying and to bury the dead. He announces the end of tricenaries.[207]

The Cellarer (117[208]) (note: read St. Benedict's chapter on the cellarer,[209] one of the most important in the *Rule*: the virtues of

---

206. *Regulations*, 282 (n. 595).

207. *Regulations*, 284 (n. 600); tricenaries are the thirty-day commemoration of a dead member of the community (*Regulations*, 238–39 [n. 503]).

208. *Nomasticon*, 207–208.

209. "*Cellararius monasterio eligatur de congregatione sapiens, maturus moribus, sobrius, non multum edax, non elatus, non turbulentus, non injuriosus, non tardus, non prodigus, sed timens Deum, qui omni congregationi sit sicut pater. Curam gerat de omnibus; sine jussione abbatis nihil faciat; quae jubentur custodiat; fratres non contristet. Si quis frater ab eo forte aliqua irrationabiliter postulat, non spernendo eum contristet, sed rationabiliter cum humilitate male petenti deneget. Animam suam custodiat, memor semper illud apostolicum, quia qui bene ministraverit, gradum bonum sibi acquirit. Infirmorum, infantum, hospitum, pauperumque cum omni sollicitudine curam gerat, sciens sine dubio quia pro his omnibus in diem judicii rationem redditurus est. Omnia vasa monasterii cunctamque substantiam ac si altaris vasa sacrata conspiciat. Nihil ducat negligendum. Neque avaritiae studeat, neque prodigus sit et stirpator substantiae monasterii; sed omnia mensurate faciat, et secundum jussionem abbatis. Humilitatem ante omnia habeat, et cui substantia non est quae tribuatur, sermo responsionis porrigatur bonus, ut scriptum est: Sermo bonus super datum optimum. Omnia quae ei injunxerit abbas, ipsa habeat sub cura sua; a quibus eum prohibuerit non praesumat. Fratribus constitutam annonam sine aliquo typho vel mora offerat, ut non scandalizentur, memor divini eloquii, quid mereatur* qui scandalizaverit unum de pusillis. *Si congregatio major fuerit, solatia ei dentur, a quibus adjutus et ipse aequo animo impleat officium sibi commissum. Horis competentibus et dentur quae danda sunt, et petantur quae petenda sunt: ut nemo perturbetur neque contristetur in domo Dei*" ("As cellarer of the monastery let there be chosen out of the community a man who is prudent, of mature character, temperate, not a great eater, not proud, not headstrong, not rough-spoken, not lazy, not wasteful, but a God-fearing man who may be like a father to the whole community. Let him have charge of everything; let him do nothing without the abbot's orders, but keep to his instructions. Let him not vex the brethren. If any brother happen to make an unreasonable demand, he should not vex him

the cellarer—*maturus moribus*[210]): he can speak to all the brothers, guests, familiars, travellers, etc. The only people he cannot speak to are monks and choir novices. He provides the food for the various kitchens, sees to it that the sick and the *"minuti"* get proper relief, {and} gives relief to others with permission of {the} prior. He sees that the guests are well taken care of. {He} weighs out bread for the meals and provides wine or cider. He goes around the tables at least once during dinner and supper. He sends out {the} remains of meals to the gate for the poor. He assists the brother novices at the time of their profession. When the cellarer is occupied with more important business, this is all done by the subcellarer.

---

with a contemptuous denial, but reasonably and humbly refuse the improper request. Let him keep guard over his own soul, remembering always the saying of the apostle that *he that hath served well, secures for himself a good standing* [1 Tim. 3:13]. Let him take the greatest care of the sick, of children, of guests and of the poor, knowing without doubt that he will have to render an account of all these on the Day of Judgement. Let him look upon all the utensils of the monastery and its whole property as upon the sacred vessels of the altar. Let him not think that anything may be neglected. Let him neither practice avarice, nor be wasteful and a squanderer of the monastery's substance; but let him do all things with measure and in accordance with the instructions of the abbot. Above all things let him have humility, and if he have nothing else to give, let him give a good word in answer; for it is written: *A good word is above the best gift* [Ecclus. 18:17]. Let him have under his care all those things which the abbot has assigned to him, but presume not to deal with what he has forbidden to him. Let him give the brethren their appointed allowance of food without any arrogance or delay, that they may not be scandalized, mindful of what the Scripture saith that he deserves *who shall scandalize one of these little ones* [Mt. 18:6]. If the community be a large one, let helpers be given him, so that by their assistance he may fulfil with a quiet mind the charge that has been committed to him. Let those things which have to be asked for and those things which have to be given be asked for and given at the proper times; so that no one may be troubled or vexed in the house of God") (c. 31 [McCann, 80, 82; 81, 83]).

210. "mature in behavior" (McCann, 80).

The Sacristan and his helper (114[211]): the sacristan's first charge is to be the timekeeper of the monastery (*horologium temperare*[212]). As soon as the community rises, he goes down to church to provide light for them. He also opens the church doors for the community (i.e., those into the cloister). He rings the bell for chapter, mixt, *biberes,* collation (reading before compline) and all the hours. He indicates to {the} cantor when to speed up the office. He makes candles, provides ashes, palms, etc., when needed, provides {a} stole and crozier for {the} abbot when needed, keeps {the} holy oils, etc. {He} assists {the} abbot in the blessing of a monastic crown, is in charge of missals, etc., washes and irons the altar linens, irons corporals {while} vested in {an} alb. Vested in {the} alb {he} makes altar breads, in perfect silence, aided by two brethren in scapular. He washes the chalices once a week, and sweeps the church.

The Weekly Reader[213] gets his blessing after the major Mass {on} Sunday. {He} enters the refectory and has the book open on the *analogium*[214] when the prior enters, and sits during the prayers before meals. {He} sings what he reads, as in church: homilies from the Fathers mostly, or scripture that is not finished in the office. He could be corrected by the prior; if he did not understand the correction, he had to begin the verse over again until the prior growled at him some more and he caught on.

The Sick:

1. *De vementibus et sanguine fluentibus* (89[215]): (a) if a priest gets a nosebleed while saying Mass, the server brings water to {the} altar in a basin; if the deacon or subdeacon {should} get a nosebleed, they retire to one side and it is taken care of there; (b)

---

211. *Nomasticon,* 202–203.
212. "be in charge of the clock".
213. C. 106 (*Nomasticon,* 194).
214. The lectern.
215. "Concerning those vomiting or having a nosebleed" (*Nomasticon,* 172).

if someone leaves choir to vomit, a specially appointed person follows with a light and helps him until he is cleaned up and comes back to choir. If someone leaves {the} refectory to vomit, the servant of these sick does not leave but sends the servant of {the} refectory or someone else to help him.

2. *Those who have been bled* (90[216]): (1) they should not be bled in harvest time, Advent, Lent, Christmas, Easter, Pentecost (three days after), nor when they are hebdomadary[217] or servant of {the} refectory; but the brethren are normally bled four times a year, or can be bled four times a year—usually in February, April, September and around the Feast of St. John {the} Baptist; (2) they are bled between tierce and sext on ordinary days, between sext and none on fast days; immediately after being bled they go to the refectory and take some food and drink, then they go and lie down or sit in the cloister or chapter room; this they do when the office is not being said; during the time of office they go to the choir of the infirm; they do not go to work; (3) they get special food—in winter a pound of white bread, plus ordinary bread, plus a pittance (eggs or fish); they take mixt every day, including fast days; (4) the third day they return to choir for day hours and sit down for two psalms of the little hours (although the others remain standing), but they still do not go to work or to the night office until the fourth day—even then, on the fourth day, they are given lighter work.

3. *De Infirmis extra Chorum* (91[218]): these are the sick who are not bad enough for the infirmary but who do not come to choir. When one has to stay out of choir for sickness, one makes the reason known before the community in chapter, and the abbot then tells whether one continues to stay out or not. The abbot decides what regime he is to follow, what work, etc. If someone is just temporarily out of choir, he sits in the infirm choir and does not take mixt like the more seriously sick. If one's sickness

---

216. *Nomasticon*, 172–73.
217. The weekly celebrant of the conventual Mass.
218. *Nomasticon*, 175–76.

is uncertain, if he does not get better after a couple of days, he goes to the infirmary.

4. *The Sick in the Infirmary* (92[219]): they can speak with the infirmarian but only in certain places, and quietly, {and} only about necessities. They take care not to speak during meals or when the office is going on in church. Those in the infirmary, as far as possible, say the office together, if they can get up—not those in bed, however. If able, they can go to church for the day hours, and for professions. They can serve Mass in harvest time. They must not be in church or cloister during intervals, or make signs to the other monks. They work if work is assigned to them.

---

219. Nomasticon, 176–77.

Constitutions of the Order of Cistercians of the Strict Observance

Choir Novitiate
Abbey of Gethsemani

The Constitutions of the Order of Cistercians of the Strict Observance[1]

1. {The} meaning of the word "constitutions": {a} rule {is} the norm of living by which the monk attains to his end, union with God. Constitutions are particular statutes, added to the *Rule*, approved by the Holy See. They *define* how we are to understand the *Rule* of St. Benedict, and in what particular ways we are to carry out the prescriptions of the *Rule*. The *Constitutions* interpret and apply the *Rule* to our way of life, to the government of the Order, and especially to our choice of special means to our end. Both the *Rule* and the *Constitutions* are simply ways of showing how in our Order we live the evangelical counsels and follow Christ and His gospel teachings. Other differences {are that} the *Rule*, emanating from our Holy Founder, has a very special weight {and therefore} deserves very special reverence; the *Constitutions* emanate from our General Chapter, {and} are more modern, less venerable. The *Rule* cannot be changed in itself. It can be adapted by constitutions which are themselves changeable. The *Rule* is a *permanent* norm.

---

1. *Constitutiones Ordinis Cisterciensium Strictioris Observantiae a Sancta Sede Approbatae et Confirmatae* (Westmalle, Belgium: Ex Typographia Ordinis, 1925); *Constitutions of the Order of Cistercians of the Strict Observance* (Dublin: M. H. Gill & Sons, [1925]).

The *Rule* guides all the Benedictine families; the *Constitutions* are for us alone. Usages—particular practices observed in the Order—can be changed by the General Chapter or locally modified by {the} superior or visitor; {they are a} mode of observance.

2. *Outline*: {the *Constitutions* consist of} three parts: (1) the government of the Order; (2) the observances; (3) admission into the Order. Part 1 includes not only {the} General Chapter, {the} Abbot General, {the} abbots and their election and deposition, but also rules for visitations and for the foundations of new monasteries. Part 2 prescribes concerning {the} office, mental prayer, reading, silence, work, studies, fasting, sleep, habit, enclosure and the care of the sick. Part 3 governs above all the admission of postulants, the novitiate, simple and solemn profession, change of stability and the reception of fugitives and apostates.

NOTES ON THE *CONSTITUTIONS* of the Order of Cistercians of the Strict Observance

1. The Apostolic Letter *MONACHORUM VITA* (August 20, 1924):[2] a very special interest is attached to the terms in which the Church herself has approved our *Constitutions*. We learn from them how the Church looks at our vocation. We understand what she expects of us. The document begins by an outline of the history of the Order of St. Benedict, from the point of view of its various reforms. The monasteries of the Order "have never been without zealous members, who kept vigilant watch over monastic observance."[3] The different reformers "have been raised up from time to time by the providence of God, in order to recall the monks to the primitive fervour of their institute—*priscos sanctitatis mores*—and to the royal way of salvation marked out for them by the prescriptions of their holy founder and legislator."[4] First it is clear that all these monastic reforms within the Order

---

2. Included as a preface in the English translation of *Constitutions* (1–6); not found in the Latin *Constitutiones*.

3. *Constitutions*, 1, which reads: "were never without . . ."

4. *Constitutions*, 1, which does not include the Latin phrase.

of St. Benedict have the following characteristics: (a) they are the work of providential instruments of God; (b) by which God Himself recalls monks to (1) the primitive holy way of life—*priscos sanctitatis mores* (hence it is a return to the sources of monasticism—our obligation is then to study those sources and conform our life to the sanctity of the Fathers); (2) the *salutarem principemque viam*[5]—the main highway, the way open to *all kinds* of men (can one detect here an implicit contrast with the more special and restricted vocation of the Carthusians?); (3) this royal way is the way of St. Benedict, our founder. We have then a call to return as closely as possible to St. Benedict—that is the aim of our *Constitutions*. They are to be understood in this light. Reforms in the *Constitutions* are also to be seen as adaptations by which we aim to return still closer to the royal way of St. Benedict. Note: it is not for the rank and file of the Order to excogitate new ways of reforming the *Constitutions*.

Various Reforms: the letter first praises in detail the reform of CLUNY;[6] St. Odo,[7] St. Mayeul[8] and St. Odilo[9] are expressly mentioned. The Cluniac discipline is praised. So too is the liturgical life of Cluny. Above all the silence of Cluny is praised: "Now, silence, by excluding worldly tumult, fosters the interior life, and disposes to prayer, that is, prepares the monk for the due discharge of the 'Work of God' which St. Benedict has so especially enjoined on his disciples."[10] This praise of silence, though directed to Cluny, applies of course especially to us. A passing reference is made in praise of St. Romuald[11] and the foundation of the

---

5. "the royal way of salvation".
6. For a brief overview of Cluny, founded in 910, see Thomas Merton, *The Silent Life* (New York: Farrar, Straus & Cudahy, 1957), 72–74.
7. St. Odo (c. 878–942), second abbot of Cluny (927–942).
8. St. Mayeul (Majolus) (906–994), fourth abbot of Cluny (965–994).
9. St. Odilo (962–1049), fifth abbot of Cluny (994–1049).
10. *Constitutions*, 2.
11. St. Romuald (c. 950–1027) founded the monastery at Camaldoli in about 1012.

Camaldolese hermits.[12] One asks why this detailed praise of Cluny {appears} in the document that approves *our Constitutions*. Perhaps it is because there has been a tendency IN THE PAST FOR Trappists to exaggerate the virtues and value of Trappist austerity by running down other observances, notably the Benedictine.

Cîteaux: the letter however admits a decline in the observance of Cluny, which led to the foundation of Cîteaux by St. Robert,[13] with Sts. Alberic[14] and Stephen Harding.[15] Robert, "under the inspiration of divine grace [*Dei gratia inspiratus*] and with the consent of [the legate]"[16] abandons Molesme "to the end that he might be able to fulfil his monastic obligations by the exact observance of the Holy Rule."[17] Here the language of the *Exordium Parvum*[18] is followed almost verbatim: "They unanimously resolved to put in practice the Rule of St. Benedict without alleviation or mitigation: to live there in absolute poverty, 'rejecting whatever was opposed to the *Rule*' [*quidquid regulae refragabatur*]."[19] A few clauses

---

12. For an extensive discussion of the Camaldolese, see *Silent Life*, 144–71.

13. For a brief biographical sketch of Robert (1027–1110), the founding Abbot of Cîteaux, see Thomas Merton, *In the Valley of Wormwood: Cistercian Blessed and Saints of the Golden Age*, ed. Patrick Hart, ocso, Cistercian Studies Series [CS], vol. 233 (Collegeville, MN: Cistercian Publications, 2013), 143–53.

14. For St. Alberic (d. 1109), Robert's successor, see *Valley of Wormwood*, 37–52.

15. For St. Stephen (c. 1056–1134), third Abbot of Cîteaux, see *Valley of Wormwood*, 262–77.

16. *Constitutions*, 2, which includes the name of the legate, Hugh, Archbishop of Lyons.

17. *Constitutions*, 2.

18. *Exordium Parvum*, c. 15: "*Regulam beati Benedicti in loco illo ordinare, & unanimiter statuerunt tenere; rejicientes a se quidquid Regulae refragabatur*" ("They unanimously decided to establish and keep the *Rule* of blessed Benedict in that place, rejecting whatever was opposed to the *Rule*") (*Nomasticon Cisterciense, seu Antiquiores Ordinis Cisterciensis Constitutiones A.R.P.D. Juliano Paris . . . Editio Nova*, ed. Hugo Séjalon [Solesmes: E Typographeo Sancti Petri, 1892], 62).

19. *Constitutions*, 2, which reads: ". . . resolved, Robert and his associates, to put in practice in that place the Rule . . ."

develop the history—St. Bernard develops the Order; {the} Holy See approves Cîteaux and the *Charter of Charity*. The growth of the Order "was of great advantage to monastic discipline, to the honour of the Church, and to the spiritual advantage of the faithful,"[20] mainly because of the countless bright examples of *"humility, obedience, sanctity, patience in labour and frugality of life."*[21] Further approbations of the Holy See {are} then mentioned.

La Trappe: "The monks fell away from their original austerity"[22] and once again God "inspired holy men"[23] to labor for the restoration of primitive observance. Here all the Strict Observance movements are included, but that of La Trappe is singled out for special mention, without de Rancé[24] being named.

The Strict Observance Reunion: the three congregations in the nineteenth century are mentioned, then the reunion of 1892.[25]

The Aim of the OCSO—now we reach the most important passages of the letter:

1. The end of the Order: LIKE THE PRIMITIVE MONKS OF CÎTEAUX, THESE REFORMED CISTERCIANS, FOR THE GREATER GLORY OF GOD, SEEK BY A PENITENT LIFE THE PERFECTION OF THE SPIRITUAL MAN [*spiritualis hominis perfectio*] ESPECIALLY BY SILENCE, LABOR AND PRAYER.[26] Notable points {include}: (a) return to the early

---

20. *Constitutions*, 3, which reads ". . . spiritual interests of the faithful."
21. *Constitutions*, 3 (emphasis added).
22. *Constitutions*, 4.
23. *Constitutions*, 4.
24. Armand-Jean Le Bouthillier de Rancé (1626–1700), reforming Abbot of La Grande Trappe; for a discussion of de Rancé and the Trappist reform, see Thomas Merton, *The Waters of Siloe* (New York: Harcourt, Brace, 1949), 32–49, 303–308.
25. See *Waters of Siloe*, 146–52 for a discussion of the 1892 reunion that led to the formation of the Order of Cistercians of the Strict Observance.
26. *Constitutions*, 4, which reads: "Like the primitive monks of Cîteaux, these Reformed Cistercians strive after spiritual perfection, for God's greater glory, by a life of penance, being particularly devoted to silence, manual labour, and prayer."

Cîteaux—imitation of {the} first Cistercians; (b) for God's glory, above all—God is the end in view, not our perfection alone; (c) the perfection of the *spiritual man*—living "in the spirit"[27] and not in the flesh; (d) by *silence, labor* and *prayer*, characteristic means singled out as essential to us. There follows an analysis of the Benedictine spirit, *quoad nos*:[28] (a) *orare et laborare*[29]—prayer and work are for us the essence of Benedictinism, according to this letter; (b) both prayer and work are of course only means to the great end—*seeking God*; (c) seeking God will mean for us in practice a love for the divine office: Nothing is to be preferred to the Work of God;[30] the letter uses the expression *schola divini servitii*[31] as applying chiefly and above all to the fact that we chant the office each day—a school of *praise* therefore; (d) our liturgical prayer is our chief way of following Christ and uniting ourselves with Him who "spent the night in the prayer of God";[32] (e) everything we do must be ordered to the glory and praise of God, but especially and above all "the sons of St. Benedict and St. Bernard are called to carry out

---

27. Rom. 8:9; Gal. 5:25.
28. "with regard to us".
29. "to pray and to labour" (*Constitutions*, 4); this phrase, often considered the unofficial motto of Benedictine life, is not found in the *Rule*, but apparently was first used in the nineteenth century by Maurus Wolter, osb, a German abbot: see M. D. Meeuws, "Ora et Labora: Devise Bénédictine?" *Collectanea Cisterciensia* 54 (1992): 193–214.
30. "*Ergo nihil operi Dei praeponatur*" ("Let nothing, therefore, be put before the Work of God") (*Rule*, c. 43 [*The Rule of St. Benedict in Latin and English*, ed. and trans. Justin McCann, osb (London: Burns, Oates, 1952), 102/103]); the Work of God ("*opus Dei*") is the divine office (*Rule*, cc. 7, 22, 43, 44, 47, 50, 52, 58, 67 [McCann, 46, 70, 102, 104–106, 108, 116, 118, 130, 152–54]).
31. "a school of divine service" (*Constitutions*, 5); cf. "*Constituenda est ergo nobis dominici schola servitii*" ("Therefore must we establish a school of the Lord's service") (*Rule*, Prologue [McCann, 12, 13]).
32. *Constitutions*, 5, which reads: "passed the whole night in the prayer of God" (quoting from Lk. 6:12).

the work of God night and day, and to see that the sacrifice of praise is offered to God without ceasing."[33]

SUMMARY: "FAR FROM WORLDLY THINGS, LIVING PIOUSLY, LABORIOUSLY AND PENITENTLY IN THE MONASTERY, THE CISTERCIANS OF TODAY CARRY OUT THE WORK OF THE PSALMIST WHO WOULD HAVE ALL THE WORLD ADORE GOD AND SING PSALMS TO HIM—a thing which the forgetful men of this world easily omit."[34] Here the stress is also on the enclosure, stability, retirement and solitude which make our praise perfect and pure; also on the note of reparation. {Among} other items, the *Little Office*[35] is singled out here for special mention as a characteristic Cistercian observance. *Eucharistic devotion* is also mentioned as primary—we chant our office before the Blessed Sacrament. We pray that the faithful may come to love and adore Jesus in this sacrament of His love.

CONSTITUTIONS, {PART} 1: THE GOVERNMENT OF THE ORDER

The General Chapter[36] {is} "the supreme authority of the Order."[37] {The} meaning of the word "chapter" (*capitulum*) {is} "a legitimate gathering of those members of a religious order who have power of voting to determine matters of importance in the life of the order."[38] N.B. above the General Chapter is the

---

33. *Constitutions*, 5, which reads: "the disciples of SS. Benedict and Bernard are called in a special manner to discharge the Divine Office night and day, so that the sacrifice of praise may be offered to God without intermission."

34. *Constitutions*, 5, which reads: "Far removed from worldly affairs, living in their monasteries a life of piety, labour, and penance, the Cistercian monks of to-day continue with the Psalmist to call upon all creatures to praise and bless the Creator, a duty so little regarded by the forgetful people of our age."

35. I.e., the office of the Blessed Virgin Mary: see below, pages 80–81.

36. Chapter 1 (nn. 1–14) (*Constitutiones*, 3–5; *Constitutions*, 7–9).

37. "*Summa Ordinis potestas*" (*Constitutiones*, 3); *Constitutions*, 7.

38. "*Capitulum appellatur 'adunatio plurium religiosarum legitime convocatorum pro negotiis ad Religionem ipsorum pertinentibus definiendis'*" (Ludovicus Fanfani, OP, *De Jure Religiosorum ad Normam Codicis Iuris Canonici* [Rome: Marietti, 1920], 26 [n. 43]); Fanfani goes on to define a conventual or local

Holy Father (canon 499, #1: "All religious are subject to the Roman Pontiff as to their supreme superior and they are bound to obey him even under the vow of obedience;"[39] Sacred Congregation—Fr. Larraona;[40] the religious usually contact {the} Congregation through our Procurator General [cf. *Const.*, #36[41]]). "Its decision is final in all *purely Regular* causes which are brought

---

chapter: "conventuale *seu* locale, *si unius Conventus membra vocem activam in Capitulis habentia convocantur*" ("conventual or local, if members of one religious house having an active voice in chapters are called together"). See also Gordian Lewis, CP, *Chapters in Religious Institutes: An Historical Synopsis and Commentary*, The Catholic University of America Canon Law Studies, 181 (Washington, DC: Catholic University of America Press, 1943), 2–3.

39. "*Religiosi omnes, tanquam supremo Superiori, subduntur Romano Pontifici cui obedire tenentur etiam vi voti obedientiae*" (*Codex Iuris Canonici*, ed. Petrus Cardinalis Gasparri [New York: P. J. Kenedy & Sons, 1918], 143).

40. Msgr. Arcadio Larraona (1887–1973) was the Secretary for the Congregation of Religious in Rome. For his visit to Gethsemani in August 1952, see Thomas Merton, *A Search for Solitude: Pursuing the Monk's True Life. Journals, vol. 3: 1952–1960*, ed. Lawrence S. Cunningham (San Francisco: HarperCollins, 1996), 10–11; for his being named a cardinal in November 1959, see *Search for Solitude*, 344. Larraona was very involved in Merton's various plans to seek a life of more solitude away from Gethsemani: see Merton's October 18, 1955 letter to Cistercian Abbot General Dom Gabriel Sortais mentioning Larraona's advice not to join the Carthusians (Thomas Merton, *The School of Charity: Letters on Religious Renewal and Spiritual Direction*, ed. Patrick Hart [New York: Farrar, Straus, Giroux, 1990], 92); see also Merton's September 8, 1959 letter to Larraona (Thomas Merton, *Witness to Freedom: Letters in Times of Crisis*, ed. William H. Shannon [New York: Farrar, Straus, Giroux, 1994], 205–7), as well as references to the December 7, 1959 letter sent by Cardinals Valerio Valeri and Larraona turning down Merton's request for an indult of exclaustration to move to Dom Gregorio Lemercier's monastery in Cuernavaca, Mexico (*Search for Solitude*, 358–59 [December 17, 1959 journal entry]; *Witness to Freedom*, 211–12 [December 17, 1959 letter to Lemercier]; *Witness to Freedom*, 216–19 [January 2, 1960 letter to Valeri]; Thomas Merton, *The Hidden Ground of Love: Letters on Religious Experience and Social Concerns*, ed. William H. Shannon [New York: Farrar, Straus, Giroux, 1985], 134–35 [April 21, 1960 letter to Jean Daniélou, SJ]).

41. *Constitutiones*, 8; *Constitutions*, 13.

before it"[42] (i.e., not matters of faith and morals belonging to the Holy Office,[43] nor other matters belonging to other congregations).

What the General Chapter does (#2): six points[44] ({for} examples of laws conformable to the Holy *Rule* and *Constitutions*, compare {the} statute of 1903, #2[45] on poverty with {the} *Rule*,[46] and 1904, #1[47] on enclosure—no missions).

42. "*Idem extremo judicio statuit de causis mere regularibus ad ipsum delatis*" (*Constitutiones*, 3); *Constitutions*, 7 (emphasis added).

43. I.e., the congregation of the Roman Curia assigned to make rulings on doctrine and morals, once known as the Sacred Office of the Inquisition, now called the Congregation for the Doctrine of the Faith.

44. The General Chapter elects the Abbot General and definitors and watches over their administration; accepts the resignation of the Abbot General, abbots and titular priors, and if necessary deposes them; authorizes new foundations and grants permission to sell, alienate or borrow; makes laws conformable to the *Rule* and *Constitutions*; judges and punishes infractions of the law; corrects abuses pointed out by visitors (*Constitutiones*, 3; *Constitutions*, 7).

45. "The General Chapter calls the attention of Superiors to the abuses which tend to be introduced into certain houses in regard to poverty. Religious try to have superfluous or too precious objects, like chalices, books, vestments, watches, etc. They have parents or friends give them things which they desire or which they need, and they regard them afterwards as their own, and they look askance when they are put to the use of others. These abuses, so contrary to the spirit of poverty and to what the Holy Rule prescribes in chapters 33 and 54, must be extirpated from our monasteries, and those guilty should be serverely punished" (*Decisions and Definitions of the General Chapters of the Order of Cistercians of the Strict Observance, 1895–1950*, translated at St. Joseph's Abbey, Spencer, MA [mimeograph] [Dubuque, IA: Our Lady of New Melleray, 1951], subsequently continued through 1965).

46. *Rule*, c. 33 (McCann, 85, 87) is the general prohibition of ownership; c. 54 (McCann, 123) refers particularly to tokens and gifts from parents or friends.

47. "Our order vowed to the contemplative life, should not accept any mission or ministry properly so called. If circumstances demand a partial ministry, we shall submit but only with the reserve of observing habitually

#3: When and where it assembles: Cîteaux, {on the} twelfth {of} September.

#4: Who are the members; their obligation to attend, "postponing all other business";[48] exceptions {are made for} illness and distant countries (see General Chapter of 1905, #8: European houses {must be represented} every year, {the} Far East every five years, America twice in five years, plus the plenary General Chapter[49]).

#5: The Plenary Chapters.[50]

#6: Who else assists: {the} Procurator General and {the} definitors.

#7: Who presides.[51]

#8: Precedence.[52]

#9: Requirements for a decisive vote {include an} absolute majority, until the third scrutiny, in which a relative majority is sufficient; in {the} case of an abbot, {an} absolute majority is strictly required.

Here the rules are being given for conventual chapters as well as for the General Chapter. Numbers 1 and 2 can apply, for instance, to the nomination of a definitor or a *censor librorum*;[53]

---

the community life in our monastery. It will not be allowed to look for any exterior ministry of our own accord. The General Chapter will be the judge of the cases in which we should accept this permanent partial ministry, and will outline the limits."

48. *"omni postposita occasione"* (*Constitutiones*, 3–4); *Constitutions*, 8.

49. The General Chapter specifies China and Japan (as well as the Congo and Marianhill, in South Africa) as required to attend every five years, and "the Orient" (unspecified) along with America as twice in five years.

50. Held every five years (*Constitutiones*, 4; *Constitutions*, 8).

51. The Abbot General (*Constitutiones*, 4; *Constitutions*, 8).

52. Precedence is established according to the rank of the abbey—abbots, then titular priors, then others; procurator general and definitors at the end, in that order unless a definitor is an abbot emeritus, then taking precedence before the procurator, unless he himself is an abbot (*Constitutiones*, 4; *Constitutions*, 8).

53. "a censor of books".

number 4 would apply to the election of the General in the General Chapter or the local abbot in a conventual chapter (see 1896, #19).

#10: Canonical deposition—a two-thirds vote {is} required.
#11: When the votes are taken in secret: 3 cases.[54]
#12: The visitor's reports—and action taken.
#13: Acceptance of penalties.
#14: Poor communities (n.b. *Carta Caritatis*;[55] examples: 1896, #9[56]).

Constitutions, chapter 2 (nn. 15–28[57]): *The Abbot General* (N.B. {according to} general law, the power of superiors, {whether the} chapter, major superiors {or} local superiors, is *local* and *personal*: {it} touches {the} subject wherever he may be; {it} is dominative [governing] over not only {the} professed but novices and familiars). {According to} canon 501, n. 1,[58] in {an} exempt religious order {there} is also {the} power of *ecclesiastical jurisdiction* in {the} external and internal forum—i.e., {to} replace the ordinary in such functions as giving faculties to confessors, in lifting certain excommunications, etc. Canon 502[59] says that the supreme head of the religious order has power on all provinces, houses and subjects, according to the norm of the constitutions.

#15: *Besides* the General Chapter: {the} General Chapter remains supreme, but {the} Abbot General {is} a supreme *representative* who "at all times"[60] (i.e., between General Chapters)

---

54. I.e., in every election, when prescribed by law or when requested by a Chapter member (*Constitutiones*, 5, which mentions only the last, evidently omitting the first two inadvertently; *Constitutions*, 9).

55. C. III (*Nomasticon*, 71); see above, pages 12–13.

56. This statute refers specifically to assisting poor monasteries of women: "Unhappily from the temporal point of view, there are some very poor houses. The Abbot General engages all the Capitular Fathers whenever they have any alms to dispense, to send them by preference to these houses."

57. *Constitutiones*, 5–7; *Constitutions*, 10–12.

58. *Codex Iuris Canonici*, 144.

59. *Codex Iuris Canonici*, 144.

60. "perpetuo" (*Constitutiones*, 5); *Constitutions*, 10.

maintains observance of rules and settles affairs of the whole Order—*negotia expediat*;[61] {this} does not imply that he overrules the General Chapter but that for convenience the General Chapter leaves him to settle pressing business. {It is} explicitly stated that he is *assisted by his council*.

#16: Limitations of his power: (1) he cannot enact laws; (2) cannot dispose of persons or property of communities (over {the} head of {a} local superior); (3) can only take temporary measures, and {only} when necessity requires.

#17: If possible, {he} puts off to {the} General Chapter any case that falls within its province.

#18: How far is he bound to follow the definitors? (cf. #32[62]).

#19: {An} account {is} to be given to {the} General Chapter of his administration.

#20: {He has the} right to confirm {the} election of abbots.

#21: {He has the} right to visit all monasteries {and the} obligation to visit those houses that have no Father Immediate.

#22: {He has the} right to hear {the} confessions of all.

#23 {He may have} free communication with all.

#24: {He} imposes penalties with {the} same authority as {the} General Chapter.

#25: {The office is} perpetual—{he becomes} Abbot of Cîteaux (how about the one who rules Cîteaux?).

#26: Qualifications, and how {he is} elected.[63]

#27: {He} does not need to be confirmed by {the} pope.

#28: {The} Vicar General: {this is an} annual appointment of the General Chapter.

Constitutions, chapter 3 (nn. 29–34[64]): *The Definitors* ({according to} general law, superiors, especially major superiors, have

---

61. *Constitutiones*, 5; "settle any affairs" (*Constitutions*, 10).

62. See below, page 69 (*Constitutiones*, 7–8; *Constitutions*, 12).

63. He must be professed at least ten years, legitimately born, at least forty years old, elected with a majority at a Plenary General Chapter (*Constitutiones*, 6–7; *Constitutions*, 11).

64. *Constitutiones*, 7–8; *Constitutions*, 12–13.

a *council* of advisers, which must be fixed, and who cannot be replaced by others in certain affairs—according to the constitutions of each order. The function of a council is to *help* the superior and to *guide* him, but it can never direct him. However in certain cases—v.g., the dismissal of a religious under perpetual vows [{see} canon 655[65] or 646[66]], the council and the superior function together, the superior being the *praeses*.)

#29: How many definitors? representing what languages?[67] {They are} elected for five years.

#30: What {are their} qualifications?[68]

#31: Their functions—to give advice when asked.

#32: Cases when they have a deliberative vote—i.e., when they function as a decisive body.[69]

#33: {They} cannot make {a} visitation unless {they are} abbots.

#34: {They have} free communication with *first superiors*, not with subjects, {and only} concerning affairs of {the} Order, not just anything.

Chapter 4 (nn. 35–40[70]): *The Procurator General*

#35: {He} is one of the definitors {and} is named Procurator General by the General Chapter.

---

65. *Codex Iuris Canonici*, 190.
66. *Codex Iuris Canonici*, 187.
67. Five definitors, two for French language houses, one each for German, English and the Low Countries (*Constitutiones*, 7; *Constitutions*, 12).
68. Solemnly professed priests, not necessarily abbots, at least thirty years old (*Constitutiones*, 7; *Constitutions*, 12).
69. Dismissal and elected replacement of a definitor; approval of new foundations; granting permission to sell, alienate or borrow; convoking an extraordinary General Chapter; accepting resignations of abbots or titular priors, or granting faculties for their deposition if such business cannot wait for a General Chapter; dismissal of a religious in temporary vows, if referred to the Abbot General; dismissal of a religious in solemn vows (*Constitutiones*, 7–8; *Constitutions*, 12–13).
70. *Constitutiones*, 8–9; *Constitutions*, 13–14.

#36: His function {is that he is the} ordinary medium of transaction of affairs of {the} Order with the house superiors. Everyone not expressly prohibited has the right to seek a rescript from the house superior—has a right to go over the head of the local superior, but that latter's power is not suspended; however, he should not mix in the affair without grave reason and without informing the higher superior (canon 204[71]). Canon 517 says that every order of men *juris pontifici*[72] must have a Procurator General. (The business may be of the whole order, of different houses {or} of individuals.) The congregation, ordinarily, will consult the procurator about any affair of the order that comes through another source. However in matters of the *internal forum*, the religious will directly contact the Sacred Penitentiary[73] (especially if {the} seal may be violated).

#37: He informs the Abbot General and definitors *of all the affairs* entrusted to him {and is} guided by {the} advice and instruction of the Abbot General.

#38: {He} asks no faculties for a member of the Order unless {the} petition is approved by {the} Abbot General or {the} local superior of the subject.

#39: {He} transcribes decrees {and} notifies superiors {of them}.

#40: {He presents an} account of {his} expenditure; all contribute to pay his expenses.

Constitutions, chapters 5–6 (nn. 41ff.)—*The Fathers Immediate*:[74]

#41: How the order is divided: not {by} provinces but {according to} motherhouses and filiations.

#42: {The} functions of {the} Father Immediate: (1) annual visit to filiations; (2) charge of {a} filiation that has no abbot or

---

71. *Codex Iuris Canonici*, 51.

72. "of pontifical right" (*Codex Iuris Canonici*, 149).

73. The tribunal or dicastery of the Roman Curia assigned to decide matters relating to the sacrament of penance.

74. Chapter 5 (nn. 41–42) (*Constitutiones*, 9; *Constitutions*, 14).

titular prior; (3) presides at {an} abbatial election; (4) appoints {the} superior of {a} foundation and administers {the} same until {the} election of {an} abbot; (5) *may* hear confessions of subjects in filiations; (6) {has} free communication with members of filiations; (7) visitors delegated by him may also hear confessions.

The Abbot:[75] {according to} general law, an abbot can be (a) *nullius*[76]—i.e., {he} rules not only an abbey but a territory including some parishes; he is the *ordinarius loci*[77] of this territory; (b) *de regimine*:[78] {he is} legitimately elected by the conventual chapter, blessed by {the} local bishop, {and} has complete spiritual and temporal government of his abbey and its dependencies, plus the privilege of conferring minor orders (canon 964, n. 1[79]), {with a} right to *pontificalia*[80] in the churches of the Order, but not {to a} violet zuchetto; {he} can perform all consecrations reserved to {a} bishop except that of a bishop himself—i.e., {he} can bless chalices, altars, etc., but with oil blessed by the bishop. {With regard to} general obligations, every abbot is *gravely* obliged to lead religious to the end of their vocation, to perfection, and to the particular end of the Order (prayer and penance). {He} must see that the *Rule* is known and kept. He is to reside in the abbey, to carry out decrees of the Holy See, and to instruct subjects, {as well as} to report to the Holy See. {He is} as *gravely* obliged as {a} bishop to see that unworthy subjects are not advanced to orders (*Quantum Religiones Omnes*[81]).

75. Chapter 6 (nn. 43–53) (*Constitutiones*, 10–12; *Constitutions*, 15–18).

76. I.e., "*nullius dioecesis*"—"of no diocese"—exempt from diocesan control and having governing responsibilities over specific territory surrounding a monastery; see canons 319–27 (*Codex Iuris Canonici*, 85–86).

77. "the ordinary of the place".

78. "in charge," i.e., an abbot who has jurisdiction only over the members of his community and those attached in some way to his monastery.

79. *Codex Iuris Canonici*, 273–74.

80. I.e., the ceremonial ornaments of a bishop (pectoral cross, ring, miter and crosier); the zuchetto is the skullcap worn by bishops.

81. December 1, 1931, Instruction of the Sacred Congregation of Religious (*Acta Apostolicae Sedis* 24 [1932], 74–81); in a May 10, 1953 letter to Fr.

#43: {He} exercises *spiritual jurisdiction* and has charge of the temporal administration. Spiritual jurisdiction {means that} he is the *ordinary* of his subjects. That is to say, that by virtue of his office he has the divine power of Christ Himself to govern, to teach, to administer sacraments—and he can delegate this power to others. He is responsible for all *appointments* of officers, etc. (#44). He *admits* candidates to {the} novitiate {and} to profession. He gives dimissorials for ordination, and chooses those he wants to be ordained. He can *dispense* from {the} *Rule* in particular cases—he *interprets* the *Rule* as he thinks best. He can *command* under pain of mortal sin. He can impose and lift *excommunications*. He is responsible for all the spiritual and temporal affairs of the monastery and can appoint anyone he sees fit in the community to help him discharge this responsibility.

Voting: read carefully nn. 45–46:[82] in matters of importance and in cases specified by sacred canons, HE ASKS THE OPINION OF THE COMMUNITY.[83] After hearing the opinion of the brethren, the abbot may do what he considers to be most expedient. This is the general rule, the basic principle. The abbot is the one representative of God. The community is not a democracy, in which the abbot is the representative of the members. The abbot is entrusted by God with the responsibility for all the decisions—EXCEPT the cases in which the abbot is bound to limit his decision by the decision of others—the conventual chapter; the General Chapter; the Holy See: (a) ALL three must be consulted when

---

Augustine Moore, OCSO, Merton refers to this decree, writing that the master of scholastics "has no disciplinary function" and that "the Fr. Prior also takes care of the investigation of candidates before ordination, as directed by the instruction of the S.C.R., 'Quantum religiones omnes'" (*School of Charity*, 57).

82. These provisions are spelled out in the rest of this paragraph (*Constitutiones*, 10–11; *Constitutions*, 15–17).

83. For a consideration of this aspect of the *Constitutions* in the context of the *Rule*, see Thomas Merton, *The Rule of Saint Benedict: Initiation into the Monastic Tradition* 4, ed. Patrick F. O'Connell, Monastic Wisdom [MW], vol. 19 (Collegeville, MN: Cistercian Publications, 2009), 98–100.

there is question of a very large sum ($50,000?) of money (and, in practice, the making of a new foundation) ($10,000); (b) the conventual chapter and the General Chapter must also approve large money transactions ($5,000 to $15,000) and the undertaking of an industry; (c) {the} conventual chapter shall have {a} deliberative vote on money transactions over $500 (????) on lawsuits, power of attorney, and admission of {a} novice to profession, or new stability. In these cases, it is to be noted that the vote of the community is not fully and completely decisive, in the same sense that a favorable vote means that the thing *must be done*. The abbot can still *not* incur expenditure, not make the new step, etc. {It is} different however in the case of profession. The novice has {a} strict right to profession if voted by the community. Hence the community vote is only a check on the abbot to prevent unwise moves, but it is in no sense an expression of what must be carried out. The abbot remains the supreme head of the community, solely responsible before God, but limited in his power in these particular ways.

#46, n. 4 refers in matters of contracts to canons 536[84] (on the obligation of the community to meet debts incurred, on the care to be taken in contracting debts), 1529[85] (whatever civil law provides in connection with contracts is to be observed by the Church, unless it is contrary to the law of God) {and} 1543[86] (contracts involving a loan of commodities [?]—responsibilities?).

#47: Who has the right to vote in chapter (note: is there an *obligation* to vote? yes, in {the} case of a novice admitted to profession [General Chapter, 1899, #5[87]]; yes, even when the vote is

---

84. *Codex Iuris Canonici*, 155.
85. *Codex Iuris Canonici*, 445.
86. *Codex Iuris Canonici*, 448.
87. "The General Chapter decides that there is an obligation to vote for the admission of a novice to profession, in view of the inconvenience which would result if abstention were permitted."

only consultative [General Chapter, 1920, #15 [88] mentions explicitly the case of solemn profession]; it would seem that the obligation to vote exists in all cases, but one can renounce one's right to vote and then the obligation ceases also.) All who vote must be stabiliated—hence when there is {an} election of a superior at a foundation, the Father Immediate first receives the stability of the voters (General Chapter, 1908, #3 [89]).

#48: The matter must first be previously laid before the chapter; to what extent does one have to know the ones proposed for profession? ({there is} no discussion here, except in council.)

#49: {The} abbot, etc. {are to} scrutinize and announce {the result}.

#50: {The} decision {is} entered in the book of acts.

#51: {The} private council ({here,} usually the prior, {the} father masters, {the} guest master and Dom Vital [90]).

#52: {The} accounts.

#53: Absences of {the} superior, and permission required. [91]

Regular Visitation: [92]

---

88. "The religious have no right to abstain from voting, when the vote is only consultative, for instance, when the Superior asks the vote prescribed for the solemn profession of a religious."

89. "In conformity with the Constitutions, when we proceed to the election of the first Superior in a new foundation, the Rev. Father Immediate or his delegate first of all receives the stability of electors."

90. Vital Klinski, ocso (1886–1966) "was born in Poland and entered the Cistercian abbey of Achel in Belgium in 1904; he was elected Abbot of Achel on August 29, 1920, but resigned his office in 1927 and entered Gethsemani on November 19, 1927. . . . [He] died at Gethsemani on June 3, 1966" (*School of Charity*, 9–10 [headnote to Merton's August 29, 1947 note and drawing to Dom Vital, who was his confessor at the time, on the occasion of the silver jubilee of his abbacy]).

91. Permission from the Abbot General to be absent for more than twenty days is required; notification must be given to the Father Immediate for absence between ten and twenty days (*Constitutiones*, 12; *Constitutions*, 18).

92. Chapter 7 (nn. 54–58) (*Constitutiones*, 12–13; *Constitutions*, 18–19).

#54: {It} must be annual ({this} supersedes General Chapter, {1905,} #7[93]—America {and the} Orient {are to be} visited twice in five years—{the} present situation).

#55: Visitation of Cîteaux—who does it? (two abbots of the first four houses[94]).

#56: Who visits other monasteries?

#57: {The} importance of visitations and {the} manner of proceeding: {it} must follow {the} *Carta Caritatis* (mostly about precedence)[95] {and the} *De Forma Visitationis*[96] (see later); {according to} canons 513, #1,[97] {the} visitor has the right to ask questions regarding matter of visitation, and those asked are obliged to reply truthfully, and no one can impede visitation (n.b. {this is a matter of} excommunication in our Order) ({canon} 2413[98] concerns the same thing, aimed at nuns). See the General Chapter, 1920, #27 on the duty of a visited abbot to the visitor.[99]

#58: {An} accurate report {is} to be forwarded within two months to the Abbot General ({the} visitor uses {a} questionnaire and really goes into details).

Election of Abbots:[100]

---

93. This specified that Mistassini (Canada) and Our Lady of the Valley (Rhode Island) were visited annually, as in Europe, while the Congo, Marianhill, China and Japan were visited once every five years; copy text reads "1904".

94. The first four daughter houses of Cîteaux were La Ferté (1113), Pontigny (1114), Clairvaux (1115) and Morimond (1115).

95. *Nomasticon*, 69–70.

96. *Instituta*, n. 33 (*Nomasticon*, 219–20).

97. *Codex Iuris Canonici*, 147.

98. *Codex Iuris Canonici*, 659–60.

99. The local abbot is to explain the statute "*De Forma Visitationis*" on the Sunday preceding the visitation and to read the chapter on visitations from the *Spiritual Directory* in the reading before compline. "In a word, the visited Abbot should remember that he will give an account to God of what he shall have omitted to do in order to facilitate the Visitation."

100. Chapter 8 (nn. 59–68) (*Constitutiones*, 13–14; *Constitutions*, 19–20).

#59: A superior dies (see General Chapter, 1908, #7:[101] papers must be sealed until {the} arrival of {the} Father Immediate; he has full charge until after {the} election).

#60: How long before an election? (a) {the} ordinary {period is} fifteen days to three months; (b) {the} extraordinary {period can be up to} three years (with {the} consent of {the} Father Immediate and the Abbot General) {or} over three years (with the approval of the Holy See).

#61: Who can vote? (n.b. *no one can validly vote for himself* [canon 170[102]]); all who can vote must be summoned. (Examples of canonical impediment: the insane; those under censure; {the} infamous [apostates who have signed up with other sects]; bigamists [clerics with an excommunication]; deprived of {a} vote by sentence {are} those who introduce women into {the} enclosure {or} those who resist the authority of the Holy See. Others deprived of active and passive voice, *ipso facto, jure communi*,[103] {include} apostates from the Order [even though returned]; those guilty of simony in ecclesiastical affairs; *those with {an} indult of exclaustration* [canon 639[104]]; *those with {an} indult of secularization* [canon 640, #1[105]]; religious who have been made cardinals or bishops, even after {a} return to religion; {the} temporary professed; [General Chapter, 1899, n. 2: those who leave *cum animo non revertendo*[106] lose {their} vote[107]]).

#62: {Among the} *necessary conditions for the exercise of {the} right to vote is the presence of the voter: physical* presence is required—in the *house* ({one} can vote in the infirmary).

---

101. Originally in 1906, n. 1; 1908, n. 7 specifies that the Father Immediate cannot remove or destroy any of the papers without written instructions to that effect from the deceased superior.

102. *Codex Iuris Canonici*, 42.

103. "automatically, by common law".

104. *Codex Iuris Canonici*, 185.

105. *Codex Iuris Canonici*, 185.

106. "with the intention of not returning".

107. N.B. from that time onward, even if they make their stability elsewhere.

#63: {It is necessary to} follow canon law and {the} *Ritual*[108] as to {the} form of the election.

#64: {An} absolute majority of the votes is required.

#65: *Who are eligible?*[109] Must their abbot be a priest? #65 does not say, but canon 154[110] says that offices initiated in order to care for souls in external forums cannot validly be conferred upon clerics who are not priests.

#66: {Voters} can elect from religious and abbots of filiations, but not vice versa (can postulate?)

#67: Acts must be transmitted to the Abbot General for confirmation.

Foundations:[111]

#69: Permissions {are} required (also the conventual chapter {must concur} if there is a question of money outlay).

#70: {A foundation should be} "remote from {the} haunts of men"[112] (cf. old legislation[113]).

#71: {It must include} twelve persons and a superior—four {of them} priests.

#72: {It is to be} dedicated to Mary.

---

108. *Rituale Cisterciense ex Libro Usuum Definitionibus Ordinis et Caeremoniali Episcoporum Collectum* (Westmalle, Belgium: Ex Typographia Ordinis, 1948), 288–304 (VIII, vi, 1).

109. Those who are thirty-five years old, legitimately born, solemnly professed, at least ten years from first profession (*Constitutiones*, 14; *Constitutions*, 20).

110. *Codex Iuris Canonici*, 38.

111. Chapter 9 (*Constitutiones*, 14–15; *Constitutions*, 20–21).

112. *"in locis a conversatione hominum remotis"* (*Constitutiones*, 15, which reads: *"semotis"*); *Constitutions*, 21.

113. *"accessui hominum insolitus"* ("unaccustomed to the coming of men") (*Exordium Parvum*, c. 3 [*Nomasticon*, 55]).

CONSTITUTIONS—PART II: OBSERVANCES

#73: Uniformity of Observances:[114] {this chapter} refers back to the *Carta Caritatis*:[115] {the} "very nature of the Order"[116] requires uniformity ({it} quotes {the} *Carta*[117]). Nevertheless each house retains its own physiognomy—{the} customs of {the} house are to be respected when legitimate. {This is} not to be taken in an extreme and absolute sense. {There is a distinction between} differences *de facto* (probably some {are to be} regarded as undesirable) {and} differences *de jure* (exceptions for hot climates, etc.). Some clarifications {are provided}: 1913, #13 says that the *Ritual* is the norm in liturgical things, but when {the} *Ritual* is not clear we go back to {the} *Consuetudines*.[118] {According to} 1913, #2: "The General Chapter reminds all of the duty incumbent upon us of preserving the spirit of simplicity of our Fathers in all that concerns the furniture, the adorning and construction of our monasteries."[119] {This is} to be interpreted how? Later[120] the General

---

114. Chapter 1 (nn. 73–75) (*Constitutiones*, 16; *Constitutions*, 22).

115. "*Quatenus in actibus nostris nulla sit discordia sed una caritate, una regula, similibus vivamus moribus*" ("May there be no discord in our acts, but may we live with a single charity, under a single *Rule*, with common customs") (*Nomasticon*, 69).

116. "*ipsa Ordinis nostri natura*" (*Constitutiones*, 16); *Constitutions*, 22.

117. "*Itaque, in actibus nostris nulla sit discordia, sed una caritate, una regula similibusque vivamus moribus*" (*Constitutiones*, 16 [n. 73]); "Let there be no discordance, therefore, in our actions, but let us live united in a common charity, under one and the same Rule, and observing the same customs" (*Constitutions*, 22).

118. "It is now understood that for the correction of our Liturgical Books we must take as authentic principle and rule the text itself of the Ritual, each time that the Ritual is clear and does not contradict itself. But when there is obscurity or contradiction in the Ritual, then it will be necessary to have recourse to the ancient Missal, i.e., to the rubrics of the *Consuetudines*."

119. Text reads: ". . . spirit and simplicity . . . and the construction . . ."

120. The text, written by Dom Jean-Baptiste Chautard (1858–1935), Abbot of Sept-Fons, was approved by the General Chapter in 1925.

Chapter issued the *Spirit of Simplicity*,[121] {which was} not always followed. {In} 1902, #1, "The General Chapter, informed that in certain monasteries public exercises of devotion are multiplied, which is *harmful to regularity*, recommends the greatest discretion to superiors, and engages them not to prescribe too long ones, or permanent ones"[122] (examples: at Gethsemani after the war, {the} rosary, weekly Benediction on Friday, {and} litanies {were} suppressed in {the} visitation—also Stations on Good Friday). {According to} 1909, #3, visitors cannot forbid devotions for months of Mary, St. Joseph, etc., "if these are not harmful to regularity,"[123] but {it} reminds superiors of 1902 above, {and} adds that our houses do not have to undertake public devotions prescribed by the bishop (except *imperata*[124]).

#74: Changes due to poverty or local conditions must be made only with {the} express permission of {the} General Chapter—cf. 81 below:[125] {the} Father Immediate and {the} local abbot decide if some hours are not to be sung.

#75: Modifications can be made by the local superior in individual cases, and this for any one of his subjects who requires a change due to health, age or "any other just cause."[126] Modifications of what? of {the} *Constitutions*, regarding work, fasting, vigils, abstinence.

---

121. *The Spirit of Simplicity Characteristic of the Cistercian Order—An Official Report, Demanded and Approved by the General Chapter, together with Texts from St. Bernard of Clairvaux on Interior Simplicity*, translation and commentary by a Cistercian Monk of Our Lady of Gethsemani [Thomas Merton] (Trappist, KY: Abbey of Gethsemani, 1948).

122. Emphasis added.

123. The actual wording of the text is: "provided that these practises do not harm the regular observances."

124. "except for the collect *imperata, intra missam*" ("what has been commanded, within the Mass").

125. *Constitutiones*, 17; *Constitutions*, 23.

126. "*aliam justam causam*" (*Constitutiones*, 16); *Constitutions*, 22.

Office:[127]

#76: {The} Apostolic Letter of Pius IX, "*Quae a sanctissimis*" (February 7, 1871), is at the beginning of our *Pars Hiemalis*,[128] approving the modified Cistercian liturgy of the present time (n.b. {the} decree of the Congregation of Rites of 1934[129] allows {the} new arrangement of psalms).

#77: {There is a} most serious obligation to recite the divine office daily in choir, no matter how few monks {there are}. ({The} *obligatio chori*[130] binds {the} superior above all, and only {the} superior directly. A religious could sin gravely against this *obligatio* if he refused to attend choir when his presence was strictly necessary for celebration of {the} office.) {The} obligation to attend choir can be *imposed* on a novice by the abbot or father master, and then they are bound also under sin (Schaefer 1203[131])—otherwise not. {What is} required {includes the} proper time and place ({the} church)—{the} right hours (more or less)—n.b. not in {the} chapter room (in {the} novitiate chapel???).

Office of the Blessed Virgin:

#78: Background and history: {the} General Chapter of 1185, statute 28,[132] prescribes {that} in {the} community and in the infirmary (*in conventu et in infirmatorio*), the office of the Blessed Virgin Mary shall be said as follows: matins and lauds in the interval between vigils and lauds of {the} canonical office, the other hours immediately after the canonical hours—all to be

---

127. Chapter 2 (nn. 76–82) (*Constitutiones*, 16–17; *Constitutions*, 22–23).

128. *Breviarium Cisterciense Reformatum*, 4 vols. (Westmalle, Belgium: Ex Typis Cisterciensibus, 1951), *Pars Hiemalis*, iii–iv.

129. *Breviarium Cisterciense, Hiemalis*, vii.

130. "the obligation of choral recitation [of the office]" ("*hac obligatione*" [*Constitutiones*, 17]; *Constitutions*, 22).

131. Timotheus Schaefer, OFM cap., *De Religiosis ad Normam Codicis Juris Canonici*, 4th ed. (Rome: Typis Polyglottis Vaticanis, 1947), 717.

132. J.-M. Canivez, ed., *Statuta Capitulorum Generalium Ordinis Cisterciensis ab Anno 1116 ad Annum 1786*, 8 vols. (Louvain: Bureaux de la Revue d'Histoire Ecclésiastique, 1933–1941), 1.101–102.

"sung" (recited) as at {the} office of the dead; {the} community sits during psalms and lessons. The office of Our Lady {is} to be omitted: (a) from {the} first Sunday of Advent to {the} Octave of Epiphany; (b) from Palm Sunday to {the} Octave of Easter; (c) from Holy Saturday to {the} end of Easter week; (d) within {the} octave of {the} Assumption (probably the only feast of Our Lady that had an octave then); (e) on all feasts of twelve lessons (repeated: 1195, #102[133]). 1191, #75[134] says that the office of the Blessed Virgin Mary is to be said in {the} infirmary at all times except {the} feasts of Our Lady, {the} octave of {the} Assumption, Christmas, Easter and Pentecost ({the} day not the octave). The office is optional for those outside the monastery, but not for those in the monastery, {who} must be present at the hours (cf. 1194, #1[135] and notes). However there is an earlier reference which says that those on a journey may say the office of the Blessed Virgin Mary together. Does this indicate that it was only allowed to be said privately when they were in community? In 1200 (#4),[136] a commemoration of St. Bernard was introduced into the little office at lauds and vespers, at the same time as St. Bernard was inserted into the litany. Returning to the present: private recitation of the little office and the office of the dead is prescribed. The simple professed are not bound to private recitation of the divine office when they miss choir, but are bound to private recitation of the Blessed Virgin Mary office. (Novices are not bound—what should they do?) {The} General Chapter of 1953[137] decreed that the office of the Blessed Virgin Mary should be omitted when the canonical office is *de beata*.[138]

---

133. Canivez, 1.197.
134. Canivez, 1.144–45.
135. Canivez, 1.171.
136. Canivez, 1.250.
137. N. 2 of "Propositions Presented by the General Chapter and approved *ad experimentum* by the Sacred Congregation of Religious."
138. "for the Blessed [Virgin Mary]".

Gregorian Chant:

#79: Singing of the office: the office is to be sung every day in Gregorian chant—excluding nocturns and lauds. Background: 1134, #73 [139] {is the} earliest recorded legislation on chant "*de falsis vocibus*": [140] "men should sing in a virile voice, not like women or like actors. . . . Modesty {is} to be kept in chant, so that it should savor of gravity, and devotion should be preserved." [141] 1217 [142] {contains the} first reproof against polyphony. The abbots of Dore and Tintern {were} accused of introducing polyphonic chant "*more saecularium*"; [143] the matter is entrusted to {the} abbots of Neath and Flaxley to go personally to these monasteries and find out what has been going on and report to the General Chapter what they have done to "diligently correct" [144] the abuse. {Rules were made} against changing the books {by} adding marks and rhythmic signs: {this was} prohibited first in the *monitum*, [145] then by the General Chapter of 1908 ({#2}), [146] then again in 1938, as follows (#1): "The General Chapter renews its strict prohibition against the changing of anything whatever in the notation of our books of chant or adding thereto any marks or conventional signs. Our chant in the future shall not be altered in any way without the permission of the General Chapter." [147] 1946 [148] en-

---

139. Canivez, 1.30.

140. "in false voices" (i.e., in falsetto).

141. "*virili voce cantare, et non more femineo tinnulis . . . veluti histrionicam imitari lasciviam. . . . mediocritatem servari in cantu, ut ad gravitatem redoleat, et devotio conservetur.*"

142. Canivez, 1.472 (#31).

143. "in the manner of seculars".

144. "*diligenter corrigant.*"

145. The "instruction" included at the beginning of the Cistercian chant books: see *Graduale Cisterciense* (Westmalle, Belgium: Ex Typis Ordinis, 1934).

146. Copy text reads: "#22."

147. Text reads: ". . . whatsoever . . . of Plain Chant . . . in future . . . permission or approbation of . . ."

148. 1946, #8.

trusts this to a chant commission[149] (Dom Louis,[150] chairman: {cf.} his remarks at visitations; steps had been taken here—v.g., the cantor of Oka,[151] etc., various other cantors).

#80: The conventual Mass {is} to be sung every day after tierce or none.

#81: Who decides where and when some of the singing is to be omitted? {the} Father Visitor, after consulting the local abbot. {If the} number of monks {is} small, {this is a} reason for not singing—either because a small number means more work, and more work time is necessary, or because chant cannot well be rendered in its more elaborate parts by a small choir (?). (Note the "brackets" in the *Graduale*.[152])

#82: The obligation to attend choir: no one whatsoever shall be regarded as exempt from {the} obligation of choir unless he is detained elsewhere by a sufficiently grave cause. {It is necessary to} distinguish: *habitual* absence from certain hours would require a very grave cause. {It is} permitted tacitly in the case of the Master of Laybrother Novices at the present time, {and for} others in the past. *Occasional* absence nevertheless requires a serious cause: (a) sickness is the most usual one; (b) other duties—v.g., hearing confessions of seculars on retreat, preparing altars for secular priests, serving Reverend Father's Mass, care of the sick, watching by a body, making up sleep after the fire watch. {The}

---

149. The Abbots of Westmalle, La Grande Trappe, Diepenveen, with consultors.

150. Dom Louis Le Pennuen, Abbot of Melleray and Father Immediate of Gethsemani.

151. I.e., the Abbey of Notre Dame du Lac, near Montreal; for a brief discussion of its founding and later development, see *Waters of Siloe*, 143–45, 188–89.

152. See the "*monitum*" in the *Graduale*: "*Variis in cantibus, saepe super lineas reperientur duae virgulae rubro colore, impressae, modoque opposito dispositae ❮ ❯; haec signa partes neumarum quae omitti possunt de licentia superioris includunt*" ([iii]) ("In various chants, above the lines two virgules often will be found, printed in red and placed on opposite sides ❮ ❯; these signs enclose the parts of the neums which can be omitted with the permission of the superior").

principle {is} "to let nothing be preferred to the Work of God."[153] When God's will manifestly calls us to something else temporarily, then we are not preferring that to the office. Regard the office as a privilege—as a burden, no. Permission should be asked of a superior, and {the} cause of absence made known.

Mental Prayer:[154]

#83: Twice daily, "All shall apply themselves to mental prayer in choir."[155] It became more necessary in proportion as *lectio divina*[156] fell into disesteem—"intervals" {became} just "time in between." St. Benedict in the *Rule* {writes}: *in conventu omnino brevietur oratio*.[157] We need to get back to the attitude which regards the time of *lectio divina* as also {a} time of mental prayer. {The} *Consuetudines*[158] encouraged it during the intervals. Gilbert of Hoyland[159] encouraged it after the night office (precisely the

---

153. See above, page 62, n. 30.

154. Chapter 3 (nn. 83–85) (*Constitutiones*, 17–18; *Constitutions*, 23).

155. "*omnes orationi mentali in choro vacent*" (*Constitutiones*, 17); *Constitutions*, 23.

156. "sacred reading"; for an extensive discussion of *lectio*, see Thomas Merton, *Monastic Observances: Initiation into the Monastic Tradition* 5, ed. Patrick F. O'Connell, MW 25 (Collegeville, MN: Cistercian Publications, 2010), 149–53, 155–56, 165–69; and Thomas Merton, "*Lectio Divina*," *Cistercian Studies Quarterly* 50.1 (2015): 5–37.

157. "In community, however, let prayer be very short" (*Rule*, c. 20 [McCann, 68/69, which reads: "*In conventu tamen omnino . . .*"]).

158. *Ecclesiastica Officia*, c. 71 (*Nomasticon*, 150–52).

159. Gilbert of Hoyland, *Sermo 23 in Cantica*, n. 3 (J.-P. Migne, ed., *Patrologiae Cursus Completus, Series Latina* [*PL*], 221 vols. [Paris: Garnier, 1844–1865], vol. 184, col. 120CD): "*Sed nec ipsa communium horarum intervalla nocturna vacant. Deus bone, hora illa noctis, quam sine nocte est, quam nox illa illuminatio in deliciis! Orationes illae privatim fiunt, sed privata non petunt. Submissior quidem vox, sed mens intensior, et preces tacitae multum habent acuminis. Denique frequenter vocem eripit oratio vehemens; et verbis nec eget, nec utitur, quae puro et pleno fertur affectu. Amor in auribus Domini solus obstrepens, corporalium strepitus dedignatur verborum, quae sicut inchoanti excitamenta sunt, sic impedimenta solent esse perfecte oranti*" ("But the nocturnal intervals between the hours of communal prayer are not empty themselves. Good God, how that

period that was later occupied by the little office of the Blessed Virgin Mary).

#84: Twice {a day} "*some time* shall be spent in examination of conscience."[160] (It does not say "together," but this seems to be implied.)

#85: Every year, all shall make a spiritual retreat. The General Chapter of 1920, #28,[161] counsels {a} *monthly* retreat (it counsels: for developing {the} interior life in our communities). *Usages* 524[162] prescribe that all who hold an office should make a day's retreat each month. {The} house custom {here} encourages weekly retreat days for certain officers and a monthly day of recollection for all.

Confession:[163]

#86: "According to the ancient definitions [*secundum antiquas definitiones*]"—this refers to the *Libellus Antiquarum Definitionum* (1239), Dist. vii, c. 4: "*Abbates insuper et monachi semel ad minus in hebdomada confiteantur si copiam habuerint confitendi.*"[164] A note on the power of confessors in our Order: it is limited to the internal forum. General Chapter, 1937, #2 {says}: "The General Chapter

---

hour of night is taken away from night, is an illumination in delights! Those prayers are made privately, but do not seek private benefits. Indeed the voice is more subdued, but the mind is more attentive, and silent prayers have a great deal of intensity. Indeed passionate prayer often goes beyond the voice; carried along by pure and full affection, it neither wants nor uses words, Love alone, filling the ears of the Lord, scorns the noise of bodily words, which, while they are a spur for the beginner, are generally impediments to one praying perfectly").

160. "*aliquid impendatur temporis in examine conscientiae*" (*Constitutiones*, 18); *Constitutions*, 23 (emphasis added); the times specified are before dinner and after compline.

161. "The monthly retreat well made is also an excellent means to favor greatly spiritual progress" (§7).

162. *Regulations of the Order of Cistercians of the Strict Observance Published by the General Chapter of 1926* (Dublin: M. H. Gill & Sons, 1927), 247.

163. Chapter 4 (nn. 86–88) (*Constitutiones*, 18; *Constitutions*, 24).

164. "Let abbots as well as monks confess at least once a week if they have matter for confessing" (*Nomasticon*, 419).

formally declares that the superior and superioress alone, and not the confessors or the chaplains, have authority to dispense from the regular observances. They may likewise declare void every injunction of any external act or observance whatever proceeding from the confessors or chaplains."[165]

#87: The appointment of confessors (canon 518[166]): (a) for the community, {the} qualifications {are that} they should be learned, prudent and charitable. {There should be} *several*—that is to say, at least two. They have power to absolve from sins reserved in the Order as well as from censures (*"cases"* covers both sins and censures). *Censure* {is a} medicinal penalty; {it} deprives a baptized person who is deliberately delinquent and *contumacious* of certain spiritual benefits until he is absolved from the censure. {It} can only be inflicted for a mortal sin committed with contumacy. A *censure latae sententiae*[167] is incurred when one who knows the law commits the sin prohibited by the law. A *censure ferendae sententiae*[168] is committed when one who has been formally warned and menaced at least once by the superior deliberately commits what was forbidden; the censure is then inflicted with or without judicial process. A *reserved sin* is one for which the jurisdiction to absolve is limited to certain confessors. Who can reserve a sin? the pope, {the} bishop in {a} diocese, {the} superior general in an order, an abbot in his monastery and dependencies. In 1916, the Holy Office decreed[169] that in religious orders and dioceses only a *small number of sins* could be reserved. Canon 897 declares: "Let reserved cases be altogether few, three that is, or at most four, from the most serious and atrocious ex-

---

165. The text reads: ". . . any external act or observance whatsoever . . . or the chaplains."

166. *Codex Iuris Canonici*, 149.

167. "sentence [already] given"—i.e., imposed automatically without judicial process.

168. "sentence to be given".

169. *"Super Casuum Conscientiae Reservationibus,"* Acta Apostolica Sedis 8 (1916): 313 (#2).

ternal crimes, specifically determined";[170] and {it} adds that the reservation should remain in force only as long as it is necessary to extirpate the evil and restore discipline. When canon 518[171] declares that some confessors must be appointed with power to absolve from reserved cases, the only force of this is to imply that the superior can also appoint others who do not have these faculties. (N.B. any confessor with faculties from the bishop of the diocese also can absolve from cases reserved in the Order.) Examples of excommunication {include the following}: most special—profanation of the sacred species {is} most specially reserved to the Holy See; special—apostasy from the faith {is} specially reserved, {as are} reading heretical books which propagate heresy {and} simulated celebration of Mass; simply—violation of papal enclosure {or} attempt at sacrilegious marriage (by a religious with solemn vows); to God—marriage out of the Church, baptism of children out of the Church, abortion, marriage of a religious attempted while in simple vows; *nemini*[172]—publishing books on scripture without authorization, forcing someone to embrace the religious state; suspensions—hearing confessions without permission, absolving reserved sins without jurisdiction, an abbot exercising his functions without the abbatial blessing, a religious superior who gets his subject ordained by the bishop of another diocese. N.B. EXCEPTIONS: {according to} canon 2385,[173] apostates *ipso facto* incur excommunication reserved to their *own religious superior*. Confessors have no power of themselves to absolve from this. Canon 2386[174] {specifies that} fugitives incur a suspension, and loss of office—*suspensio a sacris*[175] is reserved to their own

---

170. "*Casus reservandi sint pauci omnino, tres scilicet vel, ad summum, quatuor ex gravioribus tantum et atrocioribus criminibus externis specifice determinatis*" (*Codex Iuris Canonici*, 257).

171. *Codex Iuris Canonici*, 149.

172. "to no one".

173. *Codex Iuris Canonici*, 653.

174. *Codex Iuris Canonici*, 653.

175. "suspension from sacred rites".

major superior. Confessors cannot lift this censure. In our Order, they all incur *excommunication*. {In} canon 2388,[176] solemnly professed religious and clerics *in sacris*[177] attempting matrimony incur excommunication reserved *simpliciter*[178] to the Holy See; simple professed incur excommunication reserved to the ordinary of the place. Reserved cases in our Order—what are they? The General Chapter of 1899 {states}: "The excommunication of Palm Sunday remains in force and only the Superiors and those to whom they have delegated this power, can absolve from it."[179] In 1907, #6,[180] a religious who goes to Rome to visit someone in the Holy See without permission of his own higher superiors is a fugitive and incurs excommunication *ipso facto*. {See} *Constitutions*, 184 {to} distinguish {the following}: apostates and fugitives incur all the penalties imposed by common law, and in addition, by *particular law* fugitives incur excommunication. The most notable examples of "reserved cases" in the Order are, then, sins mentioned in the Palm Sunday excommunications, and flight from the monastery (as well as apostasy). Palm Sunday excommunication {is} inflicted on *conspirators, incendiaries, property owners, thieves* {and} *fugitives (vide supra)*. {For} others, {see the} *Liber Antiquarum Definitionum*, D. vii, c. 6: "All persons of the Order who try to impede the process of their visitors or judgements handed down by the General Chapter, in visitations, in ordinations, corrections or excommunications, or who stubbornly and maliciously oppose the visitors or Fathers Immediate, or who side with those who do this by themselves or through others,

---

176. *Codex Iuris Canonici*, 654.
177. "in holy orders".
178. "simply"; "exclusively".
179. 1899, #3.
180. "It is forbidden for any religious of the Order to go to Rome without the permission of the Abbot General. The religious who contravenes this prohibition will be considered as a fugitive, and consequently will incur excommunication *a jure ipso facto*."

through letters, requests, threats, etc., etc.,"[181] fall under the same excommunication; also (*Liber Antiquarum Definitionum, ibid.*) laying violent hands on a monk or laybrother, laying violent hands on an abbot, or imprisoning him, or having him expelled, or prohibiting his entry into the monastery. To what extent do these remain in force???

Confessors of Novices:

1. There are to be "one or more ordinary confessors, according to their number."[182] This is the exact wording of canon 566, #1.[183] The canon here refers back to canon 519, which provides that in spite of constitutions which say that a religious must go to certain confessors, the subject is *always free* "for the peace of his conscience" to go to any confessor "approved by the ordinary of the place,"[184] and the confession is valid and licit; also the confessor can absolve from sins and censures reserved in the order. This applies both to professed and novices, but only in orders of men. It is disputed whether a confession so made dispenses from {the} obligation to make the regular confession prescribed in the constitutions. The permission of a religious superior is *not necessary* for this confession, but it does not follow that the religious can violate a rule in order to make this confession—v.g., leave {the} enclosure without permission. It only applies to confessors with faculties from the ordinary of the place. Canon

---

181. "*Omnes quoque personae Ordinis, quae processum visitatorum suorum aut judicum a Capitulo generali concessorum, in visitationibus, ordinationibus, correctionibus seu exsecutionibus impedierint, vel ipsis visitatoribus aut patribus Abbatibus procaciter & proterve se opposuerint, aut ista facientibus consenserint per se vel per alios, litteras, preces, minas, insidias vel auxilia parentum . . .*" (*Nomasticon*, 422).

182. N. 87 (*Constitutions*, 24; the section on confessors of novices is not present in the Latin text).

183. "*Pro novitiorum numero unus vel plures . . . ordinarii confessarii*" (*Codex Iuris Canonici*, 164 [this is actually canon 566.2, n. 1]).

184. "*ad suae conscientiae quietem . . . ab Ordinario loci approbatum*" (*Codex Iuris Canonici*, 149).

519 [185] revokes all other privileges to the contrary, i.e., which made it impossible for {a} religious to confess outside his monastery without the knowledge of the superior.

2. The ordinary confessors must live in the same house—{there is} no difficulty {about this} *apud nos*. [186]

3. "Several others" shall be appointed, to whom they may "freely have access in particular cases." [187] This is the wording of canon 566, #3, [188] which adds that the father master must not show any displeasure or place any difficulties in the way. Those to whom novices have access at the moment are: Fathers Lambert, Amandus, Edward and Vianney. [189] {It is} sufficient to make a sign or write a note, but the note goes through the ordinary channels. One cannot normally make one of these his ordinary confessor. If one goes to one of these, he does not have to go to the ordinary confessor in the same week.

4. The extraordinary confessor {comes} "at least four times a year" [190] (wording of canon 566.2, #4 [191]); it is customary in most

---

185. *Codex Iuris Canonici*, 149.

186. "among us."

187. *Constitutions*, 24 (once again, this section on confessors of novices is not present in the Latin text).

188. *"designentur aliqui confessarii, quos novitii in casibus particularibus adire libere possint"* (*Codex Iuris Canonici*, 164).

189. Lambert Enslinger, ocso (d. September 22, 1960); Amandus (later Roger) Reno, ocso (d. December 6, 1977); Edward Knecht, ocso (d. February 19, 1983); Vianney Wolfer, ocso (d. November 16, 1993). Merton mentions Fr. Lambert in an April 14, 1960, journal entry as "dying in the infirmary, after a stroke" (*Search for Solitude*, 384), and describes his death, after a second stroke, in a September 23, 1960, journal entry (Thomas Merton, *Turning Toward the World: The Pivotal Years. Journals, vol. 4: 1960–1963*, ed. Victor A. Kramer [San Francisco: HarperCollins, 1996], 51–52); in a January 3, 1968, journal entry, he calls Fr. Roger (Amandus) "a local sage and oracle" whom he consults about the upcoming abbatial election (Thomas Merton, *The Other Side of the Mountain: The End of the Journey. Journals, vol. 7: 1967–1968*, ed. Patrick Hart [San Francisco: HarperCollins, 1998], 32).

190. *Constitutions*, 24; not included in *Constitutiones*.

191. *"Quater saltem in anno"* (*Codex Iuris Canonici*, 164).

places for the extraordinary to come at ember days—{this is} not a matter of law, though. One must present oneself at least to receive his blessing.

5. The father master and undermaster do not hear sacramental confessions of novices unless the latter for grave and urgent causes ask it of their own free will in particular cases, {which are}:

   a) grave and urgent—certainly not *ex devotione*;[192] {this} seems to imply two things: (a) a serious problem; (b) which needs to be settled in {the} sacramental forum; (c) and it is difficult or impossible to go to another confessor;

   b) {the} novice himself must ask to make this confession;

   c) in particular cases.

The reason for this {is that} the master is bound to make a decision in the external forum which would be hampered by this knowledge, perhaps.

Difference Between {the} Functions of Father Master and of {the} Confessor: canon 561, #1 {says}: "The novice master alone has the right and the duty to watch over the formation of the novices, and to him alone the job of running the novitiate belongs [*novitiatus regimen*] so that no one else is permitted, under any pretext whatsoever, to meddle in these things except those superiors who are permitted to do so by the constitutions."[193] Therefore the confessor has nothing to do either with the formation of the novices or with running the novitiate. The formation comprises three things: instruction, exercise, proving. The confessor has no business meddling in any of these, although of course he will naturally give a little instruction and suggest practices of virtue. But the novice should never feel obliged to follow any such instructions, except what strictly pertains to the sacrament (v.g., avoiding occasions of sin, taking steps to avoid falling back into

---

192. "for reasons of devotion".

193. "*Uni Magistro ius est et officium consulendi novitiorum institutioni, ad ipsumque unum novitiatus regimen spectat, ita ut nemini liceat hisce se, quovis colore, immiscere, exceptis Superioribus quibus id a constitutionibus permittitur*" (*Codex Iuris Canonici*, 163).

sin, etc.). The father master should know everything in the internal forum which will help him to make a correct judgement regarding the fitness of the novice for the life, his spirit, and the manner in which he fulfills the obligations of the Order. The father master is the spiritual father of the novice and has a special grace of state to help him correct his difficulties and prepare for the religious life—or guide him to some other state.

#88: "Superiors can hear the confessions of their subjects who freely and of their own accord ask them to do so"[194] (cf. canon 518, #2[195]).

A. *Confessions*:

a) Our superiors have the power to hear confessions of their subjects. Indeed, the *ordinary power* to absolve from sin is in the hands of the abbot, and consequently the other confessors receive faculties and jurisdiction from him.

b) Canon 518, #2 says the subject must ask "*sponte sua ac motu proprio*"[196]—that is to say, not moved by threats and violence, or *even by persuasion* (v.g., human respect—{he} feels that the superior would like to hear his confession, would treat him nicer if he went to confession, etc.).

c) The superior should not hear these confessions habitually, but *he may do so* if there is a serious reason (*cum gravi causa*[197]). A serious reason would be that the subject could not find peace in going to another confessor, or he prefers a confessor of his own order (the superior being the only such), or he makes remarkable progress with him, etc. Hence the superior *can* be the ordinary confessor of his subjects, as distinguished from the novice master, who must hear confessions only in an isolated case.

---

194. "*Superiores possunt confessiones audire subditorum qui ab illis sponte sua ac motu proprio id petant*" (Constitutiones, 18); Constitutions, 24.

195. *Codex Iuris Canonici*, 149.

196. "by his own will and personal decision".

197. The canon says this should not be done "*sine gravi causa*" ("without serious cause"), as does *Constitutiones*, 18.

d) The purpose of this {is} that the superior be not impeded in the external forum by knowledge acquired under the seal, which he cannot use.

e) The restrictions on going to confession to the superior apply to the subjects, not to guests, etc. There is no restriction for them.

f) A confession made under force etc. by a subject would be valid but not licit. "They shall bear in mind the prohibitions of canon 518, #3."[198] Canon 518, #3 reads: "Superior shall take care not to induce any subject to make a confession of sins to him by violence, fear or importunate persuasions, either by himself or through others."[199]

B. *Manifestation of Conscience*: "They shall in no way whatever induce any of the religious to make manifestation of conscience to them."[200] "Manifestation of conscience" is broader than sacramental confession. *Schaefer* (684) defines it: "A revelation of the state of one's soul outside of confession, in which one makes known those matters which proximately pertain to virtue or vice. It is a revelation of habits, affections, inclinations, propensities, temptations, dangers and passions, made in order to receive help and counsel for the doubts and difficulties of the spiritual life and to make progress in the way of perfection."[201] Schaefer adds[202] that self-accusation in chapter is not manifestation of conscience

---

198. N. 88 (*Constitutions*, 24; not included in *Constitutiones*).

199. "*Caveant Superiores ne quem subditum aut ipsi per se aut per alium vi, metu, importunis suasionibus aliave ratione inducant ut peccata apud se confiteatur*" (*Codex Iuris Canonici*, 149).

200. *Constitutions*, 24, which reads: ". . . Religious subject to them to make . . ." (not present in *Constitutiones*).

201. "*aperitio status animae extra confessionem et quidem earum rerum, quae proxime ad virtutes vel vitia se referunt. Est revelatio morum, affectuum, inclinationum, propensionum, tentationum, periculorum, passionum alicui facta, ut quis in dubiis et difficultatibus vitae spiritualis consilium et auxilium acquirat et certius in via perfectionis ducatur*" (Schaefer, 364).

202. Schaefer, 364.

(because it is not private and does not concern the interior); discussion of difficulties in prayer or in keeping external rules are not a manifestation of conscience. THESE CAN BE DEMANDED BY THOSE SUPERIORS WHO ARE NOT OTHERWISE ALLOWED TO ASK MANIFESTATION OF CONSCIENCE. Confession is not, strictly speaking, a manifestation of conscience, because it is ordered not to receiving *advice* but *absolution*. Our *Constitutions* are quoting canon 530, #1, which reads: "All religious superiors are strictly prohibited to induce the persons in their care to make manifestation of conscience to them in any way whatever." [203] This is all-inclusive. It is more strict than the prohibition to induce one to go to confession:

a) ALL superiors—therefore not only nuns, but also men, priests; the question arose with regard to superiors of nuns who tried to make manifestation of conscience *obligatory*;

b) "strictly prohibited"—therefore under pain of mortal sin, though it admits parvity of matter;

c) but it applies only to superiors properly so-called—not to {the} novice masters, nor masters of students;

d) in any way whatever—this excludes not only threats, but also flattery {or} promises of reward, direct or indirect;

e) subjects—that means not only professed but also novices and postulants;

f) the superior cannot urge manifestation of conscience *to himself* in public exhortations, but he can exhort *to openness as such*;

g) there is nothing to prevent the novice master, or a preacher, or someone, *to urge all to be open with the superior*, since this has distinct advantages, but they must not act in collusion with the superior in doing so;

h) all prescriptions in religious rules and constitutions making manifestation to the superior obligatory are abrogated by canon 530, #1;

---

203. "*Omnes religiosi Superiores districte vetantur personas sibi subditas quoquo modo inducere ad conscientiae manifestationem sibi peragendam*" (*Codex Iuris Canonici*, 152).

i) SUPERIORS RETAIN THE RIGHT AND INDEED THE OBLIGATION TO INQUIRE ABOUT VIOLATIONS OF RULE AND BREACHES OF DISCIPLINE EVEN WHEN THESE TOUCH UPON SPIRITUAL MATTERS— this is not a manifestation of conscience.

530, #2 reads: "However the subjects are not prohibited from freely and spontaneously opening their soul to their superiors; indeed it is expedient that they should approach their superiors with childlike confidence, if the superiors are priests, and make known to them their doubts and anxieties of conscience."[204] These words are quoted verbatim by our *Constitutions*.[205]

{Note} *the advantage of openness* with superiors. The superior still has a special grace of state, especially in Benedictine life. We cannot say it is obligatory to manifest one's conscience to Reverend Father but it is certainly worthwhile. The abbot has graces of state to judge his subjects. He should be regarded as Christ in the monastery. However, it is not true to assert that the superior alone, for example, is the sole judge whether or not one has a vocation, etc., etc.

#89: *Holy Communion*:[206]

1) Days on which Holy Communion is prescribed are to be regarded as days of *general communion* for the community, when the community goes to communion at the high altar and all who are well disposed are urged to receive the Body of Our Lord: all feasts of sermon, all feasts of two Masses (on these days, general communion {takes place} at the matutinal Mass; what is done

---

204. "Non tamen prohibentur subditi quominus libere ac altro aperire animum suum Superioribus valeant; imo expedit ut ipsi filiali cum fiducia Superiores adeant, eis, si sint sacerdotes, dubia quoque et anxietates suae conscientiae exponentes" (*Codex Iuris Canonici*, 152).

205. *Constitutions*, 24, which reads: "The Religious, however, are not forbidden to open their hearts freely and spontaneously to their Superiors; nay, more, it is to their advantage to have recourse to them with filial confidence, and also to expose to them their doubts and troubles of conscience"; not present in *Constitutiones*.

206. Chapter 5 (nn. 89–91) (*Constitutiones*, 18–19; *Constitutions*, 24–25).

now in other houses? {See} *Usages* 184–188:[207] communion is at the matutinal Mass when there is one, at high Mass on work days in winter and Lent, at private Masses in the summer); on days when there is a plenary indulgence to be gained in the Order—for instance, Saturdays in Lent, feasts listed in the *Ordo*[208] (most are {of} two Masses and Sermon, but some are three lessons or twelve lessons—v.g., St. Maurus, St. William, Sts. Fabian and Sebastian, St. Scholastica, Bl. Juliana, St. Placid, St. Malachy, St. Edmund, rogation days, St. John Lateran, St. Peter of Tarentaise, St. Lutgard, St. Cajetan, St. Catherine, St. Nicholas, St. Lucy).

2) For the individual, these regulations have a directive force: they are *counsels*. The individual is *invited*, but not commanded, to go to communion.

3) For the individual, {he should} follow the direction of a confessor with regard to frequent communion. Daily communion is promoted now, but all should take care not to go to communion merely out of routine or human respect.

#90: *Daily Communion*: {according to} canon 863, all the faithful are to be urged to receive communion frequently and even daily.[209] Canons 595, #2[210] and #3[211] are reproduced textually in our *Constitutions*, #90 and #91: "Superiors shall promote frequent and even daily communion."[212] ({The} obligation of {the} superior {is} not merely to urge a great number of communions but *to foster a eucharistic life* in the community, because this is the safeguard of the community itself; in a sense this obligation is more

---

207. *Regulations*, 88–91.

208. *Ordo Divini Operis Persolvendi Sacrique Peragendi ad Usum Cisterciensium Reformatorum seu Strictioris Observantiae* (Westmalle, Belgium: Ex Typis Ordinis, 1949).

209. "*Excitentur fideles ut frequenter, etiam quotidie, pane Eucharistico reficiantur*" (*Codex Iuris Canonici*, 247).

210. *Codex Iuris Canonici*, 172.

211. *Codex Iuris Canonici*, 172.

212. "*Superiores suos inter subditos promoveant frequentem, etiam quotidianam, sanctissimi Corporis Christi receptionem*" (*Constitutiones*, 18); *Constitutions*, 25, which reads: "Superiors shall promote among their subjects the frequent and even daily reception of the Most Holy Body of Christ."

important than any other, because if the monks lead a true eucharistic life they will live united in fervor of charity and will spontaneously keep all the rules. They will aid one another to rise to high perfection.) But the decree *Quam Singulari*[213] emphasizes the fact that communion is always a free matter for the individual and that one who wishes to abstain for some motive may do so and should do so without fear of arousing suspicion of brethren or superiors. {With regard to} right dispositions, {the} Decree *Sacra Tridentina Synodus* (Pius X) says {it includes the} state of grace and right intention.[214] Right intention consists in the fact that the one going to communion does not go out of *mere routine* or prompted by *vanity* or *human considerations*, but *desiring to please God*, and *to be more closely united with Him in charity*, and *to receive from Him the divine remedy* for our infirmities.

#91: For grave scandal or grave external fault, the superior can prohibit the subject from receiving communion until he has gone to confession (595, #3). Some authors hold that a public disobedience, even though not grave, is sufficient here. More probably it requires a mortal sin.

VI. Spiritual Reading:[215]

#92: {This chapter} makes clear that spiritual reading (*lectio divina*) is the next in importance of the monk's obligations after the divine office. However, this obligation is fulfilled by prayer also: "prayer or reading."[216] The monks of our Order are obliged to nourish a private contemplative life of their own. Reading, meditation and prayer go together (cf. {the} *Scala Claustralium*[217]).

---

213. This decree of August 8, 1910 (*Acta Apostolicae Sedis* 2 [1910], 577–83), on the reception of holy communion by children, does not in fact deal with the question of abstaining from communion.

214. *Acta Sanctae Sedis* 28 (1905): 400–409.

215. Nn. 92–94 (*Constitutiones*, 19; *Constitutions*, 25).

216. "*orationi aut lectioni*" (*Constitutiones*, 19); *Constitutions*, 25.

217. *Scala Claustralium sive Tractatus de Modo Orandi* (*The Ladder of Monks, or Treatise on the Way to Pray*) (PL 184, cols. 475A–484D); for a discussion and analysis of this text, see Thomas Merton, *An Introduction to Christian*

#93: The place of reading is designated. Traditionally, preference belongs to the cloister. The local superior designates other places. Usually the scriptorium is one of these places (but it is not to be regarded as the traditional or ordinary place of reading—the custom is a modern one). In European monasteries, it seems, monks do not ordinarily *read* in the garden. They may walk and pray there. Here, reading in the garden and the woods is allowed (cf. visitations of 1955, 1953).

#94: The reading must be *spiritual*. This paragraph controls the matter to be read, and guards against the introduction of secular curiosities or other things that do not pertain to the contemplative life.

a) The abbot is the one responsible for providing good books. Monks of course may make suggestions. The "necessary" books {are most appropriate}. Today more are necessary than in the past, but we do not have to accumulate all the latest publications in every field. Recommended by the General Chapter of {1920,} #28 [218] are the *Holy Rule* and the *Spiritual Directory*. [219] {Books should be} "such as contain sound doctrine." Note also that monks should not get involved in matters savoring of controversy.

b) "*He shall take care that the monks do not waste their time reading newspapers and useless books.*" [220] Newspapers are banned in general. The abbot remains the judge of what is a "useless" book. This depends on some circumstances: v.g., *Relax and Live*

Mysticism: Initiation into the Monastic Tradition 3, ed. Patrick F. O'Connell, MW 13 (Kalamazoo, MI: Cistercian Publications, 2008), 332–40.

218. "The good desire of reading books and especially the practical use of the Holy Rule and of the Directory which contains the whole program of our spiritual asceticism" (§2) (copy text reads: "1921").

219. [Vital Lehodey, ocso,] *A Spiritual Directory for Religious* Translated from the Original French Text "*Directoire Spirituel à l'Usage des Cisterciens de la Stricte Observance*" by a Priest of New Melleray Abbey, Peosta, Iowa (Trappist, KY: Abbey of Our Lady of Gethsemani, 1946).

220. "*Qui Abbas invigilet ne tempus terant monachi legendo ephemerides librosve inutiles*" (*Constitutiones*, 19); *Constitutions*, 25 (emphasis added).

by J. A. Kennedy.[221] The statutes of the General Chapter give further precisions: 1906, #13 {reads}: "Our religious are forbidden to have recourse to *L'Ami du Clergé* or to other reviews in order to obtain decisions contrary to our Constitutions, etc., *and are forbidden to try to impose them on their Community*. The General Chapter invites Superiors to *show themselves severe in their permission to read these reviews*."[222] (*L'Ami du Clergé* corresponds to the *American Ecclesiastical Review*. Hence even in such reviews, permissions to read are granted sparingly.) *No magazines* were admitted to the Gethsemani community under Dom Frederic.[223] Just the *American Ecclesiastical Review* and one or two others (*Catholic Biblical Quarterly* and *Bible et Vie Chrétienne*) get into the common box today (1956). Still others are permitted in special departments: *Vie Spirituelle*, *Theological Digest* and *Theological Studies*. 1920, #21 {notes that} while there was a certain latitude allowed in permitting newspapers during World War I, "it is now time to react and superiors should not allow newspapers, periodicals or profane reviews to penetrate into our communities."[224] 1938, {#14}[225] states that radios and movies are forbidden in our monasteries, but whether it is the receiving, broadcasting or both that is prohibited is not clear.

221. Joseph A. Kennedy, *Relax and Live* (New York: Prentice Hall, 1953); see Merton's mordant comment on this book in *Conjectures of a Guilty Bystander* (Garden City, NY: Doubleday, 1966), 156: "Brother G—, a postulant who has come to the end of his rope and wants to leave, but who has been dissuaded (not by me), stands in the novitiate library leafing through a book called *Relax and Live*. Sooner or later it comes to that."

222. Text reads: ". . . Constitutions, rules and customs . . ." (emphasis added).

223. Dom Frederic Dunne (1874–1948), fifth Abbot of Gethsemani (1935–1948).

224. Text reads: "The General Chapter most explicitly reminds all the Superiors that it is now time to react and that they should . . ."

225. "The use of the radio, as well as moving pictures are equally prohibited in our monasteries" (copy text reads: "#13").

What reading is encouraged in the Order? The General Chapter of 1921, #10 says: "To hold in greater esteem the *meditated reading of the Holy Scriptures and of the holy Fathers*, the General Chapter decrees: (a) public readings should be chosen to encourage this taste, especially our Father, St. Bernard; (b) the religious should have at their disposal "manuals and commentaries on the Holy Scriptures."[226] In the spirit of this legislation, those with sufficient talent should be trained early to read and study {the} scriptures and the Fathers, especially those of our Order, in order to communicate this taste to others. From the Circular Letter of Dom Gabriel[227] (1952):

a) Our time of reading is a time of serious devotion to the things of the spirit, not a mere amusement, still less a mere formality to salve our conscience. It implies *serious thought*—a real activity of the mind and heart.

b) {For} *lectio divina*, the *matter must be "divine"*: Scripture, Fathers, lives of saints, writings of masters of spirituality, ancient or modern. The *intention must be "divine"*—to seek God.

c) It is not only useful but *essential* to the spiritual life. "IS IT NOT BECAUSE SO MANY OF THE MONKS AND NUNS OF OUR ORDER DRAW FROM THEIR READING SO LITTLE TO GAZE UPON AND CONTEMPLATE AND LOVE, THAT THERE ARE SO FEW REAL CONTEMPLATIVES EVEN IN AN ORDER LIKE OUR OWN WHERE EVERYTHING IS ORGANIZED TO LEAD SOULS TO CONTEMPLATION? One of the reasons for these numerous failures, without a shadow of a doubt, is the lack of a solid diet of doctrinal nourishment. This need causes prayer to become empty, sleepy, reduces it to dry, fruitless drudgery. The mind has no truth to catch a solid grip on. God is not in the soul, so how can it help see-sawing back and forth

---

226. Text reads: ". . . General Chapter judges that we could (1) utilize the public readings in order to have the Holy Scriptures and the Holy Fathers, especially our Father Saint Bernard, better known; (2) put in the hands of the religious manuals and commentaries of the Holy Scriptures."

227. I.e., Dom Gabriel Sortais (1902–1963), Abbot General of the Cistercian Order of the Strict Observance from 1951 until his death.

between disenchanting aridity and hollow sentimentality." He then goes on to show the proper atmosphere in which reading must be carried out, the right way to read and pray, etc. He ends up by saying the term *interval* is probably an unfortunate one, leading religious to think it is just an in-between time in which to rest and do nothing.

VII. Silence: [228]

#95: "There is nothing which conduces more to the practice of regular discipline than the religious practice of silence."[229] Note: {this is} a rare statement, worthy of attention. Usually in the *Constitutions* there are no ascetic explanations or statements of spiritual policy. The *Constitutions* are not the place for the formulation of the ideal, but simply for statements of fact—we do this; we don't do that. However, when an observance like silence is so closely related to the very essence of an order, then a reserved but fundamental pronouncement like this one may be called for. It merits all the attention it attracts by its unusualness.

a) The background: this is the common teaching of theologians; it is practically speaking the teaching of the Church on silence for religious. {See} Cassian: "HIC EST PRIMUS DISCIPLINAE ACTUALIS INGRESSUS" (*Conf.* 14, c. 9);[230] St. John Climacus: "Silence is prudent, the mother of prayer, the former of contemplation, liberation from captivity, hidden progress in virtue, the keeper of divine fervor, hidden ascent to God, etc., etc.";[231] Cluny (statutes of Peter the

---

228. Nn. 95–98 (*Constitutiones*, 19–20; *Constitutions*, 25–26).

229. "*Regularis disciplinae observantiam nihil magis fovet quam religiosus silentii cultus*" (*Constitutiones*, 19); *Constitutions*, 25, which reads: ". . . to the observance of . . ."

230. "This is the first stage of practical training" (*PL* 49, col. 967A, which reads: ". . . *est enim primus* . . ."); for a discussion of this conference, including this chapter in particular, see Thomas Merton, *Pre-Benedictine Monasticism: Initiation into the Monastic Tradition* 2, ed. Patrick F. O'Connell, MW 9 (Kalamazoo, MI: Cistercian Publications, 2006), 45–51.

231. "*silentium prudens est parens orationis, a captivitate liberatio, ardoris divini custodia, . . . contemplationis informator, occultus in virtutibus profectus,*

Venerable): "*Summe necessaria in omni religione silentii utilitas sine quo modis congruis observato,* NEC DICI RELIGIO, NEC ESSE POTEST";[232] Vatican Council (schema): "Care must be taken lest religious be disturbed by inordinate visits of outsiders to the cloister, which brings danger of waste of time and violation of the rule"[233] (this is for *all* religious); Clement XIV (Constitution *In Vinea Domini* [1772]): "The superior must admonish and punish publically the religious who break silence so that all may learn to hate talkativeness and love silence, which is the most safe guardian of solitude, peace and charity, FOR WHEN SILENCE IS NOT OBSERVED THE MONASTERY IS A BEDLAM AND NOT A SOLITUDE."[234]

b) Silence is therefore an obligation to us (1) for its own preeminent value in the life of prayer; (2) as the guardian of all our regularity; (3) as the guardian of charity and peace; (4) it is therefore intimately connected with our striving for monastic perfection.

{As a} consequence, the *Constitutions* now apply this principle: since silence is so important, "conversations are not permitted to

---

arcanus in Deum ascensus" (*Scala Perfectionis*, 11.3 [J.-P. Migne, ed., *Patrologiae Cursus Completus, Series Graeca* [PG], 161 vols. (Paris: Garnier, 1857–1866), vol. 88, col. 851BC]).

232. "In all religious life silence is very necessary and useful, and without its being observed in suitable ways the life can neither be called, nor be, religious" (*PL* 189, col. 1031D).

233. "*Cautum namque est, ne Religiosi ex nimia ad claustra hominum frequentia, a solitudinis quiete cum magna temporis jactura, aliorum admiratione, ac periculo transgrediendi regulam exturbentur*" ("*Schema Constitutionis de Clausura,*" in *Omnium Concilii Vaticani Quae ad Doctrinam et Disciplinam Pertinent Documentorum Collectio*, ed. Conrad Martin [Paderborn: Ferdinand Schoeningh, 1873], 241).

234. "*Loquaces fratres superior moneat, corrigat, et ubi opus fuerit coram omnibus puniat, ut discant ipsi, discant caeteri loquacitatem odisse, et amare silentium, quod integerrimus est solitudinis, pacis, et charitatis custos, quo sublato charitas aliquando detractione violatur . . . coenobium tumultus est, non solitudo*" (*Bullarii Romani Continuatio Summorum Pontificum Clementis XIII, Clementis XIV . . .* , vol. 4 [Rome: Camera Apostolica, 1841], 452).

us, *even by way of recreation*."[235] This means there is no recreation provided for in our rule. We are practically the only order where there is no official recreation—the Camaldolese and Carthusians have it, as do also the Carmelites, etc. We have to take special care that the talking permitted to us does not become a recreation—talking off the subject. *Conversations are not permitted*—to converse is to violate the rule. {There is an} exception of course with superiors and directors, but if we deliberately seek mere recreative conversations with these we may lose the spirit of silence. However, here as elsewhere, in cases of necessity and for special reasons, the superior may permit conversation, for instance with someone sick in the infirmary. Cultivate silence, but not mutism. Practice silence in a spirit of discipline, but be able to speak when you have to.

96: *Permissions to Speak* (among the religious themselves): it is obvious that permission to speak will sometimes be necessary. It is also obvious that permission to speak cannot lightly be given when it is not necessary. To be too free in getting permissions to speak opens the way to disorder. In principle, permissions to speak are to be granted *rarely*. See {the} *Usages* for further practical details.[236] "Those who break silence should be punished."[237] The fact that this is specifically mentioned in the *Constitutions* indicates that violation of silence is considered a serious breach of discipline in our Order, and lends weight to the view of some that violation of silence can be a venial sin. "When the religious meet—salute in silence"[238]—perhaps to make sure there are no illusions about *Memento mori*.[239]

---

235. "*colloquia nobis non permittuntur, nequidem recreationis causa*" (*Constitutiones*, 19); *Constitutions*, 25 (emphasis added).

236. *Regulations*, 156–60 (nn. 323–31).

237. "*Puniri debent qui taciturnitatis regulam absque licentia transgrediuntur*" (*Constitutiones*, 19); *Constitutions*, 26, which reads: "Those who, without permission, transgress the rule of silence should be punished."

238. "*Cum sibi obviant, invicem salutent cum silentio*" (*Constitutiones*, 19); *Constitutions*, 26, which reads: "When the Religious meet, they shall salute one another in silence."

239. "Remember death"; the reference is evidently to the traditional Trappist practice enjoined by the Abbot de Rancé of being continually mindful

97: Permissions to speak to outsiders: they "shall never speak or converse in any way with outside persons."[240] This forbids signs, presumably. Should we salute the guests? Yes, and smile at them. Be pleasant, but do not communicate with them. If they speak, you can indicate politely by sign that you are not allowed to reply. "Whoever they may be"[241]—this seems to indicate that bishops etc., are not excepted. To speak to *any outsider*, permission of one's superior is required. {It} can be legitimately presumed, for instance, if one sees women walking innocently (or otherwise) into the enclosure, or in case of serious accident. But do not be too free about presuming permission! Note {the} danger of scandal! When one is outside the monastery, in town for business, etc., it is presumed that the permission to speak when necessary is included in the permission to go out for that purpose.

98: *Letters and Visits*: "Letters shall not be opened nor sent out without the permission of the Superior."[242] This prescription of the *Constitutions* is the one that seems to have received the most elaboration from the General Chapters in recent years.[243] There are a large number of statutes on this matter of letters, and others concerning the contacts of monks with the outside. We group all this legislation together here, although some of it concerns the prescriptions on enclosure.

a) Letters may not be *opened*—that is to say, if one were to receive an unopened letter that did not come through the superior's office, one would still require permission to open and read it. (The exceptions to this rule are listed later.)

---

of one's mortality, which would not be interrupted by this silent acknowledgement of one another.

240. "*Cum extraneis personis, . . . nullo modo conversentur nec loquantur*" (*Constitutiones*, 19); *Constitutions*, 26, which reads: "The Religious shall . . . speak to . . ."

241. "*quaecumque illae sint*" (*Constitutiones*, 19); *Constitutions*, 26.

242. "*Epistolae nec aperiantur neque transmittantur sine Praelatorum licentia*" (*Constitutiones*, 20); *Constitutions*, 26, which reads: ". . . opened or sent . . ."

243. 1954, ##3, 4.

b) Letters may not be *sent out*. This means, in practice: (1) Permission of the superior is even required for the letter to be *written* ({see the} Visitation Card, {1953}[244]); letters merely handed to the superior without any permission to write or send them out are to be torn up and thrown away, even if handed in open (cf. 1907, n. 9: permission must be gained to *write* a letter). (2) To send or receive a letter without the permission of the superior is a *mortal sin* (General Chapter, 1934, n. 5[245]). "The General Chapter declares that it does in no way intend to change its interpretation or its will in regard to the point of our Constitutions which prohibits the *Sending* or *Receiving* of letters unknown to the superior. This prohibition is binding by its very nature under pain of mortal sin."[246] (3) "Letters" covers all kinds of communication. "The General Chapter declares that the term 'letters' in *Const.* n. 98 *includes any communication by writing with the outside*. Telephone communications are classed with letters. . . . Such correspondence without the knowledge of {the} superior is of its nature a grievous sin, admitting however of lightness of matter."[247] Hence, to send a note by hand, to make a phone call, to send a telegram, to communicate by short-wave radio (v.g., {at the} fire tower[248]) against the will of the superior is a sin, {and} can be a grave sin. Lightness of matter

---

244. The visitation card is the letter from the Father Immediate (here Dom Louis Le Pennuen, Abbot of Melleray) summarizing the results of the visitation and prescribing instructions for particular changes; Merton was generally the secretary for the French-speaking Father Immediate and made the English translation of the visitation cards (typescript reads: "1955").

245. "the right to control the correspondence belongs to the first Superior alone. The Father-Masters may do so only if they have received a delegation to do so."

246. 1930, #2.

247. Text reads: ". . . cited in # 98 of the Constitutions . . . correspondence carried on without the knowledge (consent) of the Superiors is of its very nature . . ."

248. Nelson County had erected a fire tower at Vineyard Knob on the monastery property; before being appointed master of novices in 1955, Merton had been offered the opportunity by the abbot to live in solitude at

would be something trivial, like desiring to find out a baseball score, or some trifling family news. Gravity of matter {entails}, for instance, in order to go against the will of the superior in an important matter, concerning, for instance, one's own vocation, or the vocation of another, or some project of one's own having a certain magnitude—v.g., to give advice in a big family problem or etc. (General Chapter, 1954, n. 3). (4) "On a trip, i.e., when out of the monastery, the religious remain subject to the Superiors, and may not carry on a correspondence with a third party except in accordance with the directions or permissions they have received or can legitimately presume."[249] The above prescriptions bind us, therefore, even when we are out of the monastery.

Letters Exempt from Control: in principle, the control of letters by superiors is an application of the law of enclosure. If the religious is allowed to have free communication with everyone, uncontrolled by {the} superior, then the enclosure is failing at least in one respect. However the general law of the Church guarantees that the religious, however strict may be the constitutions of his order, must *always* be allowed certain privileges in the matter of communication. This communication is guaranteed by canon law, and it permits the subject, whoever and wherever he may be, to communicate with his higher superiors *without any control* on the part of the local superior. What is the meaning of the phrase *exempt from all control*?

1. They can write a letter and send it without asking permission of the superior. They can hand it to him closed, and he must send it.

2. They do not even have to present the letter to the superior. They can send it out without his knowledge, and have no obligation to pass it through the hands of any member of the Order (General Chapter, 1905, n. 3[250]).

---

the tower as a fire watcher. For details see Michael Mott, *The Seven Mountains of Thomas Merton* (Boston: Houghton Mifflin, 1984), 286–88.

249. Text reads: ". . . permissions that they . . ."

250. "Decisions & Definitions" section "For the Superiors."

3. They can receive letters from these same persons, and the letters *must* be handed to them unopened. 1932, n. 4[251] {says} it is a mortal sin for {a} superior to open one of these letters, but the letter must be marked clearly in such a way that it will not be opened by mistake.

What does our General Chapter say on these points? {According} to 1906, n. {15}: "The General Chapter invites the Fathers Immediate to be watchful that liberty of correspondence with higher Superiors be assured our monks and nuns. He or she who wishes to write to higher authority *does not have to ask permission."* [252] So much for the first part of the statute—liberty is guaranteed. However, there is a qualification made, which is important. The superior has no control over this correspondence, but the *subject himself is held responsible.* It is not a case where an irresponsible liberty is allowed. The subject is bound to see that he writes only on necessary and useful matters. He must not abuse his privilege. So the General Chapter continues: "But we remind the religious that they ought not to write except for just and serious causes. If they act otherwise, they can be liable for punishment by the General Chapter." Comment {on} just and serious causes: *subjectively*, the desire to open one's heart to a higher superior is a just and serious cause, or indeed merely to write to him out of friendliness is sufficient; any reasonable or virtuous motive makes the correspondence licit. *Objectively*, these words are probably aimed against unreasonable and unjust complaints. A religious who in writing to superiors does not weigh his words, who carelessly lets himself go into detraction or calumny or unjust complaints and accusations, *commits a serious fault* (in grave matter) and can receive a notable punishment from the General Chapter. Note {concerning} anonymous letters: an added note of gravity is added if an unjust accusation is written anonymously or under the name of some other religious (for instance the forged name

---

251. Text reads: "A grave fault is committed for a . . ."
252. Text reads: ". . . assured to our monks . . ." (emphasis added) (typescript reads: "16").

of an officer in a community). This would be a very serious fault, which in certain cases might deserve expulsion from the Order. 1906, n. {16}[253] prohibits "collective letters" signed by many. Individuals retain the right to send their observations to higher superiors, but not collectively. This applies only to letters containing protests. It is to "prevent agitation."

To whom can these letters be written: (1) the *Holy See*—{the} Holy Father, any one of the Sacred Congregations, any cardinal or prelate who holds office as head or secretary of a Congregation; (2) {the} *papal legate* ({the} Apostolic Delegate {in} Washington); (3) {the} *Cardinal Protector* (we do not exactly have one; Fumasoni is protector of {the} S. O. Cist.[254]); (4) {the} Abbot General; (5) {the} Father Immediate; (6) Reverend Father, when he is absent or when we are absent from our own monastery and in another.

Manual Work:[255] n. {99}[256] lays down that the source of our income should be *chiefly* manual labor, agriculture and the rearing of cattle—chiefly, not exclusively. Begging is tolerated but discouraged. Members of the Order are not allowed to go out and beg themselves. Begging by mail is frowned upon {as} not {in accord with} the spirit of the Order. To beg means in some sense to become dependent on benefactors, and they can then influence the spirit and observance of the Order. One of the main reasons for manual labor is to make us independent of powerful benefactors and thus free to live a purely monastic life. This was one of the reasons for the break from Molesme to Cîteaux. *Hence it is*

---

253. Typescript reads: "17".
254. Peter Cardinal Fumasoni-Biondi, one-time Apostolic Delegate to the United States and Prefect of the Sacred Congregation of Propaganda Fide, who contributed a prefatory letter to the translation and Merton's commentary on the encyclical *Doctor Mellifluus*: see Thomas Merton, *The Last of the Fathers: Saint Bernard of Clairvaux and the Encyclical Letter, Doctor Mellifluus* (New York: Harcourt, Brace, 1954), 17.
255. Chapter 8 (nn. 99–102) (*Constitutiones*, 20; *Constitutions*, 26).
256. Typescript reads: "90".

one of the fundamental points of our Constitutions. Manual labor includes all kinds of manual work, even an industry, but farming is singled out for special mention. Farming and the raising of stock (sheep, pigs, cattle), dairy farming, forestry, etc. are the normal means of support for a Cistercian monastery. *Industries* are considered abnormal, and are subject to control by the General Chapter (cf. *Const.*, n. 46, ii, 5;[257] cf. Statutes {of the} General Chapter, 1898, n. 1); n. 101 reiterates this.[258] *Crafts* are allowed according to the *Rule*.[259] The various trades are an integral part of the monastic life and no real distinction between them and farm work is to be made, except the ascetic note, reminiscent of the *Rule*, that the dispositions of the individual must be considered.[260] The one exercising a craft must do so in all humility. It puts him on an "exceptional" basis, {and he is} not {to} desire this. {With regard to} *parochial ministry*, sometimes our monks are compelled by circumstances to undertake active works of the ministry. But this is against the spirit of the Order and can only be tolerated when absolutely unavoidable. When it creeps in, it must not be allowed to become habitual. {The} General Chapters of 1920[261] and 1923 take up the question of parochial work done by the monks during World War I: 1923, n. 2 {says}:

257. This specifies that *"de negotiatione artificiali aggredienda"* ("The undertaking of an industrial enterprise") is permitted only with the approval of the General Chapter, after a majority of the conventual chapter of the house has voted in favor (*Constitutiones*, 11; *Constitutions*, 16).
258. *Constitutiones*, 20; *Constitutions*, 26.
259. C. 57 (McCann, 128/129).
260. *"Quod si aliquis ex eis extollitur pro scientia artis suae, eo quod videatur aliquid conferre monasterio, hic talis erigatur ab ipsa arte et denuo per eam non transeat, nisi forte humiliato ei iterum abbas jubeat"* ("But if one of them be puffed up because of his skill in his craft, supposing that he is conferring a benefit on the monastery, let him be removed from his work and not return to it, unless he have humbled himself and the abbot entrust it to him again").
261. 1920, #24 (*bis*).

With regard to the exterior ministry taken up during the war by many of our houses, it is to be observed that we must distinguish between the accidental, rare and temporary ministry asked as a necessary and urgent service, and the prolonged and permanent ministry. In the first case, whenever it is necessary, it is proper to render the service asked of us. In the second case, if any of our houses have been obliged to exercise an exterior ministry up to now, the General Chapter invites them to suppress this state of affairs as soon as possible, i.e., as soon as circumstances will permit without grave injury to souls. We wish to observe on this point that the religious of our Order not being called to the exterior ministry, the Superiors must not easily acquiesce to the solicitations of the Rt. Rev. bishops; and if they must sometimes grant these requests, let them choose the most capable and pious religious and not those who ask for it or desire it. Besides the General Chapter declares that in all cases our religious must abstain from parochial work during the week.[262]

Observe the following points:

1. This again is a most fundamental point of our *Constitutions*; {it} goes back to the early days of the Order when our Fathers refused to be supported by the revenue of parishes, etc., to undertake responsibility for parishes or the direction of nuns. We are obliged to *defend our status as monks*. {The} apostolate {is} not our vocation (only {the} apostolate of prayer).

2. The superiors are placed under grave responsibility to protect the regularity of the Order in this matter.

---

262. Text reads: ". . . state of things, . . . without any grave . . . called to the exercise of the exterior . . . too easily acquiesce . . . and most pious . . . grant their request . . ." Text of 1920, #24 (*bis*) reads: ". . . necessary and urgent . . . ministry till today, . . . state of things, . . . permit it without any grave . . . the exercise of the exterior . . . acquiesce too easily . . . solicitations of the Bishops grant their requests . . ."; it is lacking the final sentence.

3. Where there is an urgent and unusual need, then we can and indeed must consent to help out where there is {a} question of grave danger to souls.

4. We cannot make a foundation in a place where we would be forced by circumstances to undertake missionary work for souls outside the monastery.

5. A permanent state of activity is not to be countenanced. If necessary, the monastery would have to move elsewhere to avoid it.

6. Note—the General Chapter recognizes that there are souls in the monastery discontent with the contemplative life which they are perhaps unable to lead, and desirous of getting into activity. This weakness should not be encouraged. Note that vocations should be well screened in order to make sure that only those who can seriously live the monastic life are allowed to make profession.

7. In any case, whether work is temporary or not, the monks can only work in parishes on weekends, never during the week.

Closed Retreats: not mentioned in our *Constitutions* and not developed to any great extent in many of our monasteries of Europe, closed retreats have been specifically praised and encouraged, in our monastery, by the Holy Father. The retreat "movement" should not become too much of a "movement" with publicity and ballyhoo surrounding it. (Here the work is conducted by laymen; the monks take care of the guests and give the retreats, but do none of the organizing and they should not do any of it.) Note {this could become a} danger to {the} vocation of monks, overworked in contact with seculars, who get no intervals or interior life. (In many houses of Europe when group retreats come, the monks just provide the quarters and the retreatants bring their own retreat master.)

N. 102: The duration for the work (for the choir religious) {is} *not less than three hours* (morning and afternoon), {and} not ordinarily more than six hours. The work is never less than three hours on a full work day; it can be over six hours when there is extra work.

Studies: [263]

N. 103: {This specifies} the prescribed course of studies, for those to be ordained to the priesthood. Note—our studies are to conform to canon law. This presupposes that the one admitted to study of philosophy in our monastery has previously finished his humanities (high-school education roughly covers this—we hope!!). Canon 1364 [264] particularly mentions *training in religion and in Latin as well as in the language of the country*. {It} also {includes} the usual training in other branches of learning expected of an educated man in the region. Canon 1365, [265] n. 1 prescribes the study of philosophy for two full years; n. 2 prescribes four years of theology, which means moral and dogma, plus sacred scripture, Church history, liturgy, canon law, sacred eloquence and Church music; n. 3 also prescribes pastoral theology and training in practical methods, which is usually overlooked in Trappist monasteries for obvious reasons. Notes: the "two full years" of philosophy mean twenty-one months (three months allowed for vacations). Four years of theology means forty-five months of study. General Chapter, 1908, n. 5 [266] says a decree of the Holy See on studies binds *"sub gravi"* [267] ({a} reference to a decree of {the} Sacred Congregation at that time). {An} examination {is made} "in the presence of the abbot," [268] since the abbot is the one chiefly responsible for the fitness of those to be advanced to orders.

N. 104 (cf. canon 588, n. 2 [269]) {specifies that} scholastics ought not to hold any office which interferes with their studies. This

---

263. Chapter 9 (nn. 103–108) (*Constitutiones*, 20–21; *Constitutions*, 27).

264. *Codex Iuris Canonici*, 397.

265. *Codex Iuris Canonici*, 398.

266. "On the subject of the students in our houses, the Reverend Fathers of the Chapter insist that the studies be made conformably to the Constitutions, and as far as possible according to the program adopted. The Decree of the S. Congregation on studies obliges *sub gravi*."

267. "under pain of serious sin."

268. *"coram Abbate"* (*Constitutiones*, 21); *Constitutions*, 27.

269. *Codex Iuris Canonici*, 170.

means at least that they should not have a job which demands their attention during the morning work and prevents their getting their intervals and, of course, getting to choir. Hence a scholastic ought not to be prior or subprior, infirmarian, submaster of novices (this can be done but is not encouraged where others are available), *a fortiori* cellarer or guest master. {A} dangerous situation {can arise} where there are few priests and scholastics have many jobs. They suffer from the lack of time and attention in studies. It is above all necessary to have priests in the monastery with a solid theological and spiritual formation. Incalculable harm can be done by a well-meaning but befuddled priest with misguided zeal and no knowledge, especially if he wins {the} confidence of souls by his piety.

Time for study: *all the tempus lectionis*[270] is to be allowed for study, including intervals during the grand silence, if necessary. But the student should not neglect his spiritual reading and prayer life. {There is a} danger of over-anxiety about studies, wasting effort on useless things and missing the important points. {There is a} necessity to *learn how to study and use time well*. Classes are not always held during the morning work. In some monasteries there are classes in the interval after the afternoon work.

Our *Constitutions* say nothing of a master of scholastics, prescribed in canon 588. His function is to continue their religious formation and especially to form them for the priesthood. He should continue their novitiate formation. Not all of our houses have a master of scholastics. In the larger houses, the office has been instituted for obvious reasons. He is not necessarily the director of all the scholastics, but he gives them public direction and exhortations (conferences) and they have access to him privately. He has no function in the exterior forum.

---

270. *Constitutiones*, 21, which reads *"tempus lectioni"* ("time for reading"); *Constitutions*, 27.

Note: Pius XI insisted on the special importance of studies in {a} contemplative order {in} *Unigenitus Dei Filius*[271] (19 March 1924):

1. The primary obligation of *all* religious is the obligation of prayer and contemplation. For this, sound theological studies are absolutely essential.

2. But such sound studies are most of all important for those who lead an enclosed contemplative life: "We would have those who lead an enclosed and contemplative life take note of this more than anyone else [says Pius XI] for they make a serious mistake if they imagine that they can easily ascend to the heights or reach intimate union with God if they have neglected or abandoned their theological studies, and have deprived themselves of the most helpful knowledge of God and the mysteries of faith which is drawn from the sacred doctrine."[272]

{*The*} *General Chapter on Studies*: 1895, n. 8 {says}: "The General Chapter has adopted the following program of studies which should be followed in all our houses": preliminary studies: Latin, the elements of Greek, literature, geography, the general history of the country, mathematics (this given to the child oblates where they are received??); philosophy: "at least a year" (this is out of date—supplanted by {the} Code—see above—{there} must be two years {of} philosophy); theology: "dogmatic and moral for at least three years"[273] (supplanted by the Code—four years {of} theology); courses in scripture, Church history and canon law are to be taken "simultaneously with philosophy and theology." Examinations {are to be given} twice a year at least, plus exams

---

271. Pope Pius XI, *Unigenitus Dei Filius*, *Acta Apostolicae Sedis* 16.4 (April 1924), 133–48; ET: *Review for Religious* 11 (1952): 183–98.

272. "*Quod velimus eos in primis attendere, qui umbratilem in caelestium rerum contemplatione vitam degunt; errant enim, si putant, theologicis studiis aut ante neglectis aut postea depositis, posse se, copiosa illa destitutus, quae e doctrinis sacris hauritur, Dei mysteriorumque fidei cognitione, facile in excelsis versari atque ad interiorem cum Deo coniunctionem efferri atque evehi*" (*AAS* 16.4, 137).

273. Text reads: "dogmatic and moral theology. . ."

before ordination. General Chapter, 1920, n. 6[274] adapts legislation of 1895 to the prescriptions of the Code—NO *studies in the novitiate*; 1895, n. 9 {says} studies properly so-called {are} forbidden during the novitiate "except for those who do not know sufficient Latin."[275] The *Constitutions* (n. 156[276]) declare that there are to be *no studies during the canonical year of the novitiate*, and indicates that studying is discouraged during the second year also, but it is permitted. ({The} Father Immediate stopped all studies during {the} novitiate at Gethsemani in {the} visitation of 1951.[277]) In 1920, n. 19, the General Chapter expressly praises the program of studies in force at Westmalle, and asks that it be communicated to other houses. (I have never seen it.)

N. 105: *Studies in Rome*: "From all parts of the Order":[278] the definitory is especially anxious to get men from *all parts* of the Order, so that directors, professors and future superiors may receive a full and solid formation in theology and in the spirit and history of the Order. This is very necessary if the Order is to hang together and not break up into separate congregations. It keeps distant houses (v.g., America) in contact with the head of the Order more fully. It provides future definitors and abbots, etc. "Some of the religious":[279] {the} General Chapter of 1946, n. 2 decides that they must have *solemn vows*. Religious under temporary vows may be sent only in certain exceptional cases, to be judged by the Definitory. In point of fact, most students in Rome go there after

---

274. "We will follow actually the Codex which prescribes 2 years of philosophy and 4 of theology."

275. Text reads: "However, novices who do not know sufficient Latin, may be allowed to give some time to the study of this language."

276. *Constitutiones*, 30; *Constitutions*, 36.

277. For Dom Louis Le Pennuen's first visitation at Gethsemani (which led directly to Merton's being appointed Gethsemani's first master of scholastics), see the journal entries of May 7 and June 13, 1951 (Thomas Merton, *Entering the Silence: Becoming a Monk and Writer. Journals, vol. 2: 1941–1952*, ed. Jonathan Montaldo [San Francisco: HarperCollins, 1996], 457–58, 458–60).

278. "*ex omnibus Ordinis partibus*" (*Constitutiones*, 21); *Constitutions*, 27.

279. "*nonnulli*" (*Constitutiones*, 21); *Constitutions*, 27.

ordination and take graduate work at the Gregorian University (v.g., Fr. Deodat De Wilde's thesis on Bl. Guerric,[280] Fr. Pacificus Delfgaauw on St. Bernard,[281] etc.—not very many so far!). "To pursue *at Rome*": {the} General Chapter of 1946, n. 2 also specifies that we do not send students elsewhere than to Rome to work for degrees. In "extraordinary and exceptional cases a request can be presented to the Definitory"[282]—not, for instance, to Catholic University. Who should be sent? They must be (1) good religious; (2) good students (cf. St. John of the Cross: "religioso y estudiante, religioso por delante"[283]). {Note the} importance of sound formation in piety and {a} solid religious vocation. Those who are bright are not always solid or even necessarily mature. Often "intellectual" monks are quite unstable and fickle, easily affected by new circumstances and conditions. However, we must not be so afraid of intellectuals that we keep the Order immersed in blind stupidity. Risk is sometimes worthwhile!

How are these students chosen?

1. The local abbots suggest men whom they think fit, in their own community.

2. The Abbot General and definitors make the final selection. Note that generally the Abbot General himself and quite probably one of the definitors at least would know each candidate.

---

280. Deodat De Wilde, *De Beato Guerrico, Abbate Igniacensi eiusque Doctrina de Formatione Christi in Nobis* (Westmalle: Typis Abbatiae, 1935).

281. Pacificus Delfgaauw, *Saint Bernard, Maître de l'Amour de Dieu: Étude de Théologie Monastique* [1952]; later published as *Saint Bernard, Maître de l'Amour Divin* (Paris: FAC-Éditions, 1994).

282. Text reads: ". . . extraordinary (exceptional) . . ."

283. Merton quotes this couplet in *The Ascent to Truth* (New York: Harcourt, Brace, 1951), 145, and translates it: "A man of prayer and a man of study: / But primarily a man of prayer" (339, n. 2; citing Bruno de Jésus-Marie, OCD, *Saint Jean de la Croix* [Paris: Plon, 1932], 122). See also Crisógono de Jesús, OCD, *The Life of St. John of the Cross*, trans. Kathleen Pond (New York: Harper, 1958), 64: "the educative methods of the Rector [John] . . . could be summed up in an aphorism which from that time became classic in the colleges of the Reform: 'Religious and student, but religious first.'"

What are they to do?

1. They are to go to Rome and pursue a course of studies *higher* than the ordinary course. This is interpreted as graduate work; they study for doctorates, etc.

2. ({N.} 106) They live in the house of the Abbot General.

3. They follow a rule of life compatible with their studies. For instance they talk together at certain times, mostly in Latin. The *horarium* is not that of an ordinary monastery, etc. (N.B. {there is} singing {of the} night office sometimes at Tre Fontane).

4. They are under the direction of a pious and competent religious (of our Order necessarily?) who may be a definitor.

N. 107: *the obligation of the priest to continue his studies*: the fact that most priests of the Order are not sent to Rome for post-graduate work does not mean that in their case, study stops forever after the end of the ordinary four years of theology;

1. The Code (canon {1365}[284]) expressly says that the two years {of} philosophy and four years {of} theology are only a *minimum* (*"saltem"* [285]). This *saltem* refers to {the} injunction that many should go on to higher studies.

2. However, it is the mind of the Code that every priest should continue his theology. Hence canon 590[286] prescribes examinations in dogma and moral during the first five years after ordination. Here too, the exam is prescribed for "at least" five years, so that it may go on for longer. It is prescribed once a year—here we have it twice. Exempt from these exams are young priests who teach theology, canon law or scholastic philosophy. Exempt also are those whom religious superiors exempt for some grave cause. Professors, obviously, continue to study! Note: this legislation is more strict than that for the secular clergy (canon

---

284. *Codex Iuris Canonici*, 398 (text reads: "canon 1380," which is concerned with sending clerics on to higher studies in philosophy, theology and canon law [402], referred to in the following sentence).

285. "at least".

286. *Codex Iuris Canonici*, 171.

130[287]). The seculars need to take {an} exam only for three years and they can be exempted for a "just cause" (religious require a *gravis causa*[288]). Those who are studying for the doctorate in theology, etc. need only take their university exams, but those studying in lay universities are not exempt from the quinquennial exams. N.B. if the religious superiors are negligent in holding these exams, the bishop of the place *cannot* himself examine the young priests of the said order—the case must be brought to the Sacred Congregation of Religious (cf. Schaefer, 1042[289]).

Our *Constitutions* do not merely prescribe studies for the young priests:

1. *All* priests must continue throughout *all* their religious life to study.

2. As contemplatives, they are urged to study not primarily moral, or canon law, but above all dogma and scripture. The term "theology" is used here, but the primacy seems to be given to dogma, with moral included in so far as it leads the monk himself to perfection, rather than in so far as it pertains to the care of souls. However it is very important that the Trappist priest know his moral theology and be able to direct others in the monastery. Here is one of the few places where our *Constitutions* quote scripture.[290] The passage is classical—from Malachi 2 (v. 7): the priest is "the angel of the Lord of Hosts" and the people shall "seek the law at his mouth." Hence this clearly states that the rest of the monastic community is dependent on the priests for knowledge of the things of God, although this is incumbent upon the abbot above all. Any priest should be prepared to be abbot as far as this question of sacred learning is concerned. The priest in the Trap-

---

287. *Codex Iuris Canonici*, 31.

288. "*gravem ob causam . . . exempti*" ("exempt for a serious reason") (canon 590).

289. Schaefer, 620.

290. "*labia eorum custodiant scientiam ut lex possit requiri ex ore ipsorum*" ("let their lips keep knowledge, so that the law may be sought from their mouth") (*Constitutiones*, 21; *Constitutions*, 27).

pist monastery should not desire to be abbot, should not seek to become abbot, and can legitimately avoid preparing himself deliberately for the charge in material matters, but every priest is bound, as far as he is able, to be proficient enough in sacred doctrine to fulfill the requirements of an abbot in that particular matter.

How are we to understand this obligation?

1. It is not satisfied merely by *lectio divina*, in the sense of meditative or contemplative reading (*Const.* #92[291]).

2. It is a *real study* of sacred science.

3. It is not satisfied, by the junior priests, merely by the quinquennial exams.

4. In practice, every priest should reserve for himself certain periods at which he applies himself to the study of theology or scripture or both—not necessarily every day or every week, but certain seasons should be set aside for a more concentrated study. For instance, one of the long intervals on Sundays or feast days could be devoted habitually to theology or scripture. More time could be given to these studies in Lent, for example. The "study of theology" here aimed at should not be understood as being limited to the study of *theological textbooks*. On the contrary, it would be better for the priest after his ordination to study St. Thomas Aquinas or patristic theology, especially St. Augustine or St. Gregory, *a fortiori* St. Bernard and the Cistercian Fathers. In other words, it is advisable for the priest to *go to the sources*, for by this time he should have enough background to be able to do so. It is unfortunate that in fact so many priests are either so busy or so taken up with other concerns that they do, in fact, abandon almost entirely the study of theology or scripture. The truth is that they have little taste for these things, since they have unfortunately never experienced the profit that comes to the soul from application to study of the great Doctors of the Church—or anything else beyond the theological manual. It is very sad to see a

---

291. *Constitutiones*, 19; *Constitutions*, 25.

contemplative priest frittering away his reading time in silly or useless preoccupations with material or bodily concerns—or sign-making.

N. 108: *The Monthly Conferences*: canon 591 [292] prescribes that in every *domus formata* of religious, once a month there must be held a *moral or liturgical case*, which must be attended by (1) all clerics studying theology; (2) all who have studied theology. A *domus formata* is one in which there are at least six religious (professed), four of whom are priests. [293] (Note: in Rome, twice a month there are conferences—one liturgical case, one moral case, plus spiritual exhortation. These must be attended by all secular clergy of the city who have faculties for confessions, under pain of not having their faculties renewed.) Hence Schaefer says (1043 [294]) religious are obliged to solve *both* {the} moral and {the} liturgical case, and the superior may add one of dogma. This was so under Dom Frederic, {but is} not the usual practice in the Order. Now we have moral and dogma, and Dom Vital does the liturgy. Our *Constitutions* [295] and the General Chapter (1913, #3) prescribe in addition to the moral/liturgical conference of canon {591}, [296] a conference in *scripture* once a month. This is binding by virtue not of canon law but of the particular law of the Order. General Chapter, 1913, #3 reads: "With regard to the monthly conferences of Theology and Holy Scripture . . . we are bound to two conferences a month, one of Scripture and one of Theology." [297] These two *may* be held successively on the same day. They may be dispensed with in the summer when work is pressing, on condition that they are made up again in the winter. In other words, it is *not* legitimate to have a conference of scripture

---

292. *Codex Iuris Canonici*, 171.
293. Canon 488, n. 5 (*Codex Iuris Canonici*, 140).
294. Schaefer, 621.
295. *Constitutiones*, 21; *Constitutions*, 27.
296. Typescript reads: "519".
297. Text reads: ". . . bound by the text of the Constitutions to . . . of Holy Scripture . . ."

one month and one on theology the next month. In any case this would be against canon law. There must be twelve conferences a year in theology *and* twelve in scripture, but they need not follow one another month by month. These prescriptions are not fully understandable to us when we remember that our conferences take little more time than the usual morning chapter. Under Dom Frederic, the whole mornings of half-holidays were devoted to the conferences—in *addition* to the morning chapter. Hence they took up the time of morning work in those days when work was short due to the matutinal Mass after prime. It seems to have been the general idea in the Order that this was the thing to do. However it seems to be rather universal now to have it at the morning chapter.

How are the conferences to be conducted? Should there be disputations? 1912, #1 recognizes the fact that Trappists are not very good at disputations. Due to our silence, when we talk on subjects which seem for some reason to arouse emotion, the discussion easily degenerates into a free-for-all, at least in some communities. The General Chapter permits: (1) that a religious be appointed to raise objections; he addresses himself to the moderator, {and} the superior directs the debate "so that it does not degenerate into a dispute";[298] (2) other religious are allowed to make observations, but each one must speak in his turn, not as the spirit moves him, and when he feels like it; (3) the superior may be the one who raises the objections; then the others respectfully address *him*. At Gethsemani the house rule is: (1) after the conference, the one who gave the conference returns to his place ({he} does not answer objections); (2) each religious may speak in turn to offer observations; he should avoid criticizing the person giving the conference, and attempt to throw light on the matter discussed rather than to discredit the one who spoke; (3) the moderator sums up; no one should speak twice; in practice there are few remarks. Note: our *Constitutions* call the theology

---

298. Text reads: "so as not to allow them to degenerate . . ."

sessions *conferences* and the scripture sessions *lectures*, which assumes that there is less of the character of disputation in the scripture sessions.[299]

X. ABSTINENCE:[300]

109: All shall abstain from flesh meat. Abstinence from flesh meat always {has been} an important element in monastic life. A monk does not eat meat without special reason and dispensation. In some orders they take {a} vow to abstain from meat always, however sick. St. Benedict[301] allows meat to the *sick* and to the *weak*—two classes—that is to say, to anyone who really needs it. The *Constitutions* say, "the Abbot shall have consideration for their weakness."[302] In other words it depends on the abbot, guided usually by {the} professional advice of a physician, not by the imaginary needs of those who feel themselves to be "weak" or sick. The matter of abstinence is one on which a monastery should be strict, because of the weakness of imaginations, which is greater even than the weakness of bodies. Note that meat is not strictly necessary to one who can get protein from milk, cheese and eggs. Note also that *fish* is not mentioned in the *Constitutions*. {The} General Chapters of 1892 and 1922, #3[303] forbids the serving of fish in the common refectory as an indulgence. Fish was commonly served as a pittance to our Fathers; the ban on fish dates from de Rancé? or de Lestrange?[304] {In the} *Usages*, #372 {says}: "The use of meat, fish and eggs is forbidden

---

299. "*collationes aut disputationes Theologicae . . . lectiones Sacrae Scripturae*" (*Constitutiones*, 21); *Constitutions*, 27.

300. Nn. 109–12 (*Constitutiones*, 21–22; *Constitutions*, 28).

301. *Rule*, cc. 36, 39 (McCann, 90/91, 96/97).

302. "*quorum imbecillitas ab Abbate consideranda est*" (*Constitutiones*, 21); *Constitutions*, 28.

303. "The decision of the General Chapter of 1892 forbidding the use of fish as an indulgence in the common refectory is maintained."

304. Dom Augustin de Lestrange (d. 1827), leader of the exiled Trappists during the French Revolution (see *Waters of Siloe*, 50–62, 80–82, 90–93, 185–86, 301–303).

in the portions of the community";[305] #378: "Milk and eggs may be given at all times as an indulgence";[306] #476: "The use of meat is permitted to the infirm. Ordinarily it is served only at dinner; the Superior may, however, in certain particular cases grant it at other meals. . . . Meat {is} forbidden on days when abstinence is prescribed by the Church, from Septuagesima to Easter, etc. . . . But the Superior can permit meat to be served at all times to those having a real need of it"[307] (i.e., a more serious need than the "real need" which is required anyway). "Fish and eggs may be given to the sick all the year round, even in Lent."[308]

Meat on a journey: {according to} *Usages*, #404, {a} religious on a journey "may eat eggs and fish, but not meat, unless he is ill, or unless he obtains each time the permission of his Superior. Meat, however, may be eaten on a sea voyage"[309] (n.b. also, *a fortiori*, on a plane—{it is} hardly necessary to eat meat on a modern ocean liner when dishes are so plentiful). {In} General Chapter, 1899, #14, the General Chapter recalls that we should maintain abstinence while on a voyage, and that religious should not use meat without asking the permission of the superior each time.

110: Oil and butter {are} permitted as seasoning. That is, you can cook in oil and butter.

111: {The} prohibition of milk products on all fasts of {the} Church, during Advent, etc., is now modified by the General Chapter of 1953, prop. 4: "Milk products are allowed as food even during Advent and Lent, except three days a week—Monday, Wednesday and Friday."[310] This is to be understood of course

---

305. *Regulations*, 177, which reads: ". . . forbidden for the portions . . ."

306. *Regulations*, 179.

307. *Regulations*, 223, which reads: ". . . to the sick. Ordinarily, it is only served . . . Superior, however, may, . . ."

308. *Regulations*, 223.

309. *Regulations*, 190, which reads: "Meat may, however, be . . ."

310. Text reads: ". . . Lent, with the exception of . . ." (this is a regulation permitted *"ad experimentum"*).

that they are not allowed on Monday, Wednesday and Friday in Advent and Lent, but are allowed on those days at other times of the year. We still abstain from milk products on all Fridays out of paschal time.

112: Fridays in Lent: {on the} first three Fridays, {there is} one portion, with the accustomed drink; {on the} last three Fridays, bread and water. *Usages*, 374 say: "Potatoes may be added to the bread at all times, except on Good Friday"[311]—hence a supplement of potatoes is given on the fourth and fifth Friday of Lent. Potatoes rate as bread. But there must not be a "portion" of potatoes—usually, two baked potatoes. Coffee could be given on Good Friday for a good reason, for instance {on} Good Friday of 1947, when Dom Dominique[312] was here for visitation and ordered coffee {to be} given to the community because of the cold weather. {The} Lenten fast sometimes has to be suspended because of epidemics—v.g., 'flu. In all these things remember that St. Benedict leaves the *application* of the rule of fast and abstinence in the hands of the individual abbot,[313] who must judge what seems necessary in special circumstances. The abbot is bound not to introduce a spirit of useless mitigations and softness, but *he* is the judge, and it is *his* conscience that must decide. It is not for the community to resist or complain at his decisions. Reasonable and humble representations may be made to the Father Visitor. The visitors usually support the abbot in these matters. {There has been a} tendency of recent visitations to suggest {an} increase in quantity and quality of food in this monastery. {The} situation now is to be regarded as quite satisfactory. Surely no one need complain.

---

311. *Regulations*, 178.

312. The Cistercian Abbot General, Dom Dominique Nogues; for his visitation to Gethsemani (March 25–April 5, 1947), see *Entering the Silence*, 52–60.

313. *Rule*, c. 49 (McCann, 114/115).

XI. *Fasting*:[314]

113: {The} general principle:

a) The fasts laid down by St. Benedict would today prove to be "beyond the strength of a great number."[315] In St. Benedict's time, and in the twelfth century, the monks fasted until noon always, until 2 p.m. in winter and 4 p.m. in Lent. In the time when Gethsemani was founded (1848), in the fasts of the Order, dinner was taken at 2 p.m., but there was a mixt in the morning (optional, however). There is no question that the "greater number" in this monastery would be unable to fast until 2 or 4 p.m. Even fasting until 12 would be a great difficulty for most, on top of all the other fasts. Undoubtedly we must not go too far and exaggerate the "weakness" of modern man. Possibly it has a psychological origin in many cases, but it is none the less real.

b) In the time of St. Benedict and St. Bernard, the common faithful observed the same hours as monks for their meals, eating only at vespers in Lent, etc. The Order therefore assumes that it is sufficient to fast *proportionately* to the rest of the Church. Our fast remains stricter, but is proportionately diminished.

c) The strong are still encouraged to do more.

N. 114: Prescribing that dinner be taken at noon in Lent is superseded by {the} General Chapter prescriptions of 1955,[316] putting dinner at 11:30 all the year round.

115: This remains the same—dinner at 11:30 in the time of fasts of the Order. *Collation* {is} taken in the evening. In the *Consuetudines*,[317] *biberes* were prescribed in the evening—just a drink. *Collatio* was the ancient term for the reading before compline—because Cassian's *Conferences* were suggested at that time by the *Rule*.[318]

---

314. Nn. 113–16 (*Constitutiones*, 22–23; *Constitutions*, 28–29).

315. *"vires multorum superare"* (*Constitutiones*, 22); *Constitutions*, 28.

316. 1955, #2.

317. *Ecclesiastica Officia*, c. 80 ("*De Bibere post Vesperas*") (*Nomasticon*, 161–62); see above, page 32.

318. *Rule*, c. 42 (McCann, 100/101).

{The} *Usages*[319] say {that} collation should consist of six ounces of bread, plus a small side dish, for instance, salad or fruit, and the same quantity of drink as {is} given at dinner. Cheese, oleo, etc. are given at collation. On fast days of the Church it should not exceed eight ounces. A little latitude is tolerated at other times. When there is extra work, the superior can give a full portion at collation.

116: Outside {the} time of fasting, mixt is prescribed. It is not optional. One should take the mixt at these times. {With regard to} mixt, General Chapter, 1920, n. 25 prescribes:

1. Superiors should see that there be uniformity with regard to frustulum or mixt: "Though granting to each one what is necessary according to places and circumstances, the frustulum should not become a mixt, nor the mixt a full meal. The *Usages* specify that a soup or some bread with a beverage may be given as mixt."[320] English and Irish houses have {a} larger mixt. One American house had cereal. Our "relief" at mixt {is} okay in summer heat—not just to celebrate a feast day. 1922, #12[321] says all wash hands before mixt and collation as at other meals. Dinner is at 11:30 (not 11) (General Chapter, 1955[322]). Supper {is} "in the evening."[323] Supper and collation are now always at 5:15. "At supper two portions are served, one of which may be cheese" (*Usages*, 373[324]).

XII. *The Measure of Food*:[325]

117: "All shall take their meals at the common table."[326] {Note the} importance of eating in common at the same time. {It

---

319. *Regulations*, 178 (n. 375).

320. Text reads: ". . . beverage can be . . ."

321. "All agree that before taking the mixt or collation, we wash our hands at the fountain near the refectory as before the principal meal."

322. 1955, #2.

323. *"ad seram"* (*Constitutiones*, 23); *Constitutions*, 29.

324. *Regulations*, 178.

325. Nn. 117–21 (*Constitutiones*, 23; *Constitutions*, 29).

326. *"Omnes in communi mensa . . . vescantur"* (*Constitutiones*, 23); *Constitutions*, 29.

is} an expression of common life—sharing the fruits of our labor together—{an} expression of unity and peace in the community. This makes eating together a supernatural act, blessed by special prayers and graces. Christ is in the midst of us in the refectory, as everywhere else. {There} should be an atmosphere of peace, recollection, decency, modesty, joy, {a} family spirit. The refectory should not become merely a place of clatter and tension in which the assembled victims develop ulcers.

118: Always, except for certain special fasts in Lent, we get two portions at dinner, that is to say two cooked portions. It is not specified that one must be soup, but this is normal and usual. {The} *Usages* say: "if soup is given it counts as one portion" (373).[327] On days that are not fasts of the Church and Fridays, we may also add salad and/or dessert. It does not say whether this should be limited to just fruit without salad, {if} one can have both fruit *and* salad, or both salad and some cooked dessert which presumably does not count as a cooked portion (v.g., jello). Ice cream is perfectly permissible, but should, it seems, be reserved for special occasions.

119: Restrictions are however imposed at supper: two portions *only*. Here milk can count as one portion and cheese as another. Cheese rates as a cooked portion; hence it would not normally be right to give a cooked portion and cheese, because only one cooked portion is supposed to be given at supper. Exceptions can of course arise.

120: A "sufficient quantity"[328] of bread shall be given; where no measure is prescribed you can eat all the bread you need. This applies more to Europe where people are accustomed to eat large quantities of bread. In America most monks leave a part of their bread even at mixt. But you should eat it if you can. Do not feel obliged to leave anything, or leave it out of human respect. Wine, cider or beer are given in most houses of the Order—not in America,

---

327. *Regulations*, 178, which reads: ". . . counts as one."
328. "*sufficiens quantitas*" (*Constitutiones*, 23); *Constitutions*, 29.

but they could be; and sometimes {they} are served on feast days, but not here today.

121: {The} measure of collation—see above.

XIII. *Of Sleep*: [329]

122: All shall sleep in a common dormitory, including the abbot, "those only excepted who, by reason of infirmities or employments . . ."[330] *Infirmities* {refers to} snorers especially; loud talkers in their sleep; one or two who cannot get to sleep in {a} common dorm at all (this however would be {a} sign of lack of vocation in a novice); the sick in the infirmary. *Employments* {include} gatekeeper, infirmarian, guest department; {the} furnace man, {who} sometimes sleeps in the tailor shop in winter; brothers concerned with livestock, etc. It would however be a very bad principle for a brother to sleep outside the enclosure. This all depends on the judgement of the abbot.

123: Dormitory cells—{their} purpose {incorporates} "modesty and decorum."[331] Note the black Benedictines, students and novices, have a common dormitory *without* partitions; the priests have rooms. There is nothing to indicate that our cells should not have walls reaching completely up to the ceiling. The only prescription is that they should be "not completely closed in front"[332]—that is to say, shut off only by a curtain. In many monasteries the partitions are high, with no wall at all in front, only a curtain. This last point is more in accordance with the *Usages*.[333]

---

329. Nn. 122–26 (*Constitutiones*, 23–24; Constitutions, 29–30).

330. "*illis tantum exceptis quos infirmitatis causa vel ratione officiorum suorum*" (*Constitutiones*, 23); Constitutions, 29, which reads: ". . . of their infirmities or of their employments . . ."

331. "*ob majorem modestiam et vitae honestatem*" (*Constitutiones*, 23); Constitutions, 30.

332. "*nec omnino ex anteriori parte occlusum*" (*Constitutiones*, 23); Constitutions, 30, which reads: "which shall not be entirely closed in front."

333. *Regulations*, 146 (n. 295).

124: The couch {has a} straw mattress; {there is} no mention of planks here, but it is understood (cf. *Usages*, 295[334]). Blankets {are allowed} "according to need."[335] {The} *Usages* adds:[336] no other furniture but {a} holy water stoup, {a} crucifix and two pictures.

125: Sleeping in the habit: *Usages*, 296 {reads}: "We sleep in the regular habit, including the cowl, unless the Superior dispense therefrom on account of the heat, or infirmities; we take off our shoes. The novices always remove their cloaks, and the oblates their capes."[337] The superior may allow a night cowl and a night scapular. Permission is required to go without any part of the habit in time of sleep. It is quite usual to go without socks, but even this requires permission. In this house, and others with similar climate conditions, {the} General Chapter allows notable changes in the clothing worn during sleep: (a) we may have a special night robe and sleep in that alone without underwear; (b) or we may sleep in shirt and drawers, without {the} robe. This permission goes into effect each year when the superior announces it, and ceases on his announcement that the time is over. Outside these times, if individuals need to use the dispensation further, they must get permission personally for their own needs. These should be real and serious, but inability to sleep constitutes a serious enough need. The purpose of this relaxation is to make sure that the religious get their sleep. Hence it is not really a mitigation but an adaptation. {It is} an adaptation because the *Rule* allows seven hours sleep,[338] and in some places {a} change of clothing may be necessary for the religious to get the sleep allowed by the *Rule*. Mitigation would go much further—would make the sleep much more comfortable and long, would go beyond the purposes of the *Rule* in providing comforts not strictly

---

334. *Regulations*, 146.
335. "*juxta necessitatem*" (*Constitutiones*, 24); *Constitutions*, 30.
336. *Regulations*, 146.
337. *Regulations*, 146, which reads: ". . . in our regular . . ."
338. See *Rule*, c. 8 (McCann, 48/49).

necessary. Note {that} the *Usages* assume [339] that heat is an ordinary and reasonable cause for dispensing from some articles of clothing in the dormitory or elsewhere.

126: {The} time of sleep {was} changed by the General Chapter of 1955. We always retire at seven; we always rise at two-fifteen or two o'clock (two when the night office is sung, with or without responsories). {As to} "the meridian after dinner,"[340] a half-hour meridian is permitted after dinner in some houses. In others, according to the discretion of the abbot, the old practice of going to bed at eight in summer and taking an hour's meridienne still continues—it is up to the local abbot.

XIV. *The Regular Habit*:[341]

127: The religious habit, properly so-called, consists of robe, scapular, cincture and cowl. These are the articles blessed in chapter.

128: Everything above must be white wool ({a} leather cincture of course), except the scapular, which is black. There is a pattern approved by the General Chapter and which must be followed by all houses. Particularly, our cowl is different from that of the Common Observance, who have their hood separate. *Scapular*—our scapular has all the privileges of the scapular of Mount Carmel, the Immaculate Conception, the Seven Sorrows, the Most Holy Trinity, the Passion (see General Chapters, 1909, #6 [342] and 1910, #1 [343]). Hence we gain all the indulgences attached to these scapulars without having to be received or inscribed. 1930, n. 4 adds that the scapulars of *oblates* have the privileges of

---

339. *Regulations*, 146.

340. "*post prandium meridianas*" (*Constitutiones*, 24); *Constitutions*, 30.

341. Nn. 127–30 (*Constitutiones*, 24; *Constitutions*, 30).

342. This statute specifies that the first two privileges have been given by Pontifical Rescripts, and that the Order seeks to receive the same for the other three.

343. This statute actually says that the Order was not able to obtain from the Sacred Congregation of Rites indulgences attached to the scapulars of the Passion, the Seven Sorrows or the Holy Trinity.

the scapulars of Mount Carmel and the Immaculate Conception; they must be "regularly imposed."[344]

129: {We have} "shoes such as are worn in the country where we live."[345]

130: {The} monastic crown {is} renewed once a month.

XV. *The Sick*:[346] the attitude taken toward the sick, the care given to them and the charity shown to them are of the greatest importance in the monastic life. If a community takes a harsh and indifferent attitude towards its suffering members, it is a sign of a bad spirit. We must remember that the sick and the weak are perhaps not always able to measure up to the standards we set for them. We do not know what they are going through, and we do not know if perhaps we would be far worse off in their situation. Remember—the sick are very often those who have reached the end of their course. They are completing their gift of themselves to God, and are at a crucial point in their lives: (a) help them by charity not to lose their morale; (b) support them—give *aid* for their spiritual life; their sickness is their sacrifice—our penances will make up for what they cannot do; (c) {do} not forget and reject them! All should read the beautiful letter written by our Most Reverend General on the sick (June 12, 1953).

131: There shall be a common infirmary, where the sick shall have separate cells—not just a dormitory, but rooms, "cells entirely separated from one another."[347] Above all the infirmary must have a chapel where the sick can hear Mass and receive communion. It does not say that the Blessed Sacrament must be reserved there; this is a privilege which most houses enjoy however.

---

344. I.e., according to the original text of the rescript of 1874 and canon 50 of the Code of Canon Law (*Codex Iuris Canonici*, 10–11).
345. "*Calceis utimur secundum consuetudinem locorum*" (*Constitutiones*, 24); *Constitutions*, 30, which reads: ". . . are commonly worn . . ."
346. Nn. 131–36 (*Constitutiones*, 24; *Constitutions*, 30–31).
347. "*cellae omnino separatae*" (*Constitutiones*, 25); *Constitutions*, 30–31.

132: Cleanliness should be "perfect"[348]—all suitable furniture and utensils. The infirmary does not have to have all the equipment and gadgets of a modern hospital. Cleanliness is very important, both for the bodily and {the} spiritual health of the patients. Their "needs and comfort"[349] shall be provided for. Remember that most really sick people can hardly be made comfortable at all. It is all very well for monks in perfect health to demand absolute poverty in the equipment of the infirmary, but they should consider the weakness of the sick. However, the sick are also *monks*. We should not expect everything and anything that would be given to secular patients.

133: Use of flesh meat {is} permitted to the "sick and those who are very weak."[350]

134: The sick shall have a straw couch, "only softer";[351] and in special cases a woolen mattress is allowed.

135: The infirmarian should be:

a) God-fearing—that is, have a high sense of responsibility and a true charity for the sick, considering their needs more than his own comfort and opinions. He *serves the sick*—{he is} not just the head of a little community which he "rules."

b) experienced—not necessarily a doctor or a trained nurse, but at least with some experience of first aid, etc.

c) prudent—to understand and carry out doctor's orders; he will work with the doctor. This prudence also implies a certain initiative and resourcefulness when accidents arise—sometimes there are very serious accidents at work in a Trappist monastery.

136: {The} abbot shall often visit the sick. He shall see that they suffer no neglect in their sickness. This means not only physical but spiritual. The sick should be cared for in every way, so

---

348. "*nitida*" ("shining") (*Constitutiones*, 25); *Constitutions*, 31.
349. "*commoditates necessitatesque*" (*Constitutiones*, 25); *Constitutions*, 31.
350. "*infirmis omninoque debilibus*" (*Constitutiones*, 25); *Constitutions*, 31.
351. "*sed leniorem*" (*Constitutiones*, 25); *Constitutions*, 31, which reads: "but softer."

that their burden may be lightened and they may continue as far as possible a normal spiritual life. They should not be parked in the infirmary and forgotten. Especially the abbot is held gravely responsible to see that the sick receive the last sacraments and are assisted by a priest in their last hours.

XVI. *Enclosure*:[352] this is another very important chapter of the *Constitutions*. For us it is one of the most essential, for we are a contemplative and monastic order, and for us separation from the world is even more strict and more vital than it is in other religious orders. In *Sponsa Christi*[353] Pius XII remarked severely that if contemplative religious do not live up to the obligations of their state (separation from the world, prayer, etc.), there is no longer any reason why they should enjoy its privileges. A "contemplative" monk who misuses the leisure which the Church gives him for contemplation, and channels it to his own amusement and diversion, especially in constant visits, letter-writing, and concern with secular affairs, to the point of neglecting his *lectio* and the rest of the interior life (*a fortiori* the office!)—such a one is not fulfilling his obligations and has no right to his privileges. He ought to be spending his time in a useful apostolate, rather than fooling himself with his own projects, dreamed up to keep him amused and diverted. This goes for those who through their own fault become so engaged in monastic business ventures that they spend an unnecessary amount of time outside with seculars. They have no longer any right to feel that they are fulfilling a more worthy function in the Church than the members of the "active orders."

What is the enclosure? *Materially*, it is that space immediately surrounding and including a religious house and which is clearly

---

352. Nn. 137–39 (*Constitutiones*, 25–26; *Constitutions*, 31–32).
353. "If the canonical contemplative life under strict regular discipline cannot be habitually observed, the monastic character is not to be conferred, nor, if it is already conferred, to be retained" (Pope Pius XII, *Apostolic Constitution "Sponsa Christi"* [Derby, NY: Daughters of St. Paul, Apostolate of the Press, 1955], 41).

designated as set aside for the exclusive use of the religious. *Formally*, it is the law which obliges the religious not to leave these premises without permission. *Active* {enclosure is} where the religious can go without special permission (v.g., St. Ann's[354]). *Passive* {enclosure is} strictly protected by law and {the} penalty of excommunication.

137: The necessity of permission to go outside the enclosure at any time {is explicit}. {The} STATUTE ON ENCLOSURE (General Chapter, 1927, n. 1) must be read once a year in chapter:

1. All stealthy going out at night is always a mortal sin.

2. Legitimate permission to go out during {the} day ends at night. One who stays overtime without permission commits a mortal sin.

3. Going out during the day without permission is at least a venial sin.

4. In some circumstances, to be determined by {the} local superior, going out even during the day may be a mortal sin, if done without permission. No such case exists here. But there is a strict prohibition against entering the *Blue Jay Inn*[355] when one's relatives are here (*a fortiori* at other times). The question of vehicles, machines, etc., which can hardly be used except with the assumption that one leaves the enclosure, may now be taken up, although perhaps it belongs under the heading of travel. In former days the use of automobiles was forbidden to us. In 1920, {#10},[356] autos were prohibited as contrary to simplicity and to the spirit of the enclosure. Official recognition of the automobile and the bicycle by the OCSO dates back to 1946, n. 14. The statute

---

354. The old tool shed which served as a "hermitage" for Merton in the 1950s (see *Search for Solitude*, 14, 27, 29–41, 64, 181; Thomas Merton, *The Road to Joy: Letters to New and Old Friends*, ed. Robert E. Daggy [New York: Farrar, Straus, Giroux, 1989], 25; *Witness to Freedom*, 184).

355. A roadhouse, which later burnt down, located just south of the monastery property.

356. Typescript reads: "#9".

Constitutions of the Order of Cistercians of the Strict Observance 135

reads: "The General Chapter authorizes the possession and use of automobiles and bicycles. However the possession of luxurious autos is to be avoided." In Europe, generally conceded would be the use of an MG, a Citroën, a *Volkswagen*. A jeep is certainly not a luxurious auto. {A} Ford, Chevy, etc., though from a certain viewpoint luxurious, are relatively out of that category, as anyone of moderate means may own one. Cadillacs, Packards etc. seem definitely to be excluded by this statute and the spirit of the Order. It would certainly be a scandal for monks supposed to be poor to possess and maintain a car used distinctively by the rich. The thing may be a gift, but that is not the point.

Other points that come under this heading of enclosure: (1) *newspaper reporters*: in general, we should be very suspicious of reporters and allow them to look into our private affairs only with very great reserves. Obviously if an abbot dies, or a new abbot is elected, it is right that the papers be allowed to make the fact known. But the General Chapter says (1951, n. 5): "The General Chapter warns our communities against the indiscretion of newspaper reporters and photographers." *Indiscretion*: in modern America, due to the abuse of {the} privilege of freedom of the press, etc., and the tabloid or yellow press, papers think they have a right to know and print anything. They will try to get all they desire and when they have it they will try to print it. The press fosters a most unhealthy spirit of prying into the privacy of others for no good reason—as if knowledge of things that in the past were regarded {as} strictly private was some kind of advantage. This is a queer trait in the psychology of our time which is definitely morbid and pathological. It is not that the papers want to make unfriendly suggestions about the nature of monastic life. Trappists are regarded as good copy, to some extent—copy for the back pages where one also finds features about the zoo, child prodigies, circus freaks and other characters. *The point is, we must try to become dimly aware of the fact that this kind of publicity does us no good. We should not desire it and we should not encourage it.* The desire of *publicity* of *any* kind is extremely dangerous and can easily ruin the monastic spirit because ours is *a hidden life*. Publicity is a curse for a monk. *Photographers*: no recognizable picture of a living Trappist monk or brother is allowed to be published (abbots are an exception to this). 1905, n. 3 {notes}: "In certain of our houses there is a real abuse in regard to picture postcards, in which one can make out perfectly recognizable religious. Such as have been printed may be disposed of; others may not be printed in the future."[357] 1938, n. 14 confirms this and adds: "It extends this prohibition to all pamphlets edited in our monasteries. [In such pamphlets] not only the text but also the illustrations are subject to the approval of the [censors]." The warning against indiscretion of photographers in 1951 (above) doubtless includes a *warning against letting them take recognizable pictures which will then be printed in magazines and newspapers*. The only way in which we can control what appears in such publications is to make it impossible for them to get pictures of us. Once they get them they will use them without consulting us, although some magazines are obliging enough if one makes representations to them (however, {there was} trouble with *Paris Match* in 1954). Note: Reverend Father has ordered that even our relatives cannot take pictures of novices; pictures may be taken after profession. *Radios*, etc.: in 1938, n. 14, the General Chapter also forbade the "use of the radio and moving pictures."[358] This was the way the text was translated and read here. In 1951, n. 6, however, we read: "The General Chapter retains the prohibition of {1938} which forbids the having of *radio stations*."[359] These statutes will be clarified by inquiry to the definitors. Meanwhile, we can say the following:

1. It appears that broadcasts should not emanate from Cistercian monasteries, including the broadcasts of our chant. Re-

---

357. Text reads: "In certain of . . . . religious. The General Chapter allows those that have already been printed to be disposed of but it forbids others being printed in the future."
358. Text reads: ". . . radio as well as moving pictures."
359. Text erroneously reads: "1928".

cords, however, are permitted, and once recorded they can be broadcast. Is there then no difference? Yes, there is still a great psychological difference from the point of view of the monks, who would realize that in singing the Mass of a certain feast they were "going on the air." This kind of psychology is entirely incompatible with {the} Cistercian spirit of enclosure. It would be ridiculous to be hidden within the enclosure and present in everybody's living room by radio, or worse still, TV.

2. It appears that movies should not be *taken* in Cistercian monasteries. One would suppose that mere shots of the buildings would be tolerated. Obviously, one's friends can take home-movies here. But movies to be distributed commercially should not be taken, showing the community. This at least is our opinion. Movies are sometimes *shown* in Trappist monasteries (v.g., *Collectanea*, July 1956[360]—in a British monastery).

3. It also seems quite obviously foreign to our spirit of enclosure to allow radio programs, or worse still, TV programs, however holy and sublime, to be heard or watched inside a Cistercian monastery. There is no question that radio, TV and the movies would quickly reduce our enclosure to a mere ridiculous formality.

4. How about phonograph records?

    a) Recordings have been made of the chant at Cîteaux and at Gethsemani. There are of course many disadvantages. During the time of recording it brings the world and its gadgets and its confusion into the cloister. It produces a spirit of upheaval and worldliness in those who have to perform. However it may be said that the good that is done may excuse these aberrations. Prudence is required!!

---

360. There is no reference to such an event in the issue of the Order's French-language magazine, *Collectanea Cisterciensia*, for this date; the information had perhaps been included in an earlier issue among the "chroniques" of news from various monasteries (which Merton himself wrote for Gethsemani from 1951 through 1955) that had been included regularly in the magazine in previous years but were discontinued in 1956.

b) Can monks listen to records? Obviously records of Gregorian chant and other good Church music are permissible and laudable; they can do much to form the taste of the monks and thus help their spiritual life indirectly. Records should not be played in the refectory instead of spiritual reading—or only in very exceptional cases. There is so far no legislation on these points.

Conclusion of n. 137: no one may leave the enclosure without permission *even in order to visit a higher superior* (cf. General Chapter, 1907, #6[361]). Although one has the right to go to confession to any priest in the diocese with faculties, one does not have the right to leave the enclosure without permission to reach that priest; he must be within the enclosure.

N. 138: *Violation of the enclosure by women*: there are two aspects of enclosure: *active*, {which} prohibits the egress of religious, {and} *passive*, {which} forbids the ingress of externs, especially of {the} opposite sex. {In accordance with} canon 597, n. 1,[362] we are an order with solemn vows; hence our enclosure is *papal*, and this means in all our *regularly erected houses* the entrance of women of whatever age, kind or condition, and under whatever pretext, is forbidden under pain of excommunication, simply reserved to {the} Holy See (canon 2342, n. 2[363]). *The excommunication does not reach girls under twelve* (Schaefer, 1160[364]). Anyone who admits, invites or otherwise induces them to enter also incurs excommunication. {This is an} *extremely strict obligation*. Let us look closely at canon 2342, n. 2: excommunication simply reserved to {the} Holy See is incurred *ipso facto* by (a) women who violate the cloister of religious men; (b) superiors and others, whoever they may be, who introduce or admit women of no matter what age; (c) beyond the sentence of excommunication, religious who admit women are also to be *deprived of office*, if they have one, and of

---

361. See above, page 88, n. 180.
362. *Codex Iuris Canonici*, 173.
363. *Codex Iuris Canonici*, 638.
364. Schaefer, 689.

active and passive voice. Comments: (a) all females who violate enclosure knowingly commit mortal sin (if they are of {the} age of reason; {those} under seven {are} supposed not to incur guilt); *impuberes*, girls under twelve, do not *incur excommunication* for entering enclosure (canon 2230[365]) but can commit mortal sin by doing so; unbaptized women are excused from the penalty of excommunication; (b) *introducentes vel admittentes*:[366] to introduce means to invite, to open the door and {to be} cooperating in the induction of {a} forbidden person; to admit is to fail to prohibit, not to close the entrance if it can easily be done. Whoever they may be, even laypersons employed by the monastery, are not allowed to admit women. *Of no matter what age*: whereas girls under twelve do not incur excommunication for violation of enclosure, men who introduce them do incur excommunication. Note: to introduce a boy under twelve into an enclosure of nuns does not involve excommunication; the wording of the law is different in their case; (c) deprived of office—*by a sentence* of their superior, *not ipso facto*. *Wives of heads of state* {are a separate matter}. Commenting on this, Fr. Augustine, OSB,[367] one of the outstanding commentators in {the} USA, declares that in America there are no rulers who can be considered supreme heads of state in the sense implied by the Code. Since Dom Edmond,[368] at Gethsemani the governor has been considered a "supreme head of the state"[369] and his wife, with suite, has been admitted to the enclosure. Though this is evidently not the mind of the legislator for us, the practice has been started and could not be stopped without serious difficulty, perhaps. Fortunately it does not

---

365. *Codex Iuris Canonici*, 603–604.

366. "bringing in or allowing in" (*Codex Iuris Canonici*, 638).

367. Charles Augustine [Bachofen], OSB, *A Commentary on the New Code of Canon Law*, 3rd ed., 8 vols. (St. Louis: B. Herder, 1931), 8.372.

368. Dom Edmond Obrecht, fourth Abbot of Gethsemani (1898–1935).

369. Canon 598, #2: "*qui supremum actu tenent principatum*" (*Codex Iuris Canonici*, 174).

occur too often. ({The} last time {was in} 1949 {at the} centenary celebration.[370])

139: *The dedication of a church*: {there is} one great exception to the law of enclosure. When a church is dedicated, for nine days women can visit the church, cloisters, chapter room and refectory in {the} absence of {the} community. {They} cannot enter any other places in {the} enclosure, and must never be in the enclosure after nightfall. Why does the Church allow this? Because when a church is dedicated the sacred rites concern the whole Mystical Body, and therefore all should be able to enter the church and see it, at least some time.

The meaning of the legislation on enclosure {is} to protect the monks against undue disturbance and distraction from outsiders, to allow them to live their life of prayer and solitude which are with us serious obligations. Hence frequent visits in the parlor etc. are as much a violation of enclosure as frequent journeys outside and should not be tolerated unless there is a sufficiently grave reason. A monk should never allow himself to envy those who have to go out or have much to do with outsiders. Still less should anyone, by suggestions and hints or other means, try to procure for himself a job in which he will have contact with visitors or other seculars.

Chapter XVII: JOURNEYS:[371]

140: If one is to go on a journey, there is required:

a) a grave reason *or* necessary business of the house: *necessary business of the house*—this is left rather broad, and remains to be judged ordinarily by the local superior. He is the one who must take responsibility and it is usually he personally who sends anyone out on business.

b) General Chapter, 1906, n. 12 explains what is meant by "very serious reasons." This does *not* include: first Mass; family

---

370. For a description of the Gethsemani centenary celebration (June 1, 1949), see *Entering the Silence*, 320–21.

371. Nn. 140–43 (*Constitutiones*, 26; *Constitutions*, 32).

affairs; sickness or death of a near relative—but it adds: "except in a particular case which is judged worthy of exception." Thus again the local superior *can*, if he sees fit, permit a journey for one of the above reasons. It is never done here. General Chapter, 1907, n. 6 {says}: a religious *may not go to Rome* without the permission of the Abbot General. "The religious who contravenes this prohibition will be considered a fugitive and consequently will incur excommunication *ipso facto*."[372] General Chapter, 1927, n. 2 again begs superiors not to permit journeys except for "most grave reasons." General Chapter, 1947[373] repeats {the} statute of 1906, n. 12, and urges observance of it. General Chapter, 1947, n. 4 says that when a *nun* goes out she must be accompanied by an extern sister, and permission to go out does not include permission to visit friends or go into stores, etc. Apparently with monks the prohibition is not literally so strict, but one should interpret the law in the light of the will of the superior. General Chapter, 1910, n. 3 {reads}: "In order to suppress {the} gyrovague spirit of some religious, we declare that superiors ought not to allow change of houses except for reasons of exceptional gravity, and of these they shall be the sole judges,"[374] and recalls {the} statute of 1906, n. 12—as above. General Chapter, 1920, n. 29 {reads}: "There must be most grave circumstances to authorize anyone of the Order to take a cure at a health resort."[375] This seems quite exceptional—European health resorts (v.g., Vichy, Nice, Trouville, Interlaken, etc.) are, some more, some less, places of vacation and pleasure, and would not seem to be appropriate places for a Cistercian monk to take a cure. However the General Chapter admits that in grave illnesses when such a cure has been prescribed by a doctor, the journey and cure may be permitted.

---

372. Text reads: ". . . considered as a . . . *a jure ipso facto*."

373. 1947, #1.

374. Text reads: ". . . suppress the gyrovague . . . allow the change . . . of an exceptional . . ."

375. Text reads: ". . . of our Order to take a course at any . . ."

141: {The} abbot should give the one going on a journey letters or {a} recommendation or an "obedience"—"stating the place to which he is sent, the length of his sojourn and the time of his return."[376]

142: (In Europe) the regular habit is worn while travelling, with a black cloak over it. In {the} USA this is not customary; we wear {a} roman collar etc., if clerics, {a} black suit if not.

143: Ordinarily, flesh meat is not to be eaten on a journey. It can be eaten (a) with permission of {the} superior—his *own* superior; (b) in case of necessity; (c) {on a} sea (or air) voyage.

PART III—ENTRANCE TO THE ORDER

Having studied the organization of the Order and its observances we now turn to the final section, on the admission of new members, on profession, dismissal of members and the readmission of those who may have left.

Chapter 1: *The Admission of Postulants*:[377]

144: "The greatest care shall be taken in the admission of novices."[378] Here we consider the mystery of our vocation from a canonical point of view, rather than from the viewpoint of spirituality. It may seem cold and heartless, but this aspect of the question is vitally important. Vocation is an expression of the inner life of the Church, and consequently it belongs to the Church herself to say whether or not an individual belongs in this or that state of life. Unless we allow ourselves to be guided by her, the Order cannot remain for long in a healthy state.

---

376. "*litteras commendatitiae, in quibus determinetur locus ad quem mittitur, et praefigatur tempus ac terminus itineris et reversionis*" (*Constitutiones*, 26); *Constitutions*, 32.

377. Nn. 144–50 (*Constitutiones*, 27–29; *Constitutions*, 33–36).

378. "*In admittendis novitiis summa diligentia exhibeatur*" (*Constitutiones*, 27); *Constitutions*, 33.

Theologians have a familiar axiom: *facilis admissio est pessima candidatorum selectio.*[379] The Church has insisted, especially since the Council of Trent, that religious vocations be carefully tested, and that candidates for the religious life receive a thorough and intensive formation. These two points cannot be neglected, and in either case the obligation is extremely serious. It is useless to try to form a candidate who cannot receive the desired form. Hence it is first of all necessary to discover whether the postulant has the necessary aptitudes and the right intention, before he is even admitted to the monastery. Our higher superiors insist strongly on the obligation to *select our vocations* even before they enter the monastery, and not to regard the novitiate itself as a time of selection. As far as possible the vocations should be on a solid basis before the candidate enters the novitiate or even the postulancy. We are therefore obliged as far as we can to find out as much as possible about our postulants and to try to decide the question of their vocation even before they enter. Canon 545, n. 4[380] prescribes that testimonial letters, sent by the bishop, must be based on a diligent investigation, especially of the candidate's regularity, studies, reputation and previous history. The Decree *Quantum Religiones Omnes* (December 1, 1931) says, "Superiors must take the greatest care not to receive subjects too hastily, but to accept only those in whom signs of a *divine vocation* are found."[381] Superiors are bound above all not to make rash declarations that a person "has a vocation," especially when the candidate himself is still in doubt on the point. The candidate

---

379. See Ladislaus ab Immaculata, CP, "*De Vocationum Selectione*": "*Facilis candidatorum admissio est pessima vocationum selectio*" ("Easy admission of candidates is the worst selection process for vocations") (Sacra Congregatio de Religiosis, *Acta et Documenta Congressus Generalis de Statibus Perfectionis: Romae 1950*, 4 vols. [Rome: Pia Società San Paolo, 1952], 2.628).

380. *Codex Iuris Canonici*, 158.

381. "*Superioribus adhibenda erit ut adolescentes, non gregatim, neve festinanter adsciscantur, sed ii soli, in quibus divinae vocationis indicia deprehenduntur*" (quoted in Schaefer, 811 [#1360]).

should be interviewed at the monastery by more than one person, and if possible the superior should get to know his family. It is by no means sufficient to decide a vocation by letter, nor is a flying overnight visit to the monastery enough. Even after careful investigation and favorable consideration of the candidate, it might be advisable to delay his entrance still further in order to test his resolution. In any case it is necessary that no doubtful candidate be admitted to the monastery.

What are the exterior and canonical signs of a religious vocation?

1. Basic requirements (canon 538[382]): the candidate must be a Catholic; not detained by any legal impediment (negative aptitude); moved by the right intention; capable of assuming the obligations imposed by the order (positive aptitude). (For the impediments, see *Constitutions*, n. 145, *infra*[383]). *Right intention* {means} one must desire to attain to the end of the religious life by means of the *Constitutions*, {the} *Rule* and observances of our Order. That means he must understand, in a general way, what the monastic life is, what our idea of perfection is, what means we use to attain it, and to freely choose those means for himself. *Defects in intention* {include a} *lack of knowledge*—a person does not really know what kind of life he is trying to embrace; *lack of objectivity*—he has a wrong or exaggerated idea of himself, and is entering to aggrandize himself or compensate for feelings of inferiority; *lack of positive motives*—{he} enters out of {a} negative desire to escape something he does not like; *lack of supernatural motive*—{he} enters with no positive desire to serve God; *lack of volition*—{the} personal *will* {is} not sufficiently engaged. {With regard to} *capacity (aptitude)*, we have to be able to serve God in our chosen vocation *with everything we have*—with body, heart, mind, will and our whole being. If we are so constituted that one or other of these *cannot* be used, we generally lack aptitude for a given vocation. For instance a choir monk should be expected

---

382. *Codex Iuris Canonici*, 155.
383. *Constitutiones*, 27–28; *Constitutions*, 33–34.

to *sing* and understand the liturgy, etc. {Aptitude includes the} *bodily* (health, voice, strength, stamina); {the} *psychological* (balance, right temperament, solid background); {the} *intellectual* (studies—especially Latin, {an} IQ of 115 or 120); {the} *spiritual* ({an} interior life {that is} at least beginning to deepen, {an} ability to keep the three vows).

2. *Special capacity for our life*: in one entering our Order, we must find not only the general signs of a religious vocation, but more particular signs of a vocation to *our life*:

a) *Special signs of a contemplative vocation* are *required in our life*—{the willingness to live} a life for God alone—{a} desire to seek God above all else (not merely a love for the *concept* of seeking God, but for the reality and the sacrifices this involves, {including} the absence of consolations that belong to the active life); {there must be a} *love of prayer*, especially of the divine office, something more than {the} desire of {the} active life.

b) *Signs of a Benedictine and Cistercian vocation* {include} love of {the} common life, with emphasis on simplicity and strictness and greater solitude, {as well as} love for our special poverty, silence, manual labor, etc. Note the signs given by St. Benedict in the *Rule*[384]—*seeking God*, zeal for {the} *office*, {for} *obedience*, {for} *humiliations*. If we take people who lack these qualities, we will ruin the Order.

3. *A divine vocation*: we must distinguish, with Schaefer (758[385]), between the external signs which give a person a "juridical" vocation. That is to say, when one has negative aptitude (freedom from impediment), is a Catholic, and has also positive aptitude for the life, then humanly speaking one has a vocation—i.e., a *potential* vocation. The *divine vocation is to be judged by other more important signs*, which make it morally certain that one is called by God. These are *right intention* with a *firm will to persevere*, together with the favorable decision of the proper superior—

---

384. *Rule*, c. 58 (McCann, 130/131).
385. Schaefer, 409.

this of course in addition to aptitude, etc. When all things add up to a divine vocation, then clearly the person should enter and do everything he can to persevere. Investigations are for this purpose above all—to discover whether the person is *called by God*. N. 144 concludes: "Those only shall be received who, by their good character, conduct, reputation, condition and education, can contribute to the advantage and credit of the Order."[386] What does this mean? It should not be interpreted as if the postulant entered the Order for the advantage of the Order and not for his own. We do not select our postulants on human considerations alone—taking only young men of noble blood and university education, or those whose parents are in a position to give financial help to the monastery, etc. Such a procedure would be altogether unworthy of a monastery. *Good character* {or} conduct means at least good will, basic humility, the firm intention to lead a good life and seek God, even though there may have been past sins—the postulant who is willing to expiate these and seriously reform his life can be said to have these qualifications. *Reputation* {means} a person who has given grave scandal should not be received without proper measures to show that he has changed his life. This {is} particularly {important} to combat the reputation of the Order as a refuge for criminals, etc. {With regard to} *condition and education*, social rank in itself is of no importance, but a postulant should not come from the underworld (!) without a period of transition; {as for} education, at least secondary education should be completed for the choir, with sufficient Latin and {a} background in the humanities. This lineup can be supplemented from the *Usages*: "It is forbidden to receive persons who are weak-headed, wrong-minded, badly disposed characters, inconstant, eccentric, obstinately scrupulous, or melancholy, no matter what temporal advantages may be hoped for from them" (#2).[387] This bears on another and most important aspect of aptitude—the *psychological* side. The above

---

386. "*qui bonis moribus, vita, fama, conditione et educatione cedere possint ad Ordinis utilitatem et honorem, recipiantur*" (Constitutiones, 27); Constitutions, 33.

387. *Regulations*, 1–2.

list seems to exclude morons, those who are notably immature in their emotions, and schizoid or schizophrenic types especially. All authorities agree that the worst possible mistake that can be made in this field is to admit into the religious life someone who shows *paranoid* tendencies; these are characterized by (a) an *extremely suspicious* nature, amounting sometimes to delusions of persecution, seeing evil everywhere; (b) an *extremely critical* disposition, constant murmuring and fault-finding, with subversive tendencies and resistance to authority; (c) {a} *hostile and withdrawn* {disposition, marked by} cold silence, sometimes giving way to a voluble flow of seemingly brilliant but very obscure and abstruse reasoning, with big words and complex logic which eventually proves to be utterly meaningless; (d) {a} *subjective and self-centered* {perspective, one} extremely prone to judge everything by the way it affects their super-sensitive feelings ("ideas of reference"); (e) {a} *jealous and ambitious* {attitude, with an} extreme avidity to achieve extraordinary brilliancy and fame {and a} hostility and envy towards others who seem to threaten this climb to fame; (f) sometimes {there is an} *extreme authoritarianism*, laying down the law and correcting everyone, but not accepting correction from anyone; (g) sometimes {there is} *excessive and eccentric religiosity*, {a} showy piety. Many of these things are felt by everyone, but in the paranoid they dominate and form his life, and they make him sometimes outwardly noticeable. He may be a real cross in a community, and indeed when paranoia blossoms out, the patient becomes a terrible troublemaker—he can ruin the whole monastery with his weird activities (suspicions, denunciations, even acts of violence). It is quite evident that these types should be excluded at all costs.

Canonical impediments: n. 145 {discusses} negative aptitude for religious life—freedom from impediments. (*Note*: there are other impediments, from natural law, not mentioned here. The *natural law* excludes "*amentes,*" mentally sick persons who do not have the use of their faculties; it also excludes psychotics. Infants and minors are prohibited by the natural law from entering religion without the consent of their parents up to the age of fifteen, though they can *validly* do so [not licitly]; after fifteen, a minor can validly and licitly enter religion without {the} consent of his parents, even though the civil law still subjects him to them [Schaeffer, 757[388]]. Natural law as well as canon law both prevent the entrance of *slaves* [without {the} consent of {their} masters], of those under *infamy*, and those who are liable to punishment for a crime or other damage.) *Canon law* {specifies}:[389]

1. *Invalidating* {*impediments*}: THE NOVITIATE IS *INVALID* in the case of the following, if they receive the habit without dispensation from the Holy See:

Those who have joined a non-Catholic sect (i.e., after having first been Catholic). This affects a *Catholic* who has *externally* and publically affiliated himself with some sect. Formal signing up seems to be required (*adscriptio*). Baptism, with the Baptists, is enough! Those who have joined an atheistic organization are also under this prohibition (Commission for Interpretation of {the} Code—response: 30 July 1934[390]). It does *not* affect converts from a non-Catholic sect, or Catholics who were baptized by parents but (in good faith) educated out of the Church in a sect, or Catholics who have joined the Masons (Schaefer, 781[391]).

Those under age (fifteen years completed) (canon 555, n. 1[392]): however, in orders where there are two years' novitiate, one of which only is canonical, a postulant can enter at fourteen and finish one year of novitiate, then take his canonical year after reaching the age of fifteen (Schaefer, 784[393]). It hardly seems advisable to do this in our Order, especially since our tradition was always so strong against admitting very young boys (cf. Notes on the *Consuetudines*[394]). However, in order to do this an *indult*

---

388. Schaefer, 408–409.
389. Canon 542, n. 1 (*Codex Iuris Canonici*, 156).
390. See Schaefer, 423 (#780).
391. Schaefer, 424.
392. *Codex Iuris Canonici*, 161 (canon 555.1, n. 1).
393. Schaefer, 426.
394. See above, pages 46–48.

would be required because normally the first year is the canonical year. If one too young is admitted by mistake, the validity of his novitiate can count from the day he reaches the age of fifteen.

Those induced by violence, grave fear or fraud—because the religious state must be embraced freely. *Violence* {refers to} a force, either moral or physical, which cannot be resisted; {it is} reducible in practice to *grave fear* (which may be relatively grave—i.e., not so bad in itself but formidable for a weak person). If inflicted by another person, by threats or browbeating, it invalidates the act; this goes for admission to one or {an} other category (v.g., if one would be willing to enter the monastery, but not as a brother, and is forced to do so). There is therefore no case in which a person can justly be compelled by another to enter religion. Examples of "grave fear"[395] {would be} fear of death, of injury, of great humiliation, of greatly displeasing a person on whom one is somehow dependent or by whom one can be influenced, etc. Grave fear inflicted by {a} subject on {a} superior, or vice versa, both invalidate {the} novitiate. {With regard to} *fraud (dolus),*[396] the fraud can be on either side—that of the ones admitting the candidate or on the part of the candidate himself. Fraud here means any kind of deception that involves deliberate means to enter religion or cause one *to enter religion on a false basis*, for instance if a candidate conceals an impediment which he knows he has. *Excommunication* {may result}: the sin of forcing another *quoquo modo*[397] to enter the novitiate or to take vows is punished by an excommunication (not reserved). This applies to entrance to {the} novitiate, not to postulancy (canon 2352[398]). It is licit to *persuade or induce* someone to enter religion, provided there is no fault in the manner of persuasion, but it would be a fault to persuade someone to enter a less perfect order when it was clear he

---

395. "*metu gravi*" (*Constitutiones*, 27); *Constitutions*, 33.
396. *Constitutiones*, 27; *Constitutions*, 33.
397. "howsoever".
398. *Codex Iuris Canonici*, 642–43.

was called to something higher (cf. Schaefer, 789[399]). Note also {that} it is a sin against justice to induce a person by violence, fear or fraud *not* to enter religious life. Restitution is required in such a case.

Married persons, during the lifetime of the partner: marriage is an impediment even if the partner consents to the other's entering religion. A non-consummated marriage is no impediment and is dissolved by solemn profession, or by dispensation. According to Schaefer, divorced persons may receive a dispensation to enter religion (Schaefer, 791[400]).

Those with religious vows in another institute: those who have been *secularized or dispensed* from vows still need permission of {the} Holy See to enter another novitiate. {A} *transitus* from one institute to another is provided for by law (canon 632ff.[401]). *Novices and postulants* from other institutes are not impeded *per se*, but special permission must be obtained from the Holy See if they were *dismissed* from the novitiate, or dismissed from a seminary or religious college (Decree *Ecclesia Christi*: September 7, 1909[402]). This holds not only for a formal dismissal but for an *equivalent* {to} dismissal ({i.e., if} persuaded to leave by {one's} superiors). Dispensation is also required for someone who left another institute *after the expiration of simple vows*. But profession *in articulo mortis*[403] during the novitiate does not create an impediment since its effect is purely spiritual and not juridical; if the novice recovers, he may enter another novitiate not affected by this impediment (Schaefer, 795[404]). *Note on the admission of subjects from a society without vows*: (1) these societies, though not religious institutes, are subject by the Church to the obligations of religious in certain matters; one of these is the passage to an-

---

399. Schaefer, 430–31.
400. Schaefer, 432.
401. *Codex Iuris Canonici*, 183–84.
402. See Schaefer, 434 (#794).
403. "at the point of death".
404. Schaefer, 435.

other society or religious order; (2) members of these societies are therefore bound by canon 632 (Schaefer, 1663[405]): "*Religiosus nequit ad aliam religionem . . . transire sine auctoritate Apostolicae Sedis*";[406] (3) Canons, 633, 634 and 635[407] also apply (cf. Schaefer, 1648ff.,[408] re: {the} nature of these societies without vows).

Those threatened with punishment for a grave crime of which they have been or can be accused—for obvious reasons: they may be entering to get away from the police, and they may bring discredit upon the order and the religious life. This applies to accusations before civil or ecclesiastical judges, but only affects those who have committed a *grave* crime. It presupposes that the law is legitimate (not an unjust law against the Church, for instance). If the crime is ecclesiastical, it must be *public*; an occult crime is not an invalidating impediment. If a person is *innocent*, then even though he may be accused and brought to trial, his novitiate will be valid.

Bishops, whether residential or titular, even though only designated: the bishop is "married" to his diocese, and is in the "state of perfection" (*exercendae*), while the religious is only in that state where one tends to perfection.[409] Hence for a bishop to become a Trappist is not considered a step up by the Church, but a step down, and would require special permission from Rome (Schaefer, {798}[410]). A resigned bishop can certainly enter religion validly without impediment.

Clerics bound by vow to serve their diocese or the missions: this does not refer to canon 981, n. 1,[411] where there is {a} question of

---

405. Schaefer, 996.

406. "Religious cannot transfer to another religious order without the authorization of the Holy See" (*Codex Iuris Canonici*, 183).

407. *Codex Iuris Canonici*, 184.

408. Schaefer, 988–89.

409. See Schaefer, 437 (#798); the distinction is between the bishop, who is in the state of exercising perfection, and the religious, who is in the state of acquiring perfection ("*status perfectionis acquirendae*").

410. Schaefer, 437; typescript reads: "789".

411. *Codex Iuris Canonici*, 280.

{a} promise to serve the missions as a title for ordination. This promise does not invalidate admission to {the} novitiate. Canon 542, n. 1 [412] and our *Constitutions* [413] are speaking of vows taken by graduates of certain Roman colleges and others (v.g., the College of the Propaganda; {the} German-Hungarian College; {the} North American, Irish, Scotch College, etc.) {who are} bound after ordination for three years, or some other period, to serve in their territory. (N.B. if a seminarian during his studies begins to plan to enter religion he is not bound to manifest it to his bishop unless the latter is paying his expenses—and even here it would be a question of liceity and not of validity. However, that is purely from the point of view of his entrance. *De facto* he would have to beware of sinning against justice.)

Conclusions: *if any one of the above impediments is found after one has begun the novitiate, the novitiate is invalid*. Even if the subject and the superior are in perfectly good faith, it makes no difference—the novitiate is invalid. *Ignorance of the law does not excuse* in this case, because no provision is made for it. Dispensation for any one of these impediments must be sought from the Sacred Congregation of Religious before one can validly begin the novitiate (n.b. *sanatio* [414] {is} possible).

2. ILLICIT {Impediments}—*the following impediments do not affect the validity of the novitiate, but it is illicit to begin the novitiate until they have been dispensed*:

Clerics in major orders, without consulting the bishop—because their departure may mean grave harm for souls, and of this the bishop remains the judge. The impediment affects priests, deacons and subdeacons. The law says: without *consulting* the bishop, and does not demand that the bishop's permission be

---

412. *Codex Iuris Canonici*, 156.

413. *Constitutiones*, 27; *Constitutions*, 33–34.

414. I.e., a "*sanatio in radice*" ("healing at the root"), a papal dispensation that does not require the repetition of one's profession (see Schaefer, 909 [#1527]).

granted. However it would not be advisable in most cases to admit a cleric without permission from his bishop, even though it might be licit. Schaefer says: "In practice it would seem to be *most seldom* proper for the bishop to refuse permission on these grounds alone—the priest will serve souls more effectively in religion" (803[415]). If the bishop opposes the priest's entry into religion, he *can* apply to the Congregation, and the Congregation *may* petition the bishop to allow him to enter religion.

Those with debts which they cannot pay: {the} reason {is that} a work commanded by the natural law takes precedence of a counsel. The debts implied here must be juridical, that is, they must be a matter of contract, or loan, or just restitution—not just a matter of promise. In a word they must fall under strict justice, not charity or liberality. How serious a sum {must be} involved? The impediment no longer exists if the creditor(s) decide to take no action (even though his obligation still exists). A dispensation may be sought if it is absolutely impossible for the person to pay his debts, if the order will not get into a lawsuit on his account, and if the person is likely to lose his soul in the world (Schaefer, 805[416]). If a superior knowingly receives a man with debts, without dispensation, and in bad faith, he is bound to pay the man's debts.

Those who are liable to furnish accounts, or are implicated in other temporal affairs,[417] from which the order may have reason to fear lawsuits or difficulties—for instance, an executor of a will, a manager of a business, etc. As soon as he is freed from his responsibility, the impediment no longer exists.

---

415. "*In praxi rarissime videtur expedire, ut Ordinarius loci deneget ob hanc solam causam Clerico licentiam amplectendi Statum perfectionis. Etenim talis Clericus, postquam factus est Religiosus, solet adhuc efficacius laborare pro salute animarum, quam si remansisset clericus saecularis*" (Schaefer, 440–41).

416. Schaefer, 441–42.

417. "*Reddendae rationi obnoxii aut aliis saecularibus negotiis implicati*" (*Constitutiones*, 28); *Constitutions*, 34.

Sons who are bound to support their parents in grave necessity, and parents whose help is necessary for the maintenance and education of their children.[418] Again the principle is the same as in the case of those with debts. *One cannot undertake to do something more perfect, which is a matter of counsel, while neglecting that which is prescribed by the natural law.* Such "perfection" would be illusory. Read Matthew 15:1-9:[419] it is necessary that in honoring God we do not neglect the honor and love we owe our parents. This is not in conflict with Matthew 10:37 (He that loveth Father or Mother more than me . . .). It is not a question of loving them *more* than God, but of the basic love commanded by God, without which our "love" for God is hypocrisy. *Grave necessity* is less than extreme necessity, which of course constitutes a graver obligation still. Grave necessity means real poverty—a serious lack of {the} necessaries of life periodically, or else a more or less permanent state of indigence. Even *one who has made a vow* to enter religion is not exempted from this duty of the natural law. Furthermore, the necessity can be *relative* to the parents' state of life, and even if the necessity is not absolutely grave, delay in entering religion can be advised. *Parents* means father and mother, grandfather

418. "*Filii qui parentibus . . . in gravi necessitate constitutis, opitulari debent, et parentes quorum opera sit ad liberos alendos vel educandos necessaria*" (*Constitutiones*, 28); *Constitutions*, 34, which reads: "Sons who ought to support their parents . . . who are in grave necessity . . ."

419. "Then came to him from Jerusalem scribes and Pharisees, saying: Why do thy disciples transgress the tradition of the ancients? For they wash not their hands when they eat bread. But he answering, said to them: Why do you also transgress the commandment of God for your tradition? For God said: Honour thy father and mother: And: He that shall curse father or mother, let him die the death. But you say: Whosoever shall say to father or mother, The gift whatsoever proceedeth from me, shall profit thee. And he shall not honour his father or his mother: and you have made void the commandment of God for your tradition. Hypocrites, well hath Isaias prophesied of you, saying: This people honoureth me with their lips: but their heart is far from me. And in vain do they worship me, teaching doctrines and commandments of men."

and grandmother—nothing is said in the Code about brothers and sisters. If they are in extreme necessity, and depend on the candidate, he is obliged by the natural law to take care of them. However, if they depend on him for their education, he is not obliged to remain in the world, but may be counseled to do so. *Dispensation* from the impediment can be given, for instance, if remaining outside places the candidate in an extraordinary danger of sin. {With regard to dispensation} from vows, {the} grave necessity of parents can be a just cause for exclaustration or dispensation from temporary vows. {The} obligation to leave does not exist unless {the} need is extreme, and the order itself should be encouraged to help out.

Parental objections: {this} is no impediment, but sometimes civil law makes it necessary to ask their consent in {the} case of minors. Church law leaves {a} minor free to enter religion without {the} consent of parents. {A} candidate may enter religion if there are other children capable of supporting the parents, or if it is certain that his remaining in the world will not effectively aid the parents, or if some other way of helping them can be arranged—also, as mentioned above, if there is extraordinary danger of sin (cf. Schaefer, 807–809[420]).

Those who would be ordained to the priesthood in the order, but who are barred by an irregularity or other canonical impediment to ordination. {An} *irregularity* {is} a permanent impediment to ordination; {a} *simple impediment* {is} a temporary impediment to ordination. First, let us consider irregularities; there are two kinds of irregularity: *ex defectu*[421] (canon 984[422]) {and} *ex delicto*.[423] Irregularity *ex defectu* {involves the following}: *illegitimate birth* is very common in our time of divorces and broken homes. Note that this impediment *ceases automatically when one makes solemn profession*, and of course

---

420. Schaefer, 443–44.
421. "due to defect" (see Schaefer, 445 [#811]).
422. *Codex Iuris Canonici*, 280–81.
423. "due to wrongdoing" (canon 985 [*Codex Iuris Canonici*, 281–82]; see Schaefer, 446 [#812]).

it ceases when the marriage of the parents is fixed up. It can also cease by rescript, but in practice we do not usually have to go to Rome in cases where this impediment exists. {Also excluded are} those who are *crippled or deformed*, and thus unfit to minister at the altar without scandal, {as well as} *epileptics, psychotics* {and} those who are or have been possessed by the devil; *bigamists* ({who have had} two marriages contracted successively and validly by civil law) {are also in this category}. {Included under the heading} *infamia juris*[424] {are} for instance those who have signed up with a non-Catholic sect (this comes under {the} previous section), {those} who have desecrated the sacred species, or robbed a grave, {or} attacked the Holy Father, {or} fought a duel, or acted as a second in one, bigamists (again), those *convicted by law* for sins against purity with minors (under sixteen), or for rape, incest, etc. The above are infamous *ipso facto*; others require the sentence of an ecclesiastical court—namely religious committing sins of rape, sodomy, etc. as enumerated above. {Also barred are} *judges who have passed {a} sentence of death*, {as well as} those who have exercised the function of *executioner* in inflicting capital punishment. In all these cases the Church is thinking of the public dishonor that would be brought, in such cases, upon the most Holy Sacrifice of the Altar, and it is not a question of interior or hidden sins. The Church does not want the Holy Sacrifice to be associated even by chance in the minds of men with such things as these.

Irregularity ex delicto (canons 985, 986[425]) {includes}: (1) apostates, heretics, schismatics (partly covered by *Constitutions*, {145}, i:1,[426] but goes a little further); (2) {those} who received baptism from a non-Catholic by their own choice, outside {the} case of extreme necessity ({this} does not apply to infant baptism); (3) those who have been married before a civil authority, or who have attempted marriage when in religious vows, or with someone under vows; (4) those who have committed voluntary ho-

---

424. "infamy in law".
425. *Codex Iuris Canonici*, 281–82.
426. *Constitutiones*, 27; *Constitutions*, 33 (text reads: "144").

micide, or have procured an abortion or cooperated in doing so, *effectu secuto*;[427] (5) those who have mutilated themselves or others, or who have attempted suicide; (6) clerics exercising {the} art of medicine forbidden to them, if it results in the death of the patient; (7) those who exercise the functions of holy orders when they are not in orders, or are canonically incapable of doing so. (In all these cases there must be a true *mortal* and *external* sin.)

Simple impediments to orders (i.e., temporary) {include}: (1) children of non-Catholics, as long as these remain out of the Church (this is one of the most common difficulties of those entering our monasteries; it is no longer law that one whose parents *die* in error is impeded); (2) married men, while {the} wife is still alive ({this is} already covered by 145, i:4,[428] above—hence for us this is an *invalidating* impediment); (3) those who exercise some office forbidden to clerics—this would not of course apply practically to anyone entering a Trappist monastery, {since} to do so he would have to leave his job; (4) slaves properly so-called, unless they receive their freedom; (5) those who are bound to military service, until they have fulfilled their obligation; (6) neophytes not yet sufficiently steady in the faith (the ordinary may be the judge of this, says Schaefer [813][429]); (7) those under *infamia facti*[430] as long as this lasts (in the judgement of the ordinary).[431] *Orientals* must receive special permission from the Congregation of the Eastern Church before they can enter a religious institute of ours (canon 542, n. 2[432]). Orientals here means Catholics of the Eastern rite united to the Holy See. {It is} not necessary that they come from the territory where the Oriental rite flourishes—there are churches of the Oriental rite in the US. *However,*

---

427. "with the result having followed" (see Schaefer, 446 [#812]).
428. *Constitutiones*, 27; *Constitutions*, 33.
429. Schaefer, 446.
430. "infamy in fact" (for the distinction between *infamia iuris* and *infamia facti*, see canon 2293 [*Codex Iuris Canonici*, 623]).
431. Canon 987, n. 7 (*Codex Iuris Canonici*, 283); see Schaefer, 446 (#813).
432. *Codex Iuris Canonici*, 157.

when there is {a} question of Orientals who, retaining their own rite, intend to found provinces and houses of the Oriental rite, they can make their novitiate in an order of our rite without dispensation (Pontifical Commission for Interpretation of the Code, 10 November 1925[433]). Finally, Schaefer adds[434] one more impediment which is not included in our *Constitutions*, but which comes under the natural law: *anyone who has done serious injury to another which cannot be repaired except by remaining in the world.* IF ANY OF THE ABOVE IMPEDIMENTS WHICH RENDER THE NOVITIATE ILLICIT IS KEPT HIDDEN OUT OF MOTIVES OF FRAUD BY THE CANDIDATE, THE IMPEDIMENT *IPSO FACTO* BECOMES INVALIDATING (cf. *Constitutions*, 145, i:3[435] above).

Punishments for those who violate these prescriptions of canon 542 regarding impediments {are as follows}:

a) Superiors are to be punished for receiving candidates in violation of canon 542 according to the gravity of the fault. Deprivation of office can be a punishment for this. Canon 2411[436] prescribes this punishment, and also for receiving candidates without testimonial letters, or violating {canon} 571, n. 1[437] regarding the requisites for profession.

b) The punishments are to be inflicted either by the higher superiors or by the Holy See. No punishments are prescribed by the Code for the candidate violating these prescriptions. It is sufficient that his novitiate be invalid or that he take the measures demanded to make it licit.

146: The motives for entering the Order shall be carefully inquired into. We have seen this already. Here emphasis is placed on finding out the intentions of the candidate, what makes him seek this particular form of life, and there is a suggested indica-

---

433. *Acta Apostolicae Sedis* 17 (1925): 583 (see Schaefer, 447 [#815]).
434. Schaefer, 447 (#816).
435. *Constitutiones*, 27; *Constitutions*, 33.
436. *Codex Iuris Canonici*, 659.
437. *Codex Iuris Canonici*, 165.

tion of what a true vocation consists in: "whether they are actuated by a true desire of a higher and more perfect life, and of being able to serve God with greater freedom."[438] Wrong motives are also suggested: inconstancy, "or some merely human or ill-regulated attraction."[439]

147: {The} *period of probation*: three things are required before the postulant can be admitted to the habit in our Order:

a) One-month postulancy (for the choir), prescribed "in secular clothes."[440] Here, when it seems that there may be a long wait for certain papers and that the postulancy will consequently extend longer than a month, we give the oblate's habit, as is done for the brother postulants. Otherwise, the postulant spends a month in his secular clothes.

b) A spiritual retreat of *at least* eight days ({it} can be longer).

c) {One is} admitted to the novitiate by the abbot, with the consultative vote of his council. It is the abbot alone who *admits* the candidate to the novitiate—that is to say, accepts him and decides that he shall receive the habit. This can take place before the habit can legally be given. The novitiate itself only begins with the reception of the habit. (The vote of the council is consultative only.) There is very little prescribed regarding the period of postulancy. It can be spent in various ways, according to the discretion of the superior. It is permitted to give postulants studying Latin a special *horarium*. They can study {while} living in the guest house, or in the novitiate, following all, some or practically none of the novitiate exercises. Many systems have been tried out here. It is at present felt that it is best not to have postulants study Latin here if it can be avoided, and to have the postulants

---

438. "*num zelo melioris frugis ac perfectioris vitae, et ut Deo liberius famulari possint*" (*Constitutiones*, 28); *Constitutions*, 34–35.

439. "*humano aliquo affectu aut inordinato animi*" (*Constitutiones*, 28); *Constitutions*, 35.

440. "*in suo habitu*" (*Constitutiones*, 28); *Constitutions*, 35, which reads: "in their secular dress."

follow as far as possible the ordinary exercises of the community and of the novitiate. Thus their probation can be carried on more effectively.

148: *Testimonial Letters*: three classes of candidates are here considered; each class has its own requirements: laymen, clerics and religious from another institute.

1. *Laymen* must furnish first of all certificates of baptism and confirmation ({along with a} marriage certificate of {his} parents, because of {the} impediment of illegitimate birth—{see} above). In addition, we must get testimonial letters from the ordinary of their place of birth and of any other place in which they have spent more than one morally continuous year after the completion of their fourteenth year. The candidate himself can apply for and bring the certificates of baptism and confirmation, but the superior admitting him must himself seek the testimonial letters from the competent authorities. (If records have perished, v.g., in war, and certificates cannot be obtained, it is sufficient for the candidate to provide one witness to his confirmation or to take an oath that he was confirmed, in {the} presence of the superior: cf. canon 800. [441]) If {a} candidate is not yet confirmed and there is no way of getting him confirmed, he may be admitted in expectation of a future opportunity, *epikeia* [442] being practiced (Schaefer, 824 [443]). The obligation to get testimonial letters is *grave*, and failure to do so can mean deprivation of office for the superior (canon 2411 [444]). The concept of *testimonial letters* {means that} these are documents provided by a competent Church authority, testifying to the candidate's *qualities and juridical aptitude* for admission into religion (cf. canon 545 [445]). *Juridical aptitude* means absence of censure, irregularity or other impediment. *Place of*

---

441. *Codex Iuris Canonici*, 230.
442. A principle allowing for a flexible interpretation that is assumed to respect the intent of a law in situations not explicitly addressed by it.
443. Schaefer, 452.
444. *Codex Iuris Canonici*, 659.
445. *Codex Iuris Canonici*, 158.

origin means the place where his parents had their domicile at the time of his birth. If the parents had no domicile, then it is the place where the child was actually born. If the child was abandoned, then it is the place where he was found. {With regard to the} *morally continuous year* after the fourteenth year, thirty days interruption is sufficient to break moral continuity. Thus if a person is away at school for nine months out of the year for four years, testimonial letters are not asked from the diocese where the school was located, only from that where he had his domicile. If he has been a *vagus*,[446] never remaining for more than a few months in any diocese, no testimonial letters are asked except from the ordinary of his place of origin. Under Pius IX,[447] the legislation was that a man who had been a year in the army had to provide testimonials from the military ordinary, but this is no longer the law.

2. *Seminarians, clerics, religious*: *clerics* provide {a} certificate of ordination and testimonial letters from ordinaries of dioceses in which they have spent more than one morally continuous year *since ordination* (this holds {as well} for those in minor orders). *Seminarians* or novices from other orders provide letters from the rector or the religious superior of the last institute where they have been; this is *in addition to the testimonial letters of the bishops*, as in 1 above. {For} *religious under vows*, it is sufficient that the major superior of their institute give his approval and testimony (when they transfer with an apostolic indult). Prümmer[448] holds, however, that if they have been out of religion for a year, in passing over, a new testimonial letter is required from the ordinary under whom they spent that year (cf. Schaefer, 830[449]).

---

446. "a wanderer" (see Schaefer, 453 [#825]).
447. Decree of November 5, 1852 (see Schaefer, 453–54 [#825]).
448. Dominicus M. Prümmer, OP, *Manuale Iuris Canonici*, 5th ed. (Freiburg: Herder, 1927) 275 (q. 207), cited in Schaefer, 458, which reads: "271".
449. Schaefer, 458.

Chapter 2: THE NOVITIATE:[450]

151: *The novitiate begins* with the reception of the habit, and this cannot be done except in a house of our Order, by a member of the Order (ordinarily the superior, who accepts the novice for his own house, or someone delegated by him). {The terminology used is} "receive or bless":[451] {the} distinction {is that} reception means formal acceptation to become a novice; bless means to give the novice habit in {a} public ceremony. It is possible that "receive" may also mean to give the habit privately. A superior may accept an aspirant as a *postulant* outside a house of the Order, but definitively to receive him as a novice cannot be done outside a Trappist monastery. The implication is that one cannot definitively accept one for the novitiate who has not and is not undergoing the probation required by law in a monastery of the Order. Note that the vote of the private council is required for the novice to be received. Actual reception of the habit is not required by common law for the *validity* of the novitiate (Schaefer, 869[452]). In practice, no one begins the novitiate in our Order except by reception of the habit (however special conditions—wartime and persecution—might make things different). Giving the habit before the month of postulancy is over is illicit, but does not invalidate the novitiate. If a novitiate is begun with an invalidating impediment, then the novitiate begins when the impediment is removed.

152: The habit of the novices.[453]

153: The novices have the same food as the monks, except that those under twenty-one do not fast. They observe the same *horarium*. We allow the postulants a period of adjustment in which they sleep late. Relief (indulgence) is given to novices for

---

450. Nn. 151–58 (*Constitutiones*, 29–30; *Constitutions*, 36–37).
451. "*recipere aut benedicere*" (*Constitutiones*, 29); *Constitutions*, 36.
452. Schaefer, 485.
453. The habit consists of robe, scapular, girdle and cloak, all (except the scapular) of white wool (*Constitutiones*, 29; *Constitutions*, 36).

the same reason as it is given to the monks—in case of special need. Novices do not get the indulgence merely because they are novices (except in the first month of postulancy and perhaps a little after that). It is desirable that the novices should learn to live the life just as it is lived by the professed, and it is above all beneficial to them to keep the whole rule exactly. The novitiate, a period of formation, demands by its very nature that the novice test his strength and capacity to live the life just as it is lived by the community. Inability to keep the rule would be a sign of lack of aptitude. However, if the father master or abbot in a particular case feels that a temporary alleviation is necessary, the novice should accept it, in a spirit of docility and abandonment, and leave the judgement in this matter to his superiors.

154: In the refectory, church and elsewhere, they take their rank just like the professed. *Usages*, n. 14 [454] explains this: our rank is determined by the time of our *definitive entrance into the community* as postulants. The *Usages* further state: "This order cannot be changed either by the clothing or the profession," [455] but in this house we interpret it in the sense that when a novice makes profession before one who entered before him, he precedes that one in rank until the latter makes profession; but this does not apply to one who receives the habit before another postulant who entered earlier. "Priests and clerics take precedence of the other novices in the church" [456] (*Usages*, 14; cf. 93: "Priests and those in Orders, even those who have received only the tonsure, take precedence in choir and the ecclesiastical ceremonies only": [457] this explains the precedence given here to the professed, because monastic tonsure is in fact equivalent to clerical tonsure). Novices are supposed to remain in the lower stalls, but in this house we have the custom of putting novice priests in the upper stalls.

454. *Regulations*, 7.
455. *Regulations*, 7, which reads: ". . . clothing or by the profession".
456. *Regulations*, 7.
457. *Regulations*, 47–48, which reads: ". . . have only received . . . and in ecclesiastical . . ."

155 and 158: *The location of the novitiate.* These two numbers seem in some measure to duplicate one another: 155—"The novitiate shall be separated, as far as possible, from that part of the house occupied by the professed";[458] 158—"A place shall be set apart for the novices, where they shall apply themselves to their reading and attend the instructions of the Father Master."[459] It would seem that 158 represents the ancient legislation of the Order and 155 is simply a quotation of canon 564, n. 1[460] (canon 564, n. 2[461] also prescribes a separate place for the novitiate of the brothers). Canon law is mostly concerned with the "novitiate house" in provinces of religious. In monastic orders, each monastery normally has its own novitiate. In orders like the Carthusians, where there are small numbers, novices are trained only in a few houses. They are sent to their proper house for profession. In monastic orders, the monastery has no need of permission from the Holy See to start a novitiate once the house itself is canonically erected, but if the monastery is to serve as a *common novitiate* for several other monasteries, then permission of the Holy See is required. We do not have {a} common novitiate in our Order. The *Constitutions* and canon law (564) demand that there be as little communication as possible between the novices and the professed. This is true even of houses where the novitiate is separate from the rest of a province; in such houses exemplary religious only are supposed to be placed, and even with these the novice must have very little communication. *A fortiori* in our monasteries there should be no communication with the professed. The novitiate is supposed to be spent under as near as possible ideal conditions. The novice receives many graces, is in

---

458. "*Novitiatus ab ea parte domus, in qua degunt professi, sit, quantum fieri potest, segregatus*" (*Constitutiones*, 30); *Constitutions*, 36.

459. "*Sit etiam pro novitiis locus deputatus, ut lectionibus vacent et instructiones Magistri audiant*" (*Constitutiones*, 30); *Constitutions*, 37, which reads: ". . . they may apply . . . the instructions of their Father-Master."

460. *Codex Iuris Canonici*, 163.

461. *Codex Iuris Canonici*, 163.

a state of special fervor {and} is very receptive to instructions and example, and less desirable influences may make a deep and harmful impression on him. The work of his formation may be seriously impaired by the wrong kind of influences. Another reason for this separation is to guarantee *unity* in the novice's formation. He should not be subjected to various conflicting influences and opinions. Obviously conflicts and differences of opinions are inevitable, but during the time of formation, a time requiring special care and protection, the novice would not be able to understand these conflicts too well.

1. It is thoroughly undesirable for a novice to form a special relationship of intimacy with a professed, for instance by reason of their work, especially if they have permission to speak. Hence it is desirable that as far as possible permissions to speak with professed be kept at the absolute minimum. It is also desirable that the novices should work separately and not with the professed. The danger is here that a special little area of the novice's spiritual life may be subtracted almost completely from novitiate influences and control, and this would seriously harm his formation.

2. Novices should not be too easy to write "tickets" to the professed for slight reasons, especially when these lead to a regular "correspondence" by notes.

3. Sign conversations with {the} professed are forbidden, and even necessary signs should be avoided if there is some other way—v.g., through the undermaster, etc. {To} salute the professed and smile {is} okay: "*seniores venerari.*" [462]

Studies and offices must not interfere with the novitiate:
156: "The novices shall not be appointed to any office. They shall discontinue their studies at least during the canonical year." [463] The chief business of the novitiate is in the regular life

462. "seniors are to be shown respect" (*Rule*, c. 4 [McCann, 30]).
463. "*Novitiis nulla committatur administratio. A studiis cessabunt, durante saltem anno canonico*" (*Constitutiones*, 30); *Constitutions*, 36, which reads:

itself and the exercises. The first obligation of the novice is to keep the *Rule* and follow the common exercises; without this his formation cannot be perfect. Nothing that interferes with regularity must be allowed to become part of the novice's life. (N.B. sicknesses and temporary needs of course understandably call for exceptions, but these are only temporary and do not really affect the novice's formation. If the novice has such poor health that he needs many and constant exceptions, then it is a sign that he does not have a vocation.) Canon 565, n. 1 says that the purpose of the novitiate "is to form the soul of the novice by the study of the *Rule* and of the *Constitutions*, by holy meditations and zealous prayers, in learning above all those things which pertain to the vows and the virtues, in undergoing opportune exercises destined to pull out vices by the roots, to discipline the passions of the soul and to acquire virtues";[464] n. 3[465] adds that during the novitiate the novices should not preach or hear confessions (if they are priests), nor engage in the *exterior works* of the order, nor should they engage in the study of the humanities, science or the arts. Clement VIII decreed[466] that the novitiate should be given over *exclusively* to spiritual exercises (19 March 1603).

N. 157: *The Novice Master*:

a) One of the most grave obligations {is} to see that the novices are in the care of a capable novice master. The Church legislates on this point with the greatest care. Canon 559, n.1[467] prescribes that there must be a father master, aged at least thirty-five, at least ten years professed in the order (from first pro-

---

"Novices shall not . . ."

464. "*ut informetur alumni animus studio regulae et constitutionum, piis meditationibus assiduaque prece, iis perdiscendis quae ad vota et ad virtutes pertinent, exercitationibus opportunis ad vitiorum semina radicitus exstirpanda, ad compescendos animi motus, ad virtutes acquirendas*" (*Codex Iuris Canonici*, 163).

465. *Codex Iuris Canonici*, 164.

466. *Cum ad Regularem* (see Schaefer, 515 [#909]).

467. *Codex Iuris Canonici*, 162.

fession), and he must be a priest (in a clerical order). He must be, according to this canon, noteworthy for his prudence, charity, piety and observance of the rule. N. 2[468] speaks of the submaster, who must be at least thirty years old, and who is immediately subject to the father master in matters pertaining to the novitiate. He must be professed five years from his first profession. {According to} n. 3,[469] both the father master and the submaster must be free from every other duty which would impede their functions in the novitiate (cf. General Chapter, 1938, #3:[470] the master must be free from *all other offices*, including the hearing of confessions in the community [visitation, {1947}[471]]). Our *Constitutions* resume the wording of canon 559, n. 1, changing it slightly in certain points: the father master should be "one who has previously distinguished himself by an exemplary life,"[472] and instead of merely saying that he is exact in observance of the *Rule*, our *Constitutions* say "he must be given to prayer and works of mortification."[473] These changes come from the wording of a decree of Clement VIII (March 19, 1603). In other words, the novice master must be deeply imbued in the spirit of the Order and must be able to impart that spirit to others, not only by words but above all by example. {This is} a terrible responsibility. (Nothing is said in our *Constitutions* about the submaster of novices. The *Usages* [n. 547[474]] admit the possibility of a submaster who

---

468. *Codex Iuris Canonici*, 162.

469. *Codex Iuris Canonici*, 162.

470. This statute does not include mention of confessions, which was specified by the visitation.

471. Typescript reads "1946" but the correct date is evidently 1947; see the journal entry for April 5, 1947: "One of the results of the Visitation is that I must go looking for a new confessor. The Masters of Novices have been forbidden to hear confessions as it keeps them too busy" (*Entering the Silence*, 60).

472. "*vitae anteactae exemplo praestantior*" (*Constitutiones*, 30); *Constitutions*, 37.

473. "*orationi praeterea et mortificationis operibus addictus*" (*Constitutiones*, 30); *Constitutions*, 37, which reads: "who should . . . be given . . ."

474. *Regulations*, 258.

replaces the father master in his absence. The submaster usually has nothing to do with the spiritual direction of the novices.) {According to} canon 560,[475] the novice master is appointed according to the norm of the constitutions. Our *Constitutions* make clear that the novice master is chosen by the first superior. There is no definite term of office.

b) *The juridical condition and duties of the novice master*: canon 561, n. 1[476] makes very clear that the *novice master alone* is in charge of the formation of the novices and the regimen of the novitiate. In this Order, of course, the novice master simply represents the abbot in this matter. But all other members of the community are strictly excluded, and must not interfere with novitiate affairs in any way. The first function of the novice master is to *form the novices* by *instruction*—imparting doctrine about the *Rule*, monastic life, {the} virtues, etc.; *training*—giving them things to do, showing them how to do them well; *probation*—testing their virtue and their spirit. The area of his jurisdiction {includes both} (1) the *external forum*: how they keep the *Rule*, exterior conduct, etc. {and} (2) the *internal non-sacramental forum*—that is to say, his proper province extends into the conscience of the novice in all that regards his spirit, his progress, his manner of understanding and fulfilling the obligations of the monastic life. In practice this even would extend to the matter of confession, in so far as the novice master *should* know of any habitual deordination in order to form a proper judgement. But the novice master need not know of isolated lapses that are immediately repaired. In any case, since he is the director of the novice, he should know in general what pertains to the novice's soul, so as to be able to direct him objectively and well. He has therefore the right to ask for a manifestation of conscience. (3) In isolated cases the novice master may also be called into the *sacramental* forum, but only by the spontaneous request of the novice himself. To what extent is the master depen-

---

475. *Codex Iuris Canonici*, 162.
476. *Codex Iuris Canonici*, 163.

dent on the first superior in the exercise of his functions? General Chapter, 1923, n. 4 says: "With regard to the question . . . is it proper to trace out for the Father Masters a uniform direction as to their dependence on the first Superior in the formation of the novices . . . ? The General Chapter is of the opinion that it is not possible to give such a common rule, and that it is sufficient to establish that the Father Masters in our Order . . . are under the dependence of the Superiors."[477] In other words, and in practice, the novice master has as much to do in the formation of novices as the superior wills him to have. No doubt there is not much variation from house to house, although it is obvious that in a large house the novice master will be left with a more complete and total responsibility for the novices and the novitiate. In any case by common law and by virtue of the *Usages* (n. 543[478]), the novice master is clearly the spiritual director of the novices. He holds repetitions explaining the *Rule*, {the} *Constitutions*, monastic history and "everything relating to monastic education" (*Usages*, 545[479]). He holds {a} chapter of faults when he thinks {it} proper. He customarily gives public and private penances, distributes {the} work of the novices, grants permissions, procures all that is necessary for them, and sees that they are properly cared for when they are sick (*Usages*, 546[480]). In our community, training in the ceremonies, books etc. and other external matters are left in the hands of the submaster, who can also hear accusations and give penances. (4) The novice master has *a grave obligation* to apply himself with all diligence to exercising the novices in religious discipline according to the *Rule* of the Order. He must in other words form them first of all in *a spirit of obedience and regularity*. The future of the Order depends on the right formation of the

---

477. Text reads: ". . . question of knowing whether it is proper . . . out to the . . . novices the General . . . Order in virtue of the Codex and of the Holy Rule are under . . ."

478. *Regulations*, 256–57.

479. *Regulations*, 257.

480. *Regulations*, 258.

novices. It is {a} question of directing the powers of their souls to serve God with generosity and love in this manner of life, and carrying on the traditions of the founders of the Order, in order to attain the end proposed by them. If the novice is formed with a true monastic spirit, then he will be able to live as a monk and pass on the monastic way of life to future generations. The training of the novice in the monastic way of life is a *disciplina* which is learned more by doing what is right than by merely hearing it told to him. Hence the father master is bound most seriously to see that the novice cultivates the fundamental monastic virtues and outlook which are set down in the *Rule*. In practice, this means seeing that the novice is in all things humble, obedient, mortified, charitable, a lover of silence and of prayer, devoted to manual labor, to holy reading and meditation, reverent and pious, zealous for the work of God, etc., etc. The father master must avoid extremes—not being either excessively severe and rigorous or too gentle and complacent towards fallen nature.

c) *The juridical condition and duties of the novice*: although the novice master does not strictly have *potestas dominativa*,[481] nevertheless the novice is held to obey him, and this depends either on a domestic power (some authors) or on a kind of derived *potestas dominativa* (Larraona;[482] cf. Schaefer, n. 899[483]). The novices are bound to obey the *Rule* and *Constitutions*, not under sin but in view of their formation. In practice, an irregular novice exposes himself to dismissal and is bound in conscience to accept the judgement

---

481. See canon 501.1: "*Superiores et Capitula, ad normam constitutionum et iuris communis potestatem habent dominativam in subditos*" ("Superiors and chapters, according to the norm of constitutions and common law, have dominative power over their subjects") (*Codex Iuris Canonici*, 144); for the juridical meaning of this term and its distinction from domestic power, see Thomas Merton, *The Life of the Vows: Initiation into the Monastic Tradition* 6, ed. Patrick F. O'Connell, MW 30 (Collegeville, MN: Cistercian Publications, 2012), 258–60.

482. A. Larraona, CMF, "*Commentarium Codicis: Can. 560*," *Commentarium Pro Religiosis et Missionariis*, 24 (1943): 25–40, especially 38.

483. Schaefer, 508.

of the novice master in that case. It is most important for the novice to take regularity very seriously; although perfection does not consist merely in the exterior observance of the rules and usages, nevertheless the fundamental duty of the monk is to obey his rule and *use it as a means to perfection*. This is impossible if he neglects it in order to prefer his own will and his own fancies.

TEMPORARY PROFESSION:[484] this section of the *Constitutions* is naturally one which is most important for novices studying the laws of the Order, since temporary profession is the immediate term of the novitiate training.

159 prescribes that temporary vows are to be made when the following requirements have been met with (cf. General Chapter, 1928, n. 1): (1) a two-years' novitiate (of which the first is the canonical year); (2) the deliberative vote of the conventual chapter; (3) seventeen years completed. Concerning the vote in chapter, it is expressly prescribed by a statute of the General Chapter (1933, n. 3): "When an assembly is held to ask the votes concerning a temporary or solemn profession, *no discussion is permitted*, and the religious have no other right than {that} of secretly giving their votes."[485] There is an *obligation* for all the voters present to cast a vote one way or another when there is question of profession, whether simple or solemn (General Chapter, 1899, n. 5 and 1920, n. 15). The novitiate may be prolonged (a) until the novice attains the required age for profession; (b) for six months if there still remains doubt as to his fitness. If the novice is not accepted by the community for profession he *must leave* unless he is allowed to remain as a family brother or oblate.

What is profession? {It} is a public taking of vows of religion in an institute approved by the Church, a *juridical act* by which the professed *assumes the religious state* and becomes a religious in the strict sense of the word. By this juridical act there arises a *mutual obligation* between the religious institute and the professed.

---

484. Chapter 3 (nn. 159–65) (*Constitutiones*, 30–31; *Constitutions*, 37–38).
485. Emphasis added.

The professed is bound to live according to the *Rule* and to obey the superiors, and to participate according to his capacity in the work and prayer of the community. On the other hand the order assumes responsibility for his bodily health and all that is owed by a family to a son. *Two essential elements* make up religious profession: *traditio sui*[486]—the gift of oneself (accepted by the community) {and} the *emission of vows*. The two must go together. Mere emission of vows without the intention to give oneself, or the giving of oneself without the emission of vows, do not make a religious. By the *traditio sui* is formed a human bond between the religious and his community—a bond which can be dissolved. By the emission of vows is formed a supernatural bond between the religious and God. (Can such a vow be dissolved?) Public vows of religion are *reserved*, and can be dispensed only by the Holy See (in the case of our Order). In our Order, simple vows are made for a period of three years or more, but not perpetually (though they were made perpetually at a certain time in the past). Emission of vows {must be} a public, external act for {it to be} *valid*; {if it is} tacit {it is} not valid.

Conditions for the Validity of Profession (common law): for any profession, simple or solemn, temporary or perpetual, the following conditions are necessary for validity:

1. The legitimate age {of} sixteen years completed for temporary vows (seventeen years in our Order), twenty-one years completed for perpetual vows, whether solemn or simple. If a person under eighteen makes temporary profession in our Order, then it is understood that his simple vows are for more than three years, and he makes them with that understanding. Profession would be invalid if made on the candidate's sixteenth birthday.

2. The candidate must be admitted to profession by the legitimate superior. To *admit to* profession {means} by consenting to allow him to make profession as being a worthy candidate; this {is} done by the superior and the conventual chapter. To

---

486. "handing over oneself": see *Life of the Vows*, 175–76.

receive one's profession is the act of the legitimate superior presiding as one takes vows and receiving these vows. This act of the superior is necessary for validity, but {it} can be done by delegation.

3. He must have completed a *valid uninterrupted novitiate.* {The} validity of {the} novitiate is judged by (a) {the} absence of impediments listed above (canon 542[487]) (see separately); (b) it must have been spent *continuously in the novitiate* for *at least one year* (common law). In our Order it is expressly stated that the novitiate must last *two years*. Hence a two-years' novitiate is necessary for validity (cf. canon 555, n. 2[488]). But during the second year, the novitiate may be broken without having to be started over again from the beginning. This is not true of the canonical year. For us {there is} a two-years' novitiate: {the} canonical year {must be} *uninterrupted* (ordinarily {the} first year); {the} second year {must be} *completed*. The superiors of the Order cannot dispense from the second year of the novitiate (Schaefer, 881[489]). {With regard to the} *uninterrupted novitiate,* since *the canonical year must be uninterrupted,* we had better look closely at the meaning of this concept. The novitiate is interrupted in the following way:

a) if the novice, *having been dismissed by the superior, leaves the house*: this means formal dismissal, and takes effect the moment the dismissal is confirmed, and the interruption begins the moment the novice leaves the *house.*

b) If the novice *leaves the house without permission, not intending to return* (even though he might be out for only half an hour, and still wearing the habit). His going out must be fully voluntary. The intention must be more than merely internal. For an external sign, a declaration of intention, or the act of taking his bag and belongings is sufficient. If he leaves secretly for a few

---

487. *Codex Iuris Canonici,* 156.
488. *Codex Iuris Canonici,* 161.
489. Schaefer, 493.

days with the intention of returning, and does return, the novitiate is not interrupted (but he will probably be sent away).

c) If the novice, even with the superior's permission, is out of the house for thirty days, for no matter what reason, his novitiate is interrupted and must begin over again—out of the *house*, not out of the novitiate. Thirty days in the infirmary {is} no interruption of the novitiate. The days may be *continuous or non-continuous*. They must be days of twenty-four hours. Half a day does not count as a day. One may be out of the novitiate fifty-nine times for twelve hours or under without interrupting the novitiate. Naturally, such expeditions are not desirable, especially in an order like ours. If, after completing his novitiate, the novice is absent for thirty days, his profession can still be valid.

Suspended {novitiate}: (1) If the novice spends *less than thirty days* outside the novitiate, the novitiate is not interrupted and does not have to be begun over again, but the days spent outside are to be made up. However, if he is out for fewer than *sixteen days* (total—continuous or non-continuous), the number does not have to be made up (cf. Schaefer, 885[490]). In the case when the novice is out for sixteen days or more and these days have to be made up, the novitiate is considered *suspended* (during that time) but not interrupted. If under sixteen days, it is not suspended. *Even when compelled to be absent by necessity*, the novice finds his novitiate suspended by a stay of more than fifteen days out of the house, and interrupted by a stay of more than thirty days outside. For instance, in the case where the house could be burned down and the novice would have to remain elsewhere, the novitiate would be suspended or interrupted, according to the time spent outside a regular novitiate of our Order. (2) The novitiate would also be suspended or interrupted in case of unjust civil law (in time of persecution) or other civil legislation (military service). If the novice is out for fifteen days only, nothing has to be made up. If he is out for sixteen days, he makes up not *one* day but sixteen.

---

490. Schaefer, 497.

(3) In the case where the novice is out for fewer than sixteen days, it is not necessary for validity that he make up this time, *but it remains to the discretion of the superior whether or not he should make it up*. If during the time that the novice is absent, under thirty days, he clearly and exteriorly manifests his *intention of not returning*, his novitiate is *interrupted* from that moment. It has to be begun again. Although the superior has power to permit the novice to go out of the novitiate, it is expressly prescribed by canon 556, n. 3[491] that he must not do so without *a grave and just cause*. If he allows the novice to be out without such a cause, the *permission is illicit* (and the novice does not have a moral right to avail himself of it), but it does not interrupt or invalidate the novitiate. Sickness of the novice's relatives is considered a just and serious cause in common law, but in our Order we would be slow to allow a novice outside for this reason, in view of the fact that such permissions are not granted to the professed (see above: enclosure[492]). *The novitiate is not interrupted even by an absence of over thirty days* if the novice, with permission, goes to another novitiate of our Order during that time. *The time spent in travelling* from one house to another *would have to be computed* in the time required for suspension or interruption of the novitiate. As said above, *interruption* concerns only the canonical year of the novitiate with us. *Suspension* can also occur in the second year of the novitiate. Another fifteen days of leeway are allowed in this second year. Another *condition for validity* {is that} the whole novitiate must be spent in the habit of the novices of our Order. Time spent in the choir novitiate does not count toward fulfilling the time requirement for the laybrothers' novitiate. If one goes from the choir to the brothers, having the habit of {a} novice, the novitiate for the brothers begins on the day of the transfer. We return now to the conditions for validity of profession after this important excursus on the notion of an interrupted novitiate.

---

491. *Codex Iuris Canonici*, 162.
492. See above, page 141.

4. Profession must be made without the influence of force, grave fear or fraud being exercised upon the professed. {This is} another serious condition for *validity*. This would include a *substantial error* as to the *nature* of the obligations and the *effects* of the vow. *Grave fear*, in this case, means a fear implanted by an exterior agent. It may be relatively grave, and it may take the form of threats, veiled or otherwise, and importunate heckling. *If proved in the external forum*, the fact that such fear was implanted invalidates profession.

5. For validity, the profession must be made with an express sign of the will of the one making profession, whether in writing or *viva voce*. The taking of a public vow must necessarily be visible and external. Tacit profession (for instance, putting on the habit of the professed with the permission of the superior, the other conditions being fulfilled) is not accepted by the Church. Normally the external manifestation of profession is made by the *rule* prescribed in the order.

6. The profession must be received by the legitimate superior or his delegate. The superior can delegate any member of the order. The delegation must be more than merely presumed, but it may be tacit.

The effects of simple religious profession:
1. By giving up himself and vowing obedience, poverty, stability, etc., the professed is *incorporated in the community* ({this is the} significance of embracing at solemn profession). He is therefore considered a *sacred person*, and his religious acts are now no longer a mere matter of private devotion, but are part of the public worship offered by the Church to God. He is now a *religious*.

2. Since he now has *public vows* (i.e., received by a legitimate superior in the name of the Church, even though not in the presence of the community), his vows can only be dispensed by the Holy See (in our Order). Simple profession renders acts against the vow *illicit* but not *invalid* (v.g., marriage).

3. He is able to *participate in spiritual graces* reserved for religious and monks of our Order. In particular, {at} solemn profes-

sion, the religious is as it were purified by a *second baptism* from all the debt of punishment for his sins.

4. *He incurs the obligation to observe the rules and constitutions {and} to obey his superiors.*

5. He comes under the *dominative power* of the superior, so that the superior can command him and exact obedience under pain of sin. The superior also has the right to annul all previous private vows he may have made.

6. If he is a cleric he renounces all offices and benefices.

7. All other vows previously made by him remain suspended.

8. He cannot be a sponsor at baptism or confirmation without a special reason, and only with permission of the superior.

9. He is no longer able to belong to any third order, even if he was inscribed in one before.

10. He has a strict right to food and lodging, to be provided by the order, and to everything that one can expect in a (poor) family.

11. He is *not* bound to the canonical office.

12. He does *not* have active or passive voice in the chapter. *Renewal*: *temporary profession may be prolonged*—for three years or under—at the discretion of the abbot. In this case he can direct the professed to renew his vows; this {is to be} done in the presence of two witnesses. It *must* be prolonged if necessary for the professed to reach the required age (twenty-one) for solemn vows. When temporary vows are to be renewed, they *must* be renewed not later than the third anniversary of the first profession. They *may* be renewed within the month before they expire. *There must be no interval during which the professed is not under vows.* The renewal of vows requires: (a) a new pronouncement of the formula of vows, in the hands of the legitimate superior; (b) an explicit statement of the time for which the vows are being renewed.

In the case where religious are obliged to military service, the novice may make profession, but only up to the time when he must be called up by the draft board. As soon as he is called into the army, *his vows cease*. Yet he remains a member of the order and subject to the authority of the superiors. At the same time, however, (a) he is free to leave the order; all that is required being that he give notice to the superior in writing, before witnesses; (b) he may be dismissed by the superior for {a} just and reasonable motive. Creusen[493] notes that this applies only to ordinary military service—not to mobilization in time of war.

The DISMISSAL of simple professed:

N. 160: they can be dismissed by the Abbot General with the consent of his council, *or* by the local abbot with the consent of his council (in both cases, {by a} secret vote). Note: there are some grave crimes by which a religious, whether simple or solemn professed, is IPSO FACTO dismissed from his order (canon 646[494]): (a) apostasy from the faith; (b) running away with a person of the opposite sex—this requires *mutual agreement* of the two parties, not a chance encounter followed by {a} decision to remain together; (c) attempted matrimony. In these cases, the superior notes and declares the fact and enters it in the register, with required evidence, and the religious is *ipso facto* out of the order. If the religious is simply professed, his obligation to keep the vows then ceases entirely.

Motives for dismissal:

a) Breakdown of health is *not* a motive for dismissal, unless the ill health was concealed before profession. Neither is mental breakdown strictly a motive for dismissal, but a religious who breaks down mentally during simple vows should leave, especially if his condition upsets the community. Normally speaking it is to the mutual advantage of the professed and of the community that he leave, and the superiors should counsel him to do so.

b) Serious lack of religious spirit, to a degree that is scandalous in the community, and which is not corrected after frequent admonition.

---

493. Joseph Creusen, SJ, *Religious Men and Women in the Code*, 4th English edition, ed. Adam Ellis, SJ (Milwaukee: Bruce, 1940), 180 (#237).

494. *Codex Iuris Canonici*, 187.

c) Faults of character incompatible with religious discipline and with community life (some mental cases—v.g., paranoids—would definitely come under this heading).

d) Lack of aptitude for the work of the order (cf. Creusen, p. 267[495]).

N. 161: *No judicial process is required* for the dismissal of a simple professed. "It can be proceeded with simply on the truth of the matter being made known."[496] Canon 647, n. 2[497] prescribes the following: *the reasons must be made known to the religious*, and he must have {an} opportunity to answer, but the decision remains with the superior. The religious can appeal to the Holy See, and during this recourse the dismissal has no effect.

N. 162: *The property of the simple professed*: according to common law, the simple professed retains the ownership of his property and the right to acquire more, unless the contrary is stated in the constitutions. In our *Constitutions*, it is explicitly stated that the simple professed retains the ownership of his property (162), and implicitly that he may acquire more (163). By the simple vow of poverty, what is renounced is (a) the right to *administer* property; (b) the right to the *use of* property; (c) the right to its *usufruct* (that is to say, the right to dispose freely of revenues from property). "The administration, disposal and use of the revenues derived from it are absolutely forbidden to them" (*Constitutions*, 162[498]). Hence, before profession, they must make what is colloquially called a "will." In this document they not only state who is to inherit their property, or what property may accrue to them during profession, but they also cede the administration and arrange for disposal of revenues, etc., during the time of their profession. In

---

495. #348.

496. "*ad eam procedi potest, sola facti veritate inspecta*" (*Constitutiones*, 31); *Constitutions*, 37.

497. *Codex Iuris Canonici*, 188.

498. "*eis omnino interdicta est administratio et redituum erogatio atque usus*" (*Constitutiones*, 31); *Constitutions*, 38, which reads: "the administration from it, and the disposal and use . . ."

making their will, they may leave their property (in case of death) and make over their revenues to the monastery.

N. 163 explicitly provides for a change in the case where property accrues to the professed which has not been provided for in his will. In that case, he "shall make or renew the provision, according to the regulations laid down in Art. 162."[499] The purpose of this is to remove all doubt of the validity and liceity of this act of disposition of property during the time when he is under the vow of poverty. He *can* make the change. No special permission is required. If the simple professed wishes to *change his whole will*, he needs the permission of the Holy See (or for any notable change in the will). If recourse is absolutely impossible, in urgent cases he may approach the Abbot General or the local abbot for this permission (cf. Creusen, p. 185[500]).

NN. 164–65 tell us what we have already discussed under the effects of profession:

a) The temporary professed do not have a vote in the chapter. It is specifically stated that they have no vote in the election of an abbot, in case someone might think an exception would be possible here.

b) "They must observe the Rule and attend choir, like the solemnly professed, but they are not bound to the private recitation of the Divine Office."[501]

In effect, the time of simple profession is really a prolongation of the novitiate. It extends the time of formation and probation of the young monk. In this period he must continue to show zeal and regular spirit—if he loses them it is certainly a reason for barring him from solemn profession.

---

499. *"fiat aut iteretur secundum normas N. 162 statutas"* (*Constitutiones*, 31); *Constitutions*, 38.

500. #243, 4(b).

501. *"Regulam observare debent et choro interesse ut solemniter professi, non tenentur tamen ad privatam recitationem Divini Officii"* (*Constitutiones*, 31); *Constitutions*, 38.

Part III, Chapter 4: SOLEMN PROFESSION[502]

What is solemn profession? In what does it differ from simple profession? The question is debated among theologians. {There is} no need to go into the various opinions. In practice the following differences can be noted: (a) solemn profession is accepted by the Church as solemn, distinguished by the Church from simple vows; (b) the vows which the Church distinguishes as solemn always imply a complete and irrevocable giving of oneself—they are always perpetual; (c) these vows make *invalid* any acts which may be placed contrary to the vows. The distinction is not found merely in the greater solemnity of the rite by which the vows are publically emitted. This distinction dates from the sixteenth century. Before that time, all religious vows were considered "solemn vows" (although they did not always have the effects of invalidating contrary acts). "Simple vows" were merely "private vows." Public simple vows first came into being with the simple profession of young religious in the Society of Jesus.

Special effects of solemn profession:

a) The invalidation of contrary acts—solemn profession is a diriment impediment to matrimony (canon 1073[503]). The professed is unable to make an onerous contract without permission of his superior. It would be invalid. The professed is unable (under the vow of obedience) to undertake any serious personal obligation, whether to God or to men, which cannot be dissolved by the superior ({the one} exception {is} the vow to go to a higher life).

b) The solemn professed renounces not only the use and usufruct of his property, but also *all title to possession*. He becomes incapable of acquiring any fresh property. All that comes to him after profession in our Order belongs to the monastery.

---

502. Nn. 166–68 (*Constitutiones*, 31–32; *Constitutions*, 38–39).
503. *Codex Iuris Canonici*, 306.

c) Even when he is not a subdeacon, he is obliged to the private recitation of the canonical hours if he is not present at the choral office, *sub gravi*.

Conditions for solemn profession and other formalities:

N. 166 (1) {states that} after the three years of temporary vows and the completion of twenty-one years, the professed shall make solemn vows. If he does not make solemn vows, he must either (a) renew his simple vows (for a maximum of three years) {or} (b) return to the world or to his former institute if he came from one in which he had vows. In order to renew his simple vows, the professed "makes his vows in the hands of the superior in the presence of at least two witnesses. An official report of this act shall be drawn up" (General Chapter, 1924, n. 4[504]). He uses the same formula which is pronounced in chapter. N. 166 (2) {reads}: "The Abbot who receives the solemn profession must inform the parish priest of the place where the professed was baptised."[505]

N. 167 {specifies that} within two months before solemn profession, the candidate renounces all his property, including his basic ownership, and becomes legally "dead" as far as acquiring or disposing of property is concerned. "This renunciation comes into effect only after the profession has been made."[506] If the will is made before the two-months' period which precedes profession, the will is not valid (canon 581, n. 1[507]). The professed can make *anyone he likes* the beneficiary of his will. It is a new will and wipes out the provisions of the old one. After profession, any steps necessary to ensure the civil effect of the will must be taken (canon 581, n. 2[508]).

---

504. Text reads: "The renewal of temporary vows should be made in the hands . . ."

505. "*Abbas professionem solemnem excipiens debet profitentis parochum baptismi de eadem certiorem reddere*" (Constitutiones, 32); Constitutions, 39.

506. "*Haec renuntiatio tantum post professionem editam vim atque exitum habet*" (Constitutiones, 32); Constitutions, 39.

507. *Codex Iuris Canonici*, 168.

508. *Codex Iuris Canonici*, 169.

N. 168 {concerns} the voting. Secret votes of the chapter are required, "but in this case they are merely consultative."[509] The General Chapter of 1895 (n. 6) distinguishes the votes for simple and solemn profession. In the former case, "the Prior and Sub-Prior are scrutators and must let the voters know the number for or against."[510] In the latter case, "the superior alone counts [the votes] and he is not obliged to give out the results."[511]

The Promise of Obedience in Chapter:

1. According to our *Ritual* (Book 6, chapter 2), the candidate for profession takes the following steps "about ten days"[512] before the end of his "novitiate" (this is according to the old legislation in which solemn vows were made at the end of a year's novitiate):

a) The candidate (novice) is brought into chapter after the father master announces that the *Rule* has been read to him three times. He makes his "third petition."[513]

b) At this time, in the presence of all, he "most freely"[514] disposes of all the goods he may possess. The *Ritual* adds a counsel that it is preferable that he should do so in favor of the poor: *maxime in gratiam pauperum*.[515] There should never be any kind of pressure, even implicit, exerted on a candidate to induce him to leave his goods to the monastery. The will is drawn up later.

c) After he has made this public renunciation of his goods, the candidate kneels before the abbot and makes his promise of obedience. The formula given in the *Ritual*[516] is the one we use

---

509. "*quae tamen in hoc casu, sunt mere consultativa*" (*Constitutiones*, 32); *Constitutions*, 39.
510. Text reads: ". . . who are the scrutators must let . . ."
511. Text reads: ". . . result."
512. "*decem circiter diebus*" (VI, II, 1 [*Rituale*, 239]).
513. "*ultimam suam petitionem*" (*Rituale*, 239).
514. "*liberrime*" (*Rituale*, 239).
515. *Rituale*, 239.
516. "*Pater, promitto tibi et successoribus tuis legitimis obedientiam secundum Regulam sancti Benedicti usque ad mortem*" ("Father, I promise to you and

now. Once this promise has been made, the novice leaves the chapter room and begins his spiritual retreat—of about ten days—in preparation for public profession.

2. These are the prescriptions of our *Ritual*. Naturally, they have been greatly modified by canon law. Solemn vows are today made only after three years of simple profession. One thing remains in force from the above. Although the candidate already has a vow of obedience, he nevertheless makes his promise of obedience in chapter, to the abbot, at the beginning of his retreat for solemn vows. The General Chapter was at first a little hesitant on this point: 1924, n. 4 prescribes that the promise of obedience be "made in chapter on the day of the profession"; 1926, n. 4 changed it to the beginning of the retreat, "in order to remain more in conformity with the spirit of our Ritual"; 1931, n. 2 gives precisions about the ceremonial to be followed—the abbot explains the *Rule* as usual, then says, *loquamur de ordine nostro*,[517] {and} the candidate comes out to the middle and receives a short exhortation, after which he makes his promise.

Part III, Chapter 5: CHANGE OF STABILITY[518]

Because of our vow of stability, it is in practice almost as difficult to change from one monastery of the Order to another as it would be to change to another order. Nor is it merely a matter of "red tape." One must not get the idea that all we need in order to avoid sinning against the vow of stability is to go through the proper formalities. It is a sin against the vow even to seek to change one's stability without a very grave reason. The General Chapter of 1900, n. 9 says: "On the subject of stability, we recall that a religious should live and die in the monastery

---

to your lawful successors obedience according to the *Rule* of Saint Benedict up until death") (VI, II, 2 [*Rituale*, 239]).

517. "Let us speak of our order" (III, VIII, 2 [*Rituale*, 94]); see *Monastic Observances*, 213–15, which explains the phrase as meaning "let us speak of our observance . . . let us speak of the way we are keeping our rule" (215).

518. Nn. 169–70 (*Constitutiones*, 32; *Constitutions*, 39).

where he has placed himself, and that he CANNOT, WITHOUT GOING AGAINST HIS VOW, TRY TO CHANGE HIS HOUSE."[519]

N. 169 lays down the following conditions for {a} change of stability:

a) grave necessity—what would be a case of grave necessity? serious ill-health, requiring a change of climate; {a} genuine desire to offer oneself to help a poorer community. The mere pretext that one "cannot get along" in the present community may have to be tolerated sometimes in practice, but it often turns out that those who have this as their reason are not able to "get along" in *any* community. However, it could happen that for spiritual reasons a change would be seriously desirable; in such a case the fact would probably be evident to the superiors as well as to the monk himself. He may be *sent* by his superior.

b) the consent of their own abbot.

c) the consent of the community *ad quod*.[520]

d) the permission of the Holy See.

How does one change stability? One spends a year of probation in the community *ad quod*. He is admitted for probation with the approval of the abbot's council. The vote is taken after a year by the conventual chapter. New stability is made according to the *Ritual*.[521] If the professed has temporary vows, the new stability takes place in chapter. If he has solemn vows, he makes a new promise of obedience in chapter and then renews his stability in church. He simply goes to the presbytery step after the gospel {and} reads the act of new stability, which he signs and places on the altar in the presence of the abbot (*Usages*, n. 44[522]). {His} rank in the new community "shall be decided according to the Statute

---

519. Emphasis added.

520. "to which [one is transferring]".

521. "*Pater, promitto tibi obedientiam usque ad mortem secundum Regulam sancti Benedicti*" ("Father, I promise you obedience up until death according to the *Rule* of Saint Benedict") (VI, VII, 3 [*Rituale*, 261]).

522. *Regulations*, 24.

of the General Chapter" (*Constitutions*, 169 [523]). The statute in question is 1924, n. 7, which provides as follows: (a) "If the reason for the change is honorable and publicly known as such, the religious takes his rank of seniority"; (b) "If the reason is notoriously unfavorable, the religious takes the last place"; (c) "If any other hypothesis, the Superior shall decide what rank is to be taken." [524]

A question might arise as to the possessions which the monk has renounced in favor of the community *a quo* [525] at the time of his profession. It is according to justice, says {the} General Chapter, 1929, n. 2, that the community *a quo* should retain the property ceded to it by the monk, and that it should acquire any new property that would be coming to him. However, if the monk (by reason of age, health, etc.) might be a burden to the community *ad quod*, the superiors should reach an agreement among themselves according to justice. If after the change some property should accrue to the newly stabiliated monk which *somehow does not fall under his previous renunciation*, then this new property is acquired by the community *ad quod*.

If a monk has spent one year of probation for new stability and then does not make stability, he cannot remain longer in the community *ad quod* without the consent of that community (General Chapter, 1910, n. {4} [526]).

It is to be noted that change of stability is very likely to imply a dishonor. When we have made a vow to live and die in a monastery, this vow is to be taken seriously, for it is a promise made to God freely and knowingly, and it is to the honor and glory of God for us to keep this vow, not only as to its letter but also as to its spirit, and {to} avoid anything that savors of a "gyrovague

---

523. *Constitutions*, 39 (*Constitutiones*, 32 reads: "*in ultimo ordine monachorum monasterii pro quo postulant*" ["in the last rank of monks of the monastery for which they seek entrance"]) .
    524. Text reads: "In any other . . ."
    525. "from which [one is transferring]."
    526. Typescript reads: "3".

spirit" reproved by the General Chapter of 1910, n. 3, which decrees: (a) superiors ought not to allow a change of house except for REASONS OF EXCEPTIONAL GRAVITY; (b) and of these THEY shall be the sole judges; the responsibility is placed on the shoulder of the superiors, who are not to let themselves be persuaded easily by unstable subjects.

Chapter 6: *Admission of Religious from Another Order*:[527] the provisions of nn. 171 and 172 of our *Constitutions* regarding the admission of religious from other orders applies equally to those who belong to institutes without religious vows (v.g., {the} Society of the Precious Blood, Columban Fathers, etc.).

171: In order for a religious to pass from one order to another, the permission of the Apostolic See is required (canon 632[528]). This permission implies usually the consent of the superior of the order *from which* the religious comes, and of the superior of the order *to which* he transfers. Canon 633[529] (to which we are referred by the *Constitutions*[530]) prescribes that one who comes from another institute (1) must make a full novitiate in our Order—during this time, he retains his vows, obligations and rights which were his in his previous institute, but they are *suspended*; he is obliged to obey his superiors in our Order and even the novice master under his *vow* of obedience; (2) he shall return to his former institute if he does not make profession with us (cf. n. 172).

172 prescribes a full two-years' novitiate. If the *transiens* has perpetual vows, he immediately makes solemn vows with us, omitting the period of temporary vows. The vote for this is *deliberative*, because of the special seriousness of the decision. There is a special gravity in the choice of one who from the first will have *solemn* vows in our Order without having had the opportunity to spend three years of further probation and get to know

---

527. Nn. 171–72 (*Constitutiones*, 32–33; *Constitutions*, 39–40).
528. *Codex Iuris Canonici*, 183.
529. *Codex Iuris Canonici*, 184.
530. *Constitutiones*, 33; *Constitutions*, 40.

the life and the community better. The Code considers that his experience in religion elsewhere will suffice, but other contemplative orders, in spite of this provision of the Code, while being slow to admit men from other orders, also prolong their probationary period (v.g., the Carthusians). The probation of one from another order can be extended *for one more year in the novitiate*, but not more (canon 634 [531]). On the day of his new profession, the transient (a) loses all his rights and obligations in his previous institute and takes on those of our Order; (b) the monastery from which he came retains his goods or those which accrued to him, though in justice a certain amount of what may have accrued to him during his new novitiate may be due to us (cf. canon 635 [532]).

Chapter 7: *The Laybrothers* [533]

N. 173: There is a certain tone about this section which strikes us as a little strange today: "We receive Lay-Brethren . . . who are under our care. . . . We treat them like ourselves." [534] This is not comprehensble except in the light of the prologue of the ancient *"Usus Conversorum"* [535] in the *Consuetudines* (Section 3 [*Nomasticon*, p. 234]). Here it is stated that in the early days of the Order the laybrothers were always illiterate and required care more or less as if they were children. At the present time, though the life of a brother is simpler, more laborious and less studious than that of a choir monk, there is less difference between the two categories as far as education and background are concerned. There is in fact more equality between the brothers and the monks in our Order than in many others. In point of fact, since the brothers are usually endowed with technical skill and do in fact control the whole material side of the monastery, it would be true in a certain sense to say that the somewhat "simpler" choir religious

---

531. *Codex Iuris Canonici*, 184.
532. *Codex Iuris Canonici*, 184.
533. Nn. 173–83 (*Constitutiones*, 33–34; *Constitutions*, 40–42).
534. *"Fratres Conversos seu Laicos . . . suscipimus . . . qui sub cura nostra sunt, et sicut nosmetipsos tractamus"* (*Constitutiones*, 33); *Constitutions*, 40.
535. *The Customs of the Brothers* (*Nomasticon*, 234–41).

are in the "care" of the brothers. The brothers participate in all the goods of the community "both spiritual and temporal," share in the prayers of the Order, retreats, indulgences, etc. They have neither active nor passive voice in the conventual chapter, but recently it has been decreed (General Chapter, 1953, n. 11) that the professed laybrothers should be received in private scrutiny at the regular visitation just like the choir professed. Also, recently the laybrothers began to make solemn profession in choir like the monks, with the same ceremonies.[536] They began to be admitted to the choir of the monks during solemn Masses, and began to sing with the choir at certain functions (General Chapter, 1953, n. {9}[537]). They were given more time for reading also (*idem*, n. 10). All this indicates a movement for greater equality and greater participation on the part of the brothers in the life of the choir. {With regard to} relations with the brothers, they should be treated in every way like the choir religious. They are religious—they are not clerics or monks, and in this sense there is a lesser degree of official dignity about their state, but this does not detract from the fact that they may be personally more holy. The choir religious should not patronize or boss the brothers, nor should anyone take advantage of the fact that he is a priest in order to lord it over them. The choir should strive to give the brothers in all things a greater example of humility, charity, silence, patience and all the religious virtues. The brothers do in fact want to be able to look up to the fathers, especially the priests, and it hurts them when a choir religious is a bossy, impertinent, prying character who can think of nothing but complaints about how the brothers do their work. Relations with the brothers, as with everyone else in the community, should be marked by simple and supernatural affection and respect.

174: Rules for admission to the laybrotherhood:

---

536. See 1953, ##5, 6, 7.
537. Text reads: "8".

1. The candidate must have completed fifteen years in order to begin the novitiate. He may be received as a postulant under fifteen, {but} not under fourteen.

2. The postulancy lasts at least six months. "The Abbot can prolong the time prescribed, but not beyond a second period of six months."[538] A year postulancy is then possible. It is assumed that probation for the life of the brothers should be longer and greater care should be taken. This is not because the requirements for a laybrother are stricter than for the choir, but because the weeding-out process for the choir is already more strict, since much depends on the candidate's education. For the laybrothers there are no educational requirements, though it would seem desirable that the candidate have at least part of his high-school education finished, or even all of it, {the} reason {being that} if after two years' novitiate he returns to the world, he will be less seriously handicapped.

3. Provisions for retreat, clothing and novitiate {are the} same as for the choir.

175: {There are the} same regulations for profession, dismissal etc. as for the choir.

176: {There are the} same regulations for simple and solemn vows.

177: The habit.

178: One who has received the habit as {a} laybrother in our Order can never be transferred to the rank of the choir religious. In actual fact the transfer is possible, with a dispensation from the Abbot General, but it is very much discouraged in the Order and in particular at Gethsemani. When the transfer is made, the brother enters as a choir novice in some *other* monastery, and it is sometimes required that he make an extra-long postulancy before beginning the new novitiate. The case is very rare.

---

538. "*Abbas praescriptum tempus potest prorogare non tamen ultra aliud semestre*" (*Constitutiones*, 33); *Constitutions*, 40.

179–180: {Regarding} the schedule of the brothers, the *Constitutions* lay down only the following: (1) the brothers assist at conventual Mass and vespers on Sundays and holydays only; (2) their office consists of "prayers appointed for them in the Cistercian Ritual"[539] (*Paters* and *Aves*); (3) morning mental prayer in common is prescribed; (4) it is also prescribed that the brothers in common "hear a private Mass"[540] in the morning (to replace attendance at conventual Mass); (5) they are meant to be free from liturgical and other obligations in order to devote themselves to longer work; (6) they are also obliged to *lectio divina* (183). For the schedule of the brothers in detail, see {the} *Laybrothers' Usages*, n. 39ff.[541] This has been modified by the changes of schedule introduced by the General Chapters of 1953, 1955, etc. Roughly, the brothers live as follows: during the time when the choir is at vigils and lauds, the brothers say their office of vigils, make a meditation, and according to the season hear Mass, receive communion or else go to the workroom. When they have their communion Mass during our night office, they go to the workroom later. While they work in the workroom, there is public reading. They take their mixt earlier than the choir. They only observe the fasts of the Church, hence they get mixt in full on fast days of the Order, and more for collation (cf. 182). They have roughly seven hours of work in the winter, between eight and nine hours in the summer. They have time to read when we are in choir.

181: Confessors shall be appointed from among the priests of the community (professed). There is a master of laybrothers (cf. *Choir Usages*, 549–51[542]) charged with the "guidance and

---

539. "*preces quae illis in Rituali Cisterciensi assignantur*" (*Constitutiones*, 34); *Constitutions*, 41 (cf. *Rituale*, 177–78 [IV, xiv, 3–6]).

540. "*audita Missa privata*" (*Constitutiones*, 34); *Constitutions*, 41, which reads: "hearing a private Mass."

541. *Regulations of the Lay Brothers of the Order of Cistercians of the Strict Observance Approved by the General Chapter of 1927* (Dublin: M. H. Gill & Son, 1934), Book II: "Order of Exercises," 16–24 (##39–56).

542. *Regulations*, 260–61.

spiritual direction"[543] of the professed brothers. {He} holds repetitions and catechisms analogous to those of the novitiate {and} visits them at their work "once a week" (*Usages*, 550[544]). He makes the various appointments for chores and services around the community.

183 states the obligation for the brothers to apply themselves to prayer and *lectio divina* when they are free from work. This obligation is as serious for the brothers as for the choir, since the brothers too are obliged to lead a monastic and contemplative life. But there are graver obstacles for some of them in view of the fact that they may often have extra work, especially in planting and harvesting seasons. Also they may be to some extent exempt from supervision and able to get into bad habits more quickly. Hence a real spirit of prayer and regularity is especially necessary for the brothers who are engaged in heavy work, if they are to preserve their vocation or its true spirit. The brothers' life in general offers opportunities for great humility, simplicity and self-sacrifice. But in order to profit by these opportunities, the brother must be very serious in his search for God, his spirit of silence, recollection and obedience.

The brothers have their own scriptorium (183).

Chapter 8: FUGITIVES AND APOSTATES—DISMISSALS—RETURN TO THE ORDER[545]

Here is a sad truth which we must face. Even good and fervent religious can sometimes lose their zeal and fervor and end up in a betrayal of their vocation. It can happen to anyone, and the greatest care must be taken to lead a really interior life of faith, humility, love and utter devotion to truth. Exterior regularity is not enough, nor is a fidelity based on fear. If there is not a genuine and humble love of our vocation, we are always in danger of putting into effect the contradiction that exists hidden within us.

---

543. *Regulations*, 260 (#549).
544. *Regulations*, 260 (#550).
545. Nn. 184–92 (*Constitutiones*, 35–36; *Constitutions*, 42–43).

184–186: Fugitives and Apostates: the difference between the two {is that} a *fugitive* "is one who without the permission of his superiors deserts the religious house, but with the intention of returning *to the institute*" (canon 644, n. 3[546]). Flight is distinguished from unlawful going out (cf. {the} statute on the enclosure). Flight supposes an absence of two or three days, without the permission of superiors, or withdrawal from their control to a place unknown to them, for that time. A temporary professed who leaves *even without the intention of returning* is a fugitive but not an apostate. {With respect to} *apostates,* canon 644, n. 1 defines {an} apostate as follows: (1) "one who has made the profession of perpetual vows whether solemn or simple"[547] (hence one under temporary vows cannot be an apostate); (2) "[who] unlawfully leaves the religious house with the intention of not returning";[548] (3) "[or who] with the intention of withdrawing himself from religious obedience, does not return to the house though he has lawfully left it."[549] The Code distinguishes apostates from the faith (canon 1325, n. 2[550]), apostates from holy orders (canon 2379[551]), and apostates from religion (canon 644), with which we are here concerned. The essence of apostasy is *the desertion of religious life,* and in particular withdrawal from obedience to religious superiors in general, in the sense of the withdrawal from all religious obedience. (To refuse obedience while remaining in the monastery is not juridical apostasy.) Here we are particularly concerned with the *crime* of apostasy and not merely with the *sin.* The *sin* of apostasy can consist purely of the internal act, the intention to desert the religious life. This can be

---

546. "*qui, sine Superiorum licentia, domum religiosam deserit cum animo ad religionem redeundi*" (*Codex Iuris Canonici,* 186).

547. "*professus a votis perpetuis sive sollemnibus sive simplicibus.*"

548. "*qui e domo religiosa illegitime egreditur cum animo non redeundi.*"

549. "*qui, etsi legitime egressus, non redit eo animo ut religiosae obedientiae sese subtrahat.*"

550. *Codex Iuris Canonici,* 385.

551. *Codex Iuris Canonici,* 651.

committed without actually deserting religion. But it is purely interior and does not involve excommunication, etc. and the other consequences in the external forum. The *crime* is external, in two ways, as shown above: (1) the monastery is left illegitimately; (2) or one refuses to return when it is required to do so. In either case, there must also be an *internal malicious intention* to desert religion. If the intention to desert religion is absent, the religious is innocent of apostasy. But if the religious is absent for more than a month, and if during that time he fails to communicate to his superior his intention of returning, he is presumed by law to be an apostate until the contrary is proved. The intention of not returning is also presumed when the religious places an act which is incompatible with returning—v.g., attempting matrimony, accepting employment in a secular business, etc. The intention of not returning is clear when it is expressed by the apostate himself. If one leaves to embrace a stricter life in another order, he is not considered an apostate according to common law, but in some orders there is special legislation to that effect. It would seem that such legislation exists in our Order (cf. *Liber Antiquarum Definitionum*, Dist. XI, n. 1: that we cannot pass to the Carthusians without permission, and that if we pass to the Friars Minor or {the} Dominicans even with permission of {the} abbot we are considered fugitives—see *Nomasticon*, p. 449).

184 prescribes that fugitives and apostates, whether or not they keep the habit, incur the penalties inflicted by common law. Those penalties are laid down in canon 2385: [552] for an *apostate*, *excommunication* reserved to his superior, or, if he comes under canon 646 [553] (apostasy from {the} faith; flight with a woman; attempted matrimony), then he is *ipso facto dismissed from the order*; if he returns, he is forever deprived of active or passive voice in chapter; for a *fugitive*, the common law prescribes loss of office, if he has one, {and} suspension, if he is a cleric. *In our Order*, by

---

552. *Codex Iuris Canonici*, 653.
553. *Codex Iuris Canonici*, 187.

particular law, *the fugitive incurs excommunication* like the apostate. The *Constitutions* explicitly state that retaining or putting off the habit makes no difference. Under the old canon law, keeping the habit was taken as a sign that one intended to return to religion.

Important notes:
1. THOSE WHO COOPERATE IN THE CRIME OF APOSTASY OR FLIGHT INCUR THE SAME PENALTIES AS THE APOSTATE OR THE FUGITIVE (canons 2209, n. 3 [554] and 2231; [555] cf. Schaefer, 1572 [556]).

2. The apostate or fugitive can be absolved sacramentally before their return only if they are sincerely sorry for their sin, and are prepared to take the proper steps to get straight. This implies either (a) a promise to return as soon as possible to religion; (b) or at least the willingness to submit to directives of superiors, if a return is somehow out of the question. Superiors can permit him to remain in the world until {a} dispensation can be obtained or dismissal is decided upon.

3. A religious illegitimately out of his cloister *loses the privilege of exemption*, and hence is subject to the draft.

4. The superiors of apostates and fugitives are gravely obliged to seek them out and try to bring them back to the regular life.

5. The apostate and fugitive ARE IN NO WAY FREED FROM THE OBLIGATION OF THEIR VOWS AND THEY ARE OBLIGED TO RETURN AS SOON AS POSSIBLE TO RELIGION (canon 645, n. 1 [557]). One is never allowed to better his juridical position as the result of a crime.

6. A professed under temporary vows who leaves is strictly neither a fugitive nor an apostate if he had the intention of not returning, but even then *he must be received back* (Schaefer, 1566 [558]).

---

554. *Codex Iuris Canonici*, 594–95.
555. *Codex Iuris Canonici*, 604.
556. Schaefer, 939.
557. *Codex Iuris Canonici*, 187.
558. Schaefer, 934–35.

7. If after one has sought out the religious and he persists obstinately in his intention to be an apostate, then *dismissal is to take place*. But scandal is to be avoided (especially for the apostate himself). Dismissal requires a separate juridical act; it does not follow automatically from apostasy, even after a certain time has elapsed. In other words, there must be a process, with formal warnings (two), after which one takes legal action. The apostate does not have to be physically present at the trial (see below).

185: We now come to some points of particular law about fugitives or apostates. The old law of the Order was extremely strict. In the old days any abbot of the Order could invoke the aid of secular police or soldiers to bring an apostate back to the monastery by force, where he would then be held in custody under lock and key. The *Constitutions* of today explicitly retain only one point of the old legislation: if a fugitive or apostate presents himself at a monastery of the Order, the superior makes him wait at the gate, ascertains whether he means to return to his house, and if he does not, then he cannot stay more than one night (cf. *Nomasticon*, p. 216: *Instituta*, XVI). This goes back to the earliest legislation of the Order.

187: Satisfaction {is} to be made by a fugitive or apostate returning to the monastery:

a) Common law is to be observed: canon 2386[559] prescribes that for fugitives there is to be suspension *a sacris* and privation of office (as above), and that he is to be punished according to the constitutions, or if there is no punishment prescribed in the constitutions, the superior (major) imposes a suitable penance.

b) Particular law imposes various penances: the first is that the culprit takes the discipline in chapter in the presence of the choir religious (*Usages*, 47[560]); the second is a suitable penance imposed by the superior to fit the nature of the case; the third {is that} he is re-instated in the last place among those actually pro-

---

559. *Codex Iuris Canonici*, 653.
560. *Regulations*, 25–26.

fessed (or among the priests if he is a priest). If he has been less than thirty days out of the monastery he can be reinstated in his proper rank.

Dismissal (186): (1) canon 646[561] gives cases which involve automatic dismissal from the order *ipso facto* (see above); (2) the temporary professed can be dismissed by the Abbot General and his council, or the local abbot with his council, as we have seen above (160); (3) {n.} 186 of our *Constitutions* deals exclusively with the dismissal of solemn professed, and applies to laybrothers and choir religious alike; (4) the law states: "if any solemnly professed laybrother become *notoriously incorrigible in a grave and scandalous fault...*"[562]—notoriously incorrigible implies three grave public faults, in between which two formal warnings have been issued. The faults must be "grave external offenses against the universal law or the special law of religious" (canon 656[563]). To assume that they are incorrigible, there must be a failure to amend after {a} warning, in such a way that bad will is evident. In practice, the serious faults alluded to here must be *crimes* (a) against laws of the Church to which a canonical penalty is attached (this would hold for precepts of the *Rule* to which is attached a sanction); (b) against a formal and grave precept of the superior; (c) against the vows or constitutions in a specially grave manner, or with specially grave scandal. *Not included* as reasons for dismissal after solemn profession {are} habitual violation of the rule in disciplinary matters {or} frequent violation of the vows in light matters. *Examples* {would include} frequent violation of silence and other observances.

---

561. *Codex Iuris Canonici*, 187.
562. "*si quis monachus vel conversus solemniter professus in gravi ac pernicioso crimine notorie incorrigibilis evaserit*" (*Constitutiones*, 35); *Constitutions*, 42, which reads: "... solemnly professed monk or lay brother ..." (emphasis added).
563. "*Gravia delicta externa sive contra ius commune sive contra speciale religiosorum ius*" (*Codex Iuris Canonici*, 190).

Procedure for dismissal of a solemn professed: after a serious external offense has been verified, the superior (abbot) issues the first warning, with exhortation, public penances and other remedies to procure amendment, including removal of {the} occasion if possible. To each warning must be added the threat of dismissal. Warnings are repeated after the next two offenses, provided there is an interval of some three days between them. If two or three years elapse after the first warning and there is some sign of amendment, then a further offense cannot be considered a "second" offense in the series, but the first in a new series. The guilty one may defend himself freely (canon 650,[564] 651[565]). However, an *immediate decree of expulsion* can be given by the local superior with his council, or the superior general with his council, if the presence of the person in the community after three warnings would cause a grave exterior scandal outside the community, or cause very serious damage within the community. Serious harm must be *imminent* for this to be justified. {A} process must follow this immediate dismissal in any case (canon 668[566]). {The} *process* {is as follows}: the process of a monk to be expelled from the Order is carried out by the definitory, before the Abbot General, who appoints a religious of the Order as prosecutor (canon 655[567]). After it is clear that the three warnings were useless, the abbot of the place sends the documents of the case to the Abbot General (canon 663[568]). The "promoter of justice" (religious prosecutor) studies the documents, and if further inquiry is not necessary, he draws up an act of accusation (canon 664[569]). The accused is then informed and chooses his own advocate, or one is given him. The case is tried, and examined and decided by a vote of the tribunal. If {a} sentence of dismissal is handed down,

---

564. *Codex Iuris Canonici*, 189 (n. 3).
565. *Codex Iuris Canonici*, 189 (n. 2).
566. *Codex Iuris Canonici*, 192.
567. *Codex Iuris Canonici*, 190.
568. *Codex Iuris Canonici*, 191.
569. *"promotor iustitiae"* (*Codex Iuris Canonici*, 191).

then the acts of the trial are sent to the Sacred Congregation. The sentence is executed when the Congregation confirms the acts of the trial.

READMISSION *of those who have left legitimately*: besides the case of one who leaves when his temporary vows have expired, there are two other ways of legitimately leaving religion:

1. *By indult of exclaustration*: permission to live temporarily outside the houses of the order and without being subject to the authority of religious superiors (canon 638, 639[570]). This may be legitimately asked for when there is a serious reason to do something that cannot be properly carried out in the religious house or under obedience to superiors, for instance if one should have to leave to take care of his parents temporarily. Such an indult should never be asked for without *serious* consultation with a director who sees things objectively and supernaturally. It is a very serious matter to have such an indult, and the Holy See in granting one supposes that the petitioner is acting on a good conscience. One could interiorly commit a serious sin against the vow of stability by obtaining such an indult without sufficient reason. An exclaustrated religious (a) retains his vows and all the obligations of the rule which are compatible with his state; (b) does not wear the religious habit; (c) during the time he is out he has no active or passive voice, but he retains the spiritual privileges of the order; (d) is subject by virtue of his vow of obedience to the ordinary of the place where he resides (canon 639). An indult of exclaustration can be obtained only from the Holy See. The question of his return to the order presents no complications: he must return when the indult expires, unless it is renewed.

Distinct from exclaustration is {a} *leave of absence*. The local abbot can grant {a} leave of absence to any professed, *up to six months*. The local superiors can give a leave of absence of *longer than six months* when there is a question of studies. But apart from that case, the permission of the Holy See must be obtained (canon

---

570. *Codex Iuris Canonici*, 185.

606, n. 2[571]). The Holy See can grant a leave of absence for *more than six months*, but in the rescript two things are explicitly mentioned: (a) the superiors are obliged to see that the religious keeps his vows and observes the rule as much as possible; (b) the religious remains fully subject to his superiors and is bound to return if during the time of the indult they ask him to return. This is different from exclaustration, in which the religious is withdrawn to a great extent from the control of his superiors. The indult of exclaustration can be revoked by the Holy See at any time.

Indult of secularization: secularization is the permission to leave the religious life definitively, with complete and absolute dissolution of all bonds with the order. The religious is in effect dispensed from his vows by secularization and remains perpetually outside the order and religion. He relinquishes all the rights, privileges and obligations of a member of the order, including the vow of chastity, unless he is in holy orders. Secularization cannot be granted without *very grave cause*, of which the Holy See remains the judge. The Congregation always consults the religious superiors and in practice follows their advice. Grave causes would be {a} complete breakdown in health, mental or physical (*"mentalis religiosi dispositio"* [572]), which might include a practical loss of vocation; {or} help necessary for parents. Note: the Holy See does not favor secularization in persecuted countries in order that the religious may continue to perform necessary works—v.g., education. The Church prefers that the *religious remain a religious* even in exile or in forced inaction rather than give up the religious state in order to teach in state-approved schools, etc. The Church considers her religious as such to be a most important and fruitful part of the Mystical Body and is very loath to see the bond of religious vows dissolved, since the religious contributes so much to the sanctity and fertility of the Church, precisely by his consecrated life. We must never forget

---

571. *Codex Iuris Canonici*, 176.
572. "mental fitness for religious life".

the high dignity and worth of our calling and how much the Church values it. An *indult of secularization is not valid* if the motives on which the petition was based are *false* or *if essential facts were withheld*. The indult does not take effect *until it is accepted by the religious*. If the religious refuses to accept it, then he remains a religious with all his vows, obligations, rights, etc. If a religious who *should* leave refuses, and if the superiors feel that his decision is just another example of his inconstancy, the matter may be referred to the Holy See.

Effects of {an} indult of secularization (canon 640[573]):

a) Total separation from the order. The secularized person must put aside the religious habit. "He may wear, through devotion the garments worn under the habit of his former religious family" (Creusen, p. 256[574]).

b) He is freed from all his vows except chastity in the case of those in holy orders alone. He is freed from his obligations, except that of reciting {the} office in the case of those in holy orders alone. He is no longer bound by any of the rules and constitutions, in the internal or external forum.

c) He once again has the power to own and acquire goods, to marry, etc. (unless {in} holy orders).

d) Religious in holy orders must return to their own diocese and be received by their own bishop, unless they can get another bishop. As to the exercise of their orders, they must be under some bishop. The bishop may receive a secularized religious either purely and simply, or else for three years *ad experimentum*.[575] The three-years' probation can be extended for another three years. At the end of the probation, or at the moment when he is accepted "*simpliciter*,"[576] the priest is incardinated in the new diocese. In the case where the religious priest is accepted on trial by a bishop, the

---

573. *Codex Iuris Canonici*, 185.
574. #336.1(a).
575. "on a trial basis".
576. "simply"; "unconditionally".

Holy See does not give a definitive indult of secularization. He is then exclaustrated, but at the end of his probation, if the bishop does not explicitly send him back to his order, then he is incardinated automatically and secularized (cf. Schaefer, 1549[577]). Religious priests who are secularized cannot (a) have a benefice in a basilica or a cathedral; (b) be a professor or hold office in a seminary or university (without {a} special indult from {the} Holy See); (c) hold any office or employment in the curia or in any religious house. "The Holy See does not wish that the hope of dignities or of an honorable position among the secular clergy give rise to temptations to inconstancy" (Creusen, p. 258[578]). It also shows the "disfavor with which the Holy See regards the abandonment of . . . religion" (*ibid*.). The Church regards passage from religion to secular clergy as a "regrettable inconstancy,"[579] but the passage in the opposite direction is quite different (cf. canon 542, n. 2[580]).

Our *Constitutions* lay down the following on reception of those who have legitimately left the Order by secularization or after expiration of temporary vows: (a) a secularized monk or brother cannot return without the permission of the Abbot General and of the Holy See (188); (b) he then makes his novitiate and profession over again, and takes his new rank, all being exactly as if he had never been in the Order at all (189); (c) if he has been "dismissed"[581] or has left of his own accord after temporary vows, he also requires the permission of the General and of the Holy See for readmission.

THE CHAPTER OF FAULTS

It is true that the chapter of faults is a very important observance and that much depends on it. Regularity is important.

---

577. Schaefer, 922–23.
578. #337.2, which reads: "The Holy See shall not . . . rise to a temptation . . ."
579. Creusen, 258 (#337).
580. *Codex Iuris Canonici*, 157.
581. "*dimissus*" (*Constitutiones*, 36); *Constitutions*, 43.

Observance is important. The *Rule* must be kept in order that we may attain the end for which we have come to the community life—union with God in peace, charity, prayer. Fraternal correction is an obligation of charity, and so a proclamation of a brother is a charitable reminder of some oversight or failing, the correction of which will be profitable to his soul and to the community at large. Hence the aim of a proclamation is to *help*, to do *good*. A wise proclamation will therefore always be judged in the light of this end. By proclaiming such a one, for such a fault, in such a way—will I really help him, will I really do good? Or will I be a scandal to him, and will I do harm? We should always assume, unless there is evidence to the contrary, (1) that our brother is willing to be corrected and that he wants to be proclaimed for faults, because a good religious is glad to be proclaimed; (2) that even if we make an error of judgement, or if our proclamation is not perfect, it will be understood in good part and our good intentions will be appreciated; (3) that those who proclaim us mean well and sincerely wish our good and are not acting out of personal spite, etc.

However, much harm can be done when the chapter of faults is badly conducted and when the spirit becomes too human. Here are some of the drawbacks:
 1. {A} tendency to lose {a} sense of proportion and perspective—we become hypnotized by the little exterior faults we wish to correct in others, and they become magnified beyond all proportion.
 2. {A} tendency of unconscious personal and natural weaknesses to creep into our "zeal" for the *Rule*. We may have {a} pure intention, but there may indeed be unconscious spite and animosity against certain ones, and this will quite easily appear in the proclamation—it may be sensed by the other one. This is of course unavoidable, but it must be taken into account.
 3. A wrong spirit, a spirit of "punishment," of "exacting justice," of "correcting abuses" may come to dominate our minds. Charity cannot survive if, in the chapter of faults, we have set up

our own judgement onto a pedestal and make it our god. From this flows false zeal, which disturbs peace, leads to interminable interior arguments over nothing, increases bad feeling, shuts the soul up in itself etc., hardens it against others. Thus community spirit is destroyed. In such circumstances one proclaims in chapter uniquely in order to assert {one's} own will and judgement and impose them on others, including superiors. {These are} proclamations {intended} to force {the} superior to see things my way.

Hence, some practical norms {are}:

1. *Simple and objective* proclamations: (a) {a} plain statement of {a} fault, in simplest terms; (b) accusation only for faults clearly based on {the} *Rule*, {the} usages {or the} known will of {the} superior; (c) {a determination} to avoid as far as possible misunderstandings.

2. *Charitable* proclamations: (a) feel kind towards the person proclaimed—do not be obsessed by a hostile image of him—if you are, don't proclaim; (b) {use a} kind tone etc., based on {a} kind attitude toward the person, not merely "put on"; (c) amusing proclamations do not achieve the right result.

3. *Selfless* proclamations: (a) not {motivated by a} desire to impose my own will or interpretation of the *Rule*; (b) if I am annoyed at the way the superior handles the proclamation, then I am probably motivated by self-love; (c) not {to} be scandalized if the one proclaimed happens to commit the same fault over again; (d) not {to} proclaim, of course, for faults committed against myself; (e) not {to} proclaim because a brother does something I do not like, or in a way I do not like, or in order to make him do what I like; (f) not {to} sulk and say, "I just won't proclaim any more—that's all."

The novitiate chapter of faults {is} in part, a training ground. The proclamations may be taken apart and analyzed and criticized, so do not be upset if this happens. {Should} novitiate customs {be included}? This {is} the proper place for proclamations on these points, but should not be a seed-ground for innumerable new "rules."

APPENDIX A
Textual Notes

Additions and Alterations in Typescript

1   publishes a] *followed by x'd out* new
         General Chapter] *typed added on line following x'd out* Abbots of the Four First
         after difficulties] *preceded by x'd out* Foundations, to
         (a)] *followed by x'd out* in 1118

3   One other is] *typed interlined above x'd out* Others are
         began to] *preceded by x'd out* of
         An Early . . . Caritatis] *added on line following cancelled* Original Text of the Carta Caritatis

4   regular] *followed by x'd out* honeste

5   *nimias*] *typed interlined and marked for insertion*
         There are] *preceded by cancelled* After twenty years
         REDOLEAT] *preceded by x'd out* REDOLET

7   *Instituta*] *preceded by x'd out* Foundations
         temporal goods] poral goods *added on line*
         Here we have . . . supposed to be.] *added in lower margin*

8   *futurum*] *interlined with a caret*
         De singulari consensione] *added on line*
         in order to] *preceded by x'd out* but retains

9   BEATI] *typed interlined above cancelled* SANCTI
         (This . . . addition.)] *added on line*
         {d}] a *in text*

10   make *any*] *preceded by x'd out* do anything

12   judge] *preceded by x'd out* fault

14   Today, only . . . #10] *added in left margin*

15	before . . . plan, etc.] *added in upper margin*
16	appointments] *preceded by x'd out* officers
18	(the term] *preceded by x'd out* (They do not use the term interval)
	cf. today] *added in left margin*
	sitting] *typed interlined and marked for insertion*
19	incedant"] *followed by x'd out* et discooperto capite
	along {the} wall??] *added on line*
	term] *followed by x'd out* to
	known to the] *followed by x'd out* superior
	note . . . read {the} *Rule*] *added in lower margin*
20	Two types . . . room.] *typed following* doing penance. *and marked for transposition*
	abbot's kitchen . . . back to {the} common refectory.] *opposite page*
	one hears] *preceded by x'd out* and both are
21	Contrast La Trappe] *added in left margin*
21–22	*Usages* of . . . suppressed] *opposite page*
22	guest] *preceded by x'd out* Visitor
23	locum] *preceded by x'd out* loca proxima
	n.b. this] *preceded by x'd out* 5-
	going on.] silence of house—prayer in ch—now loudspeakers everywhere etc. *added in left margin and cancelled*
24	(although it is in the *Rule*)] *added on line*
25	power] *typed interlined above x'd out* permission
	he is . . . trusted.)] *added on line*
26	What were . . . in the church.] *typed following* family. *and marked for transposition*
	upper] *preceded by x'd out* first floor of the east wing
	Benedict . . . cells.] *added in left margin*
	(says . . . *Statutes*)] *added on line*
27	*Usages*] *preceded by x'd out* Rules
	not a formal . . . people] *added on line*
28	one quarter] *preceded by x'd out* 1/2
	for {the} reader, etc.] *interlined with a caret*
29	74 to 83] to *interlined above cancelled and*

Appendix A

      vigils] *interlined above cancelled* night office
      to be said] *followed by x'd out* dawn—lauds "apparente
          autem die pulsetur signum . . ."
      4:45 or] *added in left margin before* 5 *typed below cancelled* 4.3
      light] *preceded by cancelled* If it is not yet day,
      5:30 or] *added in left margin*
      6:00] *added in left margin following cancelled* 5:45

30   (about five hours)] *added on line*
      1:30] 30 *interlined before cancelled* 15
      2:00] *interlined before cancelled* 1.30 *followed by cancelled*
          or 2:00

31   anyone] *preceded by x'd out* they can
      provides] *preceded by x'd out* does
      knife] *followed by x'd out* or
      divina] *followed by x'd out* for about an hour and a half
          or two hours

32   If one] *preceded by x'd out* After
      another] *followed by x'd out* on
      water] *interlined below and marked for insertion*
      guest master] *typed in left margin and marked for insertion*
          to replace cancelled infirmarian
      n.b. the *Salve* . . . family] *added in lower margin and marked*
          for insertion

35   (1) possession] *preceded by x'd out* c 85
      superiors] *preceded by x'd out* or to build chapels.
      1199] *preceded by x'd out* 1203 legislates that
      4] *preceded by x'd out* 5

36   in some] *preceded by x'd out* 8-
      1186] *preceded by x'd out* 8-
      1205] *preceded by x'd out* 11

37   1259, . . . n. 10] *added in left margin*
      Magdalen] *followed by x'd out* three to six weeks

38   1211, n.] *followed by x'd out* 11
      petitioned] *followed by x'd out* that out of

39   Read . . . silence] *added in lower margin*
      nisi] *followed by x'd out* in

40   for the day.] *added on line*

	is about] *followed by x'd out* the
	presumably . . . meals.] *interlined*
	kneel] *followed by x'd out* during the collect and at the gloria patri
	seriously] *typed interlined below x'd out* gravely
41	pallet . . . lie on] *typed interlined below x'd out* straw mattress
	but . . . bedding.] *added on line*
	not . . . office] *added in left margin to replace cancelled* at (mental) prayer
	chorum.] *followed by cancelled* (So too for Office of BV.)
	Stability . . . will of God.] *opposite page*
	burden] *preceded by cancelled* penance
42	1209] *preceded by x'd out* 10
	(note . . . disobedience)] *interlined*
	is sent] *preceded by x'd out* goes to a
43	legitimate] *preceded by x'd out* a more
	Note . . . schism.] *added in lower margin*
	a sad . . . read] *added on line*
45	1233 . . . horses, etc.] *interlined*
	({A} pittance . . . n. 23.)] *added in lower margin*
46	postulant] *altered by x'ing out from* postulants
	(Note how] *preceded by x'd out* (Note how much this makes sense—the secular is in the presence
	means] *followed by x'd out* it
	younger.] *followed by x'd out* (Monks did not even want those inabi
47	in view.] *preceded by x'd out* aimed at
	1157, n. 28] *interlined and marked for insertion*
48	However . . . visitor] *interlined*
	In {the} *Libellus* . . . vocations] *interlined*
49	({In the} *Libellus* . . . fugitive.)] *interlined*
	agreed that] *followed by x'd out* the
	N.B. novices . . . Chapter] *interlined*
	do NOT . . . chapter] *added on line*
	(but in . . . refectory)] *added on line*
50	(h) if . . . lectionis] *added in lower margin and marked for insertion*

Appendix A

	i] *added in left margin before cancelled* h
	well as] *preceded by x'd out* far
51	read on *Sundays*] *interlined*
53	prior.] *preceded by x'd out* superior.
54	saying] *typed interlined above x'd out* singing
	server] *preceded by x'd out* servant
	to {the} altar] *typed interlined*
55	for day hours] *typed interlined and marked for insertion*
	the reason] *typed interlined above x'd out* it
56	able,] *preceded by x'd out* well, they are
103	venial sin] *followed by x'd out* irrespective of attendant ci
104	forbids] *added in left margin and marked for insertion to replace cancelled* excludes
	any outsider] *altered from* any outsider
	in town . . . etc.] *typed interlined and marked for insertion*
	permission to speak] *followed by x'd out* to those one meets is
	This prescription] *preceded by x'd out* This sentence is one of the
	prescriptions] *preceded by x'd out* statutes on enc
	opened] *altered from* opened
105	cf. 1907, n. 9: . . . letter] *added in lower margin*
	or receive] *typed interlined and marked for insertion*
	knowledge of {the} superior] of superior *interlined with a caret*
106	for instance] *followed by x'd out* in some business that would involve
	magnitude] *preceded by x'd out* importance.
	1954] *preceded by x'd out* 1945
	write a letter] *preceded by x'd out* send a letter
107	persons,] *followed by x'd out* without
	1932, n. 4 . . . mistake] *added on line*
108	*To whom . . . in another.*] *opposite page*
	office] *followed by cancelled* in
109	It puts . . . this.] *added on line*
110	if any] if *typed interlined*
	houses] *followed by x'd out* that
	exercise] *typed interlined above x'd out* render

	to undertake . . . prayer)] *added on line*
111	4] *followed by x'd out* This is not to
	activity] *preceded by x'd out* obligation to
	Note {this could become a} . . . interior life.] *interlined*
112	training . . . country] *altered from* training . . . country
	General . . . time)] *interlined*
	a decree] a *interlined above cancelled* the
	Congregation] *followed by cancelled* in
	cf. canon 588, n. 2] *typed in left margin*
113	especially . . . piety.] *added on line*
	Our Constitutions] *preceded by x'd out* n. 105—*Studies in Rome*
	588] *followed by x'd out* n. 2
114	intimate] *preceded by x'd out* interior
115	"except . . . Latin."] *altered from* except . . . Latin.
	directors,] *preceded by x'd out* priests
	in certain] in *interlined with a caret above cancelled* under
116	The local] *preceded by x'd out* By
	each] *typed interlined below x'd out* the
117	mostly] *preceded by x'd out* including
	forever] *preceded by x'd out* absolutely
	refers] *preceded by x'd out* is is directed to the
	the exam] *preceded by x'd out* it is
	Professors . . . study!] *added on line*
118	in theology, etc.] *interlined with a caret*
	their] *interlined above cancelled* his
	as far as] *preceded by x'd out* in
119	fulfill] *preceded by x'd out* be
	not necessarily] *preceded by x'd out* It would be suffici
	could be given] could *altered from* should
	almost] *typed before* abandon *and marked for transposition*
120	who have] *preceded by x'd out* priests
	(professed)] *typed interlined and marked for insertion*
	may] *altered from* may
121	and twelve] twelve *interlined with a caret*
	whole] *interlined with a caret*
	permits] *preceded by x'd out* prescribes

Appendix A

	returns] *preceded by x'd out* sits down.
122	cheese and] and *interlined*
	eggs] *followed by cancelled* and fish.
	also that] *followed by x'd out* the practice of
	fish] *altered from* fish
124	but are . . . days] *interlined below cancelled* not
	rule] *followed by x'd out* and
125	on top] *preceded by x'd out* in t
	as monks] *added in left margin and marked for insertion*
126	mixt, General . . . other meals.] *opposite page*
127	portions *only*] only *interlined with a caret*
	"sufficient quantity"] *altered from* sufficient quantity
128	but not here today.] *added on line*
	priests] *preceded by x'd out* professed have one
	This last . . . Usages.] *added on line*
129	cf. *Usages*, 295] *typed in left margin and marked for insertion*
	dispensation] *added in left margin to replace cancelled* mitigation
	an adaptation because] *preceded by x'd out* A mitigation
131	Remember . . . reject them!] *opposite page*
132	secular] secular the richest
133–34	What is . . . excommunication.] *opposite page*
133	*Materially*] *interlined with a caret*
134	Ann's] *followed by cancelled* sheep farm
	No such . . . other times.] *added in lower margin*
	forbidden] *preceded by x'd out* permit
	In 1920 . . . enclosure.] *added in left margin and marked for insertion*
135	*Volkswagen*] *altered from* Volkswagen
	possess] *preceded by x'd out* ride around
	to look] *preceded by x'd out* very little
	abuse] *preceded by x'd out* abusive
	private] *followed by x'd out* gave
	The point . . . encourage it.] *altered from* The point . . . encourage it.
135–36	desire of . . . a monk.] *added in left margin*
136	living] *typed interlined and marked for insertion*

	however] *interlined below cancelled* cf.
	Note: Reverend . . . profession.] *added in left margin*
	emanate from] *followed by x'd out* a
137	taken] *altered from* taken
	Movies are . . . monastery] *added on line*
	aberrations] *followed by x'd out* which are
	Prudence is required!!] *added on line*
138	taste] *followed by x'd out* and
	cf. General . . . #6] *added on line*
	or admit] *typed interlined and marked for insertion*
	deprived of office] *altered from* deprived of office
139	incur excommunication] *altered from* incur excommunication
	to admit] *followed by cancelled* not
	fail to] *interlined below and marked for insertion*
	Of no matter what age] *altered from* Of no matter what age
	by a sentence] *altered from* by a sentence
	not ipso facto] *altered from* not ipso facto
	practice] *interlined above cancelled* abuse
140	139 . . . some time.] *following* other seculars. *and marked for transposition*
	The meaning . . . enclosure] *altered from* The meaning . . . enclosure
	suggestions] *preceded by x'd out* some me
	visitors] *preceded by x'd out* outsiders
	necessary] *preceded by x'd out* What is
141	can] *altered from* can
	may . . . Rome] *altered from* may . . . Rome
	interpret] *preceded by x'd out* always
	of the superior] *followed by x'd out* except in some unusla
142–44	PART III . . . no doubtful candidate be admitted to the monastery.] *typed page followed by* skip p. 45 *in lower margin to replace cancelled* Part III—Entrance to the Order Ch I: *The Admission of Postulants*: 144: *The greatest care shall be taken in the admission of novices. Here we consider the mystery of vocations from a canonical point of view—from the aspect of* Law, *not of*

Appendix A

spirituality. It may be worth while here to resume some principles on the admission of novices, drawn from instructions given by our Most Reverend General (Dom Gabriel) to the Superiors of the Order. All might be summed up in a familiar axiom: *"Facilis admissio est pessima candidatorum selectio."*

1- It is useless to give a formation to one who cannot be formed. If a novice does not have the proper aptitude and disposition for receiving a form, then he cannot become a useful and really living member of the Order. Hence the need to see if the subject has *aptitude* and *intention* to receive the proper form.

2- Superiors are therefore wrong who judge by good will alone, or who imagine that the selection will take place automatically with time—that one who does not have a true vocation will just naturally drop out during the novitiate. No, it is necessary to study the aptitudes and background of the candidate even before he enters the monastery, then during his postulancy, and not so much during the novitiate. This last is not so much a time *of selection* as a time of *formation*. However, note that most theologians consider the novitiate also a time of *selection*. We cannot assume that all selection will take place *before* the novitiate.

3- If mistakes are to be made, said Dom Gabriel, it would be better to err in sending away a good vocation than in accepting a doubtful one, because if God wills, the good one will come back. But the presence of a few misfits can disturb seriously the peace of entire communities.

4- Can. 545 n. 4 prescribes that those who send testimonial letters at request of Superior, must make a *diligent investigation*, under serious obligation of conscience as to the truth of what is said, especially as to irregularities, studies, reputation, and previous history.

n. 3- The Superior himself is supposed to complete incomplete information by an "accurate investigation."

The Decree *Quantum Religiones omnes* (Dec. 1, 1931) says "Superiors must take the greatest care not to receive subjects too hastily, but to accept only those in whom signs of *a divine vocation* are to be found." (see below)

5- Advantages of proceding carefully—a) The aspirant is prevented from uselessly breaking off with his present state, and upsetting his life when he has no real vocation. b) It is much better for the postulant to enter morally certain that he is called, and not just "trying out." Note however that it is extremely difficult in some cases to say, before they enter, whether they really seem to be called in a way that is morally certain. It seems *likely* indeed, and as far as one can judge they have the aptitudes . . . c) It is advantageous for the community not to regard the novitiate as a time in which to study one's vocation. Many such candidates leave, and then this affects the reputation of the monastery—talk about the monastery, many "Ex-Trappists" from such and such a house are seen here and there—creates a bad impression.

For all these reasons, the Abbot General wishes that we try as far as possible to study and decide the question of vocation *before the candidate enters*.

So far at Gethsemani this has been found to be almost impossible except in some cases. The novitiate in practice, will always remain a place in which vocations are sifted + selected.

6- A very important point: Dom Gabriel says: "IT SEEMS TO ME THAT YOU'D HAVE TO BE PRETTY HIGHLY FAVORED BY GOD OR ELSE ALTOGETHER PRESUMPTUOUS TO ANNOUNCE PEREMPTORILY THAT PEOPLE HAVE A VOCATION WHILE THEY THEMSELVES ARE STILL IN DOUBT ABOUT IT"—the great danger of telling someone, after he has been two days in the Guest house: "God wants you here." Such rash statements have led to great tragedies.

7- *Gathering information*—Testimonials etc. are often unsatisfactory or incomplete. One cannot usually meet the candidate's family or see him in the home though this would be ideal.

One must get much of the information from the person himself.

Appendix A

Inquiry by letter is not enough. One must *interview* the candidate—here he is seen by at least the Novice Master and the Abbot, and perhaps by a third interviewer. It is likely that three interviews will be the general rule in future.

The subject himself must also see the monastery and its community. Hence it is *by no means sufficient to decide a vocation by letter*.

There should be a "few days' contact."

Not an overnight, flying visit. This is not enough. If it is all that is possible the candidate should return later for a more prolonged visit.

A written Questionnaire to the candidate?

Dom Gabriel holds that though it is *usually insufficient and unnecessary*, it may "sometimes be useful," and should be used prudently.

Nothing is prescribed or suggested about *psychological tests*. The use of such tests at Gethsemani is in an experimental stage. They can and do help. Other orders use them very effectively. But even in religious life as a whole, they are still in the experimental stage.

There is always a danger of trusting too much in tests and techniques. It is much better just to go slow and get to know the candidate thoroughly by visits and interviews.

8- Contacts inside the community? (Inviting the candidate to spend a time on retreat *in the novitiate*.

Pro—the subject gets a better look at the community.

Con—The community however does not have a chance to form an objective judgement of the candidate, says Dom Gabriel.

Furthermore, the candidate, sifting everything critically, may render himself incapable of a real supernatural judgement, and keep from giving himself entirely to God.

Conclusion—Dom Gabriel however feels that *retreats inside the community may be allowed in countries like USA where candidates have no clear idea of the monastic life, and contacts may serve to dispel prejudices.*

9- After the decision that the candidate has a vocation, *a delay is recommended in order to test his resolution and progress*. But in individual cases it might perhaps be better to let him enter immediately. In practice, circumstances often settle this question.

10- What is the real point at issue in studying a vocation? To DISCOVER THE WILL OF GOD.

11- Things to be particularly avoided—

Admitting too easily subjects without aptitude, because of small numbers or some other natural reason.

Asserting that the subject has a *duty* to enter, especially when he is not altogether willing to do so.

> Here we . . . spirituality] *interlined*
> All might . . . *selectio."*] *interlined*
> Hence . . . form.] *interlined*
> and not so much] *added in left margin below cancelled*
>   as well as
> However, note . . . *selection.*] *interlined*
> We cannot . . . novitiate.] *added in left margin and marked for insertion*
> *a divine vocation*] *altered from* a divine vocation
> (see below)] *added on line*
> The novitiate in . . . selected.] *interlined*
> *Gathering information*] *altered from* Gathering information
> prolonged visit.] *followed by cancelled* The written questionnaire—is essential (prescribed by Gen. Chapter of 1947). But the questionnaire so prescribed is sent out for the purpose of obtaining detailed testimonial letters.
> *A written Questionnaire*] *altered from* A written Questionnaire
> *A written*] *added in left margin*
> usually . . . *unnecessary*] *altered from* usually . . . unnecessary
> or suggested] *interlined with a caret*
> *psychological tests*] *altered from* psychological tests
> (Inviting . . . novitiate.] *added on line*
> says Dom Gabriel.] *added on line*

Appendix A

	retreats . . . prejudices] *altered from* retreats . . . prejudices
	like USA] *preceded by x'd out* where
	a delay . . . progress] *altered from* a delay . . . progress
	especially . . . do so] *added on line following cancelled* even when
143	serious] *followed by x'd out* It is use
	by the bishop] by *typed interlined above x'd out* through
144	*exterior and canonical*] *interlined with a caret*
	intention] *followed by x'd out* (positive aptitude)
	assuming] *preceded by x'd out* bearing the
	and to freely choose those means for himself] *added on line*
	Defects in intention] *altered from* Defects in intention
	objectivity] *interlined and marked for insertion to replace cancelled* humility
	enters . . . serve God] *added on line*
144–45	we have . . . liturgy, etc.] *opposite page to replace cancelled* for the special end of our life—contemplative life
145	stamina] *added on line*
	intellectual] *added in left margin to replace cancelled* Mental
	120] *followed by x'd out* (?)
	2] *preceded by cancelled* A divine vocation?
	in one . . . our life] *interlined above and below cancelled* In an instruction to the General Chapter of 1953, Most Rev. Dom Gabriel went beyond the general signs of vocation to the religious life
	required in our life] *altered from* required in our life
	something more . . . life] *added on line*
	Benedictine] *followed by x'd out* Vocation
	Note . . . ruin the Order] *interlined*
	to say] *followed by x'd out* a
	right intention] *altered from* right intention
	firm . . . persevere] *altered from* firm . . . persevere
146	postulant] *preceded by x'd out* Order were an ins
	noble] *preceded by x'd out* good families and
	Good character] *altered from* Good character

            who is willing] *preceded by x'd out* should be willi
            Reputation] *altered from* Reputation
            condition and education] *altered from* condition and
               education
            a period] *preceded by x'd out* serious evidence

147   evil] *preceded by x'd out* faults everywhere
            types] *interlined below and marked for insertion*
            negative . . . from impediments] *added on line*
            it also excludes psychotics.] *added on line following*
               cancelled But it also certainly excludes those we
               have just mentioned who may be, in the main quite
               sane, and who function normally at least to all
               outward appearances
            by the natural law] *typed interlined and marked for*
               insertion

148   Formal] *preceded by x'd out* He would
            is enough] is *interlined with a caret to replace x'd out* might
               be
            from a non-Catholic sect, or] *added on line*
            Church in] *followed by x'd out* another
            or Catholics who have joined] or *added on line*

149   mistake,] *followed by x'd out* if he
            Violence] *altered from* Violence
            Grave fear inflicted . . . novitiate] *added on line*
            (dolus)] *followed by cancelled* here
            means to] *followed by x'd out* prevent falsify the moti
            to enter. . . basis] *altered from* to enter . . . basis
            to postulancy] to *interlined with a caret*
            persuade or induce] *altered from* persuade or induce

150   is required . . . case] *added on line following cancelled*
               demanded
            marriage . . . impediment] *added in left margin to replace*
               cancelled This holds
            dispensation.] *followed by x'd out* Divorce has no power
               to affect the impediment. The divorced are bound
               impeded as well as others.
            (Schaefer, 791)] *followed by* not however one who is *added*
               on line and cancelled

Appendix A

secularized or dispensed] *altered from* secularized or dispensed
transitus] *altered from* transitus
Novices and postulants] *altered from* Novices and postulants
after . . . simple vows] *altered from* after . . . simple vows
simple] *interlined above cancelled* solemn
(Schaefer, 795)] *added in lower margin*

151   not an invalidating] *an interlined with a caret*
novitiate will be] *interlined below cancelled* admission is
"married"] *altered from* married
without impediment] *interlined*
Clerics] *altered from* Cleric

152   This promise does] promise *interlined with a caret*
Scotch College] College *interlined*
However . . . justice.)] *added on line*
if any . . . invalid] *altered from* if any . . . invalid
Ignorance . . . not excuse] *altered from* Ignorance . . . not excuse
consulting] *typed interlined above x'd out* permission of
without *consulting*] *altered from* without consulting

153   proper] *preceded by x'd out* expedient
reason] *added in left margin*
get into] *preceded by x'd out* incur
lawsuits] *followed by x'd out* and

154   whose help] *preceded by x'd out* bound to support their children.
One cannot . . . natural law] *altered from* One cannot . . . natural law
one who . . . vow] *altered from* one who . . . vow
the parents'] parents' *interlined above* the *altered to* their
means] *added on line*

155   extraordinary] *preceded by x'd out* grave dan
Irregularity ex defectu] *altered from* Irregularity ex defectu

156   to Rome] *followed by x'd out* for this.
bigamists] *altered from* bigamists
convicted by law] *altered from* convicted by law
incest] *preceded by cancelled* sodomy

	things as these] *followed by cancelled* which would be possible if men knew that the minister of the sacrifice had been in the past publically condemned for such things. The thing must however be *public* that is generally known or capable of being generally known. Dispensation can of course be granted for good reasons.
	publically condemned] *added in left margin to replace cancelled* guilty of
157	the patient] *preceded by x'd out* someone.
	canonically] *preceded by x'd out* forbidden to do so.
	(i.e. temporary)] *added on line*
	it is no . . . impeded] *added on line*
	obligation] *followed by x'd out* (In practice novices are received in our European monasteries and go to
	institute] *preceded by x'd out* order
158	novitiate in] *followed by x'd out* a hous
	prescriptions of] *followed by x'd out* the Code
159–60	have the postulants] *preceded by x'd out* all
160	Thus their] *followed by x'd out* period of
	furnish] *followed by x'd out* testimonial letters
	we must get] *interlined with a caret to replace cancelled* they must furnish
	The candidate himself . . . 2411] *following* or other impediment. *and marked for transposition*
	censure,] *typed interlined above x'd out* impediment
	other] *typed interlined and marked for insertion*
161	interruption] *preceded by x'd out* are
	is sufficient] is *added in left margin to replace cancelled* are
	the last] *interlined above cancelled* each
162	Trappist monastery.] *preceded by x'd out* house
	Actual] *added in left margin*
	validity] *altered from* validity
	invalidating] *preceded by x'd out* impediment
163	*definitive*] *preceded by x'd out* entrance into the
164	simply] *preceded by x'd out* a modern accommodation
	proper house] *followed by x'd out* after profession.

165	the wrong] *preceded by x'd out* bad influences formation, a] *followed by x'd out* delicate and should work] *preceded by x'd out* should not with {the} professed] *preceded by x'd out* and even "necessary signs with professed
166	common exercises;] *followed by x'd out* and (19 March 1603)] *followed by cancelled* Exceptions to this rule. It is not be taken to signify an absolute exclusion of all studies.

Sacred Congregation of Religious (26 August, 1910) Moderate study, for instance a little study of Latin, can be permitted, with classes three times a week (preferably conducted by the Fr Master or Undermaster) and one hour a day of study except on feast days. The Congregation adds that although this is not properly speaking a course of studies, it is not a spiritual exercise or a "mortification" but an intellectual exercise "from which some fruit is to be drawn."

The reason for this is that the constant application of the mind to spiritual things exclusively fatigues the mind and a little application to study is not only not harmful but helps the novice to adapt better and absorb his spiritual formation more easily.

What material should be studied? The congregation recommends:

    a) The language of the country

    b) Latin or Greek—including repetition of what one has learned before and

    above all, *reading of the Fathers* in the original.

In our novitiate we encourage the study of the Cistercian Fathers and of Sacred Scripture. A little study of French is not out of the question, because of the special usefulness of this language in our life (a reading knowledge of it will be valuable).

It is also recommended that the novices give papers, or seminars, on appropriate subjects. Perhaps even in Latin, it is suggested.

However, these prescriptions of 1910 seem to have been abrogated by the Code to the extent that *formal studies* cannot be carried on during the canonical year. That is a formal course of studies cannot be taken. During the second year even a formal course is permitted, but in our case, the Father Immediate prefers that no formal studying be done during the novitiate, except in special cases approved by him.

Sacred Congregation] *preceded by cancelled* On the contrary, the

language of] *preceded by x'd out* native

formal] *preceded by x'd out* study be

a] *followed by x'd out* his own qualifications

167 cf. General . . . {1947}])] *added on line*

certain points] *followed by x'd out* The changes are to be understood as significant.

come from] *interlined with a caret*

168 The submaster usually . . . novices.] *added on line*

The juridical . . . master] *altered from* The juridical . . . master

first function] first *typed interlined and marked for insertion*

novices by] by *added on line*

how they . . . conduct, etc.] *added on line*

isolated] *preceded by x'd out* isolated sins

repaired.] *followed by x'd out* He should be insist

in general what] *interlined above cancelled* everything *followed by uncancelled* that

and sees . . . sick] *interlined below and marked for insertion*

who can . . . penances.] *added on line*

hear] *interlined below cancelled* receive *following cancelled* give pen

169–70 4 . . . fallen nature.] *following* his own fancies. *and marked for transposition preceded by* (insert this above, under duties of novice master—

170 seeing that the novice] the novice *interlined above cancelled* he

The father master . . . nature.] *added in lower margin*

Appendix A

          The father master] *interlined with a caret to replace cancelled* He
          strictly] *interlined with a caret*
          to obey] *followed by x'd out* his domestic power.

171   It is most . . . fancies.] *added on line*
          obligation] *preceded by x'd out* strict
          another] *followed by x'd out* either in
          accepted] *followed by x'd out* at the end of

172   bound to] *followed by x'd out* keep the Rule
          participate] *followed by x'd out* as best
          emission of vows] *altered from* emission of vows
          (common law)] *added on line*
          completed for] *followed by x'd out* simple
          (seventeen . . . Order)] *added in right margin*
          If a person] *preceded by x'd out* 2-

173   is necessary] *preceded by x'd out* is not necessary for validity.
          uninterrupted] *interlined with a caret preceded by cancelled* and
          (common law)] *added on line*
          having been . . . house] *altered from* having been . . . house
          novice leaves the *house*] *followed by x'd out* (even for only a day or so)
          leaves . . . to return] *altered from* leaves . . . to return

174   (but he . . . away)] *altered from* but he . . . away
          continuous or non-continuous] *altered from* continuous or non-continuous
          less than thirty days] *altered from* less than thirty days
          novitiate, the] *followed by x'd out* validity
          sixteen] *typed in left margin interlined above x'd out* fifteen *and marked for insertion to replace cancelled* eleven
          the case] *preceded by x'd out* this case
          for sixteen] sixteen *interlined above cancelled* fifteen
          under sixteen] sixteen *typed interlined below x'd out* fifteen
          spent] *interlined below and marked for insertion*

175   *but it remains . . . up*] *altered from* but it remains . . . up

intention . . . returning] *altered from* intention . . . returning
It has . . . again] *added on line*
he must] he *altered from* they
he allows] *altered from* they allow
novice, with] *preceded by x'd out* novitiate
The time . . . travelling] *altered from* The time . . . travelling
from one] *preceded by x'd out* to one
would . . . computed] *altered from* would . . . computed
Another *condition for validity*] *altered from* Another condition for validity
Another] *typed interlined above x'd out* 4- The fourth
habit of the] *followed by x'd out* Order
Time spent] *preceded by x'd out* 5- Where the

176   obligations] *followed by x'd out* incurred.
in this case,] *preceded by x'd out* must
Normally . . . order.] *added on line*
simple] *interlined with a caret*
Simple . . . marriage)] *added in left margin and marked for insertion*

177   He incurs . . . superiors] *altered from* He incurs . . . superiors
previously] *following* by him *and marked for transposition*
only with permission] only *interlined with a caret*
11. He is . . . for solemn vows.] *added in lower margin*
When temporary vows] temporary *typed interlined and marked for insertion*
must be renewed] *must altered from* must
renewed not later] renewed *interlined above cancelled* made
may be renewed] *may altered from* may
requires] *altered from* required

178   to keep the vows] *interlined below and marked for insertion*
entirely] *followed by cancelled* If he is solemnly professed

179   *the reasons . . . religious*] *altered from* the reasons . . . religious
ownership of his] his *altered from* this
renounced is] *followed by x'd out* the

Appendix A

180	accrue to them] *followed by x'd out* after (in case of death)] *interlined with a caret* is required.] *followed by x'd out* Any other changes in the disposal of property that the professed may desire to make, require the permission of his Superior. Without this permission, the acts of simple professed would still be valid but they would be illicit—a sin against poverty. In effect . . . solemn profession.] *added in lower margin*
181	under the vow] *preceded by x'd out* by undertake] *preceded by x'd out* make *all title to possession*] *altered from* all title to possession
182	subdeacon] *typed interlined above x'd out* priest must either] *preceded by x'd out* can either in which he had] *followed by cancelled* perpetual
184	he nevertheless] *preceded by x'd out* to the
185	He is admitted . . . council.] *typed interlined and marked for insertion* vote is] *followed by x'd out* then after a year] *typed in left margin before x'd out* there, reads] *preceded by x'd out* sings his
186	*somehow . . . renunciation*] *altered from* somehow . . . renunciation
187	who comes from] who *altered from* whom (cf. n.] *followed by x'd out* 16
188	The probation] *preceded by x'd out* In
189	temporal,"] *followed by x'd out* same prayers, same privileges are with everyone] *preceded by x'd out* if
191	schedule of the] *followed by x'd out* Laybrother 551] *preceded by x'd out* 22
192	Here is . . . within us.] *opposite page* Here] *interlined above cancelled* This
193	644, n. 3] *preceded by x'd out* 643 n.3. Flight is] *preceded by x'd out* A state temporary] *interlined below and marked for insertion to replace cancelled* simple even] *interlined below and marked for insertion*

	without . . . returning] *altered from* without . . . returning
194	return when] *followed by x'd out* return is re
	to desert religion is absent] to desert religion *interlined with a caret*
	innocent] *preceded by x'd out* presumed
	of apostasy] *added on line*
	effect.] *followed by x'd out* Since in our Order it is a
	Dominicans] *followed by x'd out* without
	fugitives] nothing explicit about this *added in left margin and marked for insertion then cancelled*
	prescribes] *followed by x'd out* a)
195	*the fugitive . . . excommunication*] *altered from* the fugitive . . . excommunication
	taken as] *preceded by x'd out* a
	1] *interlined*
	2] *added in left margin*
	3] *added in left margin*
	4] *added in left margin*
	back to the] the *interlined above cancelled* a
	regular life.] life. *added on line following cancelled* state.
	5] *added in left margin*
	The apostate] *preceded by cancelled* But
	One is never . . . crime.] *interlined*
	6] *added in left margin*
	if he had] *preceded by x'd out* but if he had the intention of returning he must be received back. If he had the intention of not returning, he is finished.
	he must . . . back] *altered from* he must . . . back
196	7] *added in left margin*
	even] *interlined with a caret*
	has elapsed] *added on line*
	(see below)] *added on line*
	Invoke] *preceded by x'd out* call out
	187] *typed interlined above x'd out* 186
197	there must be] *preceded by x'd out* the religious m
	other observances.] *followed by x'd out* But complete

Appendix A

	disregard of regular discipline in general might be a motive.
198	two or three] *preceded by x'd out* several y
	studies the documents] *typed interlined above x'd out* documents acts
199	serious] *altered from* serious
	a director] *preceded by x'd out* someone who is a
	petitioner] *preceded by x'd out* conscious
	An indult of] *preceded by x'd out* In a case exclaustration
	up to six months] *altered from* up to six months
	longer than six months] *altered from* longer than six months
200	*more than six months*] *altered from* more than six months
	remains] *preceded by x'd out* is bound
	fertility] *preceded by x'd out* productivity
201	the petition] *preceded by x'd out* it
202	1549] *followed by x'd out* It is the bishop who
203	oversight] *preceded by x'd out* minor
204	(f) not . . . all."] *interlined*

ADDITIONS AND ALTERATIONS IN MULTIGRAPH

138	*The excommunication . . . twelve*] *altered from* The excommunication . . . twelve
150–51	Note on . . . without vows).] *multigraph only*
152	(N.B. *sanatio* . . . possible).] *interlined*
156	by civil law] *multigraph only*
171	*juridical act*] *altered from* juridical act
	assumes . . . state] *altered from* assumes . . . state
	mutual obligation] *altered from* mutual obligation
172	*Two essential elements*] *altered from* Two essential elements
	traditio sui] *altered from* traditio sui
	emission of vows] *altered from* emission of vows
	Can such . . . dissolved?] *added on line*
	Emission of . . . not valid.] *interlined*
173	(see separately)] *added on line*
	For us . . . completed.] *added on line*
	the canonical year must be] *altered from* the canonical year must be

174	*Suspended] added in left margin*
	1] added in left margin
	2] added in left margin
175	*3] added in left margin*
176	*participate . . . graces] altered from* participate . . . graces
176–77	solemn profession] *preceded by cancelled* whether at simple *or followed by uncancelled* ??
177	*second baptism] altered from* second baptism
	Renewal] added in left margin
	There must. . . professed is] altered from There must . . . professed is
	under vows] altered from under vows

APPENDIX B
For Further Reading

I. Other Writings by Merton on Topics treated in *Charter, Customs, and Constitutions of the Cistercians*

Basic Principles of Monastic Spirituality. Trappist, KY: Abbey of Gethsemani, 1957.
Cistercian Contemplatives: A Guide to Trappist Life. Trappist, KY: Gethsemani Abbey, 1948.
Contemplation in a World of Action. Garden City, NY: Doubleday, 1971.
Gethsemani: A Life of Praise. Trappist, KY: Abbey of Gethsemani, 1966.
The Life of the Vows: Initiation into the Monastic Tradition 6, ed. Patrick F. O'Connell, Monastic Wisdom [MW], vol. 30. Collegeville, MN: Cistercian Publications, 2012.
The Monastic Journey, ed. Brother Patrick Hart. Kansas City: Sheed, Andrews & McMeel, 1977.
Monastic Life at Gethsemani. Trappist, KY: Abbey of Gethsemani, 1965.
Monastic Observances: Initiation into the Monastic Tradition 5, ed. Patrick F. O'Connell, MW 25. Collegeville, MN: Cistercian Publications, 2010.
The Rule of Saint Benedict: Initiation into the Monastic Tradition 4, ed. Patrick F. O'Connell, MW 19. Collegeville, MN: Cistercian Publications, 2009.
The Silent Life. New York: Farrar, Straus & Cudahy, 1957.
The Spirit of Simplicity. Trappist, KY: Abbey of Gethsemani, 1948.
The Waters of Siloe. New York: Harcourt, Brace, 1949.

II. Other Materials Relevant to Topics treated in *Charter, Customs, and Constitutions of the Cistercians*

Alberic Altermatt, ocist. "The Cistercian Patrimony: Introduction to the Most Important Historical, Juridical and Spiritual Documents." Translated by Elizabeth Connor, ocso. *Cistercian Studies Quarterly* 25.4 (1990): 287–328.

Aust, Magdalena. "The Early Institutional Documents of Cîteaux: A First Look at Fr. Chrysogonus Waddell's Critical Edition of the *Consuetudines Monachorum Cisterciensium*." *Cistercian Studies Quarterly* 35.4 (2000): 535–47.

Bell, David N. "From Molesme to Cîteaux: The Earliest 'Cistercian' Spirituality." *Cistercian Studies Quarterly* 34.4 (1999): 469–82.

Berman, Constance Hoffman. *The Cistercian Evolution: The Invention of a Religious Order in Twelfth-Century Europe*. Philadelphia: University of Pennsylvania Press, 2000.

Freeman, Elizabeth. "What Makes a Monastic Order? Issues of Methodology in the Cistercian Evolution." *Cistercian Studies Quarterly* 37.4 (2002): 429–42.

Friedlander, Colette, ocso. "The Juridical Documents of the Cistercian Order of the Strict Observance up to the Present Day." *Cistercian Studies Quarterly* 25.4 (1990): 329–31.

David Knowles. "The Primitive Documents of the Cistercian Order." In *Great Historical Enterprises: Problems in Monastic History*. London: Thomas Nelson, 1963: 197–224.

Tescari, Augusta, ocso, Marie Gérard Dubois, ocso, and Maria Paola Santachiara, ocso, eds. *The Cistercian Order of the Strict Observance in the Twentieth Century*. 2 vols. Rome: Cistercian Order of the Strict Observance, 2008.

Waddell, Chrysogonus, ocso, ed. and trans. *Narrative and Legislative Texts from Early Cîteaux*. Studia et Documenta, vol. 9. Cîteaux: Commentarii Cistercienses, 1999.

———, ed. *Twelfth-Century Statutes from the Cistercian General Chapter, Latin Text with English Notes and Commentary*. Studia et Documenta, vol. 12. Cîteaux: Commentarii Cistercienses, 2002.

INDEX

abandonment, spirit of: xlix–l, 163
abbesses: 44
abbey(s): 71; Cistercian: xviii–xix, 2–3, 5, 35, 44, 71
abbot(s): xix–xx, xxvi–xxviii, xxxiii, xxxv, xl, xlvii, 6, 10–14, 16–17, 20, 22–23, 25–26, 32, 36–38, 41–48, 50, 52–55, 65–66, 69–74, 77, 80, 85–87, 89, 92, 95, 98, 109, 112, 118–19, 122, 124, 128, 136, 142, 159, 163, 168, 182–85, 190, 196, 198; and sick: 132–33; as Christ: xl, 95; as representative of God: 72; authority of: xl, xliv; Cistercian: xix, 14; conscience of: 124; council of: xlix, 74, 159, 162, 178, 185, 197; counsel of: 13; *de regimine*: xxxvi, 71; death of: 135; deceased: xxxvi; deposition of: xx, xxxiii, 8, 13–14, 58, 65, 69; discretion of: 28, 130, 177; duty of: xlv; election of: xx, xxxiii, xxxv–xxxvii, 7–8, 13, 58, 68, 71, 75–77, 135, 180; emeritus: 66; excommunication of: 14; faults of: 6–7; future: 115; general: xxxiii, xxxv, xli, xliv, 58, 65–67, 70, 74–77, 88, 108, 116–17, 141, 178, 180, 190, 197–98, 202; guest: 22–23; irregular: 6, 12; judgement of: 128; local: xix, 10–11, 67, 75, 79, 83, 116, 130, 178, 180, 197, 199; mercy of: 46; non-Cistercian: 7; *nullius*: xxxvi, 71; of filiations: 6; of Gethsemani: xlvi, 108; orders of: 52; permission of: 194; Portuguese: xxvii–xxviii, 45; power of: 73; pusillanimity of: 13; recalcitrant: 14; resignation of: xx, 8, 13–14, 69; respect for: xl; responsibility of: xxxvi; spiritual jurisdiction of: xxxvi, 72; temporal administration of: xxxvi, 72; visited: 75; visiting: 7, 10, 22; uselessness of: 13; will of: 6, 10, 13
abortion: 87, 157
absence, leave of: lv, 199–200
absolution: 94; of the dead: 17; sacramental: 195
abstinence: xliv, 79, 122–24; from meat: 122; Lenten: xliv
abuse(s): xxvii, xl, 11, 41–43, 65, 82, 107, 135–36, 203
accident(s): 44, 104, 132
Accioly, Inácio, osb: liii
accusation(s): 107, 151, 169, 204; act of: 198
Achel, Abbey of: 74
act(s), illicit: 176; internal: 193; invalid: 176, 181; juridical: li, 171, 196; of trial: 199; religious: 176
activity, state of: 111
adaptation: xi
administration, temporal: 72
admission, from another order: lii, 187–88; into Order: xlvii, 58, 142–61; valid: xlix
admonition: 178

231

adolescentes: 28
advantage, of Order: 146
Advent: 39, 55, 81, 123–24
advice, spiritual: 94
affairs, family: 140–41; secular: 133; spiritual: 72; temporal: 72, 153
affection(s): liv, 93, 189; full: 85; pure: 85
age, change due to: 79; legitimate, of profession: 172; of novices: 48
agent, exterior: 176
aggiornamento: viii
agitation: 108
agriculture: 108
alb: 54
Alberic, St.: 5, 33, 60
Alexander VII, Pope: 26
All Saints, Feast of: 37–39
alleviation, temporary: 163
alms: 67
altar(s): 33, 35, 54, 71, 83, 156, 185; high: 95
Amadeus of Bonnevaux, Bl.: xxiv, 21
amendment: 198; failure of: 197; sign of: 197
amentes: 147
America: 66, 75, 115, 127, 135, 139, 142
American Ecclesiastical Review: 99
Ami du Clergé: 99
amusement: 100, 133
analogium: 46, 54
Andrew, St., Feast of: 35
angel: 118
animals: 7
animosity, unconscious: 203
antiphon(s): xxxv, 12, 51
antiphoner: 18
apostasy, crime of: 193–95; from faith: 87, 178, 194; from religious life: liv; juridical: 193; penalties of: 194–195; sin of: 193–94
apostate(s): liv, 43, 87–88, 156, 192–97; definition of: 193; dismissal of: 196; from faith: 76, 193; from holy orders: 193; from religion: 193; penalties for: 194–95; readmission of: liv; reception of: xxxiii–xxxiv, 58
apostolate: 110, 133
apostolic delegate: 108
apparel, travel: xlvii
appointments, *tabula* of: 16
aptitude(s): 146; bodily: 145; for monastic life: xlviii, 143–44; intellectual: 145; juridical: 160; lack of: 179; negative: 144–45, 147; positive: 145–46; psychological: 145–47; spiritual: 145
Aquitaine: 36
archbishop: 41
architecture, Cistercian: xxv
argument(s): xix, xliii, 9; interior: 204
aridity: 101
armarium: 18, 29, 51
army: 161, 177
arts, study of: 166
Ascension, Feast of: 38
asceticism: 101, 109
ashes: 54
aspersion: 33
assent, common: 5
Assumption, Feast of: 39, 81
attitude, ambitious: 147; jealous: 147; kind: 204
attraction, human: 159; ill-regulated: 159
Aubert, Marcel: xxv, 25–26
auditorium: xxiv, 22–23, 30, 50
Augustine, St.: xii, 119
austerities: 48, 61; Trappist: 60
authoritarianism, extreme: 147
authorities, ecclesial: xlviii; higher: xlii, 107; religious: xlii
authority: xv, xix; abuse of: xl; Church: 160; civil: 156; competent: 160; of abbot: xl, xliv; of abbot

general: 68; of Cîteaux: 3; of father immediate: xxxvi; of Holy See: 76; of superiors: xxxix, 86, 178, 199; paternal: 3; resistance to: 147
automobiles: xlvi, 134–35; luxurious: xlvi, 135
avarice: 8, 53
avidity: 147

Bachofen, Charles Augustine, OSB: 139
background, solid: 145
balance, psychological: xxxviii, 145; sense of: 1
Balerne, Abbey of: 22; Abbot of: 24
Bamberger, John Eudes, OCSO: vii–xii, lvii, lxi
baptism(s): 44, 148, 182; certificate of: 160; infant: 156; outside Church: 87, 156; profession as second: 177; sponsor at: 177
Baptists: 148
barns: 7
basilica: 202
beards: 39
beds: 25–27, 33, 41, 50, 130
beer: xxvi, 32, 36, 127
begging: xliii, 108
being, whole: xlviii, 144
belfry: 26
bell(s): 16, 26–27, 31, 33, 54
Bellarmine University: xv, xxx, lx
Benedict, St.: xviii, xliv–xlv, xlix, 9, 40, 52, 57–59, 84, 122, 124–25, 145; disciples of: 63; Solemnity of: xxxii; sons of: 62; spirit of: 9; way of: 59
Benedict XII, Pope: 26; *Fulgens sicut Stella*: 26
Benedict XVI, Pope: ix
Benedictinism, essence of: 62
benediction: 79
benefactors: xliii, 28, 108
benefice(s): 177, 202

benefits, spiritual: 86
Berdoues, Abbot of: 12
Bernard of Clairvaux, St.: xviii, xxii, xxx–xxxi, xli, 61, 100, 116, 119, 125; commemoration of: 81; disciples of: 63; health of: 2; sons of: 62
biberes: 32, 34, 54, 125
Bible et Vie Chrétienne: 99
bicycles: 134–35
bigamists: 76, 156
birth, illegitimate: 160; legitimate: 49, 68, 77; place of: 160–61; time of: 161
bishop(s): xxv, 8, 23–24, 41, 48, 71, 76, 79, 86–87, 104, 110, 118, 143, 152–53, 201–202; residential: 151; resigned: 151; testimonial letter of: 161; titular: 151
blankets: 129; moss: xxv, 27
bleeding: xxix, 28, 55
Blessed Sacrament: 38, 63, 131
Blessed Virgin Mary: xviii, 81; Feast of Nativity of: 37–39; feasts of: 81; little office of: xxxv, xxxviii, 29, 63, 80–81, 85; monasteries dedicated to: xviii, 7, 77; month of: 79
blessing(s): 16, 19–20, 40, 54; abbatial: 87; of extraordinary confessor: 91; of habit: 130; of novices: 162; of travelers: 39
blood, noble: 146
Blue Jay Inn: 134
Bochen, Christine: ix
body: xlviii, 8, 144; watching by: 83; weakness of: 122
Bohemia: 48
Bonaval, Abbot of: 12
bond, human: 172; supernatural: 172
Bonnefont, Abbot of: 12
book(s): xxiv, 7, 9, 16, 18–19, 30, 51, 65, 98; censor of: 66; choir: 51; heretical: 87; Lenten: 51–52; liturgical: 78, 169; necessary: 98;

234   *Charter, Customs, and Constitutions of the Cistercians*

of chant: 82; service: xxxviii, 82; unauthorized publication of: 87; useless: 98
Bourras, Abbot of: 36
bread: xxviii, 24, 27–29, 31, 45, 53, 124, 126–27; altar: 54; and water: 11–12, 24–25, 35–38, 42, 44, 47–48; common: 28; ordinary: 55; white: 28, 55
breakdown, mental: 178, 200; of health: 178, 200; physical: 200
brethren, monastic: xx, 37, 52–53, 55, 72, 97, 203–204
brilliancy: 147
Brittany: 36
broadcasts, radio: xlvi, 136–37; television: xlvi, 136–37
brother(s): 155; family: 171
browbeating: 149
Bruno de Jésus-Marie, ocd: 116
buildings, farm: 23
Burns, Abbot Flavian, ocso: xi
business, legitimate: 43; manager of: 153; monastic: 104, 133; necessary: xlvii, 140; of novitiate: 165–66; secular: 194; worldly: 4
butter: 29, 123

Cajetan, St., Feast of: 96
calefactory: xxiv, 20–22, 39
calling, dignity of: 201; worth of: 201
Callistus II, Pope: xvii, 1–4
calumny: 107
Camaldolese: 59, 103
Camaldoli: 59–60
Canada: xi, 75
candidate(s): xlviii, lii, 72, 149, 155, 158, 160–61, 172, 184; classes of: 160–61; condition of: 146; conduct of: 146; doubtful: 144; education of: 146; entrance of: 144; family of: 144; formation of: 143; good character of: 146; history of: 143; intentions of: 158; interview of: 144; regularity of: 143; reputation of: 143, 146; resolution of: 144; schools of: 161; social rank of: 146; studies of: 143, 145; visit by: 144
candles: 54
Canivez, J.-M.: 1, 3, 11–12, 22–28, 32, 35–39, 41–49, 80–82
Canon Law, 1917 Code of: xxxiii–xxxiv, xxxvi–xxxviii, xliii, xlviii, lv, 114–15, 139, 148, 155, 158, 188, 193; 1983 Code of: lvi–lvii; old: 195
cantor: xxviii, 18, 20, 51–52, 54; as archivist: 51
capacity: 144; intellectual: xlviii; of novice: 163; physical: xlviii; psychological: xlviii; special: 145
cape: 49; oblate: 129
Capitula: xvii
cardinal(s): 38, 76, 108; protector: 108
care, solicitous: 8
Carmelites: 49, 103; history of: 49
Carta Caritatis: vii–viii, xiii, xvi–xxii, xxx–xxxi, xxxvi–xxxvii, 1–14, 44, 61, 67, 75, 78; composition of: 5–6; conferences text of: lvii; divisions of: 3, 8; early summary of: xvii, 3–4, 6–7; original text of: xvii; outline of: 8; parts of: 8–14; prologue of: 8; scholarly controversy on: xvii, xix; studies of: 1–4; summary of: 6–7; texts of: 1–4; versions of: xvi–xviii, xxi, 1–4
Carta Caritatis Posterior: xviii, 2
Carta Caritatis Prior: xvii, 1–2, 4
Carthusians: 49, 59, 64, 103, 164, 188, 194
cases, reserved: 87–88
Casey, Michael, ocso: xxxv
Cassian, John: xxi–xxii, xlii, 101, 125
catechisms: 192
cathedral: 202
Catherine, St., Feast of: 96

Catholic Biblical Quarterly: 99
Catholic University of America: 116
cattle: 109; raising of: 108
cell(s), in infirmary: 131; monastic: xlv, 25, 27, 128; of Benedictines: 128; private: 26–27
cellarer: xxvii, xxix, 31–32, 39, 45, 47, 52–53, 113
cellarium: 40
censor: 136
censor librorum: 66
censure(s): xxxix, 76, 86, 88–89; absence of: 160
cereal: 126
ceremonial, of profession: 184
ceremonies, Cistercian: xiii, 16, 34, 169; clothing: xxviii, 163, 190; ecclesiastical: 163
chalices: 44, 54, 65, 71
Châlons-sur-Marne: 2
Champagne: 36
chant: xxxviii, 9, 51; Cistercian: 82, 136–37; commission: 83; Gregorian: 82–83, 138; polyphonic: xxxviii, 24, 82
chapel, novitiate: 80
chaplain(s): 86
chapter, conventual: liii, 63–64, 66, 71–73, 77, 109, 171–72, 177, 183, 189, 194; daily: xxiii–xxiv, 19, 30, 33, 40, 49–51, 54–55, 130, 134, 182–85; local: 63–64; meaning of: 63; morning: 16–18, 121; of faults: xxix, lv, lix, 24, 93, 169, 202–204; plenary: 66; room: 16, 18, 22, 25, 29, 46, 55, 140, 184
character, faults of: 179; good: 146
charity: xix–xx, xlv, 6, 8–12, 32, 48, 78, 97, 102, 131–32, 153, 170, 189, 203; fervor of: xli, 97; obligation of: 203; of novice master: xlix, 167
Chase, Neil: lxii
chastity: 49; vow of: 200–201

Chautard, Jean-Baptiste, ocso: 78
cheese: 29, 122, 126–27
children, of non-Catholics: 157
China: 66, 75
choir: xxix, xxxv, xxxviii, liv, 12, 26, 30, 33, 40–41, 49, 51, 55, 80–81, 83, 113, 163, 180; brothers' participation in: liii, 192; of infirm: 55
chores: 192
Christ: 5; abbot as: xl, 95; adoration of: 63; as King: 8; as Lord: 8; feasts of: 28; following: 57, 62; life in: 5; love of: 63; Mystical Body of: xlvi, 140, 200; power of: 72; prayer of: xxxv; presence of: xliv, 127; teachings of: 57; work of: xxxv
Christmas: xxxii, 12, 37–39, 55, 81
Church: viii, xv, xlviii, li, 58, 73, 123, 133, 140, 143, 150–51, 156, 166, 171, 176, 181, 200–202; fasts of: xliv, 41, 123, 125–27, 191; fertility of: 200; honor of: 61; inner life of: xlviii, 142; law against: 151; sanctity of: 200; teaching of: 101; witness of: xii
church: 18, 20, 26, 30, 41, 50, 54, 56, 80, 140, 163, 185; dedication of: xlvi, 38, 140; proper rank in: 49; servant of: 29; speaking in: 23
cider: 53, 127
cincture: 130
circators: 20
Cistercians, 13, 49; Common Observance: 108; decline of: 14; first: 62; reformed: xxxiv, 61
Cîteaux, Abbey of: xviii–xx, xliii, 2, 6, 8–11, 14, 37, 45, 60–62, 66, 68, 75, 108, 137; Abbot of: xix–xx, 2, 6, 8, 10–14, 68; as mother of the Order: 10; fathers of: xviii, 9; filiations of: 13–14, 75; founders of: 4; founding of: xviii, xx, xxxiv, 5–6, 60; Order of: xiii; visitation of: 75

Clairvaux, Abbey of: xx, xxvii, xxx, 6, 14, 45, 75
classes: 113; novitiate: 50
cleanliness: 132
Clement VIII, Pope: 166–67
Clement XIV, Pope: 102
clergy, secular: 117–18, 120, 202
cleric(s): 77, 120, 142, 151, 153, 157, 160–61, 163, 177, 189; in holy orders: 88; in major orders: 152; suspension of: 194
climate(s), change of: 185; hot: 78
cloaks, novice: 129, 162
cloister: xv, xlvi, 18–19, 21–22, 26, 37, 49, 51, 54–56, 98, 102, 137–38, 140, 195
Cloisters, New York City: 25
clothing: xxv, xlv, 7, 25, 49, 129–30; ceremony: xxviii, 163, 190; change of: xxviii, 129; cold-weather: xxix; secular: 159
Cluny, Abbey of: 9, 59–60, 101; discipline of: 59; liturgical life of: 59; practices of: 33; reform of: 59; silence of: 59
coat, fur: 49
coffee: xliv, 124
collation: 32, 54, 125–26, 128, 191
college(s), German-Hungarian: 152; Irish: 152; North American: 152; of the Propaganda: 152; Roman: 152; Scotch: 152
Columban Fathers: 187
combs: 37
comfort: 132
command: 18
commandment(s), of God: 154; of men: 154
Commission, Pontifical, for Interpreting Code: 158
commitment, holistic: xlviii
commodities: 73
common box: 51, 99

communication(s): 69, 71, 105–106; between novices and professed: 164–65; forms of: xlii
communion, daily: xl, 96; frequent: 96; general: 95; holy: xxxvii, xl–xli, 20, 24, 40, 95–97, 131; of brothers: 191
community, *a quo*: 186; *ad quod*: 185–86; consultation of: xxxvi, 72; entrance into: xxviii; imperfections of: l; incorporation in: 176; monastic: xviii, xxvi, lii, 29–30, 46, 52, 55, 96, 118, 140, 185, 203; of communities: xx; poor: 67, 185; prayer of: 172; professed: xxviii; religious: li; safeguard of: xli; sense of: xviii; size of: xxxviii; vote of: 73; work of: 172
complaint(s), unjust: 107; unreasonable: 107
compline: xxv, 18, 24, 26–27, 32, 40, 49, 51, 54, 125
concerns, bodily: 120; material: 120
concessions: 36
conduct, exterior: 168; good: 146; proper: xxvi; rules for: 31
conferences, conduct of: 121–22; disputations at: 121–22; dogmatic: 120–21; for scholastics: 113; liturgical: xliii, 120; moderator for: 121; monthly: 120–22; moral: 120; observations at: 121; scriptural: xliii, 120–22; theological: xliii, 120–22
conferences, novitiate: xiii, xv, xx–xxii, xxxi–xxxiv, xxxvi–xxxvii, xli, xlvii, lii, lv; calendar for: xxii; recordings of: xxi, xxiv, xxxi; texts of: xvi–xvii, xxii, xxxi–xxxii, lvii–lix
confession(s): xxxvii, xxxix, 17–18, 68, 71, 83, 85–94, 97, 138, 166–68; faculties for: 120; licit: 89, 93; seal of: 93; valid: 89, 93

Index 237

confessor(s): xxxix–xl, 17, 67, 85–92, 167; appointment of: 86; direction of: 96; extraordinary: 90–91; of brothers: 191–92; of novices: xxxix, 88–92; ordinary: 89–90, 92
confidence: 113; filial: 95
confirmation, certificate of: 160; oath attesting to: 160; sponsor at: 177; witness to: 160
conflicts, monastic: 165
Congo: xi, 66, 75
congregation(s), religious: 65; Trappist: xxxiii
Congregation(s), Sacred: 108, 112; of Doctrine of Faith: 65; of Eastern Church: 157; of Propaganda Fide: 108; of Religious: 64, 71, 81, 118, 152–53, 199–200; of Rites: 80, 130
conscience: 47, 100, 124, 170; anxieties of: 95; examination of: xxxix, 85; good: 199; manifestation of: xl, 93–95, 168; of novices: 168; peace of: 89; troubles of: 95
considerations, human: 146
consolation(s): xxv, 27; absence of: 145
conspiracy: 49
conspirators: 36, 88
constitutions: 94; meaning of: 57
Constitutions, Cistercian: vii–viii, xiii, xx–xxi, xxxi–lvii, 13–14, 29, 57–202; annual reading of: lv; conferences text of: lviii–lvix; parts of: 58; revised: xi, lvi–lvii
Consuetudines: viii, xiii, xvi, xx–xxxiv, xxxiv, xxxix, 10, 15–56, 78, 84, 148, 188; conferences text of: lvii–lviii; *Distinctiones* of: xxiii, 15; sections of: xxii, 15; text of: 15
consultors: 83
contemplation: x, xli, 100–101, 114, 133
contemplatives: 100

contract(s): 73, 153; *Carta Caritatis* as: 3; legality of: xxxvi; onerous: 181
controversies: xix, 9–10, 98
contumacy: 86
conversation(s): xlii, 102–103; sign: 165
converts: 148
cook(s): xxiv, xxvi, 20–21, 27, 30–31, 33, 37; weekly: 20
copyists: 20
corporals: 54
correction(s): 54, 88, 147; fraternal: 203; in choir: 51
correspondence: 105, 165; exempt: xlii, 106–107; liberty of: 107
couch(es): 129; straw: 132
Couilleau, Guerric, ocso: lv
council, abbot's: xlix, 74, 159, 162, 178, 185, 197; abbot general's: 68–69
counsel(s): 18, 93, 96, 153–54; common: 5; evangelical: 57; mature: 12; of abbot: 13
cowl(s): 17, 19, 30, 32, 34, 129–30; night: 19, 129; of Common Observance: xlv, 130; of Strict Observance: xlv, 130
craft(s): 23, 109
creditor(s): 153
Creusen, Joseph, sj: 178–80, 201–202
crime(s): 193–95; ecclesiastical: 151, 197; external: 86–87; grave: 151, 178; occult: 151; public: 151; punishment for: 148, 151
criminals: 146
crippled person: 156
Crisógono de Jesús, ocd: 116
crops: xxvi; harvesting of: 35
crosier: 54, 71
cross, pectoral: 71
crown, monastic: xlv, 37, 39, 54, 131
crucifix: 129
cubicles: 26

Cuernavaca: 64
cultures, differing: xi
Cunningham, Lawrence S.: ix, xxxii, 64
cup: 31
Curia, Roman: 65, 70
curiosities, secular: 98
curtains: 27
customs, Cistercian, 7; common: 9, 78; contemporary: xi; early Cistercian: xxi–xxii; house: xxxvii, 78; novitiate: lv, 204; quaint: xxix

Daggy, Robert E.: x, xxi, lx, 134
damnation, danger of: 43
dangers: 93
Daniélou, Jean, sj: 64
day, monastic: 15
deacon(s): 54, 152
dead: 15; absolutions of: 17; burial of: 15, 52; lauds of: 33; office of: 81; prayers for: 15, 17
death(s): 17, 103–104, 135, 150, 154, 180, 184–85; fear of: 149; of abbot: 135; of guest: 15; of novice: 50; of patient: 157; of relative: xlvii, 141; of superior: 76; sentence of: 156
debt(s): 73, 153–54; juridical: 153
decadence, monastic: xxvii, 41, 43
decency: xliv, 127
deception: 149
decorum: 128
Decroix, Francis, ocso: ix
definitor(s): xxxv, 65–66, 68–70, 116–17, 136; functions of: 69; future: 115
definitory: 115–16, 198
deformed person: 156
Delfgaauw, Pacificus, ocso: 116
denunciations: 147
deposition, canonical: 67; of abbot: xx, xxxiii, 8, 13–14, 58, 65, 69
desertion, from religious life: 193–94

desire(s): 5, 185; negative: 144; to seek God: xlix, 145; true: xlix, 159; vain: xxvii, 41
dessert: 29, 127
detraction: 107
devil, possession by: 156
devotion(s): 79, 82, 91, 100; Eucharistic: xxxv, 63; private: 176; public: 79; to truth: 192
De Wilde, Deodat, ocso: 116
Diepenveen, Abbot of: 83
differences, cultural: xlvii
difficulties: 93; in prayer: 94
dignities: 202; official: 189
diligence: 169
Dimier, Anselme, ocso: 21
dining: 27
dinner: 30–33, 36, 41, 53, 123, 125–27, 130
diocese(s): 71, 86–87, 89; incardination in: 201–202; of candidate: 161; service in: 151–52
direction, public: 113; spiritual: 117, 168, 192
director(s), spiritual: 103, 115, 169, 199
discernment, vocational: xlix, 46
disciples: 154
discipline: 5, 10, 25, 87, 133, 166, 196; breaches of: 95, 103; matters of: viii; monastic: xxviii, l, 61, 170; of Cluny: 59; regular: xlii, 101; religious: 169, 179; spirit of: xlii, 103
discontent: 111
discord: 9, 78
discredit: 151
discretion: xxxviii, 79; of abbot: 28, 130, 177; of superior: 79, 175
dishonor: 186; public: 156
dismissal(s): liv, 142, 192, 195–99, 202; automatic: 197; motives for: 178–79; of brothers: 190, 197; of novice: 170, 173; of simple professed: li, 178–79, 197; of solemn professed:

197–99; procedure for: 198–99; threat of: 198; warnings of: 198
disobedience: 42; public: 97
dispensation(s): xlviii, 129, 150, 190, 195; from impediments: 152–53, 155; from *Rule*: 72; from vows: 150, 155, 176, 200–201; papal: 152
disposition(s), critical: 147; hostile: 147; right: 97; withdrawn: 147
disputations: 121–22
dispute: xliii, 121
distraction: xlvi, 140
disturbance: xlvi, 140
diversion: 133
divisions: xviii, 5
divorced persons: 150
docility, spirit of: xlix, 163
doctors, medical: 132, 141; of the Church: 119
doctrine(s): 100; about *Rule*: 168; human: 154; sacred: 114, 119; sound: 98
documents, legal: xlix; legislative: ix, lvi
dogs: 44
domicile, of parents: 161
Dominicans: 194
domus formata: 120
domus necessaria: xxv, 25
Dore, Abbot of: 24, 82
dormitory: xv, xxv, xxvii, xlv, 7, 25–27, 30, 32, 34, 45, 128, 130–31; partitions in: 26, 128; professed: 50
doubts: 93, 95
draft, military: 195
drawers: 129
drink: xxiv, 21, 27–29, 33, 55, 124–26
drinking: xxv, 24
Dubois, Marie Gérard, ocso: xxxv
duel: 156
Dumont, Charles, ocso: lvi
Dunne, Abbot Frederic, ocso: 99, 120–21

duties: 63, 78, 83; monastic: l, 16, 18, 171; of abbot: xlv; of cantor: xxviii; of cellarer: xxix; of novice: 170–71; of novice master: xxviii, 50, 91, 167–71; of reader: xxix; of religious: xxii, li; of sacristan: xxix; of subcantor: xxix
dying: 15, 52

Earll, Mary Beth: lxi
Easter: 37–39, 55, 81, 123
eating: xliv, 24, 31, 34, 48, 127
Ecclesiastica Officia: xxii–xxiii, 15, 48, 84, 125
Edmund, St., Feast of: 96
education: 200; high-school: 112, 190; in humanities: 112, 146; in Latin: 146; monastic: xiii, 169; of candidates: 146; of laybrothers: 190; of postulant: 146; outside Church: 148; secondary: 146; university: 146
eggs: 28, 45, 55, 122–23
election(s), of abbot: xx, xxxiii, xxxv–xxxvii, 7–8, 13, 58, 68, 75–77, 135, 180; of abbot general: 67–68; of superior: xxxvi, 74, 76
Ellis, Adam, SJ: 178
eloquence, sacred: 112
ember days: 28, 91
emotion(s): xliii, 121
employment(s), in curia: 202; in religious house: 202; monastic: 128; secular: 194
enclosure: xxvii, xxxiii, xxxv, xxxvii, xlvi, lviii, 7, 23, 30, 41, 58, 63, 65, 76, 89, 104, 128, 133–35, 137–40, 175; active: xlvi, lviii–lix, 134, 138; law of: 106, 140; meaning of: 133–34; of nuns: 139; papal: xlvi, 87, 138; passive: xlvi, lix, 134, 138; spirit of: 41, 137; statute on: 134, 193; violation of: 87, 138–40

England: 36
Enslinger, Lambert, ocso: 90; death of: 90
entrance, into Cistercian Order: xlvii, 142–61
environment, European: xi
envy: 147
epikeia: 160
epileptics: 156
Epiphany: 81
epistle: 20
equality: 8
errors: 6
Eugene III, Pope: xvii, 2
Europe: xliii, 75, 127, 135
evil: 87, 147
exactions, material: 8
example, to novices: 165
exclaustration: 199–200, 202; cause of: 155; indult of: 76, 199–200; temporary: lv
excommunication(s): xxxix, xlvi, liv, lix, 14, 36–37, 67, 72, 75–76, 87–88, 134, 138–39, 141, 149, 194–95
executioner: 156
exemption, military: 195
exercises, common: 166; community: 160; novitiate: 159–60, 166; opportune: 166; spiritual: 166
exhortation(s): 113, 198; spiritual: 120
exile: 200
Exordium Cistercii: xvii–xviii, 4
Exordium Parvum: xviii, xxxvi, 3–4, 7, 60, 77
expulsion: xlvii; decree of: 198
extern(s): 138; sister: 141

Fabian and Sebastian, Sts., Feast of: 96
faculties, priestly: 67, 138
failing: 203
faith: 157; apostasy from: 87, 178, 194; bad: 153; mysteries of: 114
fame: 147
familiars: 34, 53, 67
family: 42, 144; Benedictine: 58; poor: 177
fancies: 171
Fanfani, Ludovicus, op: 63
farming: 7, 109; dairy: 109
fast(s), breaking of: xxv; Lenten: 124, 127; of the Church: xliv, 41, 123, 125–27, 191; rule of: 124; special: 127
fast day(s): 7, 27–28, 33, 55, 126, 191
fasting: xxxiii, xxxvii–xxxviii, xliv, xlix, 29, 35–36, 40–42, 58, 79, 125–26, 162
father(s): 154; capitular: 67; Church: 54, 100; Cistercian: xv, xviii, xxiii, 7, 9, 15–16, 40, 78, 110, 119, 122; desert: xv; four first: xix–xx, 6, 11, 13–14; immediate: xix–xx, xxxv–xxxvi, 2, 6, 11, 13–14, 22, 68, 70–71, 74, 76, 79, 83, 88, 107–108, 115; monastic: xli, 59
fault(s): 6–7, 12, 17, 42, 133, 203–204; against oneself: lv, 204; chapter of: xxix, lv, lix, 24, 93, 169, 202–204; common: 17; exterior: 203; external: 97; grave: 97, 197; gravity of: 158; minor: 11, 25; of character: 179; proclamation of: xxiii–xxiv, lv, 17, 19, 203–204; public: 50, 197; scandalous: 197; serious: 107–108, 197
fault-finding: 147
fear: liv, 93, 150, 192; grave: 149, 176; of death: 149; of displeasing another: 149; of humiliation: 149; of injury: 149
feast(s), liturgical: xxiii, xxvi, 20, 28, 35, 40, 119, 126, 128, 137; of sermon: 50, 95–96; of three lessons: 96; of twelve lessons: 51, 81, 96; of two Masses: 20, 95–96

feeling(s), bad: 204; super-sensitive: 147
feet, bare: xxiv
ferial days: 40
fervor: liv, 97, 192; divine: 101; of charity: xli, 97; of novices: 165
festa locorum: xxvii, 44
fidelity: liv, 192
fields: 7, 30, 34–35
filiations: 3, 6, 11–14, 70, 75, 77
fire tower: 105–106
fire watch: 83
fireplaces: 26
first aid: 132
fish: xxvii–xxviii, xliv, 28, 45, 55, 122–23
Flanders: 36
flattery: 94
Flaxley, Abbot of: 24, 82
flesh: 62
flexibility: xi
flight: liv, 88, 193; crime of: 195; penalties of: 194–95; with woman: 178, 194
Fons Siccus, Grange of: 37
Fontaine Blanche, Abbey of: 48
Fontenay, Abbey of: 37
food: xxvii, xxix, xliv, xlix, 7, 27–28, 44–45, 49, 53, 55; common: 31; measure of: 126–28; of novice: 162; portion of: 31; quality of: 124; quantity of: xliv; right to: 177
force: 176
Ford, Abbot of: 11
forest(s): x
forestry: 109
formation, monastic: xl, xlviii, l–li, 163, 180; of novices: xl, l, 91, 165–66, 168–70; religious: 113, 143; sound: 116; spiritual: 113; theological: 113, 115; time of: li
forum, external: 67, 77, 91, 93, 113, 168, 176, 194, 201; internal: xxxix,
67, 85, 92, 168, 201; non-sacramental: 168; sacramental: 91, 168
foundation(s): 7–8, 74, 77, 111; location of: 7; new: xxxiii, xxxv–xxxvi, 3, 58, 65, 69, 73; of Order: xlii; twelve early: 5
founders, Cistercian: 170
Fox, Abbot James, ocso: xiv, xxxiii, xl, 95, 105, 136
Fox, Peggy: lx
France: 36, 45
Francis of Assisi, St.: xxxii
fraud: 149–50, 158, 176
freedom: xlix, 159; from impediment(s): 145, 147; of slaves: 157
Friars Minor: 194
frugality: 61
fruit: 29, 126–27
frustulum: 126
fugitive(s): liv, 7, 14, 43, 49, 87–88, 141, 192–97; definition of: 193; penalties for: 194–97; readmission of: liv; reception of: xxxiii–xxxiv, 58
Fumasoni-Biondi, Cardinal Peter: 108
furnace man: 128
furniture, monastic: 78, 129, 132

Galicia: 47
garden: 98
Gaspari, Cardinal Peter: 64
gate house: 7
gatekeeper: 128
General Chapter, Cistercian: xi, xix, xxvi, xxxiii–xxxiv, xxxviii, xlii–xliii, xlvii, l, lii–liii, 1–3, 8–9, 11–12, 14, 24, 26, 37–38, 42, 44, 47–49, 57–58, 63–68, 72–73, 78–79, 81–82, 85–86, 88, 99–100, 104–105, 107, 109–11, 114–15, 121, 123, 129–30, 135–36, 141, 169; annual meetings of: xx, 6; as disciplinary body: xix; as legislative body: xix; as supreme authority: 63; control

by: 109; decisions of: xv, xx; decrees of: xvii, xxxiv, xxxix, lvi; extraordinary: 69; function of: 12; indult of: 47; of 1116: 2; of 1134: 28, 35, 44, 46, 82; of 1152: xxiv, 22; of 1154: 23, 46; of 1157: 23, 36, 47–48; of 1159: 23; of 1160: 35; of 1175: 23, 47; of 1176: 25; of 1180: 36; of 1184: 36, 48; of 1185: 25, 36, 80; of 1186: 23, 36; of 1190: 11, 48; of 1191: 38, 44, 47, 81; of 1192: 12, 25, 41–42, 44–45; of 1193: 42; of 1194: 36, 48, 81; of 1195: 24, 36, 42, 47, 81; of 1196: 36, 47; of 1197: 47; of 1199: 35–36; of 1200: 24, 36, 81; of 1201: 47; of 1203: 35; of 1204: 36; of 1205: 36; of 1206: 45, 48; of 1208: 45; of 1209: 24, 42; of 1210: 49; of 1211: 38, 48; of 1212: 49; of 1217: 24, 45, 82; of 1219: 43; of 1224: 45; of 1233: 37, 45; of 1234: 49; of 1245: xxiv, 25; of 1252: 26, 32; of 1257: 38; of 1258: 24, 38; of 1259: 37; of 1261: 37, 43; of 1274: 49; of 1275: 43; of 1287: 38; of 1288: 38; of 1293: 38; of 1303: 39; of 1308: 49; of 1460: 43; of 1478: 43; of 1482: 26; of 1494: 43; of 1497: 22; of 1565: 26; of 1573: 27; of 1601: 27; of 1623: 39; of 1892: 122; of 1895: 114–15, 183; of 1896: 67; of 1898: 109; of 1899: 73, 76, 88, 123, 171; of 1900: 184; of 1902: 79; of 1903: 65; of 1904: 65; of 1905: 66, 75, 106, 136; of 1906: 76, 99, 107, 140–41; of 1907: 88, 105, 138, 141; of 1908: 74, 76, 82, 112; of 1909: 79, 130; of 1910: 130, 141, 186–87; of 1912: 121; of 1913: 78, 120; of 1920: xxxix, 74–75, 85, 98–99, 109–10, 115, 126, 134, 141, 171; of 1921: 100; of 1922: 122, 126; of 1923: 109–10, 169; of 1924: 182, 184, 186; of 1925: 78; of 1926: xiii, 184; of 1927: 134, 141; of 1928: 171; of 1929: 186; of 1930: 105, 130; of 1931: 184; of 1932: 107; of 1933: 171; of 1934: 105; of 1937: 85–86; of 1938: 82, 99, 136, 167; of 1946: 82–83, 115–16, 134; of 1947: 141; of 1951: 135–36; of 1953: 81, 123, 189, 191; of 1954: 104, 106; of 1955: xxxv, xlv, 125–26, 130, 191; of 1969: xi, lvii; of 2005: lvii; organization of: xxxvii; permission of: 44; plenary: 66, 68; recommendation of: xxxix, xli; regulations of: xxii, xliii; role of: xxxv; ruling(s) of: xxiv, xliv, 67; statute(s) of: xxiv–xxviii, xxxvi–xxxvii, xliii–xliv, lii, 2, 4, 23–24, 35–36, 41, 47, 99, 104, 107, 135, 185–86

generosity: 170

geography, study of: 114

Gethsemani, Abbey of: vii, ix, xi, xiii, xv, xvii, xxi, xxxv, xxxviii–xxxix, xliii, xlvi, 64, 74, 79, 83, 99, 108, 115, 121, 125, 137, 139, 190; centenary celebration of: 140

gift(s): 65, 135, 154

Gilbert of Hoyland, Abbot: xxxix, 84–85

Gill, Stephen: xxv

girdle, monastic: 162

glory, of God: 61–62, 186; to God: xxxv

God: 5, 32, 59, 61, 63, 72–73, 100; adoration of: 63; as Creator: 63; as end: 62; as love: 32; ascent to: 101; bond with: 172; call by: xlviii–xlix, 145–46; commandment of: 154; communal relationship with: xv; equality under: 8; fear of: 52; gift of self to: 131; glory of: 61–62, 186; glory to: xxxv; honor of: 154, 186; honoring: 154; house of: 53; instruments of: 59; knowledge of:

114; law of: 73; life for: 145; love for: 154; mercy of: 46; personal relationship with: xv; pleasing: 97; praise of: 62; providence of: 58; rejection of: xxxv; seeking: xlix, 62, 100, 145–46; service of: xlix, 144, 159, 170; things of: 118; union with: 57, 97, 114, 203; will of: xxvii, xxxix, 41; work of: xxxix, 40, 59, 62–63, 84, 170
good, common: xxvii, 39; of souls: 6, 8
Good Friday: 124
goods: liii; acquisition of: 201; disposal of: 183; ownership of: 201; possession of: 183; public renunciation of: 183; retention of: 188; spiritual: 7; temporal: 7
gospel: 20, 57, 185
governance, Cistercian: xxxiii, xxxv, 57–58, 63–77; monastic: xv; spiritual: 71; structures of: xxxv; temporal: 71
grace(s): xliv, 127; at meals: 31–32; divine: 60; of novices: 164; of state: xl, 92, 95; reserved for Cistercians: 176; reserved for religious: 176; spiritual: 176; state of: 97
gradual: 18
grandfather: 154
grandmother: 155
grange(s): xxv–xxvi, 7, 24, 28, 34–37, 40, 47
grange master(s): 32, 36
grave-robbing: 156
gravity: 44, 82
Greek, study of: 114
Gregorian University: 116
Gregory the Great, St.: 119
Guala, Filiberto, ocso: ix
Gualbert, St. John, Feast of: xxxii
Guardian Angels, Feast of: 39
Guerric of Igny, Bl.: 116

guest(s): 10, 20, 51, 53, 93, 104, 111; death of: 15; sick: 15
guest house: 6–7, 10, 46, 159
guest master(s): xxvii–xxviii, 32, 36, 39, 45, 74, 113, 128
Guignard, Philippe: 1, 3

habit, blessing of: 130; monastic: xxviii, xxxiii, xxxvii, xlv, liv, 46, 50, 58, 159, 173, 176, 193–94; oblate: 159; of brothers: 190; of novices: xxviii, xlix, 159, 162, 175; reception of: xlix, 159, 162; regular: 44, 129–31, 142; religious: 130, 199, 201; sleeping in: xlv, 129–30
habits: 93
hair: 37
harm: 198
Hart, Patrick, ocso: ix, xiv, xxii, lxi, 21, 60, 64, 90
harvest: xxvi, 30, 55–56
hay: xxvi, 37
heads of state: 139; wives of: 139
health: 19, 79, 132, 145, 186; bodily: 132, 172; breakdown of: 178, 200; ill: 178, 185; mental: 200; physical: lii, 200; poor: 166; spiritual: 132
heart: xlviii, 100, 107, 144
heat: 129–30
hebdomadary: 55
heresy: 49, 87
heretics: 156
hermits, Camaldolese: 60
Heschel, Abraham Joshua: xxix–xxx
hills: x
history, Benedictine: 58; Church: 112, 114; Cistercian: xiii, xvi, xviii, xxvi–xxvii, xxxi, lvi, lx, 9, 14, 41, 60–61, 115; monastic: xxxiv, 9, 169; national: 114; study of: 112
Holy Office: 65, 86
Holy Saturday: 81

Holy See: xxxiv, 9, 57, 61, 71–72, 76, 87–88, 108, 112, 138, 148, 150–51, 157–58, 164, 172, 176, 179–80, 185, 187, 199–202; authority of: 76
home(s), broken: 155; visits to: 42
homicide, voluntary: 156–57
homilies: 54
honor, of God: 154, 186; of parents: 154
hood, monastic: xxv, 18, 25
horarium, daily: 29–35; harvest-time: 34–35; monastic: xxiii, xxvi; novitiate: xlix; of postulants: 159; of students in Rome: 117; summer: 33–34; Trappist: xxxv; winter: 29–32
Horrigan, Msgr. Alfred: xxx
horse-shoeing: 44
hospital(s): 39, 132
hospitality: xxvi, 37
hostility: 147
hour(s), canonical: xxxv, 39, 182; day: 56; little: 55; liturgy of: 49, 79–80, 83
house(s), American: 66, 126; Benedictine: xviii, 7; change of: 187; Cistercian: xlvii, 41; daughter: xix–xx, 6; English: 126; European: 66; Far East: 66; Irish: 126; mother: 11, 70; of God: 53; of studies: xliii; religious: liv, 64, 133, 193, 202
Hugh of Lyons, Archbishop: 60
humanities, education in: 112, 146; study of: 166
humiliation(s), fear of: 149; zeal for: xlix, 145
humility: 53, 61, 109, 146, 170, 189, 192
Hungary: 48
hymnal: 18
hypocrisy: 154

ice cream: 127

ideals, formulation of: 101
ideas of reference: 147
idols, service of: 8
illegitimacy: 155
illness(es): 66; grave: 141
imagination, weakness of: 122
impediment(s), absence of: 160, 173; canonical: 76, 147–59; concealing: 149; diriment: 181; dispensation from: 152–53, 155; freedom from: 145, 147; illicit: xlviii, 152–53, 155, 158; invalidating: xlviii, 148–52, 156–58, 162; legal: 144; simple: 155, 157; temporary: 155, 157
incendiaries: 88
incest: 156
inclinations: 93
income: 108
inconstancy: 159, 201; temptations to: 202
indigence: 154
indiscretion: 135–36
indulgence(s): xlv, 123, 130, 162–63; brothers' share in: 189
indult(s): 47, 148, 202; apostolic: 161; of exclaustration: 76, 199–200; of secularization: lv, 76, 200–202
industries: 73, 109
infamy: 148, 156; in fact: 157
infants: 147
inferiority, feelings of: 144
infirm: 28–29, 34, 37, 55, 123
infirmarian: xlv, 20–21, 27, 56, 113, 128, 132; as experienced: 132; as God-fearing: 132; as prudent: 132
infirmary: xxix, xlv, 22–23, 37, 55–56, 80–81, 90, 103, 128, 131–33, 174; chapel of: xlv, 131; common: 131
infirmities: 97, 128–29
influences, on novices: 165
initiative: 132
injury, fear of: 149
ink: 20

instability: 42
Instituta Capituli Generalis: xviii, xxii, xxxvi, 7, 15, 48, 75, 196
institute(s), religious: 150, 171, 182, 187; without vows: 187
instruction, of novices: xlv, l, 91, 165, 168
intention(s), declaration of: 173; defects in: 144; malicious: 194; of candidate: 158; pure: 203; right: 97, 143–45
interests, spiritual: 3
Interlaken: 141
interval(s): 18, 29, 33, 56, 101, 111, 113; nocturnal: 84
invitator: 16
irregularities: 6, 155; absence of: 160; *ex defectu*: 155–56; *ex delicto*: 155–57
irritation: lv
Isaias (Isaiah): 154

Japan: x, 66, 75
jello: 127
job(s): 157; monastic: xv, xlv–xlvi, 113, 140
John Climacus, St.: xlii, 101
John Lateran, St., Feast of: 96
John of the Cross, St.: 116
John of Toledo, Cardinal: 38
John the Baptist, St., Feast of: 38, 55
John XXIII, Pope: viii–ix
Joseph, St., month of: 79
journey(s): xxvii, xxxvii, xliv, xlvii, 39–45, 81, 123, 140–42
Jouy, Abbot of: 12
joy: xliv, 127
judge(s), civil: 151, 156; ecclesiastical: 151
judgement(s), correct: xxxix, 92; error of: 203; of abbot: 128; of novice master: 168; personal: 204; proper: xxxix, 168

judgementalism: 147
Juliana, Bl., Feast of: 96
jurisdiction, ecclesiastical: 67; spiritual: 72; to absolve reserved sins: 86–87; to absolve sins: 92
justice: lii, 186, 188, 203; promoter of: 198; sin against: 150, 152; strict: 153

Kennedy, Joseph A.: 99
Kentucky, first lady of: xlvi, 139; governor of: xlvi, 139
king: 23
kitchen(s): xxiv, 20–21, 53; abbot's: 20
Klinski, Vital, ocso: 74, 120
Knecht, Edward, ocso: 90
knife: 31, 33
knowledge, lack of: 144; of God: 114; of things of God: 118
Kramer, Victor A.: xxx, 90

La Ferté, Abbey of: 6, 75; Abbot of: 47
La Trappe, Abbey of: xxiv–xxv, lvi, 21, 61; Abbot of: 83; usages of: 21–22, 28
La Val Sainte, Abbey of: xxv; usages of: 27
labor(s): xxxv, xliv, 5, 61–63, 127; manual: xviii, xxxviii, xlii, xlix, 7, 35, 108–109, 145, 170; patience in: 61
Ladislaus ab Immaculata, cp: 143
Laibach, University of: 1
laity: xliii, 37, 111, 139, 160
lambs: 35
language(s), foul: 44; study of: 112
Larraona, Arcadio, cmf: 64, 170
Latin, conversation in: 117; education in: 146; study of: 112, 114–15, 145, 159
lauds: xxiii, xxxviii, 29, 33, 80, 82, 191; of little office: 29, 80–81; of the dead: 33
L'Aumone, Abbot of: 12

lavabo: 21, 30
lavatory: 33
law(s): 65, 68, 86, 118, 134, 139, 147, 156; canon: xv, xxxix, xlvi, xlviii, l, lvi, 77, 106, 112, 114, 117–18, 120–21, 148, 150, 152–53, 156, 164, 184; Church: 106, 140, 155, 157, 162, 194, 197; civil: lix, 73, 148, 155–56, 174; common: 76, 88, 162, 169, 172–73, 175, 179, 194, 196; general: 67–68, 71, 106; ignorance of: 152; infractions of: 65; legitimate: 151; letter of: xlvi; matter of: 91; natural: 147–48, 153–55, 158; of God: 73; of the Order: li, 171, 196; particular: 88, 120, 195–97; purpose of: xlvi; special: 197; universal: 197; unjust: 151, 174
lawsuits: 73, 153
laybrothers, Cistercian: xviii, xxii, xxvi–xxvii, liii–liv, 7, 23–25, 28, 34–35, 38–39, 41–42, 45, 47, 53, 89, 128, 149, 188–92; as religious: 189; change of schedule for: 191; clothing ceremony of: 190; communion of: 191; confessors for: 191–92; dismissal of: 190, 197; education of: 190; habit of: 190; illiteracy of early: liii, 188; increasing equality of: 189; increasing participation of in life of choir: 189; *lectio divina* of: 191–92; liturgical obligations of: 191; master of: 83, 191–92; meals of: 191; meditation of: 191; merger with choir of: liii–liv; novitiate of: 175, 190; obligations of: 192; office of: 191; participation in community goods of: 189; postulancy of: 190; prayers of: 191–92; probation period for: 190; professed: 189, 192; profession of: 190; reading of: 189, 191; retreat for: 190; rules of admission for: 189–90; schedule of: liii, 191; scriptorium of: 192; simple vows of: 190; solemn profession of: liii, 189; solemn vows of: 190; technical skill of: 188; transfer to choir of: 190; vocation of: 192; work of: liv, 191–92; workroom of: 191
leadership, lax: xx
learning, sacred: 118
Leclercq, Jean, OSB: xvii, xxi–xxii, 3–4
lectio divina: xxxix, xli, liv, 31–32, 84, 97, 100, 119, 133, 191–92
Lefèvre, J.-A.: xvi–xvii, 1–7
legate, papal: 38, 41, 60, 108
legislation, Cistercian: xi, l, 7, 45, 115, 138; civil: 174; contemporary: lx, 22; early: lx, 164, 183, 196; ecclesiastical: 117–18, 161; monastic: viii, 104; special: 194
Lehodey, Vital, OCSO: 98
leisure, contemplative: 133
Leiva, Simeon, OCSO: lxi
Lemercier, Gregorio, OSB: 64
Lent: 20, 28, 38, 51–52, 55, 96, 119, 123–25
Le Pennuen, Abbot Louis, OCSO: 83, 105, 115
leprosy: 48
lessons, liturgical: 51, 81
Lestrange, Abbot Augustin de: 122
letter(s): xlii, 89, 104–108, 144; anonymous: 107; collective: 108; exempt from control: xlii, 106–108; opened: 104; receiving: 105; recipients of exempt: 108; sending: 105; testimonial: 143, 158, 160–61; traveling: 43, 142; unopened: 104; writing: 105, 133
Lewis, Gordian, CP: 64
Libellus Antiquarum Definitionum: 48–49, 85, 88–89, 194
liberality: 153
liberation: 101
liberty: 107; irresponsible: 107

Index

life, active: 145; apostolic: 49; Benedictine: xl, 95; cenobitic: xiv; Cistercian: vii, xvi, xxxvii–xxxviii, xlii, xlix, lvii, lx; common: xliv, xlix, 127, 145; community: l, 66, 179; consecrated: 200; contemplative: xli, liv, lvii, 41, 49, 65, 97–98, 111, 114, 192; Eucharistic: xli, 96–97; exterior: xxxix; frugality of: 61; higher: xlix, 181; holy way of: 59; in Christ: 5; interior: xxxix, xliii, 59, 85, 111, 133, 145; monastic: viii, xiv, xvi, xxxiv, xxxvii, xliii, xlv, xlviii, l, liv, lvii, 50, 108–109, 122, 131, 135, 143–44, 168, 192; necessaries of: 154; penitent: 61; perfect: xlix, 159; prayer: 113; regular: 165, 195; religious: xlix, lii, liv, 5, 92, 118, 143–44, 147, 150–51, 153, 155, 193, 200; rule of: 117; spiritual: xlvi, 93, 131, 133, 138, 165; state(s) of: xlviii, 142, 154; stricter: 194; Trappist: xiv; unity of: xi; well-integrated: xxxviii
linens, altar: 54
litanies: 79, 81
literature, study of: 114
liturgy: xv, xxiii, 78, 145, 191; Cistercian: 80; of the hours: liv; study of: 112; vernacular: liv
livestock: 128
Livonia: 48
loan(s): 73, 153
lodging, right to: 177
Longpont, Abbot of: 25
love: xli, 100, 170, 192; for God: 154; for parents: 154; genuine: 192; God as: 32; humble: 192; of brethren: xx; of Christ: 63; of common life: xlix, 145; of divine office: xlix, 145; of manual labor: xlix, 145; of poverty: xlix, 145; of prayer: xlix, 145, 170; of silence: xlix, 145, 170; of vocation: liv, 192

Louf, André, ocso: ix
Louis IX, St.: 26, 32
Louisville, KY: xxx, lx
Lucy, St., Feast of: 96
Lutgarde, St., Feast of: 96

machines: 134
magazines: 99, 136
Malachy, St., Feast of: xxix–xxx, 96
man, spiritual: 62
mantle: 44, 49
manual, theological: 119
manuscripts: 51
Margam, Abbey of: xxvii, 45; Abbot of: xxvii, 45; lay brothers of: xxvii, 45
Marianhill, South Africa: 66, 75
Marmoutier, Abbey of: xxvii, 45
marriage: 176; attempted: 156; bigamous: 156; certificate of: 160; non-consummated: 150; of parents: 156, 160; of religious in simple vows: 87; outside Church: 87; right to: 201; sacrilegious: 87
married persons: 150
Martin, Conrad: 102
martyrology: 16
Mary Magdalen, St., Feast of: 37
masons: 23
Masons: 148
Mass: xxiii, xxix, 15, 20, 35, 40, 43–44, 51, 54, 56, 79, 131, 137, 156, 191; abbot's: 83; conventual: xxxviii, 20, 34, 55, 83, 191; first: 140; high: 29, 33–34, 40, 96; major: 54; matutinal: 40, 95–96, 121; private: 34, 96, 191; simulated celebration of: 87; solemn: 189
master of novices: xiii, xxviii, xxxix, xlix–li, 32, 50, 74, 80, 90–92, 94, 105, 163, 166–71, 183, 187; age of: xlix, 166; as confessor: 91–92; as representative of abbot: 168; as

spiritual director: 169; charity of: xlix, 167; duties of: xxviii, 50, 91, 167–71; formal qualifications of: xlix, 167; functions of: 91–92, 168; instructions of: 164; judgement of: 168; juridical condition of: 168; jurisdiction of: 168; mortification of: xlix, 167; obligations of: 169; of laybrothers: 83, 191–92; ordination of: xlix, 167; piety of: xlix, 167; prayer of: xlix, 167; prudence of: xlix, 167; responsibility of: l, lvi, 167; rights of: 91; spiritual qualifications of: xlix, 167; term of office of: 168

master of scholastics: xliii, 72, 74, 94, 113

materials, legislative: viii

mathematics, study of: 114

matins: 33; of little office: 29, 80

matrimony, attempted: 88, 178, 194; impediment to: 181

matter, grave: 107; gravity of: 106; lightness of: 105; parvity of: 94

matters, disciplinary: viii, 197; financial: xxxvi; legal: viii; material: 119; necessary: 107; spiritual: 95; useful: 107

Matthias, St., Feast of: 39

mattress, straw: 129; woolen: 132

Maundy Thursday: 39

Maurus, St., Feast of: 96

Mayeul of Cluny, St.: 59

McCann, Justin, OSB: 7, 11–12, 20, 24, 40, 53, 62, 65, 84, 109, 122, 124–25, 129, 145, 165

McCormick, Anne: lx

Meade, Mark C.: lxi

meal(s): xv, xxiii, xxviii, xxxvii, xliv, 21, 27, 35, 40–41, 53–54, 56, 125–26, 191; portions at: 123–24, 126–27; prayers at: 15

mealtimes: 51

meat: xxvi, xlv, 36, 41, 123, 132; abstinence from: 122; on journeys: 123, 142

medicine: 157

meditation: xxxviii, xli, 27, 97, 166, 170, 191

Meeuws, M. D.: 62

Melleray, Abbot of: 83, 105

men, married: 157

mercy: 14, 31, 38; of abbot: 46; of God: 46

meridian: 33, 130

Merton, Thomas, as compiler of "chroniques": 137; as fire watcher: 105–106; as master of novices: vii, xiii–xiv, xvi–xvii, xxi–xxii, lvi, 105; as master of scholastics: vii, xvii, 115; as master of words: ix; as poet: ix; as visitation interpreter: 105; autobiography of: ix; conscientious preparation of: vii; contribution to conciliar thought and spirit of: viii; culture of: xi; enthusiasm of: viii; example of: xi; hermitage of: xiv, lvi, 134; humor of: viii, xxiv; Japanese translations of: x; journals of: ix; liveliness of spirit of: viii; novitiate conferences of: vii–xi, xiii–xvi, xx–xxii, xxix–xxxi; personal experience of: xi; private vows of: xiv; sense of responsibility of: lvi; spiritual insight of: ix; spontaneous comments of: viii; style of presentation of: viii; teaching of: xi; WORKS: *Ascent to Truth*: 116; *Cassian and the Fathers*: xv, xxi; "Cistercian Fathers and Their Monastic Theology": xv–xvi; *Conjectures of a Guilty Bystander*: 99; "Contemplatives and the Crisis of Faith": ix; *Entering the Silence*: 115, 124, 140, 167; *Hidden Ground of Love*: ix, xxx, 64; *"Honorable Reader"*: x; *In the Valley of Wormwood*: 21, 33, 60; *Introduction to Christian Mysticism*: xv, 97–98; *Last of the Fathers*: 108; *Learning to Love*: ix; *"Lectio Divina"*: 84; "Letter on the Contemplative Life": ix; *Life of the Vows*: xv, 170, 172; "Life, Works and Doctrine of St. Bernard": xvi, xxii, xxxi; "Liturgical Feasts and Seasons": xv, xxiii; *Monastic Journey*: ix; *Monastic Observances*: xiv, xxiii, lv, 17, 20, 27–28, 84, 184; *Other Side of the Mountain*: 90; *Pre-Benedictine Monasticism*: xv, 101; *Road to Joy*: xxi, 134; *Rule of Saint Benedict*: xv, 72; *School of Charity*: ix, xiv, xxxiii, liv–lvi, 64, 72, 74; *Search for Solitude*: ix, xxxii, xxxv, 64, 90, 134; *Seven Storey Mountain*: x; *Silent Life*: xxxv, 59–60; *Spirit of Simplicity*: 32, 78–79; *Survival or Prophecy?*: xxii; *Thoughts in Solitude*: x; *Turning Toward the World*: xxx–xxxi, 90; *Waters of Siloe*: 61, 83, 122; *Witness to Freedom*: 64

methods, practical: 112

Middle Ages: viii

Migne, J.-P.: 2, 84, 102

milk: 122–24, 127

mind: xlviii, 8, 100, 144

ministry: 65; accidental: 110; exterior: 66, 110; parochial: 109; partial: 65; permanent: 110; prolonged: 110; rare: 110; temporary: 110

minor(s): 147, 155

minuti: 28, 34, 53, 55

missals: 54

mission(s): 65; service in: 151–52

Mistassini, Abbey of: 75

misunderstandings: 204

miter: 71

mitigations: l, 60; useless: 124

mixt: xxiii, xxv–xxvi, 21, 27–30, 54–55, 125–27, 191

modesty: xliv, 25, 82, 127–28

Molesme, Abbey of: xviii, xliii, 4–5, 9, 60, 108

monastery: xi, xiv, xxvii–xxviii, xxxvii–xxxviii, xl, xlii, xlvi, 7, 22, 24, 28, 34, 36, 39–41, 44, 47, 58, 63, 68, 81, 89–90, 95, 102, 106, 109, 111, 146, 183–84, 186, 190, 193, 196; adorning of: 78; as school of divine service: 62; Benedictine: 45; British: 137; Cistercian: xviii, xliii, 2, 10, 13, 99, 109, 136–37, 157, 162, 184; construction of: 78; European: 98, 111; flight from: 88; foundation of: xxxiii; location of: xviii, xlv; material affairs of: liii; needs of: 42; new: xviii, 2–3, 9; non-European: xi; plan of: 15; regular places of: xxiii–xxiv, 20–23, 25–27; Trappist: xli, 112, 118–19, 132, 157, 162

monasticism, sources of: 59

monk(s): xi, xv, xxiii–xxv, xxvii, xxxvii, xli, xlvi, lii, liv–lv, 7, 16, 20–25, 28, 30, 35–36, 41–42, 50, 53, 59, 80, 83, 85, 89, 97, 125, 135, 140–41, 162–63, 170, 185, 189; as godfathers: 44; Benedictine: xxviii; choir: liii, 144–45, 159, 188, 190; Cistercian: vii, xxviii, 63, 100, 107; contacts of: 104; contemplative: 118, 133; end of: 57, 203; expulsion of: 198; fancies of: l, 171; fickle: 116; healthy: 23, 132; intellectual: 116; junior: 27; photographs of: xlvi, 136; professed: xlix–l, 49; secularized: 202; senior: 17, 20, 27; sick: xliv, 132; transferred: lii; transient: 40; Trappist: 136, 151; traveling: 43; unstable: 116; visiting: 41; weak: xliv; will of: l; young: xv

Montaldo, Jonathan: 115
Moore, Augustine, ocso: 71–72
Morimond, Abbey of: 6, 75
morons: 147
mortification: 170; of novice master: xlix, 167
mother: 154
motives, for entering Order: 158; positive: 144; supernatural: 144; wrong: 159
Mott, Michael: 106
movies: 99, 136–37
murmuring: 147
music, Church: 112, 138
mutism: xlii, 103

nature, fallen: li, 170; suspicious: 147
Neath, Abbot of: 24, 82
necessity: 24, 44; extreme: 155–56; grave: 16, 154–55, 185
needs: 129; temporary: 166; urgent: 111
Nelson County, KY: 105
neophytes: 157
New Year: xxxii
news, family: 106
newspapers: xli, 98–99, 135–36
Nice: 141
Nicholas, St., Feast of: 96
night: 134
noblemen, chapels of: 43
nocturns: 39–40, 82
Nogues, Abbot Dominique, ocso: 124
Nomasticon Cisterciense: 1, 3, 8–23, 25–27, 29–34, 37, 39–41, 46, 48–52, 54–56, 60, 67, 75, 77–78, 89, 125, 188, 194, 196
none: 30, 33–34, 55, 83
norm(s), accepted: 9; canonical: xl; Cistercian: vii; constitutional: xl; juridical: xlviii; permanent: xxxiv, 57
Normandy: 36
nosebleed: xxix, 54

notes: 105
Notre Dame du Lac, Abbey of: 83
novice(s): vii, xi, xiv, xvi, xxi, xxx, xxvii, xlvi, l–li, lvi–lvii, 15, 21, 26, 67, 80–81, 89, 94, 129, 163, 171, 183–84; admission of: xlviii, 6, 46–49, 142, 162; admission to profession of: 73; age of: xxviii, 46–48; announcements to: xxix; Benedictine: 128; blessing of: 162; brothers: liv, 45, 53; capacity of: 163; choir: liv, 53; clothing of: xxviii; confessors for: xxxix, 88–92; conscience of: 168; death of: 50; dismissal of: 170, 173; duties of: 170–71; exterior conduct of: 168; fervor of: 165; food of: 162; formation of: xl, l, 91, 165–66, 168–70; from other institutes: 150; from other orders: 161; Gethsemani: xxviii; habit of: xxviii, xlix, 159, 162, 175; *horarium* of: 162; instruction of: xlv, l, 91, 165, 168; irregular: 170; juridical condition of: 170–71; manifestation of conscience of: 168; manner of: 168; obligations of: 166; permissions to: 169; photographs of: xlvi, 136; physical maturity of: xxviii; probation of: l, 168; progress of: 168; psychological maturity of: xxviii; reception of: 15, 47–49, 162; soul of: 166, 168; spirit of: l, 168; spiritual direction of: 168; strength of: 163; studies of: xlix; training of: l, 15, 168; understanding of: 168; virtue of: l; work of: 169
novitiate: xxviii, xxxiii, xlvii–l, liii, 46–51, 58, 91, 143, 150, 159, 162–66, 183, 188, 202; admission to: 46–48, 72, 142–61; brothers': liii, 164, 175, 190, 192; business of: 165–66; canonical: 115, 148–49, 165, 171, 173; chapter of faults of: xxix, lv,

204; choir: liii, 175; common: 164; conduct of: xl; customs of: lv, 204; entrance to: 149; full: 187; illicit: xlviii, 158, 162; interrupted: 174–75; invalid: xlviii, 148–52, 158, 162; life in: 49–50; location of: xlix–l, 164; merging of: liii–liv; of brothers: 175, 190; of Orientals: 158; prolongation of: li, 171, 180; regimen of: 168; studies and: 115; suspended: 174–75; two-year: xvi, xxviii, 148, 171, 173, 187; uninterrupted: li, 173–74; valid: 149, 162, 173, 175
nuns: 75, 94; Cistercian: xli, 44, 100, 107, 141; direction of: 110; enclosure of: 139
nurse, trained: 132

oaths: 44
Obazine, Abbey of: 36
obedience: 61, 142, 170, 192–93; perpetual: lii; promise of: lii, 183–85; religious: 193; spirit of: liv, 169, 192; to superiors: 172, 177, 199; vow of: 64, 176, 181, 184, 187, 199; zeal for: xlix, 145
objections: 121, 155
objectivity, lack of: 144
oblate(s): 28, 129, 171
obligation(s): xli, xlvi, 59, 102, 133, 140, 143, 150, 153–55, 166, 168, 181; general; 71; liturgical: 80, 83, 191; military: 157; monk's: 97; mutual: li, 171–72; of brothers: 192; of charity: 203; of novice: 166; of Order: 92, 144; of professed monk: 177; of rule: 199; of state of life: 133; of vows: 176, 178, 195; release from: 201; religious: 201; relinquishing of: 200; replacement of: 188; strict: 138; suspended: 187; to confess: 89; to studies: 74, 119; to vote: 74, 171

Obrecht, Abbot Edmond, ocso: 139
observance(s), alteration of: xx; Benedictine: 60; chapter of faults as important: 202; Cistercian: xiv, xxxiii, xxxv, l, lv, 7, 9, 17, 41, 58, 63, 78–142, 144, 184, 203; exterior: l, 171; in general: 15; in summer: 15; in winter: 15; mode of: xxxiv, 58; monastic: viii, xv, xxiii, xxxvi, 15–16, 58; of *Rule*: 8, 12, 50, 60, 167, 180, 203; of rules: lvii, 68, 163, 171, 177, 200; of usages: 171; points of: 9; primitive: 61; regular: xxxix, 15, 35, 79, 86; religious: 4; silence as: 101; uniformity of: xviii, xxxvii, lvii, 8–9, 78–79; violation of: 197
observations: 121
O'Connell, Patrick F.: xiv–xv, 17, 72, 84, 98, 101, 170
Odilo of Cluny, St.: 59
Odo of Cluny, St.: 59
offense(s), external: 197–98; grave: 197; series of: 198
office, absence from: xxxviii, 84; canonical: xxxv, 41, 80–81, 177; choral: 182; divine: xxxiii, xxxv, xxxvii–xxxix, liii–liv, 15, 18, 23, 30, 40–41, 51, 54–56, 58, 62–63, 80–84, 97, 133, 180; Latin: liv; love for: xlix, 145; night: xxiii, xxix, xxxviii, 20, 55, 84, 117, 191; of brothers: 191; of the dead: 81; recitation of: xxxviii, 180, 201; vernacular: liv; zeal for: xlix, 145
office(s), deprivation of: 138–39, 158, 160, 194, 196; ecclesiastical: 177; exercise of forbidden: 157; in curia: 202; in religious house: 202; in seminary: 202; in university: 202; loss of: 87; monastic: xxvii, xxix, xxxix, 30, 41, 47, 85, 112, 167; prohibition of for novices: xlix, 165; religious: 77

officers, appointment of: 72; monastic: xxviii, xxxv, xxxix–xl, 15, 30, 108; permanent: 15; weekly: 15
oil(s): 123; holy: 54, 71
oleomargarine: 126
openness, with superiors: xl
oratory: 7
order(s), active: 133; as family: 172; Benedictine: 58–59; Cistercian: xi, xiii–xv, xviii–xx, xxx, xxxv, xxxvii, xl–xli, xlvii–xlix, li, liii–liv, lvi–lvii, lx, 7–10, 14, 32, 37–39, 44–45, 58, 61–63, 68, 70, 78, 87–88, 92, 96, 100, 108, 110, 115–16, 127, 130, 134, 141–42, 144–45, 148, 158–59, 162, 168–69, 171–72, 174, 181, 187, 190, 193, 196, 202; clerical: 167; contemplative: xlvi, 114, 133, 188; former: lii; less perfect: 149; monastic: xlvi, 133, 164; of men: 89; religious: xx, xxxvi, xlvi–xlvii, li, 63, 67, 69–70, 86, 101, 133, 151, 178, 187, 199; responsibility of: 172; third: 177
orders, holy: 88, 112, 157, 193, 200–201; major: 152; minor: 49–50, 71, 161
ordinary: 67, 157, 160, 199; diocesan: 161; local: 88–89; military: 161
ordination(s): xliii, 72, 88, 115, 117, 119, 155; certificate of: 161; dismissorials for: 72; title for: 152
ordo: 6
organization, atheistic: 148; Cistercian: lx, 78–142; of general chapter: xxxvii
Orient: 66, 75
Orientals: 157–58
origin(s), Cistercian: xvii, xxxvii; place of: 161
Our Lady of the Valley, Abbey of: 75
outlook, monastic: l, 170; of Cistercian fathers: 16

outsiders: 102, 104, 140
oversight: 203
ownership: li, 65, 179–80, 182, 201

Pairis, Abbot of: 48
Palm Sunday: 81, 88
palms: 54
pamphlets: 136
paranoia: 147
paranoids: 147, 179
parchment: 20
parents: 42, 65, 146–48, 154–56, 161; care for: 199–200; divorced: 155; love for: 154; marriage of: 156, 160; objections of: 155
Paris: 43, 49
Paris, Julian: 1, 15, 60
Paris Match: 136
parish(es): xliii, 71, 110–11; revenue of: 110
parlor: xxiv, xlvi, 22–23, 140; grand: 22
parties: 27
paschaltide: 124
passions: 93, 166
patience: 189; in labor: 61
patients, secular: 132
Paul, St., Feast of Conversion of: 39
Paul VI, Pope: ix
peace: x, xix–xx, xxiv, xliv, 6, 8–10, 12, 19, 92, 102, 127, 203–204; mutual: xviii, 5; of conscience: 89
peacocks: xxviii, 48
Pearson, Paul M.: lxi
penalties: 67–68, 88; canonical: 197; for apostasy: 194–95; for fugitives: 194–95; medicinal: 86
penance(s): xxvii, xlvi, liv, 12, 21, 37, 42, 47–48, 50, 63, 71, 131, 169; ordinary: 12; private: 169; public: 169, 198; sacrament of: 70, 91; suitable: 196
Penitentiary, Sacred: 70

Pentecost: 37, 39, 55, 81
perfection: xxxv, xli, l, 62, 71, 97, 118, 144, 154, 171; as end of monastic life: 144; monastic: 102; spiritual: 61; state of: 151; state tending to: 151; way of: 93
periodicals, religious: xli
permission(s): 18, 36, 42–44, 50, 84, 107, 129, 134, 141, 173, 175, 177, 180, 193–94; illicit: 175; legitimate: 134; of Holy See: 199–200; of superior: 83, 104–105, 123, 142, 181, 187, 193; to novices: 169; to speak: 24, 103–104, 165; to travel: 104
persecution: 162, 174, 200; delusions of: 147
perseverance: 145–46
perspective, self-centered: 147; sense of: 203; subjective: 147
persuasion: 149; importunate: 93
Peter of Tarentaise, St., Feast of: 96
Peter, St., Feast of: 38
Peter the Venerable, Abbot: xlii, 101–102
petition(s): 50; preliminary: 71; third: 183
Pharisees: 154
philosophy, scholastic: 117; study of: 112, 114, 117
phonograph(s): xlvi; records: xlvi, 136–38
photograph(s): xlvi, 136
photographers: 135–36
physician, advice of: 122
picnic: 34
pictures, holy: 129
piety: 63, 113, 116, 170; of novice master: xlix, 167; showy: 147
pigs: 109
pillows: 41
pittance(s): 28, 31–32, 45, 55, 122
Pius IX, Pope: 80, 161

Pius X, Pope: 97
Pius XI, Pope: xxxiv, 58, 114; *Monachorum Vita*: xxxiv–xxxv, 58–63; *Unigenitus Dei Filius*: 114
Pius XII, Pope: xliii, 133; *Sponsa Christi*: 133
places, regular: xxiii–xxiv, 20–23, 25–27
Placid, St., Feast of: 96
Poblet, Abbey of: 26
Poland: 48
police: 151; secular: 196
policy, spiritual: xlii, 101
Pontaut, Abbey of: 25
pontificalia: 71
Pontigny, Abbey of: 6, 45, 75
poor: 53, 183
pope: 38, 64, 68, 86, 108, 111, 156
Porion, J.-B.: ix
Portugal: 45
possessions: 4, 186
postcards: 136
postulancy: xxviii, 162–63; entrance to: 149; of brothers: 190
postulant(s): 46, 94, 146, 160, 163; admission of: xxxiii, xlvii, 47, 49, 58, 142–62; age of: 148; aptitudes of: 143; brother: 159; condition of: 146; education of: 146; from other institutes: 150; *horarium* of: 159; intentions of: 143
potatoes: 124
poverty: xviii, xxxviii, xlix, 4–5, 65, 79, 154; absolute: 60, 132; love of: xlix, 145; of equipage: 45; spirit of: 65; vow of: liii, 176, 179–80
power, domestic: 170; dominative: 177; of abbot: 73; of superior: 177
practice(s), Cistercian: vii, xi, xxv–xxvi, xxxiv; devotional: xxxviii; monastic: viii, xxxviii; Trappist: 103; unity of: xi
praise: 63; of God: 62; sacrifice of: 63

prayer(s): xxi, xxxv, xli, xliv, xlvi, liv, 16, 18, 33, 59, 61–62, 71, 84, 97, 100–101, 114, 127, 133, 140, 166, 203; at meals: 15; brothers' share in: 189; communal: 84, 172; difficulties in: 94; for dead: 15, 17; for travelers: 39–40; life of: 102; liturgical: 62; love of: xlix, 145, 170; mental: xxxiii, xxxvii, xxxix, 33, 49, 58, 84–85, 191; of brothers: 191–92; of novice master: xlix, 167; passionate: 85; personal: xxxix; public: xxxviii; silent: 85; spirit of: 192; vocal: 33

precedence: 10–11, 66, 163

Precious Blood Fathers: 187

prelate: 108

prescriptions, of *Constitutions*: 104; special: 7

press, freedom of: 135; tabloid: 135; yellow: 135

priest(s): xxix, xliii, 54, 77, 94–95, 113, 118–19, 133, 138, 152–53, 163, 166–67, 189, 197; Benedictine: 128; contemplative: 120; junior: 119; novice: 163; religious: 201–202; secular: 83; secularized: 201–202; solemnly professed: 69; transient: 40; Trappist: 118

priesthood: 112–13, 155

prime: xxiii, 29, 33–34, 121

prior(s): 6, 19, 22–23, 25, 30–32, 34, 42, 47, 50, 53–54, 72, 74, 113, 183; titular: 65–66, 69, 71

privacy: 135

privilege(s): 131, 133; abuse of: 107; of religious: li; relinquishing of: 200; spiritual: 199

probation, period of: li, liii, 46, 159–60, 162, 180, 185, 187, 190, 201–202

process, judicial: 86, 179, 196

procession: 33

proclamation(s): xxiii–xxiv, lv, 17, 19, 203–204; amusing: 204; charitable: lv, 204; norms for: 204; objective: 204; selfless: lv, 204; simple: 204; wise: 203

procurator general: xxxv, xxxvii, 64, 66, 69–70

profanation, of Eucharist: 87

professed: xlix–l, 89, 94, 163–65, 175–77, 181–82, 199; choir: 189; laybrother: 189; simple: li, 81, 88, 178–79, 197; solemn: 77, 88, 178, 180, 197–99; temporary: 76, 193, 197

profession, admission to: 72–73; definition of: li, 171; effects of: 176–77, 180; first: 167, 177; formula of: 182; *in articulo mortis*: 150; monastic: xxviii, 6, 10, 46, 50, 53, 56, 73, 111, 142, 163, 182, 187, 202; new: 188; of brothers: 190; perpetual: 172, 193; public: 184; religious: 172, 176, 193; schedules of: 51; simple: xxxiii, xlvii, li, 58, 171–72, 176, 180–81, 183–84, 193; solemn: xxxiii, xlvii, li–liii, 6, 58, 74, 150, 155, 171–72, 176–77, 180–84, 189, 193, 197; tacit: 176; temporary: li–lii, 171–80; validity of: li, 172, 174–76

professor(s): 115, 117, 202

progress, spiritual: xli; in virtue: 101

prohibitions: 43, 45, 141

promise: 153, 195

propensities: 93

property: li–lii, 53, 68, 179–80, 186; acquisition of: 179, 181–82; administration of: 179; disposition of: 180, 182; fresh: 181; of simple professed: 179–80; owners of: 88; ownership of: 179–80, 182; renunciation of: lii, 182; revenue

from: 179–80; title to possession of: 181; use of: 179, 181; usufruct of: 179, 181
proportion, sense of: 203
prosecutor, religious: 198
prostration: 40
protests: 108
providence, divine: 58
prudence: xlvi, 137; of novice master: xlix, 167
Prümmer, Dominicus, OP: 161
pruning: 30
psalm(s): 33, 55, 63, 80–81
psalmist: 63
psychoanalysts: xxi
psychology: 137; morbid: 135; pathological: 135
psychotics: 147, 156
publicity: xlvi, 135–36
punishment(s): 17, 38–39, 102, 107, 158, 196; capital: 156; for crime: 148, 151; remission of: 177; spirit of: 203
Purification, Feast of: 38
purity, sin against: 156
pusillanimity, of abbot: 13

Quarr, Abbot of: 11
Quinquagesima: 37

radio(s): 99, 105, 136–37; stations: 136
rain: x
Rancé, Abbot Armand de: 61, 103, 122
rank: 163; determination of: l, lii, 185–86; loss of: 196–97; new: 202; of abbey: 66; principle of: xlix; proper: 49, 197
rape: 156
Raymond de Bar, Abbot: 2
razors: 37
reader: xxvi, 16, 28, 30–32, 34; weekly: xxix, 27, 54

reading: xxiii, xxxiii, xxxvii, liii, 18–19, 27, 29–31, 35, 40, 49–50, 54, 58, 164; contemplative: 119; holy: 170; meditative: 119; of brothers: 189, 191; of *Rule*: 16, 50; place of: 98; private: xxxviii; public: 39, 100, 191; spiritual: xli, 97–101, 113, 138
readmission: xlvii, liv, 142, 192, 199–200, 202
rebels: 14
recollection: xliv, liv, 127; day(s) of: xxxix, 50, 85; spirit of: 192
recreation: xlii, 103
rector, of religious institute: 161
refectorian: 21, 32
refectory: xxiv, xxvi, xxix, xliv–xlv, 6–7, 10, 20–21, 27–28, 30–34, 49–51, 54–55, 122, 126–27, 138, 140, 163; infirmary: 22; laybrothers': 28; servant of: 20–21, 31, 55
reform(s), monastic: xxxiv, 24, 58–59; Trappist: xxxiv, 61
Reformation: 43
reformers: 58
regularity: xxxviii, l, 20, 34, 79, 102, 110, 166, 171, 202; exterior: liv, 192; of candidate: 143; spirit of: 169, 192
regulations, Cistercian: xiii, xx, xxiv–xxvi, xxxvii–xxxviii; current: xiv, xxiv–xxv; directive: 96; duplication of: l; juridical: xl; traditional: xiv
relatives: 134, 136; death of: xlvii, 141; sickness of: 141, 175
relief: 29, 31, 53, 126, 162
religion, apostasy from: 193; training in: 112
religiosity, eccentric: 147; excessive: 147
religious: xxxviii, li–lii, 18, 22, 27, 39, 64–65, 74, 80, 87–90, 93, 95, 99,

101–103, 106–107, 114, 118, 120–21, 123, 129, 134, 138, 141, 161, 176, 178–79, 186, 194, 196, 199–201; as tending toward perfection: 151; Benedictine: xxxiv; capable: 110; competent: 117; contemplative: 133; choir: liii–liv, 111, 188–91, 196–97; dismissal of: 69; duties of: xxii, li; fervent: liv, 192; good: 116; male: 138; of other institutes: 160, 184; pious: 110, 117; provinces of: 164; secularized: 201–202; solemnly professed: 88; vowed: li, 161
remedy, divine: 97
Reno, Amandus (Roger), ocso: 90; as sage and oracle: 90
renunciation: lii, 182, 186
reparation: 20
repetitions: xiii, 192
reporters, newspaper: 135
reputation: 146; of candidate: 143, 146; of Order: 146
requests: 89
rescript: 156, 200
resorts, health: 141
resourcefulness: 132
resources, sharing of: lii; transfer of: lii
respect: liv, 165, 189; human: 92, 96
responsibility: 153, 172; juridical: l; legislative: xix; of novice master: l, lvi, 167; of superior: 187; sense of: 132
responsories: 51
rest: xxix, 30, 49, 101
restitution: 150; just: 153
restlessness: xxvii, 41–42
restrictions: 127
retirement: xxxv, 63
retreat(s): xxix, 50, 83, 111; annual: xxxii–xxxiii, xxxix; Bellarmine: xxix–xxx; brothers' participation in: 189–90; closed: xliii, 111; for laypeople: xliii, 111; group: 111; monthly: xxxix, 85; spiritual: 159, 184; weekly: xxxix
reunion, Strict Observance: xxxiii–xxxiv, xxxvii, xliv, lvi, 61
revenues, disposal of: 179
reverence: 170
reviews, profane: 99
Revolution, French: xxv, 122
reward, promises of: 94
Rhode Island: 75
Richardson, Nelson: xxxi
rights, religious: 201; relinquishing of: 200; replacement of: 188; suspended: 187
ring, episcopal: 71
risk: 116
rite, Eastern: 157–58; of solemn profession: 181
ritual: xxiii; Cistercian: lii, 16, 77–78, 183–85, 191
robe, monastic: 32, 130, 162; night: 129
Robert of Molesme, St.: 5, 60
rogation days: 28, 96
Rome: 88, 141, 151, 156; conferences in: 120; studies in: xliii, 115–17
Romuald, St.: 59
rosary: 79
routine(s): 96; monastic: xxvi
Rozières, Abbot of: 24
rubrics: xxiii, 16, 78
rule(s), adaptation of: 129; application of: 124; common: 169; external: 94; mitigation of: 129; monastic: xxiv, xxvii, xli, l, 25–26, 57–58, 66, 97, 103, 184, 197; new: lv, 204; obligations of: 199; observance of: lvii, 68, 163, 171, 177, 200; of abstinence: 124; of fast: 124; of life: 117; relaxation of: 129; release from: 201; religious: li, 89, 94, 176; violation(s) of: 95, 102, 197

Rule of St. Benedict: viii, xiii, xv, xix, xxxiv, xxxvii, xxxix, xli, xlix–l, lv, 5, 8–10, 12, 14, 19–20, 24, 52, 57, 65, 71–72, 78, 98, 109, 125, 129, 144, 169–70, 172, 183–85, 204; adaptation of: xlv; alleviation of: 60; application of: 19; book of: 16; dispensations from: 72; doctrine about: 168; exposition of: 16, 184; interpretation of: xviii–xix, 7, 9–10, 72, 204; keeping of: 166; letter of: xx, l; mitigation of: xlv, 60; observance of: 8, 12, 50, 60, 167, 180, 203; precepts of: 197; prescriptions of: xxxiv, 57; reading of: 16, 50; sanctions of: 197; spirit of: xx, l; study of: 166; violations of: xx; zeal for: 203; Prologue: 62; c. 4: 165; c. 7: 62; c. 8: 129; c. 20: 84; c. 22: 62; c. 24: 12; c. 31: 52–53; c. 33: 65; c. 36: 122; c. 39: 122; c. 42: 24, 125; c. 43: 40, 62; c. 44: 62; c. 47: 62; c. 49: 124; c. 50: 62; c. 52: 62; c. 54: 65; c. 57: 109; c. 58: 62, 145; c. 63: 7, 11; c. 67: 62; c. 71: 19–20; c. 72: 7, 11

sacrament(s), administration of: 72; last: 133; of penance: 70, 91
sacrifice(s): xlvi, 131, 145; of praise: 63
sacristan: xxix, 16, 20–21, 26–27, 51, 54; as timekeeper: 54
saint(s), feasts of: 28; lives of: 100
St. Ann's hermitage: lix, 134
St. Bernard, College of: 43
St. John's Abbey: xxxii
St. Victor, canons of: 49
Ste. Geneviève manuscript: xvii, 4
salad: 126–27
salt: 20–21, 24, 31
saluting: 16, 19
salvation: 58–59; common: 8; of souls: xix, 12
Salve Regina: 32

sanatio in radice: 152
sanctions, monastic: xv
sanctity: 61; of Fathers: 59
Santachiara, Maria Paola, OCSO: xxxv
satisfaction: 196
Scala Claustralium: 97
scandal(s): 104, 156, 178, 196, 203–204; exterior: 198; grave: 47, 97, 146, 197–98
scapular(s), Cistercian: xlv, 30, 34, 54, 130, 162; night: 129; non-monastic: xlv; oblate: 130; of Immaculate Conception: 130–31; of Most Holy Trinity: 130; of Mount Carmel: 130–31; of Seven Sorrows: 130; of the Passion: 130
Schaefer, Timothy, OFMCap: xxxviii, 80, 93–94, 118, 120, 138, 145, 148, 150–53, 157–58, 160–62, 170, 173–74, 195, 202
schedule(s), daily: xxiii, xxv, xxxv, liii; monastic: xv; summer: xxiii, xxvi; winter: xxiii, xxvi, xxix
schism: 43
schismatics: 156
schizophrenics: 147
Schoenthal, Abbey of: 35
Scholastica, St., Feast of: 96
scholastics: 112–13
school(s), of candidate: 161; state-approved: 200
science, sacred: 119; study of: 166
scribes: 154
scriptorium: 98; brothers': 192
scripture(s): xli, lx, 54, 100; commentaries on: 100; manuals of: 100; study of: 112, 114, 118–19
scrutators: 183
seasons, harvesting: 192; planting: 192
sect, non-Catholic: 148, 156
secular(s): xlii, xlvi, 24, 40, 46, 48, 82–83, 133, 140; as hired workers: 36–37; contact with: 111

secularization: 150, 200–202; effects of: 201–202; indult of: lv, 76, 200–202; meaning of: 200; petition for: 201
Séjalon, Hugo: 1, 15, 60
self-accusation: 93
self-gift: xlv, lii, 131, 172, 181
self-love: 204
self-mutilation: 157
self-righteousness: lv
self-sacrifice: 192
self-will: 43, 171
seminarians: 152, 161
seminary: 150; office in: 202
seniority: lii
sense, common: xxxviii
sentimentality: 101
Sept-Fons, Abbot of: 78
Septuagesima: 123
sermon: 50
servant, of church: 29; of refectory: 20–21, 31, 55; of sick: 55
service(s): 192; divine: 62; in missions: 151–52; military: 157, 174, 177; necessary: 110; of sick: 55, 132; urgent: 110
sext: 27, 30, 33–34, 55
Shannon, William H.: ix, xxx, 64
sharpeners: 37
shaving: xxvi, 21, 37–39
shears: 37
sheep: 35, 109
sheep-shearing: 30, 35
shirt: 129
shoemakers: 23
shoes: xlv, 21–22, 33, 129, 131; repair of: 44
shows: xxvii, 44
sick: xxix, xlv–xlvi, 15, 23, 30, 53–56, 103, 122–23, 128, 131–33; care of: xxxiii, 39, 58, 83, 169; comfort of: xlv, 132; needs of: xlv, 132; service of: 55, 132; weakness of: 132

sickness: xxxvii, xlvi, 6, 55, 83, 131–32, 166; of relative(s): 141, 175; physical: 132; spiritual: 132
signs, Cistercian: xiii, 18–19, 21–22, 24, 30, 34, 49–50, 56, 104; making of: 35, 90, 120; necessary: 165
silence: x, xxiv, xxxiii, xxxv, xxxvii, xliii, xlix, liv, 19–20, 22–25, 28, 30, 34, 54, 58–59, 61–62, 101–104, 121, 189; as former of contemplation: 101; as keeper of divine fervor: 101; as liberation from captivity: 101; as mother of prayer: 101; cold: 147; grand: 113; love of: xlix, 145, 170; place of: 39; practice of: xlii; spirit of: 103, 192; time of: 39; violation of: 103, 197
simony: 76
simplicity: xviii, xlix, 145, 192; spirit of: 78
sin(s): 80, 93, 146, 170, 177, 184; absolution from: xxxix–xl, 92, 195; against justice: 150, 152; against purity: 156; against stability: 199; danger of: 155; external: 157; grievous: 105; hidden: 156; interior: 156; mortal: 72, 86, 94, 97, 105, 107, 134, 139, 157; occasions of: 91; remission of punishment for: 177; reserved: xxxix, 86–87, 89; serious: 112, 199; venial: 103, 134
singing: xxxviii, 51, 82–83, 117, 145
sisters: 155
slaves: 148, 157
sleep: xxxiii, xxxvii, xlv, 18, 27, 32, 34, 49, 58, 83, 128–30, 162; inability to: 129
snorers: 128
Sobrado, Abbot of: 47
Society of Jesus: 181
socks: 129

sodomy: 156
softness: 124
soldiers: 196
solitude: x, xxxv, xlvi, xlix, 63, 102, 105, 140, 145
Somerville, Mary: lx
Sortais, Abbot Gabriel, ocso: xiv, xli, 64, 100–101, 131
soul(s): xli, 100, 111, 113, 152–53, 203–204; care for: 8, 77, 118; danger to: 111; good of: 6, 8; injury to: 110; of novice: 166, 168; opening of: 95; powers of: 170; salvation of: xix, 12; state of: xl, 93
sound(s): 19, 22
soup: 28–29, 126–27
sources, Cistercian: xxxvii; judicial: xlii; monastic: vii; return to: vii; theological: 119
spa, health: xlvii, 141
Spain: 44
speaking: xxiv, xlii; in church: 23; in monastery: 23
species, sacred: 156
spirit: 62; bad: xlv, 131; Benedictine: 9, 62; Cistercian: l, 137; community: 204; family: xliv, 127; gyrovague: 141, 186–87; monastic: 135, 170; of abandonment: xlix–l, 163; of Cistercian fathers: 16; of discipline: xlii, 103; of docility: xlix, 163; of enclosure: 41, 137; of novice: l, 168; of obedience: liv, 169, 192; of Order: 108–109, 115, 135, 167; of poverty: 65; of prayer: 192; of punishment: 203; of recollection: 192; of regularity: 169, 192; of *Rule*: xx, l; of silence: 103, 192; of stability: 41; of upheaval: 137; of vocation: 192; of vows: 186; of worldliness: 137; regular: li, 180; religious: 178; wrong: 203

Spiritual Directory: xli, 75, 98
spirituality: xlviii, 142; Cistercian: vii, xi, xxxv; masters of: 100; monastic: viii–ix
spite, unconscious: 203
stability: xxvii, xxxv, 41, 63, 74, 76, 184; change of: xxxiii, xlvii, lii–liii, 58, 184–88; new: 73, 185–86; sin against: 199; spirit of: 41; vow of: 176, 184–86, 199
stairways: 26
stalls, monastic: 163
stamina: 145
state, of exclaustration: 199; religious: li, 87, 171, 200
statio: 33
stations of the cross: 79
status: liv
Statute on Unity and Pluralism: xi, lvii
Stephen Harding, St.: xviii, xx, xxiii, xxxi, 1, 3, 5, 15, 60
Stiller, Colleen: lxi
stockings: 32
stock-raising: 7, 109
stole: 54; papal gift of: ix
Stonely, Abbot of: 11
stoup, holy water: 129
straw: xxvi, 37
strength: 145; of novice: 163
strictness: xlix, 145
structure(s), Cistercian: xxxiv; of governance: xxxv
students: 115–17; Benedictine: 128
studies: xxxiii, xxxvii, xliii–xliv, xlix, 46–47, 58, 112–22, 145, 165; at Rome: xliii, 115–17; course of: xliii, 112, 117; graduate: 117; leave of absence for: 199; of arts: 166; of candidate: 143, 145; of humanities: 166; of languages: 112; of Latin: 112, 114–15, 145, 159; of liturgy: 112; of philosophy: 112, 114, 117;

of priests: 117–20; of science: 166; of scripture: 112, 114, 118–19; of theology: 112, 114, 117–20; prohibition of for novices: xlix, 115; theological: 114, 117; time for: 113
subcantor: xxix, 51
subcellarer: 53
subdeacon(s): 54, 152, 182
subject(s): xl, 71, 79, 92, 94–95, 106–107, 149, 152
submaster of novices: 91, 113, 165, 167–68; duties of: 169
subprior: 30, 113, 183
suicide: 157
Summa Cartae Caritatis: xvii, 2–4
Sunday(s): 21, 35; "Oculi": 38
superior(s): xxxviii–xl, xlii, l, 7, 16, 22, 27, 30, 35, 39, 58, 65, 68–69, 71, 74, 77, 79–80, 84, 86, 88, 90–97, 99, 102–107, 110, 121, 123, 126, 129, 138–39, 141, 144, 149, 152–53, 160, 162, 169, 173, 177–78, 182–83, 185–86, 194, 198, 200–201, 204; absence of: 74; advice of: 200; authority of: xxxix, 86, 178, 199; council of: 69, 198; death of: 76; deceased: 76; decision of: 145; delegate of: 176; directive of: 195; discretion of: 79, 175; dominative power of: 177; election of: xxxvi, 74, 76; first: 69, 168–69; future: 115; general: xxxvi, 86, 198; higher: xlii, 88, 106–108, 138, 143, 158; house: 70; legitimate: 172–73, 176–77; local: xxxiv, xxxviii, 23, 67–68, 70, 79, 98, 106, 134, 140–41, 198; major: 67–68, 88, 161, 196; obedience to: 172, 177, 199; of another order: 187; openness with: 94–95; permission of: 83, 104–105, 123, 142, 181, 187, 193; pope as supreme: 64; power of: 67; precept of: 197; punishment of: 158; religious: xxxviii, li, 87, 89, 117–18, 161, 199–200; responsibility of: 187; warning by: 86; will of: lv, 14, 105–106, 204
superioress: 86
supervision: 192
supper: 34, 36, 53, 126–27
suspension(s): 87; *a sacris*: 196
suspicions: 97, 147
Switzerland: xxv
swords: 44
synod, postconciliar: ix

table: 18; common: 126
table fellowship, monastic: xliv, 126–27
tablet: 30; weekly: 51
tabula of appointments: 16
tailor shop: 128
talking: 30, 103
taverns: xxvii, 44
telegrams: xlii, 105
telephone: xlii, 105
television: 137
temperament, right: 145
temptation(s): 93; to inconstancy: 202
tempus lectionis: xxiii, 18, 21, 50, 113
tendencies, subversive: 147
Tennenbach, Abbot of: 48
Tescari, Augusta, ocso: xxxv
theologians: 181
Theological Digest: 99
Theological Studies: 99
theology, conferences in: 121–22; doctorate in: 118; dogmatic: 112, 114, 117–18; formation in: 113, 115; moral: 112, 114, 117–18; pastoral: 112; patristic: 119; study of: 112, 114, 117–20; teaching of: 117
Thérèse of Lisieux, St.: xxxii
thieves: 88
Thomas Aquinas, St.: 119
Thomas Merton Center: xv–xvi, lx–lxi
threat(s): 89, 94, 149

Index

thurifer(s): 20–21, 57
tickets, monastic: 165
tierce: xxvi, 21, 28–30, 33, 55, 83
Tintern Abbey: xxv, 24; Abbot of: xxv, 24, 82
tokens: 65
tone, kind: 204
tonsure: xxvi, 37, 49, 163; clerical: 163; monastic: 163
tools: 30
Toronet, Abbot of: 12
trades: 109
tradition(s), Christian: xli; Cistercian: 170; human: 154; monastic: xi–xii, xvi; mystical: xv
transept: 26
transfer(s), from other orders: xlvii
transiens: liii, 187–88
transitus: 150
travel: 41, 43–45, 134
travelers: 37, 53
tree(s): xxi, xxvi; pine: x
Trent, Council of: viii, xlviii, 143
Trent manuscript: xvii, 4
trial, ecclesiastical: 196, 198–99
tricenaries: 52
trip(s): 106
Tre Fontane, Abbey of: 117
Trois-Fontaines, Abbey of: 2
Trouville: 141
truth, devotion to: 192
tunics: 30
Turk, Msgr. Josip: xvii, 1–3

underwear: 129
underworld: 146
uniformity: xi, xxxvii, xlvii, 126; of observance: xviii, xxxvii, lvii, 8–9, 78–79
union, with God: 57, 97, 114, 203
unity: xi, xix, xliv, 8, 10, 127, 165
university, office in: 202
upheaval, spirit of: 137

usages, ancient: xxiii, 15; Cistercian: xiii, xxiv, xxxiv, xxxix, xliv, l, lv, 29, 52, 58, 85, 96, 103, 122–24, 126–30, 146, 163, 169, 204; diverse: lvii; monastic: 9; observance of: 171; of La Val Sainte: 27; Trappist: xxvi, 39
uselessness, of abbot: 13
Usus Conversorum: xxii, 15, 188
utensils: 132

vacations: 112
vagus: 161
Valeri, Cardinal Valerio: 64
values, cultural: xi; monastic: vii
Van Doren, Mark: xxi
Vatican Council, First: xlii, 102; Second: viii, lvi
vegetables: 45
vehicles: 134
vespers: 19, 32–34, 125, 191; of little office: 81
vessels, liturgical: 35, 53
vestments: 44, 65
vicar general: 68
vice(s): 14, 93, 166
Vichy: 141
Vie Spirituelle: 99
vigils: xxiii, xxxviii, 28–29, 33, 79–80, 191
vineyards: 7
Vineyard Knob: 105
vintage: 35
violence: 93, 149–50; acts of: 147
virtue(s): l, 4, 93, 166, 168; monastic: l, 170; practices of: 91; progress in: 101; religious: 189
visit(s): 104, 133; of candidate: 144; to friends: 141
visitation(s): xv, xix, xxxiii, xxxv–xxxvi, xliv, liii, 6, 8, 10–11, 43, 58, 69–70, 74–75, 79, 83, 88, 98, 124, 167, 189; card: 105

visitor(s), official: 43, 48, 58, 65, 67, 71, 75, 83, 88, 124; secular: xlvi, 6, 10, 36, 140

vocation(s): 106, 111, 142, 144, 166; adult: 48; Benedictine: xlix, 145; betrayal of: 192; canonical signs of: 144; Cistercian: xlix, 5, 58, 145; contemplative: xlix, 145; divine: xlviii, 143, 145–46; exterior signs of: xlviii, 144–45; general signs of: 145; juridical: 145; lack of: 128; loss of: 200; love of: liv, 192; monastic: xiv, xxxix–xl, 7, 111; mystery of: xlviii; potential: 145; prospective: xlviii; religious: xlviii, liv, 71, 95, 116, 143, 145; signs of: 145; spirit of: 192; testing of: xlviii, 143

voice: 19, 145; active: 76, 139, 177, 189, 194, 199; low: 39; passive: 76, 139, 177, 189, 194, 199; subdued: 185

volition, lack of: 144

vomiting: xxix, 54–55

voting: xxxvi–xxxvii, 72–74, 76–77, 162, 171, 180; consultative: 159, 183; deliberative: 69, 73, 171, 187; obligation of: 74, 171; on profession: 183; right to: 74, 171; secret: 178, 183

vows: lix, 5, 122, 145, 151–52, 166, 171, 173, 177, 199–201; crime against: 197; dispensation from: 150, 155, 176, 200–201; effects of: 176; emission of: 172, 181; first: xxviii; formula of: 177; in another order: 150; letter of: 186; monastic: xv, xviii, li–lii; obligation(s) of: 176, 178, 195; of brothers: 190; of chastity: 200–201; of obedience: 64, 176, 181, 184, 187, 199; of poverty: liii, 176, 179–80; of stability: 176, 184–86, 199; perpetual: liv, 69, 181, 187, 193; private: 177, 181; public: li, 172, 176; religious: 150, 156, 181, 187, 200; renewal of: 177; simple: vii, li, 87, 150, 172, 178, 181–82, 190, 193; society without: 150; solemn: 69, 87, 115, 138, 177, 181–85, 187, 190, 193; spirit of: 186; suspended: 187; temporary: lv, 69, 115, 155, 171, 177, 182, 185, 187, 193, 195, 199, 202; to enter religion: 154; violation of: 197

voyages, air: 123, 142; sea: 123, 142

Waddell, Chrysogonus, ocso: xvii, 2, 4

Wales: 45

wanderings, of monks: 43

war: 160, 178

warning(s): 14, 86, 197–98

wartime: 162

washing: 33

Washington, DC: 108

watches: 65

water: 20, 24, 28, 32–34, 37, 41–42, 45, 54, 124; holy: 33, 129; hot: 21; warm: 21

way of life, Cistercian: vii, xi, xviii, xxxiii, xlii; monastic: 170; right: 8

weak: 122, 131–32

weakness(es): 111, 125; of bodies: 122; of imagination: 122; of sick: 132; natural: 203; personal: 203; unconscious: 203

weapons: 45; lethal: 44

weddings: xxvii, 44

well-being, spiritual: li–lii

Westmalle, Abbot of: 83; program of studies at: 115

wife: 49, 157

will: xlviii, 144, 176; bad: 197; good: 146; of abbot: 6, 10, 13; of God: xxvii, xxxix, 41; of superior(s): lv,

14, 105–106, 204; personal: l, 144, 204; to persevere: 145
will(s), beneficiary of: 182; executor of: 153; monastic: 179–80, 182–83
William of Champeaux: 2
William of Saint Thierry: 2
William, St., Feast of: 96
wind: x
wine: xxvi, xxviii, 28, 32, 36, 42, 45, 53, 127
wisdom: xxx
Wolfer, Vianney, ocso: 90
Wolter, Maurus, osb: 62
women: 104, 140; at granges: xxv, 24; Cistercian: 45; flight with: 178, 194; unbaptized: 139; violation of enclosure by: 76, 138–39
wood: 21
woods: lvi, 7, 35, 98
Wordsworth, William: xxv
work(s): xxvi, xxix, xxxiii, xxxvii–xxxviii, 18–19, 23, 30, 33–34, 49–50, 55–56, 58, 62, 79, 83, 96, 111, 120, 165, 172; active: 109; afternoon: 113; distribution of: 30; duration of: 111; exterior: 166; extra: 126; extraordinary: 29; lighter: 55; manual: 108–109; missionary: 111; morning: 113, 121; necessary: 200; of brothers: liv, 191–92; of Christ: xxxv; of God: xxxix, 40, 59, 62–63, 84, 170; of novices: 169; parochial: xliii, 109–11; temporary: 111
world: xiv, 63, 153, 155, 158, 195; affairs of: 63; return to: 182; separation from: xlvi, 133
World War I: xliii, 99, 109–10
World War II: 79
worldliness, spirit of: 137
worship, public: 176

year, liturgical: xxiii; of canonical novitiate: 115, 165, 173

zeal: li, liv, 180, 192; false: 204; for humiliations: xlix, 145; for obedience: xlix, 145; for office: xlix, 145; for *Rule*: 203; for work of God: 170; misguided: 113
zuchetto: 71

www.ingramcontent.com/pod-product-compliance
Lightning Source LLC
Chambersburg PA
CBHW020055020526
44112CB00031B/185